Dear Lord,

Dad did something wrong and they took him to jail. I don't know what happened really, but you do.

Now our lives are all messed up. Mom has to go to work so we can eat. We hardly ever see her any more. All our time is spent going to the jail to see Dad.

Mom is changing. She used to be real nice and good to us, but now she yells a lot. Her and dad don't get along very good either when we go to see him. I know she is trying, though.

People have changed. We never hear from my parents' friends, and my old friends hate me. They call me names, and sometimes fight me. Once my big brother chased them away. But it just gets worse all the time. And now a gang wants me to join them. I know it would be wrong, but they'll hurt me if I don't. I'm afraid to go to school.

God, my family's lives are really getting bad. It's very scary. Dad did something wrong, but we didn't. Please help so our lives aren't ruined!

Amen.

Ronald, age 11

OUTSIDERS L⬛⬛KING IN

HOW TO KEEP FROM GOING CRAZY
WHEN SOMEONE YOU LOVE GOES TO JAIL

Toni D. Weymouth, Ed. D.   Maria Telesco, R.N., B.A.

OLINC Publishing

0033210

OUTSIDERS LOOKING IN
How To Keep From Going Crazy
When Someone You Love Goes To Jail

ISBN 1-891261-40-1

☆ Published in the United States of America ☆

Printed in Canada

Single copies and quantity discounts are available from:
OLINC PUBLISHING
P.O. Box 6012
Fresno, CA 93703-6012
Email: olinc@earthlink.net

TABLE OF CONTENTS

PART ONE
OUTSIDERS
(Freedom)

PART TWO
INSIDERS
(The Bullet Never Stops)

WE WISH TO THANK:

Our families and friends for their patience and support during the long process of researching and writing this book;

Outsiders,

the many contributors who generously shared their experience and expertise; and

Insiders,

whose stories have inspired us, especially Amtrack, Artist, Bug, Grump, Invisible Man, Jazz, JKB, Ladies Eight, Lane, Lazarus Man and Micky Dee.

Also, we wish to give special recognition to mothers of prisoners: Rocky, Shirley, and the Mothers From Hell; and to the loyal and devoted friends of prisoners, especially Jean, Mary and Penny who come all the way from England to visit prisoners twice a year.

OUTSIDERS L👀KING IN

Is dedicated to:

Prisoners everywhere, their families and loved ones, and anyone ever accused of a crime.

HANG IN THERE!

PART ONE
OUTSIDERS

Freedom

No one has come right out and said they are now socially ostracized. It's been a more subtle kind of strangulation: unreturned phone calls, brief and awkward conversations on the street. What's worse, though, is what's happened to their marriage. All they ever talk about anymore is THE CASE. Everything else, all gestures of tenderness and intimacy, have been flattened by the weight of the impending trial . . .

Peter Blauner, *The Intruder* (a novel)

INTRODUCTION

This book is dedicated to the families and loved ones of incarcerated men and women, in the hope it will give them an understanding of problems they may encounter.

According to the Bureau of Justice statistics, more than three out of every 100 American adults were in jail or prison or on probation or parole in 1995. The United States imprisons more of its citizens than any other nation, except Russia. Each incarcerates over 600 per 100,000 population.

The perplexity of the court process, along with reports of perils lurking in overcrowded institutions, set the stage for confusion and fear. This cripples the family system, and makes it difficult to develop suitable strategies for the future of the family unit. Children whose parent or parents are in prison experience prolonged instability and uncertainty, and are three times more likely than their counterparts to run afoul of the law as they grow older.

Those who enter the court and prison systems go through periods of anxiety, trauma, shame, guilt and terror. These feelings can cause physical and mental illness and severely impair their ability to function effectively. Demystification of the process prepares the family and the accused to cope during the trial and afterwards. Learning about rules, regulations, social aspects and day to day prison life will help families conquer their fears and regain control of their lives.

Inmates, ex-convicts, family members, attorneys, correctional staff and others who work in, or have had contact with the criminal prosecution and detention system have contributed to this work, and we are grateful to them all for their assistance and input. They relate their feelings and experiences, talk about the emotional impact of incarceration, and offer practical advice and tips on dealing with the system. Any errors, inaccuracies or omissions are our own.

Most of our contributors have asked us to allow them to remain anonymous for fear of retaliation from "the system," and we have honored those requests. Names of contributors that are published, with their permission, are their actual names, except for "Marlene," who chose that pseudonym. There is one small exception: people who are quoted who were heard on talk shows. We had no way of verifying their identities.

This book is not intended to represent a scientific study, so the experiences and opinions stated are just that: experiences and opinions, anecdotal and empirical. We make no claim that the personal experiences of the authors, interview subjects and other contributors are universal, nor do we suggest that the reader should generalize from them.

Contributors and interview subjects were not selected by scientific means, but were somewhat self-selected. We started out by sending questionnaires to over 100 people of our acquaintance who had some experience with the criminal justice system. Some responded and said they wanted to participate, others responded and told us to "get lost," and many did not respond at all. Some responders recommended friends or relations, while a few others heard about what we were doing and volunteered. We refer to those who chose to participate as "self-selected," and we don't doubt that some, even many, statements and viewpoints are biased. If we could read the minds of those who declined, it's entirely possible that what they would have to say would be the diametric opposite of the opinions voiced by our contributors. In some cases, people with opposite viewpoints have expressed their views, and we have included both. In other cases, we sought out people with different viewpoints, but they didn't want to participate. In those cases, we decided to go with the single viewpoint even though we could provide none to counterbalance it.

Some portions were written or contributed by attorneys, physicians and nurses. They have expressed ideas and offered suggestions within their areas of expertise. However, these suggestions DO NOT constitute legal or medical advice and are not intended to substitute for consulting an attorney or physician.

A few contributors have made statements that could be construed as racist or classist, or may be in some way offensive to some individuals or groups. We debated long and hard about including them as written, and finally decided to do just that: include them exactly as they were written. We believe that to omit those statements would be dishonest. We would be giving the false impression that everybody in prison or in "the system" loves one another and are a bunch of "Pollyannas" who never say anything negative about anyone or anything. That's clearly not the case, so we decided to let the statements stand and speak for themselves. We don't necessarily agree with some of the statements included here, but we have allowed them to remain in the interests of journalistic integrity.

We mostly refer to prisoners as "he" and to family members as "she" because most prisoners are male and most family members who stick by them are female. However, the use of these words is not intended to be sexist, but merely to simplify writing and reading.

          *   *   *

A third house of congress shall be organized as the Delegislative Branch. It will continually review all existing laws, striking them from the books as they become obsolete, outmoded or inconsistent with the current public welfare. Furthermore, all new laws must include a date of expiration. If they are good laws, they can be renewed; if not, they expire automatically, before they can bring misery and confusion to future generations.

Allen Sherman's fantasy government in *Rape of the A.P.E.*

AN HISTORICAL VIEW

Our nomadic ancestors, always on the go, didn't have a place where they could keep wrongdoers locked up. They had no formal legal code, so justice was swift and simple. If elders thought the crime was serious, they ordered the person to be stoned to death, and the tribe moved. If the crime wasn't so bad, the offender was just banished from the clan instead of getting stoned. He could then wander the desert alone, at leisure, until he died "naturally" from hunger, thirst, sun stroke or wild animal attacks.

Then humans beings became "civilized" and invented things like codes of law, jails, prisons, police, lawyers, chain gangs, electric chairs, gas chambers and solitary confinement. The administration of justice became complicated, slow, and too expensive for most people. This was called "progress."

The British, and later the American Colonists, built jails to accommodate people who were awaiting trial. Once the person was convicted, and most were, the punishment was not incarceration. Instead, miscreants spent a spell in the pillory or stocks, were whipped, or took the plunge on the ducking stool.

Prisons were filthy and roach infested. They were reserved for two classes of inmate:
* political prisoners, meaning anyone who displeased or disagreed with the monarch, and
* debtors, who were locked up, unable to earn any money, until they could figure out a way to pay their bills. Members of the nobility were given privileges: they could entertain guests in their suites, and have their servants incarcerated along with them.

Debtors had to provide their own food and other necessities. Since they lacked the wherewithal to purchase these amenities, debtors were furnished with a tin cup and a small portal through which they could beg passers-by for coins with which to pay their expenses and bribe the guards.

Visiting policies were liberal by our standards. All prisoners were dependent upon family and friends, as the prisons provided nothing, not even food. Meals, a generous ration of wine, and clean clothes were brought in at all hours by family members.

The usual methods of dispatching wrongdoers were hanging and beheading, except for those accused of witchcraft. An alleged witch was always given a fair trial. She was thrown, fully clothed and hands tied behind her back, into a deep well. If she drowned, that proved she was innocent. If she floated, that proved she was guilty, and she was then burned at the stake.

Executions were public, and were occasions for festivity and merrymaking. This venerable custom remains a rich part of our culture today. On modern execution nights, white sheeted death penalty proponents hold "tailgate parties" in front of the prison walls. Yelling "Fry 'em," they throw rocks and beer bottles at abolitionist nuns who are quietly clacking their rosary beads and singing "We Shall Overcome."

At the end of the evening's entertainment, as the hearse departs the prison grounds, the abolitionist nuns are hauled off to spend the night in the pokey for unlawful assembly and disturbing the peace. The White Sheeted Wonders are interviewed by the media and invited to share their profound and knowledgeable views on criminal justice and The American Way with the viewers out in TV land. Afterwards they join the Governor and Attorney General at a slightly more decorous soiree at the Executive Mansion. Then everybody goes home, except in Texas. Nobody there bothers to go to executions any more because they have so many that they're no longer considered worth the effort. If anyone, even nuns, bothered to go, they wouldn't have time to do anything else, and the jails would all be full of nuns awaiting trial for the crime of disagreeing with the death penalty statutes.

In the 18th century, various reformers decided prisons were either too lax or too harsh, depending on their point of view. They introduced reforms that consisted mainly of mandatory hard labor and compulsory Bible reading. The 19th century was about the same. Prisoners were locked in solitary confinement for years on end for minor infractions such as talking. With the 20th century came a promise of enlightenment and true reform. Modern penologists realized that brutality and isolation did nothing to improve the character or behavior of convicts. Programs were introduced whereby prisoners could become literate, learn a trade, and generally improve themselves.

Politicians quickly decided these programs were "coddling" prisoners, and discontinued most of them. They set out to "improve" the system (it must have been working too well). Now many prisoners are kept in isolation in cells where they are monitored by closed circuit TV, so they don't have contact with anyone at all, even guards. Most of the various programs have been taken away, so as not to "pamper" them. The prisoners spend all day every day all alone with nothing to do except fantasize about the revenge they'll take on society when they get out.

In ancient times, the penalty for a serious offense was getting stoned to death. Today, getting stoned is a serious offense and the penalty is 25-to-life. Now, that's progress.

*   *   *

In 1971, Chief Davis of the Los Angeles Police came up with a novel idea for skyjack justice. He recommended that courtrooms and scaffolds be built at all major airports so that skyjackers could be tried and hanged on the spot, thus providing an example. Meanwhile, Archie Bunker, the lovable right-wing paranoiac of television's *All in the Family*, offered another solution: give every passenger a gun, he said. That way the skyjacker would know he's outnumbered.
Allen Sherman, *Rape of the A.P.E.*

HEARTACHES BY THE NUMBERS, TROUBLES BY THE SCORE

State and federal prison populations rose by 213 percent between 1980 and 1995, while probation rolls increased by 165 percent. The U.S. Bureau of Justice Statistics reports that the total number in jail or prison, or on parole or probation reached a record 5.3 million in 1995. This reflects an increase of 6 percent annually. A whopping 1,630,940 are behind bars, the remainder are on parole or probation.

The South averages 487 prisoners per 100,000 population. Texas leads the nation with 659, and Louisiana is a close second with 611.

The United States Department of Justice predicts that if current crime rates remain constant, five percent, or one out of every 20 residents born today, will actually be imprisoned.

The United States now has the second highest incarceration rate of any county in the world, according to the Sentencing Project. We imprison 650 of our citizens per 100,000 population. Russia imprisons 690 per 100,000, and South Africa comes in a poor third with 325 per 100,000.

When we first started researching and writing this book, about a year and a half before publication, we encountered a plethora of statistics from many sources, all of which were compiled during the last five years or so. The number of people in jails and prisons in this country has more than doubled in the last fifteen years. The first set of statistics we came across said the U.S. imprisoned about 300 people per 100,000 population, and Russia about 357. Each time we checked a new source, the U.S. numbers had grown, to 350, 500, 575, 600 and 650. Russia's numbers have kept up with ours, while the numbers in other countries have declined. By the time you read this book, God only knows what the numbers will be. Having grown tired of making revisions, we decided to call it quits at 650.

The reason for the increased prison population in the United States is not an increase in the number of crimes committed. Rather, people are being sent to prison for relatively minor crimes that would, in the past, have been dealt with by probation, fines, or rehabilitation programs. "Get tough on crime" policies and "Three Strikes" laws, not more crime, are responsible for the rising incarceration.

*   *   *

> Crime gets a lot of air time because it draws big audiences, which can be sold to advertisers. Crime is also easy to cover and requires little or no analysis or follow-up. Small wonder that TV stations are making no reduction in their crime coverage, even though crime rates nationally have been in their sharpest decline.
>   Clarence Page, columnist

MYTHS ABOUT CRIME

The Economist magazine published an article disputing widely held beliefs it calls "myths" of the crime situation which, the article claims, do not reflect "reality." Here are some "myths" and "facts" that appeared in the June 8, 1996 issue. (Statements The Economist article describes as "facts" have not been independently verified by the authors of this book.)

SERIAL KILLERS
Myth: A Justice Department official says there are 4,000 murders a year attributable to serial killers.
Fact: Only 50 people are victims of serial killers each year, and that figure has been stable for 20 years.

CRIME WAVE
Myth: The country is in the throes of a "crime wave."
Fact: According to the National Crime Victimization Survey, the crime rate has actually fallen since 1990, and murder hit its peak in 1980.

CRIMINALS
Myth: America is a nation of criminals.
Fact: While the U. S. imprisons and executes great numbers of

its citizens, the crime rate is actually lower than in many other Western industrialized countries, according to an International Crime Survey.

PRISONS
Myth: Building more prisons is the way to control criminals.
Fact: The U. S. imprisons (proportionately) more of its citizens than any European country, but the number of prisons has not brought about an end to crime.

PRISON POPULATION
Myth: The so-called "war on crime" imprisons the most violent offenders.
Fact: "Three Strikes" and similar laws imprison mostly small time drug users, drug dealers and thieves for ridiculously long sentences for relatively minor crimes, while violent criminals are hardly affected by these laws.

Research shows that children from low-income families who are placed in early childhood development programs such as Head Start have lower rates of crime and higher rates of marriage than those who are not in the program. We need to recognize that investing money in early childhood development produces a safer and healthier society over the long run. Unfortunately, the United States is the wealthiest nation on earth but has the highest child poverty rates of any industrialized country.
        The Report of the National Criminal Justice Commission

It is less evil that some criminals should escape than that the government should play an ignoble role.
Justice Oliver Wendell Holmes

LEGAL AND CORRECTIONAL TERMS

ACQUITTAL: to be declared "not guilty" in a court of law.

APPEAL: process by which defendant requests the decision of the lower court to be reviewed.

APPELLATE COURT: reviews cases that are appealed.

ARRAIGNMENT: a person accused of a crime is brought before a court, advised of the charges against him, advised of his rights and enters a plea of "guilty" or "not guilty."

CAPITAL OFFENSE: a crime punishable by death. Thirty-eight states, the U. S. Government and the U. S. Military have a death penalty. States that have a death penalty on the books but have no one under sentence of death as of this writing, are Kansas, New Hampshire, New York and Wyoming. States that do not have a death penalty on the books are Alaska, Hawaii, Iowa, Maine, Massachusetts, Michigan, Minnesota, North Dakota, Rhode Island, Vermont, West Virginia, Wisconsin and the District of Columbia.

CIRCUMSTANTIAL EVIDENCE: evidence which is inferred or deduced from known facts, but not based upon direct knowledge.

CLERK: there are several categories of Clerk who work in a court house. The Office of Records Clerk is where you go to get things like a marriage license. The office of the Clerk of the

Court is where you go to file documents and motions. Each judge, in his or her courtroom, also has a Clerk. This clerk acts as secretary and administrative assistant to that particular judge. When someone tells you to give a document to the Clerk, be sure and ask which Clerk. If you deliver it to the wrong Clerk, it will not find its way to its proper destination.

CONFORMED COPY: make an original and two copies of any document you are going to file with the Clerk of the Court. When you file, each copy will be stamped with a time and date stamp. The Clerk keeps the original and one copy to go into the court file. The second copy is for you to keep as proof that you filed it. File it away with the rest of the documents pertaining to your case.

CONCURRENT: sentences for two or more crimes are served at the same time. Five years for one crime and three years for another crime, to be served concurrently, amounts to five years.

CONFLICT OF INTEREST: occurs when a judge, attorney or juror may be unable to be impartial because of a business or personal relationship or some personal bias.

CONJUGAL VISIT: one in which sexual contact with a legal spouse in a private setting is permitted. Many jurisdictions no longer permit this practice. Several have instituted FAMILY VISITS, during which spouse, children, parents and grandparents of the prisoner can visit over night in a trailer or apartment on the prison grounds.

CONSECUTIVE: the sentences for two or more crimes are served one after the other. Five years for one crime and five years for another, to be served consecutively, effectively means ten years.

CONTACT VISIT: inmate and visitor are not separated by any barrier, may kiss or hug at the beginning and end of a visit, and may hold hands during the visit.

CONTRABAND: any prohibited item, such as drugs, alcohol, money and weapons brought into the prison. DO NOT ATTEMPT TO TAKE CONTRABAND INTO THE PRISON. IF YOU ARE CAUGHT, YOU WILL BE PROSECUTED, and will also lose your visiting privileges. The inmate you are visiting will also be prosecuted.

COURT APPOINTED ATTORNEY: may be either a Public Defender, or one who is in private practice but not on the staff of the Public Defender, who is appointed by a judge to represent an indigent defendant, and whose fee is paid by the court.

DEFENDANT: person accused of committing a crime.

DEPOSITION: testimony of a witness, sworn under penalty of perjury, and taken down by a court reporter, taking place in a location other than a court room. Your deposition and court testimony may be compared for discrepancies.

DETAINER: a legal document in a prisoner's file stating he is wanted in another jurisdiction, and should be transported there instead of being released.

DETERMINATE SENTENCE: sentence of a specific number of years.

DIRECT EVIDENCE: testimony from a witness who actually saw, heard or touched that about which he is being questioned.

DISCOVERY: legal process by which attorneys on each side of a case are required to share documents, evidence and names of witnesses with each other. Prosecutors sometimes hide or "forget" to share exculpatory evidence with the defense.

DOUBLE JEOPARDY: the rule by which a criminal defendant, after having been acquitted of a crime, cannot be tried again for the same crime in a criminal court. However, he can be tried for other, related issues. The police officers who beat Rodney King and were found not guilty of the beating were tried and convicted in another court for violation of King's civil rights. O. J. Simpson was acquitted of murder in his criminal trial, but was later charged in a civil trial and found liable for financial damages to the survivors of the two people whom he was found "not guilty" of murdering. When a defendant is found guilty, he can appeal the verdict, but when he is found not guilty, the prosecution cannot appeal that verdict.

DRACONIAN sentence: an extremely harsh or cruel sentence. Named after Dracon, a ruler of ancient Athens. Dracon "simplified" the code of law during his reign by imposing the death sentence for all offenses, no matter how petty.

ENHANCEMENT: an additional charge such as the use of a gun added on to make a crime more serious and a sentence more severe. The sentence for murder may be life imprisonment, but with the addition of rape as an enhancement the sentence may be death.

EXCULPATORY EVIDENCE: that which could prove innocence.

EXECUTIVE CLEMENCY: the rarely used power by which the Governor or President can commute a sentence to a lesser sentence.

EXPERT WITNESS: someone like a medical doctor, psychologist or scientist who did not see the crime or accident happen, but is hired and paid by either the prosecution or defense to explain technical information to the jury, such as DNA evidence, and they can review evidence and render an opinion. To qualify as an expert witness, the person generally has to have education, degrees and extensive professional experience in the subject about which he is testifying.

FELONY: a serious crime usually punishable by one year or more in a state or Federal prison.

GAG ORDER: an order by a trial judge prohibiting principals, attorneys or witnesses in a case from talking about the case outside the courtroom or to the media.

GRAND JURY: a group of people that inquires into alleged violations of the law and determines whether there is sufficient evidence to warrant a prosecution, and issues an indictment; "grand" from French word meaning "large" usually consists of 24 members.

HEARSAY EVIDENCE: evidence given by a witness who describes, not what he knows or saw, but what someone else told him or what he heard someone else say; usually not admissible at trial.

INCARCERATED: imprisoned.

INCULPATORY EVIDENCE: that which could prove guilt.

INDETERMINATE SENTENCE: a sentence with a range, such as "no less than 3 years, no more than 10 years."

INDICTMENT: formal accusation made by a Grand Jury or in a Preliminary Hearing, and brought against someone accused of a crime.

INFORMATION: formal accusation or a criminal complaint

issued by the District Attorney after presentation of evidence by police.

INEFFECTIVENESS OF COUNSEL: may be grounds for appeal, a new trial or a different lawyer if it can be shown that the trial attorney didn't do his job, for example by not calling witnesses, not investigating the case, resting the case without putting on a defense, being drunk or sleeping during the trial, or various other omissions.

JURY: a body of six, eight or 12 members that determines guilt or innocence in a trial.

M'NAUGHTON (pronounced McNaughton): a rule or test applied to determine if a defendant can claim insanity as a defense based on a mental disorder which would cause him not to know right from wrong.

MIRANDA: a result of the case Miranda v. Arizona, police are required to inform arrested persons of their constitutional rights, the right to remain silent, that anything they say can and will be used against them, the right to have a lawyer and a lawyer will be appointed at no cost if the person is unable to pay for a lawyer.

MISDEMEANOR: a crime less serious than a felony, punishable by one year or less in a county jail.

NON-CONTACT VISIT: a glass window separates inmate and visitor, they are unable to touch, and they have to talk on a phone. Occurs in jails, and in prisons if the inmate is under restriction for disciplinary or security reasons.

PAROLE: conditional release from prison, earned by work and good behavior. The remainder of the sentence is served at home or in a halfway house. Subject to many rules such as no alcohol or drug use and no association with convicted felons. Rule violation may cause parole revocation and return to prison.

PERCIPIENT WITNESS: is someone who knows or saw something relating to the crime, or to your case, someone who saw the accident happen, or an alibi witness.

PLEA BARGAIN: A process by which the defendant or his lawyer works out a "deal" with the prosecutor that is acceptable to both parties and to the court. The defendant may benefit by receiving a shorter sentence, and the state benefits by avoiding the expense of conducting a trial.

PRELIMINARY HEARING: a court hearing in which a judge listens to evidence and determines whether or not a person accused of a felony should be held over for a trial.

PRIVATE CORRECTIONS: a private, for-profit corporation such as Wackenhut or Corrections Corporation of America (CCA) that builds and manages prisons under a contract with a state.

PROBATION: a ruling by a judge that allows an offender to remain in the community under supervision of a probation officer, sometimes performing community service, instead of going to prison. Violation of probation may result in being sent to prison.

PRO PER (PRO SE): on one's own behalf, such as when a defendant acts as his own attorney.

PROSECUTOR: the District Attorney who represents the State in a criminal trial, charges a defendant with a crime and attempts to secure a conviction. In the federal system the prosecutor is a U.S. Attorney.

PUBLIC DEFENDER: lawyers employed by a county, state or Federal agency to represent defendants who cannot afford to pay a private lawyer.

RECIDIVIST: someone who, after being released from prison, commits another crime and returns to prison.

RECUSE: disqualification of a judge to serve on a particular case because of a conflict of interest or an objection by either party to the suit.

SUMMARY JUDGEMENT: a device whereby prompt disposition of a case without a trial may occur if facts are undisputed.

TRANSCRIPT: official written record of court or other legal proceedings.

WORK PRODUCT: any writing that reflects an attorney's impressions, conclusions or legal theories. Work product is not discoverable, i.e., does not have to be turned over to the other side in discovery process.

Those who become inmates are predominately Black, young, unemployed and from large cities. Those who become guards are overwhelmingly white, middle aged, from small rural towns. The process of natural selection is . . . perpetuated by prison geography. Most prisons are located in isolated areas where they often become the economic mainstay of the [area]. A reading of congressional hearings shows . . . this occupation appeals to those who like to wield power . . .
Jessica Mitford

To their keepers, [prisoners] are a sort of subspecies of the human race.
Jessica Mitford

WHO IS A CRIMINAL?

Criminologists and sociologists debate the causes of crime and criminal behavior, and the issues of prevention and rehabilitation versus punishment. Some recurrent factors they consider include poverty, lack of education, lack of meaningful work, poor impulse control, poor anger management, poor communication skills and addiction to drugs and alcohol.

And violence. Children who are abused and exposed to violence often, but not always, become violent adults, and many commit crimes of violence. Experts point out that the relationship between a violent childhood and a violent adulthood is not absolute, but there is a significantly high correlation. Many, but not all, abused children become abusers. Many, but not all, adult abusers were abused as children.

Today's scholars have a great deal to think about and a lot more to learn in this area before they come up with a formula for the causes and cure of criminal behavior. Not so our ancestors. They had it easy, espousing simplistic notions in absolute terms.

Up until about the last third of the 19th century, it was generally believed that "the Devil made me do it." In 1862, the Supreme Court of North Carolina said "To know the right and still pursue the wrong proceeds from a perverse will brought about by the seductions of the Evil One."

Around that same time, police and scientists began trying to develop "modern" methods to understand, classify and identify criminals. Identification was particularly important because any criminal could get away with anything just by giving police a false name. A more scientific way than simply asking a suspect his name was needed in order to control crime. Two Europeans lent their names to the new pseudo-science of criminology: Professor A. Bertillon, a Frenchman, and Cesare Lombroso, an Italian.

Bertillon studied over 3,000 individuals and concluded that no two are exactly alike. He also concluded that once adulthood and full growth are attained, certain measurements never change. In a system called "Bertillonage" he carefully measured height, length and breadth of the head, length of the left middle finger, length of the left foot and length and circumference of the left forearm, all in millimeters. This method, while enjoying limited success, was quickly superseded by the newer and more exact science of fingerprinting.

Then along came Lombroso, who was the first to label himself with the title "criminologist." Lombroso developed the theory that criminals are born that way, and can be spotted by their physical characteristics. He said "criminals are not a variation from the norm but a distinct subspecies having distinct physical and mental characteristics."

Lombroso studied living prisoners and the skulls of dead ones, but his unscientific method did not include the study of any other individuals as a control group. He concluded that all criminals have long, large, projecting ears; thick head and body hair but scanty beards; prominent foreheads; protruding chins; and large cheek bones.

More specifically, he classified miscreants by correlating their features with their crimes:

thieves - mobile hands and face, restless eyes, thick and closely set eyebrows, flat or twisted nose, scanty head and facial hair

rapists - brilliant eyes, delicate faces

murderers - cold, glassy eyes, large, prominent nose,

strong jaw, and dark, curly hair.

Other characteristics he associated more generally with the "criminal element" were left-handedness, epilepsy and "degeneracy," though he neglected to define the latter.

Lombroso also believed physical characteristics were representative of other non-criminal personality types:

large ear lobes - promiscuity, habitual lying

full, sensuous lips - promiscuity, generosity

thin, narrow lips - stinginess, mean spiritedness.

An English physician, Charles Goring, disputed Lombroso's findings and conducted his own study in the early 1900s. He studied a large number of prisoners, using an equal number of university students as a control group. He concluded that there was no difference between the two groups, and therefore there is no such thing as a physical "criminal type."

Lombroso, of course, did not classify "criminals" by their skin color or ethnic origin. Today, we laugh and say Lombroso was absurd to postulate that certain facial characteristics determine whether or not the owner of the face is a criminal. Nowadays, we are more modern and scientific than that: we now earnestly expostulate that a criminal is anyone whose skin is a shade darker than our own, or who was born somewhere else.

Different things are crimes and different people are labeled criminals in different times and places. Jesus and Paul were considered to be criminals in their day, Gandhi in his, Martin Luther King Jr. in his. Today's "criminals" include immigrants and single welfare mothers, people who are labeled "child abusers" because they spank their kids, people who are labeled "negligent" because they don't spank their kids, and people whose hobby is indoor gardening.

In trying to determine who is really a criminal, we need to ask ourselves who's worse:

*   the mugger or carjacker; the white collar criminal who embezzles the life savings of the elderly; or the dishonest industrialist who pays himself a few million a year while refusing to provide his employees with health insurance?

* the politician who uses his position to enrich himself, the judge who takes bribes, or the woman who took a piece of candy from the store where she worked, and ate it? (She was fired and charged with theft.)
* the TV evangelist who promises a free ride to Heaven if you'll just send all your money to Jesus (he is later discovered at the No-Tell Mo-Tel in the loving arms of the same prostitute whom he berated only yesterday as a "sinner"), or the prostitute herself?
* the destitute mother whose food stamps were taken away, so she stole a jar of baby food for her infant, or the welfare mother whose child was taken away from her because the baby was underweight and she couldn't afford to provide a nutritious diet?
* the rapist who was given probation after the violent sexual assault of a woman he did not know, but had been stalking; or the young immigrant man from a third world country who was given life in prison for statutory rape because he entered into an arranged marriage with a young girl of his ethnic group (he was 21 and unfamiliar with our laws, she was 13), with the consent and approval of her family?
* the president of the tobacco company whose product has killed thousands, if not millions, of nicotine addicts, yet he denies it's harmful; or the man dying of AIDS who is sentenced to seven years (if he lives that long) for growing a pot plant on his living room coffee table. He said the weed was to ease his pain and nausea, not to sell for profit.
* the man who repeatedly beat his wife and children, but never served a day in jail, or his wife, who finally couldn't take any more abuse and fought back, killing him, and got 25 to life? What ever happened to self-defense?
* the public official who evicted homeless people from their "welfare motel," said they were no longer eligible for General Relief and food stamps, and said on TV that it was up to churches to provide these services for the needy; or the minister who followed the mandates of his religion, fed and housed these homeless people in his church basement, and was

thrown in jail for violating a city sanitation ordinance?

Which leaves us back where we were at the beginning: nobody knows for sure who should be labeled as a criminal, or why people commit crimes, but everyone has a theory and claims to be an expert.

Two famous historical figures who were political prisoners in the early part of this century express their views about prisoners and guards. Eugene Debs, a labor organizer and president of the railroad workers union, was jailed for "conspiracy" in connection with a strike in 1894. A pacifist, he was again imprisoned during World War One for his anti-war beliefs. In all, Debs did time in three jails and two prisons. He said:

> The inmates of prisons are not the irretrievable, vicious and depraved element they are commonly believed to be, but upon the average they are like ourselves, and it is more often their misfortune than their crime that is responsible for their plight . . . a prison is a cross section of society . . .

This was written over 100 years ago, and is just as true now as it was then. Debs goes on to say:

> The guard and the inmate cease to be human beings when they meet in prison. One becomes a domineering petty official and the other a cowering convict. The guard looks down upon the convict . . . and the prisoner looks down on [the guard] as being even lower than an inmate.

Bertrand Russell, British philosopher, social reformer and conscientious objector was also imprisoned during World War One for opposing the draft. He wrote " . . . my fellow prisoners seemed in no way morally inferior to the rest of the population."

> Everyone knows who the criminal is because they've been criminalized. Young Black men. Welfare mothers. Immigrants from Asia and Latinos. It's already acceptable to assume they can be demonized. We must stop this injustice of criminal stereotypes.
> Angela Davis, 1996.

*   *   *

"No Human Being is Illegal."
T-Shirt slogan

THE DARKER SIDE OF HUMAN NATURE

Even the Justice Department has difficulty defining who is a criminal. Authorities often make errors, some ludicrous, some tragic, when they wrongfully label someone as a criminal.

According to the FBI, Richard Jewell was the bad guy. He is the security guard who risked his life at Centennial Park during the Atlanta Summer Olympics to warn others about a suspicious looking knapsack he found. After a bomb was discovered in the knapsack, Jewell went from hero to Public Enemy Number One. Jewell has since been exonerated, but his good name has been libeled across the nation's headlines, making it difficult for him to stroll into a convenience store late at night without the clerk ducking for cover.

In Virginia, the Department of Corrections publishes a list of parolees' names, gender, race, addresses, and offenses. They want every good citizen to know who their neighbor really is. The list costs $5 per zip code. Recently California began publishing a similar list of sex offenders. A computer check revealed that two-thirds of the information was incorrect. "This amounts to a third kind of punishment that wasn't included in the original sentence," the ACLU says.

Under "Megan's Law," sex offenders must register with law enforcement when they're released from prison. A CD-ROM disk contains the names, addresses and criminal profile of 63,000 registered sex offenders. California has included an additional 2,400 individuals who were convicted years ago of homosexual acts that were illegal at that time. These acts are no longer illegal, and are not registerable as sex offenses, yet the names remain on the list of registered sex offenders. The American Psychiatric Association once included Homosexuality in the Diagnostic and Statistical Manual of Mental Disorders (DSM) for diagnostic criteria in treating mental illness. It is no longer regarded as a mental illness. Homosexuality was also considered a crime by law enforcement.

Untreated sex offenders are generally acknowledged to have the lowest rate of rehabilitation among criminals, and the highest rate of recidivism. However, that does not excuse authorities when they erroneously label someone a sex offender who is not. In order for these programs to work, they must be accurate.

"Given the potentially dire consequences faced by those listed on the disk, government owes them accuracy," according to the ACLU. Numerous men on the list have already been hassled on their jobs and in their homes, and some have been attacked by angry mobs.

In San Francisco, a man associated with "Food Not Bombs" was jailed for 59 days for feeding homeless people without a permit. Law enforcement called him a criminal. He appealed, but his conviction was upheld in appellate court.

"They got me," he said as he walked out of the courtroom surrounded by his supporters. "They had me all along. I guess I'll have to go to jail, unless I decide to become an underground bagel pusher."

In Cincinnati, a grandmother was arrested and charged with disorderly conduct for obstructing official police business. She became a "criminal" when she put money into an expired parking meter, saving someone from having to pay a parking ticket. She evidently took seriously the concept of "random acts of kindness."

Recently some San Diego police officers found themselves in hot water by testifying in court that their "profile of a typical heroin dealer in the area is a Hispanic male." This led to the arrest of an innocent man. Justice James McIntyre said, "Every defendant has the right to be tried based on evidence tying him to the specific crime charged, and not on general facts accumulated by law enforcement regarding a particular criminal profile."

What about the young parents (he's 16, she's 17) who were found guilty of violating the 1921 anti-fornication law in Idaho? Are they criminals? Or the 18 year-old man who got his 17 year-old girlfriend pregnant. He decided to quit school and get a job. They planned on getting married before the baby was born. After a zealous prosecutor got a hold of him, he became a number on a court docket. Now, instead of marriage and taking care of his family, he has to register with the police as a sex offender, and has been forbidden to see his girlfriend.

The worst criminal is apparently Mom. Written in bold black letters across a morning newspaper, "Mother of infamous bank robber blames system for her troubles." In another area of the news, "Notorious serial killer's mother living in town," while yet another says, "Gag order placed on killer's mother."

Linking a mother with the alleged criminal activities of her child sets the stage for her to be recognized as an "accomplice" instead of a mother. Sometimes this has serious or even dangerous repercussions. In one case, the mother of a serial killer was fired from her job and evicted from her apartment. Even though she lived 3,300 miles from her son and hadn't seen him in 15 years, her boss and her apartment manager both viewed her as someone with whom they didn't want to associate.

Some sociologists say divorced and unmarried mothers damage their children. Politicians claim that welfare encourages women to have more children, and that single or working mothers are negligent because they're not at home looking after the kids. Mothers have traditionally been scapegoats for society's ills: welfare, poverty, latchkey kids and crime. With the changing family structure, mothers are easy to criticize.

To take responsibility for our actions is the moral and ethical thing to do, but somehow this eludes us. Instead, we point the finger at someone else. We blame the prisoner for his lack of job skills, his mother for neglecting him, and his family for creating a criminal environment. We don't look at why the inmate has no skills, or why the mother neglected him. Instead we choose to label him violent and her lazy because, otherwise, we might find that we, too, as a society, have played a part in his life.

We might have been the physician who failed to diagnose his mental retardation, or the teacher who was too busy with the gifted children to pay attention to the shy boy sitting in the back row. Maybe we sat on the board of directors where his mother was employed, and quite possibly we gave ourselves a pay raise and fired her.

In order to understand the individual, we must understand his environment. Since the individual is at all times interacting with his environment, he is at all times in a state of change.

Labeling keeps people down. It causes resentment toward groups of people such as immigrants and prisoners, and it produces negative stereotypes which limit their ability to achieve acceptance into society.

> I once asked a prisoner how he happened to be in jail, and he said he had stolen a pair of shoes. I told him if he had stolen a railroad, he would be a United States Senator.
> Mary Harris, "Mother" Jones

*   *   *

CHILDHOOD HORROR TALES
OR
How To Create A Monster Without Really Trying

The American people fear crime and criminals. Politicians fan the flames of fear for their own ends: to get elected or re-elected. Part of the "tough on crime" movement is to lower the age for trying children as adults, and for executing them. California's Governor Wilson, who wants to be President, recently suggested lowering the execution age to 13. If his suggestion becomes law, children in the midst of puberty soon will be sharing cells with hardened, vicious predators.

Younger and younger children are being charged as adults for "crimes" that were considered to be simply childish pranks a few years ago. A first grader was charged with "sexual harassment" for kissing a little girl on the cheek.

Carrying this trend *ad absurdum*, a nine year old boy in Las Vegas was arrested, strip-searched and charged with a felony for writing his name in wet cement. A construction worker at the site pointed out the newly poured cement and invited the boy to write his name in it, but that fact apparently didn't impress the police in Sin City.

In Alabama, a 12-year-old was charged with capital murder, punishable by death, in 1993. In 1995, Alabama authorities sought the death penalty for a boy aged 13. The Alabama legislature passed a bill in 1995 that could send a 7-year-old to prison for life.

Clayton Flowers, aged 15, spent three years on Alabama's death row before his sentence was reversed by the Supreme Court.

Geri Silva of Mother's ROC (Reclaiming Our Children) says:
We are there for our children who carry a criminal jacket. We are a group of mothers who meet for strength and empowerment. We mobilize our energy and make it effective as a group. Nothing happens accidentally. The group's mindset is knowing what you're doing, having a common thread everyone can tie into. We research statistics and present this information to important people. We've learned to work the system. We know how to do it smartly, wisely and with numbers, and we can change things.

California has five criteria for judging whether a juvenile is tried as an adult:
1. The sophistication of the crime
2. If rehabilitation is possible before the Juvenile Court's jurisdiction runs out on the suspect's 25th birthday
3. Previous history of deliquency
4. Success of prior rehabilitation attempts
5. The seriousness of the crime.

You don't have to be a criminal to be accused of a crime. All you
need is to be standing opposite a pointed finger.
Anonymous

STEPS TO TAKE BEFORE AND AFTER ARREST

Sara Stander, a California attorney, tells you what to do if
you are suspected of a crime, if you are arrested, or if you think
you might be arrested:
* DON'T TALK TO ANYONE. The Fifth Amendment to the
  Constitution says you don't have to say anything that will
  incriminate you. Miranda v. Arizona requires the police to tell
  you, once you have been arrested, that "You have the right to
  remain silent." So KEEP YOUR MOUTH SHUT.
* TELL POLICE YOUR REAL NAME AND ADDRESS, not
  a false name, your date of birth, and your gang affiliation, if
  any. But don't tell them anything else.
* ASK POLICE "Am I free to go now?" If they say "yes," then
  leave at once.
* MINIMIZE INTERCHANGE WITH POLICE. If you think
  you may be a suspect, say as little as possible. You can't talk
  your way out of it.
* IF YOU ARE A WITNESS, write out your statement and keep
  a copy, or tape any verbal statement you give to police.
* POLICE CAN SEARCH you, your home or car if you are
  under arrest. But if they ask permission to search, say "No." If
  they have a SEARCH WARRANT, they can search without

your permission. If you are on PAROLE, they may be able to search under some circumstances.

* LINE-UP: if police ask you to appear in a line-up, say you want your attorney to be present. Remember, all people in a line-up are supposed to look somewhat similar or the line-up is prejudicial.
* ASK FOR A LAWYER. As soon as you say "lawyer" they can't ask you any more questions.
* GOOD COP - BAD COP is the game police play to get you to confess. Watch out for the cop who tries to lay a guilt trip on you or who says "I'm your friend" or "This victim deserves a Christian burial, so tell us where the body is."

In addition to the foregoing, the following tips have been obtained from a variety of sources:

* Don't count on any help from family or friends, but be grateful and accept whatever assistance is offered. You'll need it. Instead of help, don't be surprised if you encounter hostility and ostracism from the people you thought you could count on. Some people who are arrested for or suspected of a crime are fired from their jobs, disfellowshipped from their churches and abandoned by friends and relatives.
* If you are a witness, and are not a suspect, it might not cause a problem for you to talk to the police without the advice of a lawyer, but it could. Sometimes it's easy to know which you are: suspect or witness. Other times it's hard to tell; police may say you are a witness, and later change their minds and say you are a suspect.
* If an investigator, private or otherwise, tries to talk to you, be sure he has been sent by your lawyer, not by the D.A. Warn your family and friends of this. Investigators will sometimes lie about whom they are working for in order to obtain information. Only talk to an investigator who has been sent by your lawyer. Ask any investigator who he works for, ask to see ID, and phone employer to verify.
* Don't brag about your status as a suspect to make yourself

seem like a big shot. This can cause a ton of trouble for you.

* Supervise the work of any investigators you hire. While you can't tell them how to practice their profession (presumably they are experts at what they do) you can see to it that they are working on your behalf. If you uncover a clue, insist that they follow it up. Don't let them tell you it's not important. Make sure they keep you up to date on what's happening every step of the way.

* Go check it out. If a witness says he saw the street corner where it happened from his window, take a walk down there and find out for yourself. Is it visible? Does a big tree block the view? Is there a traffic signal? Do the street lights work? What time do the street lights come on? Is there a barking dog in the neighborhood? Are kids playing outside?

* Do not bother, harass, threaten or act tough with anyone. It can only make things worse.

* If anyone bothers, harasses, threatens or acts tough with you or someone close to you, notify the police and your lawyer right away. Do NOT take matters into your own hands.

* If the police harass or threaten you, or if you are beaten up or otherwise injured by them, notify your lawyer at once. If you don't have a lawyer, get one. See a doctor and make sure your injuries are documented. Get color photos of the bruises. Ask the doctor or hospital to give you copies of your medical records (they may charge a small fee for photocopying). Contact the newspapers, radio and TV stations and tell them what happened. Contact the Internal Affairs supervisor of the police department, the Attorney General of your state, and the FBI.

Certainty is based on flimsier evidence than most of us realize.
Ellen J. Langer Ph.D., in *Mindfulness.*

With . . . get-tough advocates, the problem is how they see the problem. Seizing on sensational exceptions, they draw sweeping conclusions from anecdotal evidence.
Lane Nelson, *The Angolite* (July/Aug '96)

I see three classifications of prisoners: The rule-breakers, the offenders and the monsters. Then we have the snitches.

Former prison inmate

SNITCHES

In the immortal words of a professional snitch who is doing his time in PC (protective custody): "I heard more 'confessions' in a week than the average priest does in a lifetime."

This is how it works: the most culpable co-defendant snitches on his less culpable rappies. In exchange for his testimony, often known to the D.A. to be perjured, Mr. Most Culpable gets a "Get Out Of Jail Free" card, while Mr. Less Culpable goes to prison, sometimes even to Death Row. In a case where several judges were indicted for corruption, one judge snitched on the others in exchange for a reduced sentence.

If the snitch is a co-defendant, at least the defense knows whom they're dealing with. Sometimes they don't have the first clue. When a defendant is awaiting trial, a "professional" snitch can spend a few minutes in his cell and later testify that the defendant "confessed."

In the case of Rolando Cruz, who spent years on Death Row for a crime he didn't commit, police and prosecutor were indicted for perjury and obstruction of justice because of false "confessions." In another case, a judge gave an informant permission to lie under oath about his status as a professional snitch. Another judge ruled that informants could remain anonymous. Effectively, this means prosecution and police know who the informant is, but this information is withheld from the defense. Prosecutors use snitches when their inculpatory evidence is weak and the defendant could be factually innocent. Snitches snitch in exchange for freedom, a reduced sentence or special privileges in jail or prison such as sex, drugs, money or a television set, even illegal furloughs or placement in a witness protection program.

One notorious snitch who testified in literally dozens of

cases was such a good liar he was "passed around" from one police department to another. An informant by avocation, he was a burglar by trade. For each person against whom he testified, the D. A. "forgot" to prosecute a burglary or two. When he was ultimately found out, his police "buddies" threw him to the sharks. They marked his jacket [file folder] "unreliable." He was no longer "good enough" to be a snitch and no longer useful to them.

If you are in jail awaiting trial, or in prison, the most important rule to follow is: KEEP YOUR MOUTH SHUT. SAY NOTHING TO NOBODY ABOUT ANYTHING.

The next rule is: keep track of everyone who cells with you, especially for only a short time. Make a record of their name, and the dates and times they are in and out of the cell. Also try to learn the names of people you meet on the court bus, in the shower or chow hall. If you are moved to another tier or facility for no understandable reason, it may be to place you in contact with a snitch. Call your lawyer whenever this happens.

By keeping track of this information, and meticulous investigation, one lawyer was able to prove his client could not possibly have "confessed" to the snitch who testified against him. The snitch said they were cell mates for three weeks, while the defendant's records showed it was more like 15 minutes. In addition, this particular snitch had testified falsely in dozens of cases, using many aliases.

Some lawyers go so far as to give their clients a printed card that says something like "I do not talk to anyone because of snitching." Some lawyers write to the sheriff or warden and ask that their client not be celled with any known informant.

This advice bears repeating: KEEP YOUR MOUTH SHUT. DON'T TALK TO ANYONE EXCEPT YOUR ATTORNEY ABOUT YOUR CASE.

STRESS

According to clinical research in family therapy, doctors in the United States say that over two thirds of their office visits come from stress-related symptoms. These symptoms may be life threatening and cause family breakdown, or they may be mild annoyances. Reducing the stress in your life is vitally important. Too much stress interferes with your immune system and could cause your defenses to break down, setting the stage for serious physical or psychological problems. In each case, the symptoms of stress must be treated. In severe cases, the family member may be hospitalized. In less severe cases, stress management can be employed. This may include an appointment with a therapist or counselor.

For those who cannot afford private therapy, there are organizations and groups who use a sliding scale to determine their fees. This means they take into account your wages, your expenses and how many are in the family.

Groups such as the county mental health department, schools of psychology, and county-run mental health organizations, such as Big Bothers/Big Sisters, Indian Mental Health Services, church affiliated counseling, all use a sliding fee schedule. Some are free. Other resources for this kind of help include prisoner's rights and prisoner support groups.

*   *   *

> Fear is like a stranglehold on your senses. It shrinks your perception of the world to a narrow, suffocating black hole, and you are its only occupant.
> Eric's wife

RUMORS AND CHAOS

Excerpts from a dialogue with Eric's wife:
My husband, Eric, is on death row for murdering a convenience store clerk during a robbery. He tells me he's innocent. I'd like to believe him, but only he and God know for sure. The evidence against him was quite convincing.

When the police first came for him I was outraged. I screamed obscenities at them. If I had known there was a gun in the house, I would have used it. Eric denied the charges. He claimed innocence and produced a witness for his whereabouts that night. In my righteous indignation over his arrest, I closed my ears to the possibility of his guilt.

Eric landed on death row in May. By June I had made friends with other wives whose husbands were condemned. We'd swap war stories about our mates and pledge to fight the system we thought was so unfair.

The first rumor to reach me involved the closing of the law library. Jane called Frances, who called me. "The men won't be able to use the law library any longer."

"Why?" I asked.

"It's the Governor. You know how he's always bowing to political pressure."

"What are we going to do?"

"Let's send a hundred nasty letters to his office."

Sounded good to me. The Governor was a whiny idiot who deserved what he got. By the time I found out the law library had only been closed temporarily to fix a leaky ceiling, I had already sent six letters to the Capitol.

Two months later I received another call from Frances. "My God, they've decided to close the visiting room forever. I'll never see my husband again."

I went ballistic and wrote two more nasty letters, one to the Governor and one to the warden. Two days later the visiting room was open. It had been painted a soothing pale blue and the cracks in the floor had been fixed.

The result of blowing my mouth off cost my husband a visit from the warden for a dressing down and 10 days in the hole. Me, I suffered from a week long bout of stress-related headaches.

The third call from Frances concerned the loss of religious materials and personal belongings for our men. "They came in the middle of the night, like ninjas, and took everything my husband owned."

"Did he get it back?" I inquired, feeling a lump of suspicion in my gut.

"Are you kidding. He's lost everything. He told me they're going to kill him."

"What?" How can they execute him, he hasn't had his appeal yet."

"You don't know them. They can do anything they want."

Yes, they can, I thought, and I can't really do anything about it. Sure I can write nasty letters and I can go screaming to my congressman every time I hear a rumor about injustices on the row. But it won't get me anywhere. Innocent or guilty, my goal was to find Eric a good attorney for his appeal. I had to keep calm and focus my energy on that.

My advice to anyone who is caught up in the justice system is to keep their focus and not become unhinged by the little stuff. Do nothing which is of no use. Don't give in to the hysteria that permeates the family system. Take everything you hear with a grain of salt. Stay calm in the face of chaos. When you address the hierarchy in prison, be polite, keep your temper in the trunk of your car and never, ever let them see you sweat. Keep your head erect and your feet on the ground. Always know where you are at any given moment, know who is around you, and watch your mouth.

Open your ears to gossip, but let nothing slip by your lips that hasn't been verified by at least ten other reliable people. You are being judged by everyone, even the prisoners.

By learning to trust yourself, you will develop a strategy to overcome the hysteria in others. Physical and mental balance is the key to keeping yourself sane.

*   *   *

RUMORS RULE. They are a prison's largest commodity. RUMORS RUN RAMPANT. So in the words of a once-famous and long-gone journalist whose name eludes the authors, "Don't believe anything you hear, and only half of what you see."

Prison life begets many rules of verbal engagement: don't snitch; don't ask, don't tell (about someone's crime); and never tell the truth about anything, always lie about everything. It's these very rules that fertilize the soil in which wild rumors are nurtured and flourish.

Most rumors, like the most credible lies, start out with a small grain of truth or verifiable fact, just enough to make you wonder. Then they mushroom, and thereby create havoc among inmates, their families and prison staff.

Those of us who are in frequent contact with inmates we know and love have learned to take these rumors with a few pounds of salt. We have learned also not to act or react in response to rumors until we find out all the facts. Nothing is more embarrassing, or destroys your credibility, more than when you phone the warden's office or the governor's office, shrieking about the latest egregious violation of human rights done unto your loved one, only to be informed that it's a hoax and you've just been awarded the Gullible Sucker of the Year Award.

In the free world, it's said that truth is stranger than fiction. In the prison world fact and fiction, rumor and reality, seem to be interchangeable. While many strange and bizarre things do happen in prison, it seems things that really do happen are talked about less than the fictional figments that are rumors.

So when your loved one phones or writes with a story of the latest horror, don't go off half cocked until you check out the facts. You'll probably find, as we have, that at least half the rumors are based on imaginative speculation, not facts. Remember, though, the other half are probably true, and nobody can tell which is which.

> Funny thing, the truth. You don't hear it often anywhere. In prison it's pretty damn near extinct. But when truth rings out, it rings clear, rings true, and sounds so beautiful that it's real hard to disturb the melody with a bunch of petty static.
> Michael Hunter, a brilliant writer on San Quentin's [CA] death row.
>
>   *   *   *
>
> Power corrupts. Absolute power corrupts absolutely.
> Lord Acton

DON'T SWEAT THE SMALL STUFF

Excerpts from a dialogue with a counselor who has been working in a Mid-western prison for nine years:

Several distinct processes are operative. First, the administration is power-hungry and perpetuates itself by maintaining absolute control. They achieve this by "divide and conquer," creating chaos and dissension among their opponents. They also achieve control by secrecy, by refusing to divulge information, and by spreading disinformation. They create diversions, and they are very good at this, and they get you exercised about the small stuff, so you won't notice the big stuff. They get everyone working at cross purposes. They may let you win a skirmish or two, but you'll lose the war.

Inmates' families feel helpless, hopeless and powerless. They want and need to do something to "fix it," but they don't know what to do or how to do it. So they spin their wheels doing counterproductive things that are useless and often stupid, things that seem like a good idea at the time, but don't achieve any worthwhile outcome.

Some people thrive on chaos. If there's not enough chaos, they'll create some, to make themselves feel important and comfortable. A few guards, who are nothing more than juvenile delinquents and bullies, know which inmates are gullible, and will believe anything they hear and pass it on. They will stand in front of that inmates's cell and tell some outlandish story, just so the inmate will spread the rumor. This will result in dozens of nasty letters to the warden about something that never even took place. The prisoner and his supporters will lose any credibility they might have had with administration and become a laughing stock.

Some prisoners, not all of them, use fear of the unknown to create hysteria as a way of controlling their women. Many inmates accept whatever happens with resignation. They say "shit happens, so don't sweat the small stuff." But some of these dudes are control freaks, and they take advantage of their women's fears, and their women's desire to do something to help them, and they add grist to the rumor mill. They manipulate her into phoning and writing letters to people in authority. This way, he's still in control. He knows where she is and what she's doing, and she's doing it for him, and he's not being ignored or forgotten.

Everyone gets a payoff. The institution controls you and keeps you out from underfoot. The woman is deluded into thinking she's doing something useful. The inmate gets his jollies because even though he can't control his own environment, he manages to control her. And the guards or whoever started it get off on making fools of everyone else.

When you realize you are utterly powerless to control the system, your defense mechanisms kick in. You go into denial: "This can't be happening to us." Then you look around for some issue you can control, that you can have some impact on. So you write letters to the warden and the governor and complain about the food, the number of phone calls you're allowed, or how dirty the visiting room is. You spin your wheels dealing with these insignificant issues. All the while they're crankin' up the killin' machine or whatever, and you're oblivious. You don't see the forest for the trees.

They render you harmless, because while you're out running after windmills, they're doing whatever it was they planned on doing in the first place, but without any interference from you. You're not giving them any flack because you're all caught up with chasing your tail.

At the same time, they use you to advance their own agenda. You write letters in response to rumors, argue with the guards, call the warden names and act like a damn fool. They have maneuvered you into this behavior. Then they go to the media and say, "This person is a dangerous crackpot and we need to ban her from here for security reasons." And the public goes along with it, because you have behaved irrationally, even though that irrational behavior is the result of manipulation by the institution.

So my advice to families is this:
* Consider the source:
  How credible is the person who told me this?
  Where/with whom did it originate?
  How credible is the person who originated the story?
* When someone tries to maneuver you into some irrational act in response to a rumor or some insignificant event, ask yourself:
  What are my goals? My priorities?
  What is really the problem and is it really important?
  What are some rational solutions?
  What do I hope/expect to achieve by this action?
  Is it worth the hassle?
  Why does this person want me to do this and what's in it for him?
* Don't sweat the small stuff. If you go running off in all directions at once every time somebody yells "fire," you won't have the strength, resources or credibility left to fight the real war when it comes your way. Sooner or later, it will come your way. I guarantee it.

*   *   *

I refuse to consent to any search of my premises, the location of my arrest, my car or effects. I wish to exercise my right under the Fifth and Sixth Amendments to remain silent and to have my attorney present during any questioning or lineup. If you ignore my exercise of these rights and attempt to procure a waiver, I wish to confer with my attorney prior to any conversation with law enforcement agents on the subject of waiver.

Printed on the back of an attorney's business card.

GETTING BUSTED
A Constable's View

Excerpts from a dialogue with a police officer who has served on departments in a medium size city and a small city.

A "collar" or a "pop" is what we call an arrest. When you see the flashing lights in your rear view mirror, pull over right away. Don't make any swift or sudden movements. Stop right away or the cop will see you as a flight risk.

The officer's adrenaline starts pumping. On a traffic stop don't get out of the car, and don't walk back towards the officer's car. The officer doesn't know if he's in jeopardy, especially at night when he can't see inside the vehicle. If I see movement inside the vehicle, how do I know if you're reaching for a weapon, or hiding one? Keep your hands visible.

There are people out there who'd blow your head off just as soon as look at you. When you're in a situation with someone like that, you can't stop and think about his family and his kids. If you do, you're dead. You just have to act and react. You have to make your decision to shoot or not to shoot in three - eighths of a second. If a suspect is hiding his hand behind his back, you have to think maybe he has a weapon, and you look for a glint of metal. An officer has to be observant.

Some suspects just don't get it. If you have four cops pointing guns at you, a prudent person would put their hands up, but some of them think they're John Wayne or Wyatt Earp and they continue to conceal their hand, then they make a sudden move, and the officer can only believe the suspect has a weapon.

An officer shouldn't just rush into a situation to be a hero and get glory. That's what we call "tombstone courage." No cop who wants to go home that night would kick in the door of a crack house without waiting for back-up. You can't know how many suspects are in there.

If you get a call of a disturbance at a residence you want to defuse an anxious situation, not unlike a vehicle stop. If you see a lot of furtive movement inside the residence or a lot of people running around, you think are they stashing weapons, or what? Three times out of four these calls amount to nothing, but you have to be cautious.

But if the officer is chasing a suspect and your door is open and the suspect runs inside, the officer can legally pursue the suspect into your residence without waiting for your permission. If the police come to your door, be courteous and ask what they want. They probably want to talk to you. Officers are acutely aware of their surroundings in a house of people they don't know. Once I'm inside I look around for any door that is closed, any unusual noises. If your dog becomes hostile, the officer can ask you to put the dog in another room.

If the officer responds to a call of gunshots or screaming, he can go into the house without your permission because someone is in imminent danger of being hurt, or is already being hurt. In that case I would kick in the door, but when I go to court I better be able to tell the judge someone's life was in danger.

To an officer, different things make a person look suspicious. Wearing a flannel shirt and jacket in the middle of summer, you must be hiding something. Walking down the street, looking back over your shoulder. Beat-up cars in good neighborhoods, or trashy looking people in an expensive car or someone driving who doesn't look old enough to drive. A car with license plates that are inappropriate, like commercial plates on a passenger vehicle. The car might be stolen or might have been used in the commission of a crime.

If you are stopped for questioning, be polite and answer the officer's questions. Don't be evasive or change the subject. That's very suspicious. So is someone who is acting real nervous, pacing back and forth, smoking non-stop, or scratching all over themself.

If you are arrested, go along with the program, don't scream or struggle. Just quietly go into the cell, sit in a corner and mind your own business. Get a lawyer right away, then keep your mouth shut until he comes.

*   *   *

Once you've hunted a human being, there's nothing like it.
Allen Jacobs, bounty hunter

BAIL BONDS AND BAIL AGENTS

Excerpts from a dialogue with Dennis Justin, Bail Agent:

Bail agents are eccentric, part business and part bounty hunter. The proper name is "recovery agents." The biggest service we perform is to create jail space. By providing bail, we keep the jails from overcrowding. Bail lets you tend to your affairs and keep your job while you are on trial. When you're bailed, you waive your statutory right to a timely arraignment. If you fail to show up in court, you forfeit the bail.

Ten percent of the bail amount is cash up front. Like an insurance premium, it's non-refundable. You put up another ten percent or more, using your business or house as collateral. The cost of paperwork is additional. This is a nationwide fee except in states where you are released O. R., on your own recognizance.

In California, judges meet every six months to set bail guidelines. Florida, California, New York, Illinois and Texas are all considered trend setters in how bail is administered. Some states, such as Oregon, act as their own bail agent. Therefore, instead of contacting a private bail agent, you contact an employee of the state when you need bail.

What we look for in granting bail: ties to the community, an interest in your family, and enough equity in your home or business. We are not obliged to give everyone bail. We can put roadblocks in front of those who don't qualify by upping the cost or premium we charge. The judge can also deny bail if it's a serious crime or if you are deemed a flight risk.

Bail is a guarantee you'll show in court. A person who has run out on his bail is called a bail jumper. The courts, depending on the state involved, usually give six months before the case goes into a Summary Judgment. Then the bail agent has to forfeit the money to the court. If you are out on bail for over one year, you need to renew the bail bond contract with the bail agent.

If you skip bail, I can to go to your house and legally enter it to look for you. Law enforcement personnel need the bail agent's permission to go after a bail skipper. When we are skip tracing or bounty hunting, we can ask the court for an extension on bail, especially if we're hot on the trail of the person.

Eighty-eight percent of the people who stay in jail and don't get out on bail wind up doing time. Fifty percent of those who post bail do not do time. Think about it. People in jail show up for court with a two day old beard, chained, and wearing a baggy red jumpsuit. Those who have posted bail can show up clean shaven, wearing a three piece suit. Appearance makes a difference to a jury.

My recommendation to anyone arrested is, first, keep your mouth shut. Second, get an attorney. When arrested, you're dealing with an adversary. They keep score of how many people they've arrested. You're the one who will lose for the rest of your life if you talk. Never admit guilt and don't have diarrhea of the mouth. Never believe the cops are your friends. Be cautious.

Third, call a bail agent and get your family to come down to the jail with ten percent of the bail. Then you're out. Once out on bail, go to the courtroom where you'll be tried and watch the judge in action.

*   *   *

In order to get the booty, you have to get the body.
Scott Bernstein, bounty hunter

BOUNTY HUNTERS AND BAIL ENFORCEMENT AGENTS

You may think the Constitution protects you from search and seizure without a warrant, from being unlawfully imprisoned or transported across state lines without proper extradition. You probably think you're entitled to make a phone call to a lawyer if you're arrested and to be read your constitutional rights. And you are, unless you happen to be a bail-jumper and a fugitive, or mistaken for one, and have the misfortune of being rearrested by a bounty hunter.
Steve Kroft, on "*60 Minutes*."

Today, the bounty hunter may look like Steve McQueen:

tough as nails and determined to lock onto his prey like a spider with a fly. With search-and-arrest powers much broader than those of a police officer, this specialized hunter tracks his quarry without the added burden of regulations. He can break down the door to a house and search the premises without a warrant, arrest the occupant, detain him, and then transport him across state lines without legal repercussions.

Bounty hunters capture 87 percent of their fugitives. Cops get 20 to 23 percent.
Nancy Smith, bounty hunter, on the Oprah Winfrey Show
January 8, 1997, *How I caught the Criminal*
*   *   *

What is the face of a criminal? Is it Jim Bakker, Richard Nixon or Bill Clinton? There are dull-witted people, damaged and crazy people along with inexplicably cruel people whose sordid, secret deaths [executions] do nothing to set the universe in order. It's not the universe rebelling that lands people on death row; it's the bureaucracy plodding through it's paces.
Wendy Kaminer, *It's All the Rage: Crime and Culture*.

Is it better for ten guilty people to escape than for one innocent person to suffer? Every time a person accused of a crime is placed on trial, our legal system is on trial with him. If the law doesn't protect everybody, then nobody is safe from the danger of being wrongly convicted.
Sir William Blackstone

WRONGFUL CONVICTIONS

One and a half million people are incarcerated nationwide, the majority in California and Texas. A recent study speculated that if ten percent of them are not guilty of the crimes for which they have been convicted, that would mean 150,000 people in our prisons and jails are INNOCENT.

In 1993 Supreme Court Justice Rehnquist [Herrera v. Collins] said "Because of the very disruptive effect that entertaining claims of actual innocence would have on the need for finality in capital cases . . . the threshold showing for such an assumed right would necessarily be extraordinarily high."

Leonal Herrera was convicted and sentenced to death for the 1982 murders of two police officers. Some years later an attorney who represented Herrera's brother Raul came forward with evidence that Raul, who died in 1984, had confessed to the murders. In addition, Raul's nine-year-old son gave a sworn statement that he was an eye-witness to the crime and saw his father commit the murders. Because Texas law says new evidence must be presented within 30 days of conviction, this evidence could not be introduced and Herrera was executed.

Jesse Jacobs, another innocent Texan was executed on January 4th, 1995, for a crime the state acknowledged he did not commit. His innocence was known to the state prior to the execution, but they proceeded with it anyway because the courts said there was no legal mechanism by which the execution of an innocent person could be stopped.

The Ninth Circuit court of Appeals found the evidence of guilt against Arizona prisoner Paris Carriger was "not overwhelming," and the court had "serious doubts" about the credibility of a witness. It nevertheless held that Carriger failed to prove his innocence by "clear and convincing" evidence and failed to show that he was "unquestionably innocent."

The Supreme Court found in Carriger that a claim of factual innocence requires "clear and convincing proof." This standard requires a higher degree of proof than "preponderance of evidence," but not so high as "beyond a reasonable doubt."

"Innocent until proven guilty" is the standard in a criminal trial. Once a person is found guilty and continues to assert innocence, the standard is "guilty until proven innocent."

The court said doubt about guilt might be considered by the governor in deciding whether or not to grant clemency, but was an insufficient basis for the court to grant relief. Carriger was convicted on the testimony of a snitch who changed his story several times and who benefited from testifying.

Four men spent 18 years in prison for a 1978 double

murder they didn't commit. Two were sent to death row, one got life and the other 75 years. Recent DNA tests showed that none of the four could have been the perpetrators. It took dedicated Northwestern University Journalism students and their professor six months to investigate the case.

In a rare indictment, three former DuPage County Illinois, assistant prosecutors and four sheriff's deputies were charged with conspiracy and obstruction of justice in the wrongful murder convictions of two young Hispanic men. Rolando Cruz and Alejandro Hernandez spent eleven years on death row before being freed from prison.

In June 1996, Kevin Lee Green was released from prison after DNA evidence from state files found a match to the real killer. Green had spent 16 years in prison.

Walter McMillian won release from Alabama's death row in 1993, after spending six years behind bars for a crime he didn't commit. McMillian, 45, is Black. He was convicted of the murder of a white woman. He was freed through the efforts of lawyers from the Equal Justice Initiative of Alabama, who proved the prosecution withheld exculpatory evidence and pressured witnesses to testify falsely against him.

George Franklin, whose murder conviction was based on his daughter's "repressed-memory" testimony was overturned in 1996. He has filed suit accusing his daughter and prosecutors of conspiring to violate his rights. "I was prosecuted for a crime I didn't commit. I lost all of my life savings and spent more than 6 1/2 years in prison."

Franklin's conviction was overturned because jurors were improperly told that his silence in the face of his daughter's jailhouse accusation was tantamount to an admission of guilt.

Trial prosecutors, like police officers, are legally immune from suit, but in Franklin's case, the immunity didn't extend to pretrial matters.

Wrongful convictions don't happen only in the United States. Three men jailed for 18 years for murder in England were set free in early 1997. They had been convicted because of a confession falsified by police. This case was only the latest of several similar ones in Britain in recent years.

*   *   *

> We have allowed ourselves to become besieged by our own fear.
> Frank Black, *Millennium*

"Equal Justice Under the Law" are noble words engraved over the entrance to the Supreme Court of the United States in the Nation's Capital. If we really believe in this great democratic concept, we can hardly continue to tolerate the spectacle of a mental case charged with disorderly conduct sitting naked on the concrete floor of a bare isolation cell in a local jail while in another jurisdiction he would be in a hospital. It is equally incongruous for a minion of organized crime charged with felonious assault to be walking on the streets free while scores of minor but indigent offenders sit idly in overcrowded jails awaiting disposition.

> Richard McGee, *Our Sick Jails.*

When a guilty person is set free, some part of the community is at risk. But when an innocent person is imprisoned, the foundation of our society is placed at risk. That's a greater danger.

Greg Fallis & Ruth Greenberg, *How To Become Your Own Detective*

THE RULES OF THE GAME

Excerpts from a dialogue with a young woman who tells what happened one night:

My sister and I are in our 20's. On Christmas Eve we decided to finish our shopping. We took separate cars, but at the mall we parked close to each other. On the way home, about 7:30 P.M. since it was dark, I told Lucy to follow me.

On the freeway, I saw a bright light in my rearview mirror. It was right behind Lucy. I saw her slow down and pull over. It was a lonely stretch of road and there weren't any houses nearby, just tall pines and a lots of dark. I got scared for her so I pulled over, too. If this was a prank, I wanted to be there. Two women might scare them away.

She got out of her car and walked toward mine. I didn't see any flashing red lights, so I knew they weren't police. I tried to appear calm so Lucy wouldn't be scared, but whoever

followed us sat in their car with the bright light turned on. This
made me mad. I told Lucy to get back in her car and follow me
to the police station.

As she headed back to her car, someone grabbed her
by the hair and yanked her toward him. I didn't realize anyone
had gotten out of the car. The bright lights had blinded me. He
seized her by the waist and threw her over the hood of the car.
I could hear her ask "What's happening, what's going on?"

I got out of my car and ran to her. Out of the dark, a
second man appeared. As I turned away, he attacked. He hit
me with a long, hard object. I thought it was a bat. A warm, wet
trickle slid down my cheek and I knew it was blood. I thought we
were both going to be raped and murdered. I lost track of Lucy.
The man grabbed me and hurled me to the ground. He drug me
through the dirt and I could feel my slacks rip on the underbrush.
I screamed. He hit me again and I saw stars.

When we got near his car, I saw his uniform. Something
must have been wrong. We hadn't done anything illegal. I held
out my hand and tried to ask him what was the matter. I wanted
to cooperate. He slapped my hand and told me to "shut up." By
now more cops arrived. They put Lucy in the back of the police
car. When I tried to move toward her, the officer kicked my leg
out from under me. I fell flat on my back and I hit my head against
the concrete. I must have blacked out then.

At the police station, they claimed they saw Lucy running
and thought she was leaving the scene of a crime. They forcibly
detained her. I told them my dad was a city councilman and an
attorney. The cop said the charge was "following too close."

Dad arrived with bail. He took one look at my bloody
face and demanded to know why I hadn't been taken to the
hospital. The sheriff shrugged and said, "They weren't arrested. If
you want to take them to the hospital, go ahead."

"You hit her," my dad said, "you treat her."

"Doesn't work that way," the sheriff said. "We only pay
for the treatment of people who have been arrested and booked."

After I had an x-ray, the doctor sewed 26 painful stitches
in my head. He informed my dad that cleaning up the "sheriff's
mess" was a common occurrence in the emergency room.

"We get plenty of roughed up, bloody wrecks in here.
Some have been beaten senseless. But you don't think the
County pays for any of this do you? No sir, the County lets 'em
go so they can pay for the privilege of having the shit knocked
out of 'em by the same guys who're supposed to protect 'em.

Makes a whole hell of a lot of sense, don't it," the doctor said.

We were charged with resisting arrest and went to trial, even though we were never officially arrested. The cops threw the book at us and tried to charge us with following too close, resisting arrest, disorderly conduct and suspicion of drunk driving. None of them had a shred of evidence to prove any of those charges. One of my dad's associates, an experienced criminal lawyer, handled the trial.

How could we be charged with resisting arrest when we hadn't been arrested? Lucy had stopped voluntarily and she returned to her car voluntarily. There was no reason she should have been grabbed and pulled back. She was just somebody stopped on the road.

Lucy told them when she looked back, all she could see was bright lights. She couldn't see anybody, couldn't hear anything, so she went back to her car, not to leave, but to a position of safety.

The D.A. took it to trial because it got a lot of media attention. They had to make it seem like a real crime had happened, and the city councilman's daughters were criminals. Instead, the cops got a black eye in the media. Later, my parents got a visit from somebody high up in the sheriff's office to talk about what had happened and why. They tried to excuse what the cops did, and said young girls had no business being out late at night. They lost in court.

Cops have all kinds of fears but they can't act on every one. If the officer was concerned, he should have retreated to his car and called for more back-up. I don't believe you can eliminate the rights of citizens on the basis of cop's fear. That's why we have the Bill of Rights. A cop can't say, well he got out of his car so I shot him or I beat him up. Fear is part of their job. My sister should never have been stopped.

The district attorney spent a lot of taxpayer money to prosecute the case. It lasted two weeks. It could have cost us several thousand dollars to defend, but we had my dad's associate to help. Now my family has a great cynicism about law enforcement. I believe cops lie under oath and are capable of misbehavior just like anyone else.

After it was all over, we proceeded with a civil suit against the County, but we lost. The whole affair has badly affected both of us. We're nervous, fearful of authority, and I have serious headaches from the head injury. The incident has had residual effects on our entire family.

We took photos of the injuries. The officer said he hit my head when I was trying to escape. Baloney. I think this kind of assault is pretty common. Unfortunately, most people don't have the financial resources to hold the police responsible. It costs big money to sue. Had there been a video camera, it would have been another "Rodney King."

If you get stopped, think in terms of how the police think. Don't give them a reason or excuse to have any fear of you. If you're pulled over, stop in a well lighted area where there are lots of people, or, for your own protection and to keep the officer in line, go to the police department if it's nearby. Even if you have to drive a little distance, I don't care what they say, I always say "be careful." When the police stop you, put your hands on the steering wheel. Don't give them an excuse to say they thought you were going for a gun.

You're going to need a good lawyer, one who can present the facts, and get any supporting evidence or witnesses. If it comes down to your word against that of a police officer, there's always the presumption that the police officer is telling the truth. A person who says "I know I'm innocent so I don't need a lawyer" is wrong. Tell them to find out what life in jail is like because that's where they're going.

Even a lawyer knows better than to defend himself. A lawyer who defends himself has a fool for a client. That's why my dad's associate handled the case. My dad discussed it with him, but the associate handled it. Dad would have been too emotionally involved. That's why doctors don't operate on their own kids.

*   *   *

THE DENTIST'S DAUGHTER AND THE "SLAMMER NAZIS"

When the evening news comes on and the anchor tells how the police have apprehended a criminal, many people associate that arrest with some low-life from the "other side of the tracks."

During our investigation, we found many who didn't fit the stereotype. For the most part these were working-class professionals who'd never imagined being arrested. Unfortunately, their stories are becoming more and more commonplace.

This was written by Trudy, a mother who was pulled into

the prosecution and detention system because of someone's unwarranted desire for revenge:

It's been eight months since our daughter Elaine was wrongfully accused of a crime. Not one of her friends has been by to offer their support.

My husband and I threw a party for her eighteenth birthday. She invited her boyfriend, Jason, and some of their friends. Jason and Elaine both belong to Young Christians in America. So do most of the kids here that night, including our pastor's son.

At 8:30 P.M., a girl Elaine didn't invite showed up. This girl flirted with Jason, then invited him over to her place. He refused. Elaine found out about the invitation, got mad, and asked the girl to leave. Around midnight, the party broke up. I followed Elaine up to her room to ask about the situation. She told me everything was all right and not to worry. By 12:30 we were in bed.

About 1:00 A.M., two officers came to our door and asked for Elaine. I told them she was in bed, asleep. They told me to bring her down. They wanted to ask her some questions.

When Elaine came downstairs, they told her she was under arrest. We were stunned. My husband asked what she had done. They told us to get an attorney. Elaine was accused of assault and battery. She supposedly attacked the girl who had tried earlier to pick up on Jason, they said at about 11 P.M.

Nick explained about the birthday party and told the police Elaine had been with us the entire night. One officer told us a complaint had been made and this was a serious offense. He again said to get an attorney. It was a terrible mistake, one that could easily be rectified because Elaine had an airtight alibi. But, as we watched in horror, the police advised her of her rights. Then I realized this wasn't a crime show on TV.

My husband and I are both professionals. Nick is a dentist and I teach high school history. Neither of us had ever been arrested. Our son Ron is twelve. Elaine worked part-time in the evening as a receptionist for a rape counseling agency. During the day, she attends college. She plans on getting a degree in child development. She is not, and I want to emphasize this, a hoodlum or a fast girl. She's been brought up right and goes to church with us every Sunday. She plans to marry Jason next year.

This whole episode took us completely by surprise. The two police officers were polite. They handcuffed her but they wouldn't allow her to get dressed before they took her to the station. I ran to grab my old terry cloth robe and tossed it to her as the officers escorted her out the door. We were told that since she had turned 18, she was now an adult. We could retain an attorney for her, but nothing else. We were not allowed to go down to the station with her.

My head just exploded. I saw images of drunken prostitutes mauling Elaine, of pimps and drug dealers beating her up. Several articles I had read about jails and prisons came to mind. I didn't know if she was sitting in a filthy, roach infested cell or locked up with child killers. I couldn't stop crying. Nick had to give me a pain killer to keep me from going crazy.

Poor Ron. He didn't understand it at all. He kept saying he was going to "sic the dog on the fuzz." He called them names and threatened to kill them for taking Elaine away. After we got Ron settled, we called a lawyer, a friend Nick had known since grade school. The man explained he wasn't a criminal defense attorney, but he would call someone who would go to the police station to help Elaine.

A criminal defense attorney. My God. It sounded as if Elaine was a common criminal. I couldn't believe this was happening to us. We've always been so boringly ordinary.

An hour later the attorney called us with another nightmare. He assured us Elaine was all right, but she would have to stay in jail until Monday morning. Then she would go to court. He told us the girl who was assaulted, "the victim," he called her, claimed Elaine had threatened her with a gun. This was why bail had been set so high. We could never raise $50,000 right away. The attorney gave us the name of a bail agent who said we could put the house up as collateral. The non-refundable fee for the bail bond would be $5,000, ten percent of the bail amount.

Just as we were about to do that, the attorney called back and told us he believed Elaine would be freed on Monday. She asked us to hold off on the house, and said she'd rather sit it out in jail. It was the worst weekend I've ever experienced.

On Sunday we talked to our minister. He seemed uncomfortable with what had happened, and suggested we see a counselor who "deals with this kind of problem." Then he dismissed us like stale bread, and asked us not to return to church until "this situation is resolved." I felt so degraded and dirty, like I was somehow no longer part of the human race.

Monday, we met with the attorney at 8 A.M. He told us

the victim had given her statement to the prosecutor, but with the alibi we provided for Elaine and the rap sheet this other girl had, he should be able to prove the girl had lied. A few minutes later, Elaine was brought into the courtroom wearing an ugly, baggy red jumpsuit and chains. My little girl in chains. My heart constricted. She looked so tiny and afraid. Her cheeks were sunken, her eyes haunted. Ron started to cry and I had a hard time holding back my own tears. We waited in the courtroom until lunch time. Finally the attorney came back. He said the "victim's" roommate had signed a paper saying the victim had skipped town. All of her possessions were gone, plus she had stolen $60 from the roommate's purse.

Why did this girl come to the court house and give her statement to the prosecutor, and then skip town? It didn't make sense to me. The attorney said she probably did this to make it more difficult for Elaine. Then he took us to stand with Elaine before the judge. My stomach lurched, threatening to explode.

What if the judge sentenced Elaine to years in prison? What if he didn't need the "victim" to be there? In the end, the judge didn't dismiss the charges. He did say if the victim continued not to show up for future court dates the charges would eventually be dropped. Elaine was free to go. I felt he must have known what we were going through because he treated us with respect. By that time, we had been in the courtroom over six hours. Four hours after that, Elaine was released. When we got home, it was past the dinner hour. We all had headaches, but we certainly weren't hungry.

The toll this has taken on us as a family is beyond belief. I won't complain about the attorney fees. The man did his job. He was worth $6,000. Even though it will be hard, we can always replace the money. What we cannot replace is our trust in a system we thought was fair. We have always been an honest, law-abiding family. We mind our own business and support our community, but in the long run it made no difference. Our daughter was wrongfully accused of a crime, arrested and thrown in jail. The story about her arrest got an inch in the morning paper. But by the evening edition, a tasteless piece about our family appeared in the news: "Dentist's Daughter Arrested for Assault and Battery." The article said the police escorted her to jail "scantily clad." It didn't say the "scanty" attire was her baby doll pajamas, and didn't mention the robe.

It also said Elaine had been involved in two "violent episodes" at school, but didn't say what they were. The attorney contacted the newspaper to check their sources. The first incident happened in 1984. Elaine was seven years old. She had released two white rats into the school yard.

Elaine and her teacher were in the Principal's office and I could hear Elaine screaming, "I won't let you kill those rats. They don't deserve to die just because they're rats." Evidently someone had told Elaine that white rats were used for medical experiments. It scared her enough that she let the animals go. The second incident was in her high school biology class. She refused to cut up the frog, saying "Frogs have feelings, too." She organized a protest against murdering frogs for science. That's what the newspaper called "past violent episodes."

It's been eight months since the incident and we've still had no closure. The other day, Ron got into a fight with a kid at school. The boy designed a bunch of "business cards" with our phone number on them that said, "Got a problem with your friends? Get Elaine the Terminator. She'll pummel them bloody." He gave the cards out to everyone he knew.

Jason and his parents have been wonderful. They have consistently stood by Elaine. The rest of the town, especially those who claimed to be our friends, snubbed us. Even though Elaine was innocent, we've been treated like lepers. The kids at the party acted like they were doing us a favor by giving Elaine an alibi. You'd think they'd be happy to show she was blameless.

I've lost my job at the high school. I guess they don't want a criminal's parent teaching impressionable children. It just wouldn't be proper.

Even Nick's patients have "dwindled down to a precious few." This town used to be our home. We've lived here for 27 years. Now, I feel as if we're being blamed for every nasty incident the town has had for the last 200 years.

Elaine, blessed be, was allowed to keep her job, but after a while, they became unhappy with her alleged reputation. She quit before they fired her.

We finally decided to sell the house and the practice. That's why you saw all the boxes in the hallway. But it's not us I worry about. We have enough money to relocate. It's the kids I feel for. Elaine has carried this whole episode inside of her. She's confused and angry all the time. Last week she broke up with Jason, then after they talked, they reunited. She has nightmares and wakes up screaming. Now she's decided she doesn't want to go to college. All she can think about is her arrest record.

There are a few positives in all of this. We've become closer as a family. Standing alone against the animosity has cemented our relationships. I don't believe anyone could hurt a member of our family without all of us jumping to the defense. Before this happened, we were complacent with our belief in a just society. We thought friendship was forever. Now we're more wary. Nothing is taken for granted.

Another positive is that we've all been in therapy, and it does seem to help. Ron says he no longer hates the police, although he still calls them the "Slammer Nazis." He says it doesn't matter if you're innocent, and maybe he's right. Next time they come for us, we'll be ready.

After we get out of this town, I'm sure we'll begin to heal. For now, I can't stop thinking about others like us. Professional people whose lives have been disrupted by false accusations. According to our therapist, our situation isn't rare. He says there are support groups and activist organizations for people like us. The problem is, no one believes they will ever be arrested.

> Get your facts first, and then you can distort them as much
> as you please.
> Mark Twain

> The criminalization of drugs is immoral. Using the police to fight drugs has violated civil rights, crowded America's prisons, unfairly affected non-whites, damaged other countries and inhibited the treatment of users.
>
> Can any policy - however high minded - that has that effect ever be called moral policy?
> Milton Friedman, Nobel Prize-winning economist

Nothing in her past had prepared her for a job interview for the position of assassin for the state of Oregon [on a death penalty trial]. This job interview was technically called "voir dire" and it denoted the process by which a jury was selected

Phillip Margolin, *"The Burning Man"*

HEADS YOU LOSE, TAILS YOU LOSE
The Cost of Defense

Whether or not money was ever a problem before your loved one went to prison, it is now. It's a well known fact that there is no such thing as a "level playing field" in a criminal case. If the family or individual has substantial assets, every last dollar could be spent on a criminal defense. Even if the person is found "not guilty," he or she can be forced into bankruptcy. The most notable recent example of impoverishment by defending one's self is the case of O. J. Simpson. He had a considerable fortune, estimated by some at the time of his trial as about $10 million. When the trial was over, he had nothing left. As of this writing, his house had been foreclosed, and he was being chased for whatever he had left by both the Brown and Goldman families and the Internal Revenue Service.

Mr. Simpson was able, with his former wealth, to create the closest thing to the "level playing field" of any defendant in recent memory. Millionaire Claus von Bulow was also able to afford an excellent and successful defense against charges of attempting to murder his wife.

But what happens to the poor or middle class defendant? If the person on trial qualifies, he or she may be able to retain the services of the Public Defender or a court appointed lawyer, paid for out of public funds. However this eligibility is not automatic; the person has to pass a means test. In other words, they have to be broke. Then the law limits the amount that can be spent on the defense. So while the prosecution can spend virtually unlimited funds to prosecute your family member, the defense is restricted in how much can be spent from public funds. In some states, the defense is given as little as $1,000 to defend a murder case. If relatives and friends have money, they often mortgage the farm and give their life savings to augment the defense fund. Often they will give their last nickel to pay for private investigators and expert witnesses who would otherwise be unavailable to the defendant. So at the end of the trial, win or lose, the poor defendant and his relatives and friends of moderate means are left destitute.

If a defendant is middle class and has property or money in the bank, he or she is not eligible for the services of the Public Defender. He or she will have to hire a lawyer and pay a retainer of from $5,000 to $100,000 or more, if it's a murder defense. The house, business, cars and other assets will be consumed in defending the case.

Often, besides losing everything, the defendant and his family lose their jobs. Parents of death row inmates, in particular, have been ousted from their employment because "we can't have people like that teaching in our schools" or "taking care of patients in our hospital."

If the defendant is found not guilty, there is no legal means of getting all that money back. It's gone forever. But at least the family has the option of starting over again to rebuild the family assets.

If the defendant is found guilty, the money problems have only just begun. The family may have lost its breadwinner or a substantial contributor to the family budget. If there's a house, it will almost certainly be lost, too. The family may have to go on public assistance, and the children will have to go to day care, which is expensive, so the remaining parent can look for a job.

Then there are the expenses associated with being in prison. The state provides prisoners with bare necessities, but your loved one may turn to you for everything from shoes to cigarettes. The quarterly boxes that some inmates are allowed to receive cost on the average from $200 to $300, if you can afford to include everything on the list. In addition you may be asked to provide a TV or electric fan. If he needs to see a doctor, you may be asked to furnish money for the co-payment.

Visiting the prison can be expensive. If it's far from home there will be transportation costs, meals and motels. You will need a few dollars to buy snacks from the vending machines in the visiting room. If you are fortunate enough to be allowed family (so called "conjugal") visits, you will have to provide all the food and other items needed for that visit.

Phone calls also can be a great expense. (See "They Say Talk Is Cheap...")

Depending on your relationship to the inmate and his character, you could also be the victim of a scam. Most inmates appreciate what they get and don't abuse the privilege. But there are always the few rotten apples who will take advantage of anyone they can, any way they can. If you don't know the person too well, beware of pleas for large sums of money for legal fees, medical care or other emergencies.

Finally, if the one you love has received a lengthy sentence, or a death sentence, you will find yourself spending large sums of money on the appeals. While appellate lawyers are provided at no cost in some cases, you may want to hire an investigator and obtain copies of the trial transcripts, which don't come cheap. Transcripts can run to several thousand pages, and cost up to several thousand dollars.

*   *   *

PRIVATE INVESTIGATORS

Excerpts from a dialogue with two private investigators:
Ask the attorney if there will be an investigation and how much it will cost. If the case is through the Public Defender's Office, the court should allot some money for investigation. Get

the investigator through the lawyer. If you hire someone on your own, the lawyer may not use the information the private investigator (P.I.) develops. If you hire him on your own, you have no way of knowing if the P.I. is competent. Many are dishonest or incompetent. If money allocated by the Public Defender's Office is not enough for a good investigation, the family can contribute additional funds.

The family should urge the defendant to cooperate with his own investigator, but not the prosecutor's. Beware. The prosecutor's investigator may use subterfuge so you'll think he is on your side.

The lawyer's duty is to properly investigate the case. It's okay if the lawyer has a question or two and phones someone to ask, but overall the major investigation should be done by trained investigators. Especially in a capital case, the standard is to have a licensed investigator. If the lawyer does not hire an investigator in a capital case, get a new lawyer.

The investigator will interview family and associates. It might seem that the investigator is asking questions that will reflect negatively on the family, but these questions may help the defendant. If the investigator finds the family has problems such as alcohol, fetal alcohol syndrome, incest, lead poisoning, a history of violence or some inherited or genetic problem, this information could help the defendant by providing mitigation, so it's important to answer these questions truthfully and completely. Disclosure of these problems can help.

It's not a good idea to do your own investigation, as you don't know what questions to ask.

OBTAINING RECORDS WITHOUT A SUBPOENA

Another P.I. says:
It's vital to your survival that your attorney obtain all records pertaining to your case independently. He should not rely on the D. A. to give him all the records you're entitled to during the discovery process. Your lawyer should go to the source for each document. Later on, when he asks the D. A. for documents and evidence during discovery, he might find that some exculpatory evidence is missing. This could be a sign of impropriety on the part of public officials.

Under the Freedom of Information Act, you or your attorney, or in some cases a family member, can write to an agency and ask for a document. You don't need to tell them what it's for. They are not allowed to charge you a fee for the document. They are allowed to charge a reasonable amount for actual copying, up to about 50 cents a page, but not the salary of the worker who does the copying.

Many different documents and reports may be obtained in this way, including police reports, autopsy reports and jail records that indicate cell location and cell mates, and when you were out to court or received medical care. Guard's duty rosters are not obtainable in most cases because they are personnel records, which are exempt from discovery.

*   *   *

Excerpts from a dialogue with RICHARD BARNES, who has been a private investigator for ten years, and has had a total of 16 years in law enforcement. He specializes in search warrants, Miranda issues and ineffectiveness of counsel:

There are three phases of court: Guilt, Penalty, and Post Conviction. A family member should not help with the investigation during the guilt phase because their testimony would be considered biased. A neutral party, such as a private investigator, needs to do this.

Families can help their loved one during a death penalty case. In preparation for the penalty phase, don't wait until the last minute. The family can gather documents. What this does is present pieces of the human puzzle to the court. We sometimes go back generations, to the great grandparents and further if possible, in order to obtain a complete picture of the defendant.

A paper trail is a must. Information to include for all family members:
* Family tree, portraits of family members, birth, death and divorce records, telephone numbers and addresses of all living relatives. Where did you live, towns, houses, streets, ethnicity, relationships, neighbors.
* School records to see if there's any learning disability, IQ testing, school problems, classes taken, violence committed on or by the defendant or abuse by bullies, dating and sexual partners or preferences, adjustment problems, old teachers names, friendships with school chums and their addresses.
* Medical records including history of alcohol or drug abuse, physical or sexual abuse, violence, sexual partners, sexual diseases, head trauma, physical disabilities. Use baby

books and start as early in the person's life as possible to relate childhood incidents.
* Psychiatric records (therapists' names, addresses and phone numbers.)
* Military discharge papers (honorable, general or dishonorable), adjustment problems, combat (when and where, how long and type of training.)
* Work experience (where, how long, duties, absenteeism, performance, how much money did they make and what they did with that money.)
* Religion (what type, how long, problems, baptism, pastors, priests, nuns, names and addresses of each.)
* Recreational activities (what, where, when, how much money spent on each.)
* Close friends and relationships (who, where and for how long, any problems.)

*   *   *

There are family members who find they're in a position to help the attorney by performing some of the more mundane, but necessary, duties. This mother's exposure to her son's court transcripts, the extra work she did to make copies and to study their contents, gave her information she needed to assist the attorney during trial:

When my son called to say he was arrested, I wanted to make sure he received a fair trial.

When I arrived at the jail, a clerk handed me a copy of the jail rules and told me to wait until I heard my name.

Finally, a disembodied voice called over a loudspeaker. "Mrs..., please follow the yellow dotted line."

I headed down a long hallway. I had to wait until a guard unlocked the door, then he motioned me through. "Sit at any window," he said.

It took a few minutes for my son to arrive. When he did, I almost went into shock. His appearance had changed drastically. There were bruises under his eyes and his cheeks were translucent. I could see the blue veins under his skin. His nose was bandaged and the look on his face was apprehensive. It took me a minute or two to regain my composure before I could ask about his injuries.

He and his friends had piled into my son's car and headed for the drive-in to see Jurassic Park. The movie ended at 11:30 PM. As they drove out to go home, three girls in a convertible drove by.

The guys followed them to Mel's drive in for root beer floats. After getting the girls' phone numbers, the boys started for home, but not before burning a little rubber. "Just to impress the girls," my son said.

A cop flicked on his red lights and burned rubber in pursuit. The boys were arrested for being drunk and disorderly. When my son tried to explain that none of them had been drinking, one cop hit him in the nose with his fist, while the other pushed him to the ground. My son ended up with a broken nose and had to be taken to the hospital.

The preliminary hearing, where the prosecutor would present his case against my son to the judge, would be Monday morning.

In the courtroom, I asked his court-appointed attorney how I could help. He balked at first, said he didn't need any help. I persisted. A few days after the hearing I went to the records department in the courthouse and made copies of all his transcripts. Sometimes records or transcripts become lost or damaged. In case of a sensational trial, the material could be altered and arrest records could be modified to make the prosecution's case seem more convincing.

I was suspicious of the authorities and their methods of record keeping. I made several copies of the transcripts and had them placed in safe keeping. I even sent copies to friends and relatives living out of town. The material I copied was:
* Arrest record, including officer's statement
* Medical and hospital records
* Preliminary Court transcripts
* Criminal Complaint
* All Superior Court transcripts (after the trial)
* All Discovery Information
* Probation Report
* Private investigator's report.
* I also made a video copy of televised news about the arrest, and photocopies of newspaper articles.

After seeing my son's injuries, my paranoia about law enforcement's tactics made me wary. I studied the transcripts with a fine tooth comb. My vigilance was justified. I found the arresting officer's report contained several inaccuracies. It stated my son was intoxicated and under the influence of drugs. The medical records and the hospital report did not support this. When the prosecutor tried to use this in court, we were able to have that particular charge thrown out.

The Probation Report indicated two prior misdemeanor traffic tickets and two failures to appear for those tickets as grounds to recommend against probation. Even though these tickets happened five years earlier, they were still used to justify the D.A.'s request for prison time. The officer believed he had proof my son would be a flight risk if placed on probation.

The prosecution used the traffic tickets as enhancements when asking for a longer prison sentence. It boggled my mind at how petty prosecutors could be when going after someone. One ticket had been for a broken tail light, the other for a broken light over the license plate.

After I obtained my son's Department of Motor Vehicles records, I was able to show that the two tickets had been taken care of. The failure to appear warrants had been a mistake. I then sent a copy of the DMV printout to the attorney and one to the prosecutor. To be safe, I also sent one to the judge. By doing this I was able to eliminate the enhancements.

Most attorneys are so busy they can't do everything. Some welcome help from the defendant's family. Because I took an active role in my son's case, the attorney worked harder. He knew I cared.

Mistakes can and do happen. By having the transcripts with me, I could identify the problems immediately and take care of them before they got out of hand.

I became a tyrant to everyone I knew, telling them to make sure they and their children took care of traffic tickets and any other annoying misdemeanor type offenses. Your past can and will be used against you, no matter how trivial your crime might be.

*   *   *

When I went to pay my parking ticket I was told there was a warrent for my arrest. "Why?" I asked. "You have an unpaid parking ticket," the clerk said. I went home, found the receipt and took it back to the clerk. She said, "You were lucky. You could have gone to jail."
40 year-old therapist.

Generalized Power Of Attorney, when signed by the inmate and notarized, enables you to perform certain functions on his behalf. Obtain a do-it-yourself form at an office supply store, and fill it out. Under "Provisions," put "to act on behalf of ___ while he is in jail." Under "Terms," put, " for transcripts and other legal papers pertaining to his trial and investigations." Send two forms to the inmate. Tell him to get it notarized at the jail. Some jails don't have a Notary on the premises. In that case, tell him to just sign it and return it to you. Keep one for yourself and send one to the attorney to file.

The dead speak in riddles. It's up to the investigator to decipher the puzzle.
Anonymous

AUTOPSY REPORTS

Excerpts from a lecture given by Leslie Abramson, a well known defense attorney, and Michael Baden M.D., a preeminent forensic pathologist and coroner:

In cases of questionable death, whether of an inmate in custody, police brutality, or a homicide in which you are the defendant, the autopsy report and related documents are of great importance. From the time a body is discovered, various officials make a number of written notes and reports. When the autopsy is completed, the examining physician dictates a formal report of his findings, which is typed by a clerk.

A knowledgeable attorney or investigator knows if they ask for the autopsy report, that's all they will get. Instead, they have to request, by name, other parts of the medical examiner's file, because some of the scribbled notes may contain information vital to your case. This information may be omitted, accidentally or intentionally, from the typewritten report.

Additional documents to ask for might include:
* medical examiner's crime investigation report
* notice of death - how and by whom it was reported
* hospital or emergency room report
* family history of the victim
* crime scene photos
* autopsy photos
* x-rays
* autopsy work sheet
* microscopic slide reports
* paraffin blocks for DNA and toxicology
* bacteriology report
* neuropathology report.

It's helpful to understand some common terms:

CAUSE OF DEATH: the actual physical agent of death, for example, bleeding, poison, gunshot wound, cancer, pneumonia, suffocation.

MANNER OF DEATH: there are four: natural, accidental, suicide, homicide.

CORONER: a public official who investigates deaths, but is not necessarily a physician.

MEDICAL EXAMINER: a physician who has additional training in forensic pathology. In some jurisdictions the same person may serve as both Coroner and Medical Examiner.

PATHOLOGIST: a medical doctor with additional training in scientific diagnosing of disease, for example by studying tissue samples under a microscope.

HOSPITAL PATHOLOGIST: performs autopsies on people who have died of a natural disease, such as cancer or pneumonia. These diseases usually affect the body's internal organs and leave no-external signs like bleeding or bruising.

FORENSIC PATHOLOGIST: has additional training in the science of criminalistics, performs autopsies on people whose manner of death is accidental, suicide or homicide, is familiar with the law and with procedures involving preserving evidence in a criminal case. These causes of death usually show some outward sign of injury such as bleeding, bruising, laceration, strangulation etc.

The attorney or investigator should interview the medical examiner, and should tape the interview. They may uncover some information helpful to your case.

THE POLYGRAPH

"The polygraph is not a lie-detector, but an instrument used in conjunction with a clinical procedure designed to diagnostically determine truth or deception," says Brian C. Jayne, a polygraph expert (*The Prosecutor*, The Journal of the National District Attorney's Association, Spring 1991, vol. 24, no. 4.)

Jayne goes on to say that:
* a prosecutor has nothing to lose and a great deal to gain by offering a criminal suspect a polygraph examination
* contrary to popular belief, research consistently indicates that psychopaths are detectable with the polygraph
* the prosecutor should obtain a copy of the examiner's written report to determine exactly what questions were asked of the defendant
* it is a well established fact that victims sometimes fabricate, distort, misrepresent, and exaggerate what happened to them.

Michael Floyd, J. D., states in a brochure of Advanced Polygraph Services, a San Francisco firm he founded:

"When administered by a competent examiner [the polygraph]

is the most accurate means available to distinguish between the truth and deception. . . The most important aspect of polygraph testing is to help exonerate the innocent individual surrounded by circumstantial evidence. It is particularly helpful in those investigations that rely only on testimonial evidence."

Polygraph results are not admissible as evidence unless both sides stipulate (agree) to their admission.

*   *   *

NO REST FOR THE RESTLESS (Investigations)

Most parents say having a child injured in an auto accident is their number one fear. A catastrophic illness is number two. Few believe that one of their own could ever be arrested and thrown in jail. One mother shared her experience with us:

My son was arrested for discharging his gun on private land and "using the owner of the land for target practice." He attended Hunter's Safety Training classes and he was brought up with guns. He had been taught to shoot by my father, a retired police officer. My son was not one to take chances or flout the law.

During the preliminary hearing, I learned the farmer accused my son of shooting at him several times. He testified that he yelled at my son, but that Greg continued to shoot right at him. According to the man, the bullets barely missed his head. Knowing my boy, this sounded preposterous. If he was going to shoot someone, he'd never miss.

Outraged, I visited Greg in jail. He explained the logistics of his case. Saturday morning, he and two friends decided to go target practicing. They often went to the same rural area because no one lived near by. He'd been on an embankment by the railroad tracks, aiming his gun down at a metal pyramid target. This target was secured in the gully which butted up against the opposite embankment. Eight feet above and three hundred feet behind lay the farmer's land. The railroad tracks were on public land. Greg gave me the names of the friends who were with him.

With a camera and copies of the police report in my hand, I headed out to the property to take pictures. After getting the film developed, I went back to the jail. My son examined the photos. He pointed to the spot where he had been and to where his target had been. I circled the areas with red ink. Then I interviewed each of the witnesses and had them sign the interview statement. After that, I approached his public defender and asked about having an investigator go out to the site. He said it would be a good idea, but he had no money for this. I repeated what the farmer had sworn to, then showed the attorney the photos and the interview statements. The farmer had been fixing his fence, which had been destroyed by vandals. He claimed to have been standing next to the river, under the railroad tracks.

I pointed out that the farmer had been wrong when he said the target was hanging on his fence. I produced my son's target. It weighed 23 pounds. There was no way it could have hung on a fence. Once I placed doubt on the farmer's testimony, the attorney gave the go-ahead for an investigator.

I met the private eye at the site. He checked out my photos, police reports and witness statements, then inspected the area. It took him about 30 minutes. He saw that my son could not have shot at the farmer. The bullets would have had to travel west, then make a 180 degree turn and travel east before dropping over a cliff and heading in the farmer's direction, an impossibility.

In the end, the investigator said I had done all the grunt work. I already had the photos, questioned my son and handed over the typed interviews of the witnesses. We couldn't use the witnesses' testimony because it was considered biased, but the rest of my investigation would certainly support my son's case.

We presented all of our evidence to the D.A. and the judge. The D.A. didn't buy it. He still wanted to prosecute. Even with the evidence against the farmer, the D.A. stood firm. I knew he hadn't investigated the so-called crime scene, so how could he be so sure of winning? That's when I found out he didn't have to do any investigation. All he had to do was sit pat with the farmer's word as fact. It was actually expected that we do all the work. Lucky for us, the judge dropped all the charges.

From what I could find out, the farmer had been upset at having to fix his fence again. He had taken his frustration out on my son. If I hadn't completed my own investigation, my son would now be sitting in prison. I understand this farmer's pain at having to deal with vandals, but I can't excuse the fact that he lied. My son, even though exonerated, will have a lasting scar from this experience. He lost his job, and worse, he lost his faith in the criminal justice system, a system his grandfather had worked hard to support.

I asked the lawyer why the farmer wasn't arrested for filing a false police report. He just shrugged.

A zealous defense attorney has a professional obligation to take every
legal and ethically permissible step that will serve the client's best
interest, even if the attorney finds the step personally distasteful.
Alan Dershowitz

Only about 5 percent of criminal convictions are reversed on appeal.
Alan Dershowitz

LAWYERS

"If you get into trouble, go to a lawyer at once. Don't
wait until you're indicted. Go to a big, good law firm. Be
persistent. Don't give up. Get the best lawyer in your area. Don't
look in the yellow pages. Find out who's really good," is the
advice given by renowned defense attorney and Harvard law
professor Alan Dershowitz on the "Rolanda" TV talk show,
because "once you're in trouble, the system works against you."

Dershowitz said the government, police and prosecutors
are very corrupt, they falsify and withhold evidence, and "if
government corruption stays under cover, every one of you
is at risk."

Professor Dershowitz's rules for selecting the best
defense attorney are taken from *The Best Defense* (Random
House, 1982) and are paraphrased here:
* Be certain the attorney is only interested in achieving the best
legal outcome for the defendant
* He should have a reputation for integrity; avoid the "crooked" lawyer
* He should be competent at both trial and plea bargaining; he
should not have a reputation that he always plea
bargains, because if he says he's going to trial, the
prosecutor will know he's bluffing
* Avoid, at all costs, these kinds of lawyer: One who is too lazy
or too busy to devote the necessary time to your case. One who always
makes the same "canned" arguments without regard to
the facts or law of your particular case. One who neglects to

preserve pretrial and trial errors for appellate review.

          *   *   *

Without exception, everyone we interviewed gave exactly the same advice:

Some people think if you are innocent, you don't need a lawyer. This is a big mistake. If you are arrested, or think you might be, YOU NEED A LAWYER. Having a lawyer to advise you has nothing to do with whether you're guilty or innocent. Having a lawyer may save your life.

Get a lawyer as soon as you are arrested, or even before, the minute you think you might be arrested. Hire a good criminal lawyer, not your neighbor's uncle who specializes in real estate. If you don't know a lawyer, ask people you know, whose judgment you trust, to suggest one. Look in the classified section of the phone book, too. Some lawyers will give a free short first consultation, so even if you don't have much money, phone the lawyer anyway.

If you cannot afford any payment at all, contact the Public Defender. You'll find it in the front of the phone book in the Government pages, under "County." Even phone the reporter for the local paper who covers the court house. Ask him who people around the court house say is the best criminal defense lawyer in town.

"Any person hauled into court who is too poor to hire a lawyer cannot be assured of a fair trial unless counsel is provided for him," Justice Hugo Black wrote in the 1963 Gideon Supreme Court decision.

Today, some jurisdictions are starting to charge for the services of the Public Defender, a result of cutbacks in funding for public services. Some lawyers argue that the imposition of such fees is unconstitutional. The Public Defender is not, and never has been, available to all defendants. There is a means test, and those who are able to pay a private attorney are required to do so. In some jurisdictions, a person earning as little as $62 a week is considered not indigent and therefore ineligible for the services of the Public Defender.

Most Public Defender clients are poor, dead broke, unemployed and totally without assets or prospects. How they are expected to pay fees that range from $25 to $400 within 30 days is a mystery. Failure to pay, however, can result in the debt being turned over to a collection agency.

California attorney Sara Stander says "There's a problem with the system and there are people who fall through the cracks. The poor get the Public Defender. They are great lawyers but they are overworked and don't have the financial resources prosecutors have. They work for a government agency, and have to beg for money for important extras like hiring a jury consultant. The rich can hire the best lawyers, investigators, experts and all the rest. But the middle class falls through the cracks. They have no resources. They don't know who to ask, they have no assets, no savings. The attorney they hire has to scrimp on the defense and the client has to make payments long after the case has concluded."

Here's what Ms. Stander recommends:
* Get a lawyer who specializes in or is certified in criminal defense. These are usually, but not always, the best
* Most defense attorneys think it's not a good idea to have the defendant testify, but there are exceptions
* Most attorneys won't ask if you did the crime or not. They really don't want to know. They will review the police report and build their defense based on what the police know
* If you are guilty, or are a suspect, go about your regular life. If you flee, it will make you look bad
* Make a list of people who have information about the case and give it to your lawyer. But do not talk to the people yourself because they might think you are trying to intimidate them. Keep track of them but don't confront them
* Interview an attorney, like you would a doctor, before you hire him. Ask where he went to school, the number of years he's been in practice, the number of jury trials he's done, the types of cases, and what percentage of his cases are criminal
* Ask about his other activities like teaching, writing (is he published?), professional organizations
* Does the attorney look successful? Does he have a secretary

and other office staff? Are there other attorneys in the office?
* References from former clients are not useful, but references from other attorneys may be helpful
* Call the Bar Association and see if there are any complaints against him
* Look up in court records and see if he has ever been sued for legal malpractice.

*   *   *

The American Bar Association Standards for Criminal Justice state a lawyer's responsibilities to his client with regard to investigation, include, but are not limited to:
* conduct a prompt investigation of the circumstances of the case
* investigate the client's life history in detail
* base strategy on an intelligent choice after the consideration of relevant facts
* conduct the investigation and do not rely on other sources, such as the police or prosecution, to provide exculpatory evidence
* do not rely on the client to volunteer information about his history. It is counsel's duty to make a detailed inquiry
* make the client and his family understand that all life events, good and bad, even the most horrible, need to be disclosed to the defense lawyer
* a mental health expert is needed to determine relevant facts about the defendant's troubled past
* representation of a client demands that counsel know as much about his client's past as possible.

*   *   *

DERSHOWITZ TALKS ABOUT JUSTICE

Alan Dershowitz discusses justice and the death penalty in *Reasonable Doubts: The Criminal Justice System and the O. J. Simpson Case* (Simon and Schuster, 1996). Paraphrased and condensed, this is what he said:

Police call it "testilying." Taught in the Academy, it's an open secret among lawyers and judges. Cops lie. Prosecutors and judges pretend to believe them and let them get away with it. Even if they are caught in a lie, none are ever punished.

*   *   *   *   *

Sometimes the facts of a case say "guilty," but a jury refuses to convict because to do so would be inherently unfair. This is called "jury nullification." The Supreme Court ruled in 1895 that a judge cannot overrule an acquittal that derives from jury nullification.

*   *   *   *   *

Some prosecutors hire public relations staff and media consultants for high profile cases so their message can reach the public. The defendant cannot afford this luxury.

*   *   *   *   *

Prosecutors try to convince the defendant's allies that he is going down, so they will abandon him and sell out to the prosecution.

*   *   *   *   *

People criticize O. J. Simpson's defense because of the amount of money spent on it. Simpson spent more on his defense than most people who are accused of a crime. Most defendants are broke, and most states strictly limit the amount that can be spent by public defenders or court appointed attorneys. If these lawyers spend above the limit, it has to come out of their own pockets. Most lawyers can't afford this. The budget given them for investigation and expert witnesses is minuscule, while the prosecution has unlimited resources. This is unfair to indigent defendants.

Dershowitz compares this to a case of a very rich man who becomes gravely ill and spends much of his resources on the best available medical care. The rich man is not criticized for this. But when a wealthy man accused of a crime spends his money on an excellent defense, he is accused of "buying" justice. The remedy, Dershowitz says, is not to make the wealthy man settle for a poor man's medical care or a poor man's legal defense, but for the state to give every poor man a defense (and medical care) of the same high quality the rich man can afford.

*   *   *   *   *

The prosecution always has more resources than even the wealthiest of defendants, Dershowitz says. In Simpson's case, the defense had about a dozen lawyers. The prosecution had about four dozen. The prosecution's power goes beyond money; it can threaten witnesses or grant them immunity. Many judges are former prosecutors and favor the side of the prosecution. There is no such thing as a level playing field, though Simpson came closer than the usual defendant. Something is inherently wrong about a system that allows the wealthy to obtain better quality medical or legal services than the poor.

*   *   *   *   *

Anything that aids the defendant is unpopular, while whatever aids the prosecutor or victim is popular.

*   *   *   *   *

The courtroom skills of even the best lawyers are of less value to a client than the most thorough investigation. All the money in the world cannot change the verdict when a defendant is obviously guilty. However, no wealthy people are ever executed. The death penalty is essentially reserved for the poor. Money alone cannot buy an acquittal for a rich person who is guilty, but it can buy reasonable doubt in a clear-cut case of guilt. In a close case, however, investigation and other resources may make the difference between conviction and acquittal, or between a life sentence and a death sentence.

*   *   *   *   *

Prosecutors who are thorough and dig up incriminating evidence are praised for their zeal. When defense attorneys are equally thorough in their search for exculpatory evidence, they are criticized for trying to "buy" an acquittal.

*   *   *   *   *

It is necessary, Dershowitz says, to provide all defendants, especially those facing execution or long prison terms, with resources equal to the prosecution. Unless the prosecution is challenged in this way, they have no incentive to seek the truth.

*   *   *   *   *

A BIRD IN THE HAND

Why would anyone plead guilty or "no contest," the effective equivalent of a guilty plea, to a crime they really didn't commit? [The Latin phrase "nolo cotendere," often shortened to "nolo," is Legalese for "no contest."] Because they're afraid if they don't bargain, a jury may find them guilty and the penalty will be much more severe than the deal they were offered.

The cops and the District Attorney (D.A.) may charge you with every conceivable crime that flows from the one you're accused of. For example, if they say you took both the man's wallet and his watch, that's *two* counts of robbery.

The court appointed attorney may tell you he thinks you're guilty and he doesn't plan to conduct an investigation or put on a defense. The best he can do is negotiate a plea bargain. He says if you continue to claim you're innocent and demand a trial, you'll make the judge and prosecutor mad because you'll be wasting their time and the state's money. If you persist in your claim of innocence, they'll say that shows you have no remorse, and will *really* go tough on you.

The D. A. makes an offer your lawyer says you shouldn't refuse: plead guilty to one count and tell the judge how sorry you are. You'll get five years and be out in three. Oh, yes, he reminds you: when the judge asks if you were offered any kind of a deal in exchange for your guilty plea, or were threatened or coerced, be sure to answer "no." The fact that you've sworn an oath to tell the truth is irrelevant.

This may sound like fiction, but unfortunately it isn't. An Ohio prisoner, Little Rock Reed, published a study he conducted of 612 prisoners *(Journal of Prisoners on Prisons,* vol. 4, no. 2, 1993). The results are eye opening. Of the 612 prisoners whose cases he reviewed:
* 100% pled guilty or no contest
* 41% said they were innocent but were talked into accepting the plea because their lawyers convinced them they must "cooperate with the prosecutor" or face the consequences
* 8% said they did the crime and got a fair deal
* 51% said they were guilty of some but not all of the crimes to which they pled guilty
* 88% were overcharged with too many counts
* 100% were told by their lawyers to state, in the court room, for the record, that there was no plea bargain
* 53% received stiffer sentences than those they had been promised.

Reed concludes that "The overwhelming majority of prisoners in the United States are victims of coercive plea bargaining and have never experienced a trial."

A defense lawyer explains it this way: plea bargaining has no specific criteria or standards. It is used mainly at the discretion of prosecutors, some of whom have a policy never to offer a plea bargain, while others almost always do. Those who do see it as a way to dispose of a lot of cases with less work and without tying up the courts.

Prosecutors frequently offer to plea bargain when:

* They are certain the defendant really did the crime but the evidence isn't strong enough to prove the case in court
* a crime partner can be induced to testify against his co-defendant in exchange for a lesser sentence.

If there are several co-defendants in a case, the first who agrees to a plea bargain will benefit. He can get a reduced sentence in exchange for testifying against the crime partner who holds out and doesn't play "Let's Make a Deal." This can result in the least culpable co-defendant getting the stiffest penalty because the most culpable co-defendants have been rewarded for testifying against him.

The prosecutor generally makes an offer which the defense can accept or reject. Both sides can haggle until they reach an agreement, which is then approved by a judge. If no agreement is reached, the case will go to trial.

Some prosecutors say they will charge a defendant only with whatever crimes they are confident they can prove. Others are known to "overcharge" in order to leave room for negotiation. If a defendant agrees to testify against a crime partner in exchange for pleading guilty to a reduced charge, but later backs out, the deal is off. The Supreme Court has ruled that if this happens, it does not constitute double jeopardy to withdraw the guilty plea and go to trial.

        *   *   *

JURY SELECTION

Excerpts from a talk given by Linda Meza Ph.D., who has 17 years experience as a jury selection expert:

Important words to know when selecting a jury:

CHALLENGE FOR CAUSE: the attorney for either side may excuse any number of prospective jurors for a definite reason that involves possible bias. For example, the prospective juror is a friend or relative of someone involved in the case, has been a victim of a similar crime, or has a relative in prison for a similar crime.

PEREMPTORY CHALLENGE: the judge allows each attorney a certain number of peremptory challenges, usually about 10 or 12. The attorney can use a peremptory to eliminate a prospective juror he or she doesn't like, and doesn't have to state a reason.

VOIR DIRE: (French: to speak the truth) process by which both attorneys and/or judge question prospective jurors to determine their qualifications and suitability to serve on the jury.

Experts on the art of jury selection differ in some areas, agree in others. One area of agreement is that the attorney must be prepared for this process. He or she can't just walk into the courtroom and choose jurors willy-nilly. Experts tell lawyers not to be arrogant, don't "talk down" to jurors. Speak to them respectfully.

Experts also agree that prospective jurors should be asked to fill out a questionnaire prior to voir dire. Questions should include demographics (age, race, marital status, education), as well as personal circumstances (health, social problems, alcohol or drug use, relationship to someone in prison or law enforcement). Other questions might include religious affiliation, and what the person likes to read, watch on TV or do for recreation.

One jury expert says the most important characteristic to look for is the prospective juror's style of thinking regarding the placement of blame: does he or she believe a person commits a crime because the person is inherently bad or evil, or because the defendant was influenced by external forces beyond his control. Experts say a juror who believes the defendant is inherently bad or evil is more likely to convict, while the juror who believes external forces are to blame is more likely to acquit.

Sometimes the judge refuses to permit the use of a questionnaire in order to save time. In that case, some experts say if you can ask only one question, let it be the one about placement of blame.

"Gender makes a difference when you're picking a jury," says James Paul Linn, former prosecutor from Texas and now a defense attorney in Oklahoma City.

Linn's rules of thumb:
* Women are more compassionate than men in most criminal cases , but they can be ruthless when it comes to sex crimes.
* Men tend to be harder on defendants.
* Heterosexual men tend to respond negatively to gay men.
* Homosexuals, both men and women, are sympathetic to mistreatment. Like Black people, they are sensitive to injustice because they have experienced a lot of it.

DRESS FOR SUCCESS

"Don't dress like a 'ho, especially if you are one," a successful defense attorney admonishes his clients. "How you look in court, the image you present, will influence the outcome of your case." He goes on to say "if the Pope and Mother Teresa testify they saw you with the smoking gun in your hand, how you're dressed won't win you an acquittal, but it might make the difference between a life sentence and a death sentence."

When you dress for court, he says, "If you expect to prevail, your goal should be to make a favorable impression and appear credible and non-threatening to the jurors. The way to do this is to look and act very much like they do: conservative and middle class. The courtroom where you're on trial is NOT a forum for you to advertise your political views and contempt for the establishment, or to flaunt your sexual proclivities, gang affiliation or purple spiked hair." These are the guidelines he gives his clients:
MEN:
* Get a hair cut, conservative, not trendy
* Shave

* Follow your lawyer's advice about whether to shave off or retain a beard or mustache
* Take a bath or shower each day of the trial
* Use deodorant
* Shine your shoes daily
* Dress neatly and conservatively. For most men this means a suit or slacks and a sports jacket, dress shirt and tie. In some (very few) cases, clean denims, pressed, with a crease, may be acceptable. Also in some cases, clean, pressed work clothes may be appropriate.
* Don't wear a '70s polyester leisure suit from the thrift shop, gaudy colors or loud plaids
* Don't overdo it with expensive clothing far beyond your means or what you normally wear. If you work as a bus driver or gardener, don't show up in court in a $1,000 Armani suit. The jury will wonder where you got it
* No T-shirts with messages of any kind
* No flashy, gaudy or expensive-looking jewelry, no pinkie rings
* Nothing that could be even remotely thought to resemble gang attire.

WOMEN:
* Bathe or shower daily
* Use deodorant
* Have your hair cut and styled, conservative, not trendy
* If you hair is colored, have the roots touched up
* Wear conservative make-up
* Nails should be moderate length, not "claws;" polish is fine, but should not display art work
* Wear underwear: bra, panties, and slip
* Nylons or panty hose, no fish-nets or stockings with sculpted designs. No bare legs or leg make-up
* Appropriate dress shoes, flat or mid-height heels, no "skyscraper" heels or platforms. Sandals okay in summer
* Wear a suit, dress or skirt and blouse
* Skirt no higher than two inches above the knee
* No pants or slacks unless needed for medical reasons

* Dress like you are going to work in a conservative office, not like you're going to a party. No sequins, plunging necklines, see-through fabrics, metallic materials, backless, spaghetti straps, or slit skirts
* In other words, be modest, nothing skin tight
* No gaudy, flashy or expensive-looking jewelry.

    For both men and women, he advises:
* NO TATTOOS. Depending on the location of tattoos you may have, cover them with clothing, make-up (tear drops under the eye) or Band-aids.
* Dress comfortably, within the above guidelines. You will be sitting for hours on end
* Don't over- or under-dress, but dress appropriately for the community and your age. In San Francisco or New York, some women wear hats and gloves. In Florida or California beach communities, women may wear cotton dresses with a light sweater.

    Finally, he says, go to the court house prior to your trial. Visit several courtrooms and look at how attorneys, court clerks, court reporters, jurors, witnesses and observers are dressed. How they look is how you should look.

THE PARADOX PARADIGM

    "Damned if you do, damned if you don't" is an aphorism that must have been coined with defendants on trial in mind. Whatever you do or don't do, the prosecution and media will put the spin on it to "prove" your guilt.

    If you:
* follow your attorney's instructions and gaze straight ahead while sitting at the defense table, hands folded and face expressionless, this means you are a cold-blooded, ruthless, ferocious and emotionless killer, and proves you are guilty
* wriggle around from time to time to stretch your cramped muscles, this means you are trying to intimidate the

witnesses, shows you are a ruthless, heartless, fierce and remorseless killer, and proves you are guilty.

If you:

* laugh appreciatively at a joke made by the judge, this shows you are a brown-nosing, brutal, vicious, maniacal murderer who chortles with mirth at the thought of your victim's suffering and are totally lacking in human compassion, thus proving you are guilty

* fail to laugh at the judge's jokes, this shows you are a dangerous and vicious criminal so obsessed with your foul atrocities that you have no sense of humor, and only contempt for the judge, thus proving you are guilty.

If you:

* look at the jury, this demonstrates you are trying to intimidate them, are demented, deranged and depraved, and therefore you are guilty

* if you don't look at the jury, this demonstrates you are so ashamed of your dastardly deeds that you can't even look decent people in the eye, and therefore you are guilty.

If you:

* turn toward the audience to nod and smile at your mother, this indicates you are a sniveling, snickering, incestuous mama's boy and have a sick relationship with that wicked, controlling woman, which proves you are guilty of committing the most heinous atrocities imaginable

* don't turn and greet your mother, this indicates you are a selfish, spoiled, uncaring mama's boy who has an incestuous relationship with that evil woman, which proves you guilty of kidnapping, rape, murder, bank robbery, tax evasion and reckless driving, and of having lousy manners, besides.

If you:

* dress casually and leave your hair long, this reveals you're some low-life scum who has no respect for the court or for any other form of authority and are shamelessly flaunting your criminal lifestyle, proving you're guilty as charged

* get a haircut and dress in a three-piece suit, this reveals you are a savage cutthroat who's acting uppity, which indicates you are a pretentious, narcissistic con man with delusions of grandeur, and proves you're guilty as charged.
    If you:
* take the witness stand in your own defense, it shows you're a blubbering liar and have no qualms about committing perjury to save your own worthless homicidal hide, and that proves just how guilty you really are
* decline to testify, it shows you're a whimpering coward who doesn't have the common decency to face up to what you've done, and that proves just how guilty you really are.
    If you:
* plead Guilty, that shows you have no shame about being a rampaging, ferocious fiend and you have no compunctions about disgracing your family, which proves that not only are you guilty, but you take pride in flaunting it
* plead Not Guilty, that shows you are not only a savage, conscienceless outlaw, totally without remorse, and a smirking, surly perjurer besides, which proves that not only are you guilty, but you take pride in flaunting it.
    If you:
* seem confident, this indicates you're totally devoid of human emotion, are guilty as sin and damned proud of it
* seem nervous, this indicates you're totally devoid of human emotion, and are guilty as sin and damned proud of it.
    If there's:
* a ton of physical evidence pointing to your guilt, such as hair, fibers, blood, DNA, eyewitnesses, the bloody knife, surveillance videos and a confession, plus a motive, you know you're guilty
* absolutely no physical evidence or motive and an unshakable alibi (you were in a nuclear submarine under the Polar Ice Cap during the crime and for six months before and after it) that just shows how diabolically clever you are, to commit the perfect crime and destroy all the evidence

and set up an unbreakable alibi, and you know you're guilty.

The Paradox Paradigm doesn't apply only to the defendant, but to his witnesses, supporters and advocates as well.

If your lawyer:

* makes a statement to the press, this shows he's a devious prevaricator who manipulates the media to achieve his own nefarious ends, and is covering up the truth, which proves you're guilty
* says "No comment," this shows he's keeping his mouth shut as part of some vile conspiracy to cover up the real facts, which would nail you to the wall if all that stuff ever did come out, which proves you're guilty.

If your mother:

* cries in the courtroom, that shows she's a self-obsessed, malicious, vicious, incestuous, phony, hysterical, attention-grabbing bitch who pushed you into a life of crime in order to make you suffer for her own warped psyche and her hatred of men, and that proves you're guilty
* doesn't cry, that shows she's a cold, heartless, shallow, self-obsessed, narcissistic bitch who has no feelings for anyone but herself, and was a lousy mother besides, which drove you to do it, and that proves you're guilty.

If your alibi witness is:

* your relative, friend, pastor, physician, neighbor, employer, co-worker, acquaintance, or the captain and crew of the nuclear sub, they would certainly lie for you, because people like that who consort with common criminals like you lie all the time and you can't trust them as far as you can throw them, everybody knows that, so your alibi is totally meaningless, and you're guilty
* a total stranger, he probably doesn't know what he saw and everyone knows eyewitness identification is extremely unreliable, anyway, unless the eyewitness happens to be testifying for the prosecution, in which case eyewitness identification is extremely reliable, and you're guilty.

If a cell mate, former cell mate, ex-convict, convicted felon or jailhouse snitch:

* is a witness for the defense and has nothing to gain by testifying, everyone knows these lying jail birds can't be trusted to tell the truth, every word they utter is suspect, and if that's the best you can scrounge up in the way of witnesses you're in deep doo-doo and it absolutely proves you're guilty as hell

* is a witness for the prosecution and has a great deal to gain by testifying, such as his own life or freedom or a free ride in a witness protection program, how could anyone ask for a more reliable witness than that, it's a cinch this courageous crusader for justice is telling the truth, and nothing but the truth, out of a sense of civic duty, moral righteousness and dedication to the principles of Liberty and Democracy, all of which proves he's telling the truth about how you confessed, and proves you're guilty as hell.

The jury, too, is subject to the Paradox Paradigm. If it finds you:

* Guilty, then guilty you are and guilty you shall remain, henceforth and ever more, because everybody knows juries never make mistakes and are always right and never wrong, and if a jury of your peers finds you guilty, then by golly you're guilty, because juries can always be trusted to do the right thing, that's what it means to be an American, for goodness' sake, even if the real perpetrator confesses and the D.A. who prosecuted you asks the court to review your case, they're just bleedingheart liberals. The Supreme Court has said, once you've been found guilty, being innocent should not get in the way of execution because it confuses things. However much evidence is presented to show your innocence, it's almost never quite enough to get your sentence reversed, you could ask Leonel Herrera and Jesse Jacobs, both late of Texas, about that if they were still alive and could talk, but they aren't and can't

* Not Guilty, well, that doesn't count for much, because everybody knows juries are fickle and unreliable and make a lot of mistakes, and maybe even take bribes, so

just because some dumb old jury said you didn't do it doesn't mean you didn't do it, especially if you're an unpopular defendant like O. J. Simpson, whom the jury found Not Guilty, but everyone knows juries don't know much about anything, and by golly the man was guilty and it's our civic duty to override that sorry ass jury and destroy the man because we can't let him get away with it, so if it means taking the law into our own hands, well, then, that's what we'll have to do, because juries can't be relied on to do the right thing anymore, and it's Freedom and Democracy and the American Way that's at stake here, anyhow, dammit.

So let's stop jawin' and get on with the lynchin'.

Our minds are screwed by sensational headlines, Polly Klass Murder, Charles Manson, Robert Alton Harris, Ted Bundy. We don't read about the Joe Blow who is doing 12 years for smoking a joint after finals in the college dorm, or Jane Doe, sitting on death row, who shot her violent and sexually abusive husband after he threatened to dismember her children.

Wendy Kaminer, It's All The Rage: Crime and Culture.

We know through painful experience that freedom is never voluntarily given by the oppressor, it must be demanded by the oppressed.
Martin Luther King Jr., "Letter from a Birmingham Jail"

THE CHECKLIST THAT COULD SAVE YOUR LIFE

As soon as you or a loved one is arrested, or as soon as possible thereafter, start doing everything on this checklist. Don't wait until it's too late. If you are unable (in jail or incapacitated) give the job to a trusted family member or friend, or divide it up among several. It's a tremendous amount of work, but it's worth the effort to save your life or the life of someone you love, isn't it?

Many people who get arrested, and their families and friends, commit the inexcusable crime of being PASSIVE, of taking for granted that "things will work out." They ASS-U-ME the police will investigate, they ASS-U-ME witnesses will tell the truth, they ASS-U-ME their lawyer will take care of everything for them, they ASS-U-ME the police and prosecutor will be honest and not falsify or withhold evidence. (To ass-u-me, our teacher said, "makes an ass of you and me.")

Dumbest move of all, some ASS-U-ME they don't even need a lawyer at all if they're truly innocent. Renowned defense attorney Alan Dershowitz says "when there isn't even a case yet is often when people need a lawyer the most."

Some of these folks wind up on death row. We have met a few who still protest their innocence after 10 or 15 years on the row, and they're still waiting for the Justice Fairy to slither down the chimney and rescue them. It ain't gonna happen! If you don't do it yourself, it may not get done.

"What stage is your appeal at right now, and who's investigating your claim of innocence?," we asked a death row resident.

"Gee, I dunno," he replied. "I ASS-U-ME my lawyer's taking care of it. Isn't that his job?".

"What's the name of your son's lawyer?", we asked his mother.

"Gosh, I'm not sure," she responded, "I ASS-U-ME it's the Public Defender, I guess."

This checklist has been developed by the mothers of two inmates, working together to free their sons, both of whom have been wrongly convicted of murder. When they started, neither Mom had the slightest idea of what to do or how to do it. They just knew they weren't going to sit back passively and let "the system" kill their boys without at least giving "the system" a good run for its money. Everything they did was by trial and error. One of the mothers went to law school while the other became a paralegal. While they were learning the ropes, they nagged and pestered lawyers, judges, court clerks and everyone else who could tell them how to locate a document or file a motion. It's not surprising that around the court house, even years later, they're still known as THE MOTHERS FROM HELL.

We convinced them to put all the "how to's" down on paper so our readers wouldn't have to find out how to do it the hard way like these two women did.

* IMMEDIATELY make a memo book and write down all events surrounding the arrest, preliminary hearing or grand jury hearing, pretrial motions, investigation, attorneys, judges, witnesses, search and seizure, Miranda warnings, treatment by police, and the trial. Continue to keep a notebook or journal of everything that happens, everything that is said or done.
* Carry a small notebook at all times to make reminders or for important clues you come across.
* Carry a small, disposable camera at all times.
* If you are in jail, keep a record of cell mates, especially those

who are there only for a short time, with dates and times. LEAVE NO ONE OUT. One of them may be a snitch who will later say you "confessed."

* DON'T KEEP these logs and memos in your cell. Important documents, especially those that could prove innocence, have an amazing habit of vanishing from cells, as though they were written in invisible ink. Mail them home daily, give them to your lawyer, or mail to your lawyer via "legal mail" (uncensored) if permitted. Also send home any mail, cards or correspondence of any kind that you receive. Make a duplicate copy of your address book. Keep one and send one home.

* ORGANIZE all documents in files and boxes. If convicted, you will have a head start on the documentation for your appeal.

* OBTAIN COURT TRANSCRIPTS. The court clerk's daily notes (Minute Orders) that are kept in the court file are only a summary of daily testimony, evidence and motions. The actual transcripts, taken down by the court reporter on the Stenotype machine, are not kept in the court file. They are stored separately because of space. They can run to hundreds or even thousands of pages. They can cost as much as 50 cents or $1 per page. They may cost you hundreds or thousands of dollars. But this is so important, borrow the money if you have to, hold a cake sale, mortgage the house, do whatever it takes. It is *essential* that you buy the transcripts from either:
  1) the court reporter
  2) the clerk of the court house, or
  3) have your defense attorney obtain a copy, then photocopy them from the attorney's copy, or
  4) get them from your appellate attorney and have photocopies made

* Make friends with anyone and everyone around the courthouse who can help you: clerks, court reporters, newspaper, radio and TV reporters, attorneys.

* OBTAIN COPIES OF POLICE REPORTS.
  1) You may need to copy the private attorney's or Public Defender's file. Remember, they may not have all of the discovery

material. The D.A. or prosecutor may not have given it to them, even though they are required by law to do so. They often "forget."

2) Any statements by police or other persons taken at the time of arrest, while in jail, or during court proceedings that were not obtainable from the court file.

3) If there are any discrepancies in the reports or statements, try to obtain the *originals* (not copies). Start by asking the investigator on the case.

4) If your case involves a death, get AUTOPSY reports. (See section on Autopsy reports for a list of exactly what to ask for.)

5) Any medical or emergency room reports of anyone connected with the alleged crimes.

6) Results of any drug tests (blood, urine, saliva, Breathalyzer) on defendant or alleged crime victims.

7) Results of any Lie Detector Test (Polygraph), and the laboratory or criminalist who performed the test. Do a background check on the lab/criminalist to determine if he is independent or employed by the police department, and if he is located in or out of town. Determine if the Lie Detector Test was done with voice detection, full video and audio, just audio alone, location where test was performed and who was present during testing.

* Make sure MOTIONS are entered for PRESERVATION of DNA, ballistics or any other samples/specimens pertinent to the case. If this was not done at time of sentencing, contact the defense attorney and have him file Motions for Preservation of Evidence immediately. Follow up to be sure he does this.

* Enter Motion for a New Trial, Notice to Appeal, and Request for New Counsel.

* Enter a Motion for defendant to represent himself Pro Per (Pro Se), to relieve present attorney if ineffectiveness of counsel is an issue. (Faretta v. Cal, 422 U. S. 806).

* If INEFFECTIVE COUNSEL is an issue, make a list of what you think the lawyer did not do, or did wrong. Have the defendant make a list of what he thinks was wrong. You can also file a GRIEVANCE against the lawyer with the State Bar.

* If issues of JUDICIAL, PROSECUTORIAL or JUROR

MISCONDUCT exist, file a grievance with the Judicial Commission.

* When filing any grievance, attach facts and exhibits, not your opinions or speculations. Do not use words that are angry, vulgar, offensive or threatening. No name-calling. Always close with "Respectfully Submitted," and sign your name and the date. You may want to include the following: I (your name) certify under penalty of perjury that the contents of this letter are true to the best of my knowledge and belief.

* When you submit the grievances listed above, you may file a copy at the court house to be placed in the defendant's file. YOU HAVE THE RIGHT TO FILE ANYTHING. Include the case number, the short name of the case (People vs. Doe), and the name of the court in which you are filing the document. This does not have to be on pleading paper (special paper used by lawyers) but the information listed above must be included. There may be a fee for filing.

* Try to get all personal property not used or preserved as evidence back into your custody. This may require a Motion for Return of Personal Property through the court before sentencing. If the motion is denied, resubmit with another motion. If it's impossible to obtain these belongings, keep a written log and any pictures you may have or can obtain of the articles. Keep track of who you talked to, and how many times, regarding this.

* Get a Power of Attorney from the defendant before sentencing so you can act in his behalf. Have it notarized if the jail has a Notary Public.

* If a Notary is not available, have the defendant write a Letter of Authorization to you or some other trusted person who can take care of legal matters or documents.

* Have the defendant make a WILL. This is important. Sometimes people die unexpectedly in jail/prison. Even if he is poor and has no money/property/assets, the will is needed for instructions regarding funeral arrangements desired, who should care for any children, and who should inherit personal items of sentimental value. A *Holographic* will is legal and valid. This is a will *written entirely by hand* by the person

whose will it is, signed and dated. It's *not* valid if typewritten.

* Obtain all newspaper articles regarding the defendant's case or the defendant, from before arrest and ongoing, and any articles about the crime. Keep a binder with the date and name of the newspaper the article was in. You can get copies of the paper from a library or from the newspaper office. If you can afford it, subscribe to a clipping service. They cut out articles from *all* papers and magazines for a fee.

* Also keep clippings of any other times the defendant's name appeared in the paper: graduation, marriage, sports, activities, awards etc.

* If the defendant may be innocent, follow the news for similar crimes. Save newspaper pictures of anyone who might be the real perpetrator.

* Make friends with the local newspaper reporters who cover the courthouse and crime beats, and ask questions. They may not tell you direct information, but they are a good resource and may give you leads or suggestions.

* Keep a record of how many times the defendant's picture was in the paper or magazines prior to the trial, and his age in each photo. Did the paper use photos from driver's license, school yearbook or police mug shots? Witnesses may say they "recognize" the defendant, when they only think they recognize him because they have seen his picture in the paper so many times.

* Keep a blank tape in the VCR at all times and record any news reports or documentaries regarding the defendant's case or similar crimes. (The person who committed the "similar" crimes may also have committed the crime the defendant is accused of).

* Get friendly with radio and TV reporters and anchors.

* Obtain all medical records, psychology or mental health reports, probation reports from all sources, and inmate misconduct reports from the jail. You will need a Letter of Authorization to Obtain Documents from the defendant.

* Make a list of any defense or prosecuting attorneys who may have visited the courtroom during the trial but were not involved in it. If there is an issue of innocence or ineffectiveness of counsel, they may offer you their opinions or assistance.

* Check the County and Federal court houses to see if anyone

involved in the case has any law suits in the past or pending against them, civil or criminal, such as spousal abuse, misconduct or anything else that might suggest corruption. This includes investigators, police, defense attorney, prosecutor, judge and witnesses. Especially look for bankruptcy cases.

* Check the court Archives for divorces or old cases involving anyone listed above. Sometimes the cause of the divorce is listed, such as abuse, alcoholism, drug abuse, etc.

* Before the trial, visit the court rooms and sit in on any trials where the judge, defense attorney or prosecutor assigned to the defendant's case are involved. Most trials are public unless they are specifically sealed, and the general public has the right to attend. Sit in the back, look busy and keep quiet.

* Keep track of the defendant's file, know when material is being added or removed.

* Keep track of any files sent to the Appellate Attorney. Contact the Appellate Court. Let them know who you are and your interest in the case.

* If you get an opportunity to call other legal advisors, lawyers or paralegals, do so without hesitation. If you see or hear someone on a radio or TV talk show, perhaps a famous lawyer, professor, expert or investigator who helps defendants, call them and ask them to help with your case. You can get their address and phone number from the radio or TV station. Many of them are willing to help out. Don't be concerned that you don't know legal language. Don't be embarrassed to talk to them. Say this is all new to you and you need their help.

* While you want to take advantage of any help that's available to you, BE VERY CAREFUL WHOM YOU TALK TO. If you contact someone, they may be okay, or they may be in some way connected with the prosecution. BE EXTRA CAREFUL when someone you don't know contacts you. They may be legitimate, or they may be a "spy."

* If the defendant/inmate files a grievance with the jail or prison, have them send a copy of it home, along with the response they get. Keep this in your files.

* Have the inmate contact the Prisoner Rights Union or similar organization to obtain materials that may help with his case. The materials cost much less if the inmate sends for them than if you send for them. Send him the money for these materials if necessary. If he doesn't want to keep them after reading them, they can be sent home to you for safekeeping.
* Sometimes your loved one, especially if he is on Death Row, and particularly if he is depressed or has given up hope, will decide to relinquish his appeals. TRY AND TALK HIM OUT OF IT. TRY NOT TO LET THIS HAPPEN. He may regret it after it's too late.

   The Mothers stress that you are not paranoid; the "bad guys" probably really are looking over your shoulder. They should know. The Mothers have been followed, their phones have been tapped, and important files have mysteriously disappeared from their homes. This can happen to you, too.

CAUTIONS

* If your computer has a modem or is connected to the Internet or if you leave the computer on all the time, DO NOT leave any information about the case on the hard drive. "BIG BROTHER" is a Hacker and can get into your computer. Put any information about the case on disks, make several copies, and keep in a secure, safe place. Leave additional copies with trusted friends or relatives.
* When outside your home, watch who is watching or following you. Makes notes of description of person and/or car, and license number. Take photos if you can.
* If it's a high-profile case, be cautious and assume your phone is tapped.
* Whenever you leave your home, even briefly, let someone know where you are going, with whom, and when you expect to return.
* If you can afford it, invest in a cell phone for emergencies when away from home. It can also be useful at home if your phone lines suddenly go dead. But remember that anyone can listen in on a cell phone conversation, so be VERY CAREFUL what you say.
* If you have pets, check them for tranquilizers or poisoning. If someone wants to break into your house to look (illegally) for

"evidence," they may poison or tranquilize your dog. (This happened to the Mothers).
* Get a doggie door so your dog can have access to both the inside and outside of the house when you're away.
* THIS IS SERIOUS. IT'S NOT A JOKE! Give written instructions to family and friends about what to do if you turn up dead or missing. Put in writing that you want a private, independent *autopsy*, and have them check for earth that has been recently disturbed or freshly poured or wet cement.
* Before entering your vehicle, check completely around it for tire condition, any unidentified shiny objects, under the hood, in the trunk and under the vehicle. Check the interior of the vehicle, especially under the dash, for wiring or objects. Check in glove box and under seats; contraband such as drugs may have been "planted."
* Check the home for any new and different wiring or objects.
* If any "repairmen" that you didn't send for, from the phone or utility company, want to enter your home, call their company first and verify their identity and why they are there.
* If you hear strange noises in your house or unusual beeping or clicking noises on your phone, know you are being listened to or even watched by hidden cameras.
* DO NOT TALK ABOUT THE CASE with anyone, including the inmate, unless it's at a contact visit. Even then, be vigilant. Visiting rooms can be "bugged." In one jail, a sheriff planted a listening device in the room in which a priest was hearing an inmate's religious confession. It was illegal, but presumably the damage was done.
* BE AWARE THAT ALL PHONE CALLS FROM THE JAIL/ PRISON ARE RECORDED, AND ALL MAIL AND OTHER INFORMATION IS PHOTO COPIED. THE STATE CAN USE THIS INFORMATION AGAINST THE DEFENDANT/ INMATE. BE CAREFUL WHAT YOU SAY OR WRITE, AND DON'T JEOPARDIZE YOUR LOVED ONE. BE VERY CAREFUL WHOM YOU TRUST AND WHOM YOU TALK TO ABOUT THE CASE.

A central tenet of Western law [is] that criminals should be punished on behalf of society as a whole, not the victim . . . American judges and juries are supposed to mete out punishment whether or not the victim's family condones or condemns it.
U.S. News & World Report, June 16, 1997

A PROPOSED VICTIMS' RIGHTS AMENDMENT

In earliest times, before there were formal governments, there was no such thing as a criminal justice system. People took care of their own grievances. As civilizations developed, it was too disruptive to allow individuals to carry out their own vendettas. So they made laws, wrote them down, and made the state responsible for punishing wrongdoers on behalf of both the wronged individual and the community. They knew that people who are angry and hurt would react out of passion and revenge, not out of a desire for justice. This would harm the community by exacting punishments that were too severe to fit the crime.

Today, politicians want to change things back to the way they were in the bad old days, and let the victims select the punishment. There's a movement afoot to amend the Constitution for this purpose. The proposed amendment, backed by President Clinton and legislators from both parties, would grant victims financial restitution, speedy trials, the right to object to sentences or plea bargains, to attend the trial and parole hearings of the accused/ convicted person, and to be notified when the prisoner is released.

Most of these rights are already in place. We need to ask who's going to benefit? Politicians, not the victims. Politicians will get more votes, be elected to higher offices, and get richer, all by feeding on the desire for revenge of people who have been harmed.

The so-called Victims' Rights Movement might be called more accurately the Vindictive Revenge Movement that advocates longer and meaner prison sentences for even minor crimes, and faster executions without benefit of an extended appeal process: one appeal and you're dead. In California, the movement receives the majority of its funding from the California Correctional Peace Officers Association. This prison guards union has a vested interest in longer sentences: their jobs.

Some of the proposed changes make sense. What's wrong with court ordered restitution, anyway? Nothing. Judges already have the power to order restitution. But constitutionally mandated restitution in every case is a different story. All convicted offenders would then owe a monetary debt to their victims. But most defendants are destitute. The Chicago Sun Times reported in 1995 that only 4 cents is collected on every restitution dollar ordered to be paid, because convicts simply don't have the money.

Murder Victims' Families for Reconciliation (MVFR) [see Resources section] is a group that advocates forgiving the perpetrators who have murdered their loved ones. They actively lobby against the death penalty for those murderers, and for overall death penalty abolition. When the Vindictive Revenge faction says "You'd believe in the death penalty if it was your relative who was murdered," MVFR members can truthfully say "It was my relative, and I can forgive the person who did it." MVFR members are not a bunch of bleeding-hearts, but people who embrace the moral and philosophical ideology that two wrongs don't make a right.

Two grieving fathers, both often seen on the TV news, represent opposite ways of dealing with the deaths of their children. One spews out venom, thereby, it seems to some, actually diminishing the respect his dead son deserves. The other goes about the business of lawfully avenging his daughter's death with stoic dignity that serves to enhance the impact of her loss.

Fred Goldman, father of Ron, could be the poster boy for the Vindictive Revenge Movement. Even though O. J. Simpson was found not guilty in his criminal trial, Mr. Goldman misses no opportunity to express his hatred for Mr. Simpson and his desire to demolish the man who was accused, but not convicted, of murdering Goldman's son.

Goldman has channeled his righteous grief in such a way that it appears to hurt him more than it could ever hurt Simpson. Whenever Mr. Goldman appears on TV it looks as if his outrage has turned inward, causing the viewer to wonder how high off the scale his blood pressure has risen, and whether he will ultimately self-destruct by stroke, heart attack or ulcers.

An often-heard adage is something to the effect of "If you don't like the way things are, don't fight the system, but change it." Poster boy for this concept is Mike Reynolds of Fresno. Mike's daughter, Kimber, was brutally murdered by muggers a couple of years ago. One assailant was killed at the scene by police; the other served a short prison sentence. Reynolds and his whole family were justifiably outraged and crushed by Kimber's cruel death. Instead of destroying himself from the inside out by ruminations of revenge, Reynolds decided to change the system. That's what he did.

A professional photographer with no previous experience at politicking or law, Reynolds sat down with a group of lawyers, judges and politicians of his acquaintance, organized a statewide grass roots campaign, and gave birth to California's Three Strikes law. The authors disagree with some aspects of the Three Strikes law. That isn't relevant here. What is relevant is that Reynolds achieved a monumental task. We have intense respect and admiration for Reynolds' energy and organizational skills, which were clearly visible as he went about creating the movement, obtaining hundreds of thousands of signatures for a ballot initiative and forging alliances among all strata of society. Even though his grief was overwhelming, and rightfully so, he maintained his dignity, often choked with anguish, but never livid with anger.

ASSET FORFEITURE

Asset forfeiture: another term for highway robbery. The government came up with this idea which, like many of its cockamamie notions, sounds good in theory, but in practice it's sheer madness.

The idea was that nobody, especially so-called drug kingpins, should be allowed to profit from drug dealing. Not unreasonable. So the government should be allowed to confiscate all illicit proceeds from the drug trade. Right?

Government bureaucratic types know that drug deals are done on a cash basis, so they made a giant leap of logic: anyone who carries a large amount of cash must have obtained it by dealing drugs. Not right, but that's their assumption.

As a result, if you are caught with a large roll of bills, the cops can seize it on the spot on the mere suspicion that it's "drug money." Your protestations that you just retrieved it from under your grandmother's mattress or won big at the Indian Bingo are to no avail.

Not only can they take your cash, they can seize your car, house, jewelry and whatever else they can get their hands on. After all, if you have "drug money" then your house, car, jewelry and other things must have been purchased with "drug money" too, so they are all fair game.

They can confiscate everything you have on suspicion alone, without due process, and it's up to you to try and get it back. Good luck!

*   *   *

One such incident involved an 80-year-old grandmother who let her teenaged grandson live with her. Granny was too feeble to walk up and down the stairs, so Grandson did the laundry for them both in Granny's basement washing machine.

Also in the basement was the pot plant he was growing. When the drug-busters caught him with a joint, it took them no time at all to uncover the pot farm. Even though Granny knew nothing of the agricultural venture, she was made to forfeit her house and property.

A drug dealer hired a lawyer to represent him in a trial. He paid the lawyer a lump sum in advance. When the dealer was convicted, the government confiscated the money from the lawyer that the drug dealer had paid to him. After all, they said, it was "drug money."

The Supreme Court has ruled that asset forfeiture is not "punishment" and is civil, not criminal, in nature. Therefore it does not constitute double jeopardy. If in doubt, ask O. J. Simpson, poster boy for civil asset forfeiture. Even though he has never been found guilty of any crime, he was forced to turn over everything but the clothes on his back to the families of the victims of the crime he didn't commit.

Only in America!

*   *   *

The limits of tyrants are prescribed by the endurance of those whom they oppress.

Frederick Douglass, 1883

DON'T BLAME THE VICTIM

An 18 year old man was convicted of first-degree felony murder while attempting to steal a car. His mother-in-law spoke on his behalf at his sentencing.

"It was an accident," she said. "He doesn't deserve life in prison for that. They are making an example of the wrong guy. If Mr._____ had left him alone, this would never have happened."

According to the radio, the victim saw the defendants attempting to steal a car. When he yelled out and tried to intervene, he was shot and killed. The mother-in-law pleaded for a lighter sentence, saying the victim would still be alive if he had minded his own business. With those words she started a riot of bad feelings in the community.

The victim was the brother of a prominent politician. Both were liked and admired. Letters to the editor appeared in the morning paper, saying "If this attitude was present in the home where this boy was raised it's easy to understand how he could turn out as he did: a murderer," and "It's like saying Hitler and his Nazis were innocent victims and the millions of people who died were at fault for being in the wrong place at the wrong time."

A more appropriate remark might have been, "The shooting was wrong. This boy has never been in trouble before. He is sorry for the pain he's caused and he is asking for mercy." Blaming the victim never works.

*   *   *

A prisoner's mother said:

My son went to prison for one year for buying a quarter ounce of marijuana. It was his first offense. He never claimed some other dude did it. He admitted he was wrong and that he was guilty of the crime.

I don't believe many parents who have children in jail own up to the fact that their child is guilty, that he knowingly committed a crime. It would certainly give us more credibility with the public, our families and friends, if we did.

During the trial, I saw so many parents out in the hallway beating their chests and whining about how unfair the system is for accusing their little darling of committing a crime. I'd listen to the evidence and know the kids were guilty, but somehow that knowledge never penetrated their parent's heads. They seemed oblivious, intent on their own version of the truth.

One day, I met the mother of a convicted serial killer. She was a gentle, gracious woman who acknowledged the fact of her son's crimes. She told me her son admitted his guilt and he said it was too much of a burden for him to live with. She also said he didn't blame her or anyone else for his crimes. He held himself responsible.

Life isn't fair. When I signed up for my stint on earth, I was made aware of this. My parents raised me to tell the truth. If something went wrong and it was my fault, I fessed up and rectified the situation. That's what I taught my son.

> The man he had become was not the boy I knew. Just before he died, I told him how much I loved him.
> Serial killer's mom

SERENITY PRAYER
God, Grant me the Serenity
To Accept the Things I Cannot Change,
The Courage to Change the Things I Can,
And the Wisdom to Know the Difference.
Anonymous

DE NILE IS A RIVER...

. . . and if all the people who practiced DENIAL were to jump into it at once, it would overflow its banks.

When someone they love gets into trouble, it hurts the whole family. Some people decide to make the best of a bad situation, face reality, and get on with their lives. They have adopted the concept of the A.A. Serenity Prayer. They accept the things they can not change, try to change the things they can, attempt to recognize the difference, and make logical choices.

Others get hooked into DENIAL. They stay out there, lost in space, pretending everything is different from how it really is. Until they decide to face up to REALITY, they will be unable to get on with their lives.

Denial comes in all shapes and sizes, but its common characteristic is "My mind is already made up, so don't confuse me with facts." Fantasy prevails over reality. Until they decide to accept reality, they will continue fruitlessly to spin their wheels.

We have met a few of them:
* a woman phoned our support group for help, but every suggestion we made, she had the same answer: "No, because..." She didn't know what crime her son is in prison for, she has not obtained or read his transcripts, she doesn't know how long his sentence is, she rejected a suggestion to talk to a lawyer because "I don't trust lawyers." She wanted to visit her son, but she doesn't drive, is afraid to fly, and gets carsick on the train. She doesn't want to accept a ride with another prisoner's family because "I don't want strangers to know my business." She is "very depressed," but doesn't want to go to a therapist

because "I don't want to tell my family business to a stranger, and anyway I don't believe in them." She doesn't want to take anti-depressant medication because "It could make me an addict." She concluded the conversation with, "I need some help. Can you tell me what I should do?"

* A 48-year-old child molester, in and out of prison since age 18, whose latest arrest was for molesting a 7-year-old girl, confessed and admitted to police that he had probably molested more than 100 children during his "career." At a support group meeting, his mother demanded that "someone do something" to get "my baby" out of prison. She assured the members that she would watch over her son and "make sure he doesn't do it again." Anyway, she added "he's just a friendly guy who loves kids, and that little girl was lying."

                    *   *   *

A Marriage and Family Counselor suggests some techniques on dealing with denial:

* Find out all the facts you can about your loved one's case. Read police reports and transcripts, talk to the attorney.
* Listen and learn all you can, but avoid making statements that could be misunderstood or quoted in the media.
* If you believe your loved one is truly innocent, based on facts, not on emotion, talk to him and his lawyer. Find out what you can do, then do it. Work to get him a new trial, a reduced sentence, or whatever is appropriate and necessary under the circumstances. Don't just sit around and complain that life is "unfair." DO something about it.
* If you determine he is really guilty, accept that fact. Continue to love and support him. Do whatever you can to improve his situation if that's appropriate: a reduced sentence, transfer, necessary medical or psychiatric care. But if he is guilty, or has a serious mental illness and may be a danger to himself or others, don't try and get him released prematurely or at all. Accept the reality of his condition, while you try to make the best of a bad situation.

[Mandatory Minimum sentences] have destroyed the discretion of judges. They are grossly unfair as they apply to youthful offenders drug cases. For the most part, the sentences are excessive, particularly for first-time offenses.

Judge L. Lawrence Irving, California, 1990

MANDATORY MINIMUM SENTENCES

According to the Families Against Mandatory Minimums (FAMM) Foundation:

* The Department of Justice budget has grown 162 percent since the enactment of mandatory minimum sentences in 1987, compared to the Department of Education budget increase of 77 percent.
* Each day, American taxpayers spend $3.4 million to guard, clothe, feed and house the 60,140 drug law violators in federal prisons.
* Annually, American taxpayers spend $1.25 billion to keep drug offenders in federal prisons. It costs more to send a person to prison for four years than it would to send him to a private university for four years [including tuition, fees, room and board, books and supplies].
* Federal taxpayers spend more per year to incarcerate one inmate ($20,804) than to educate one child ($5,421).
* In 1990, more than half of the federal inmates serving mandatory minimums were first time offenders.
* Average federal sentences in 1990 were: drug offenses: 6.5 years; manslaughter, 3.6 years; assault, 3.2 years.

It makes no sense that a minor drug offender receives a sentence of 60 months while a kidnapper gets 57 months, and the penalty for manslaughter could be as little as 12 months. In 1986 Congress passed laws that forced judges to give fixed sentences to offenders convicted of drug crimes. In 1988, Congress added certain gun crimes to the list of offenses that require a minimum number of years behind bars without possibility of parole. These federal mandatory minimum sentences are determined solely by the weight of the drugs, or the presence of a firearm during a felony.

The sentences are mandatory in that judges must impose them, regardless of the defendant's role in the offense, his culpability, likelihood of rehabilitation, or any other mitigating factors. Many states have adopted similar mandatory minimum sentences.

* Mandatory minimum sentences undermine the basic tradition of justice Americans have enjoyed for 200 years, that the punishment fit the crime.

* They strip judges of their power to determine the appropriate sentence based on all the facts of the case.

* They give low-level offenders longer sentences than most kingpins. The only way to avoid a mandatory minimum is to provide substantial assistance to the prosecutor in exchange for a reduction in sentence. Unlike the organizer, the minor player seldom has valuable information to trade for a reduced sentence.

* There are sentencing disparities based on race. Studies show that Blacks and Hispanics are more likely to receive mandatory minimum sentences than whites charged with the same crime, according to The Sentencing Commission Report, 1991.

According to FAMM, the alternative to mandatory minimum sentences is to let judges consider all of the facts of each case and determine the appropriate sentence under the U.S. Sentencing Guidelines. Judges must be allowed to do what they are trained and paid to do: judge the merits of each case.

"It is hard to imagine," said U. S. District Judge J. Spencer Letts, "that there is any other nation in which a convicted rapist could get a sentence which will make him eligible for parole in a little more than three years, while a first-time offender with a spotless prior record, stands to be sentenced to 12 to 15 years [for drug possession]."

The intention of this law was to get so-called drug "kingpins" off the streets by giving them long sentences. Instead, kingpins avoid these sentences by snitching, or giving prosecutors information about their subordinates. As a result, a low-level drug dealer or user may go to prison for five to ten years or longer, while the kingpin remains free.

Unfortunately, those at greatest risk are often those who are involved the least. For example, suppose your roommate keeps drugs in your apartment without your knowledge. Your roommate is arrested, and the police offer him a deal: give us the name of a dealer, and you will get a reduced sentence. Your roommate gives them your name, even though you had nothing to do with the drugs. Your roommate testifies against you at trial, and you are convicted and sentenced, entirely on your (ex-) roommate's perjured testimony. To add insult to injury, the D. A. decides your roommate's testimony wasn't good enough, and he gets the maximum sentence anyway.

Or, how about this: a stranger standing in line at the post office asks you to mail a package for him, because he's in a hurry. You agree, and before you know it, you're arrested and convicted. The police ask you for names, but you don't know any. You get the maximum, because the judge isn't allowed to consider the mitigating factors that you have an absolutely clean record and were only being a "Good Samaritan." Tough cookies.

In all cases other than mandatory minimum drug cases judges are allowed to consider:
* the nature and circumstances of the crime
* the history and character of the defendant
* the deterrent value of the sentence and numerous other factors.

The Department of Justice acknowledges that the average petty drug offender in the Federal system receives a sentence of 81.5 months.

*   *   *

Suicide among prisoners has been on the upswing, according to a 1995 study by the National Center on Institutions and Alternatives. Feelings of hopelessness, caused, among other factors, by long mandatory sentences, could be to blame, the survey indicated.

*   *   *

This incident took place in a Courtroom in a mid-size city:
"Sir, I apologize to you for the sentence I'm about to

impose," a judge said to a man standing before him convicted of petty theft with a prior. "There was a time when I was allowed to do my job. Legislators who know nothing about anything have dreamed up these mandatory minimum sentences. If I was allowed to do my job today, I'd have given you probation. Instead, I have no choice but to sentence you to seven years. I'm sorry. What I'm forced to do is not right."

*   *   *

Any society that depends on only two sentencing options-- confinement or nothing at all--is unsafe and unjust. We need a full array of effective sentencing tools that actually suit our various sentencing purposes.
          Michael Smith, President, Vera Institute of Justice

THREE STRIKES

The "Three Strikes" law, approved by California voters in 1994, imposes heavy mandatory sentences for repeat felony convictions: double the statutory term for a second felony, and 25 years to life for a third felony, if the offender already has two or more "serious or violent" prior felony convictions. "Serious" does not necessarily mean "violent." The prior felonies may include those committed while a juvenile, committed many years ago, in a foreign country or in another state.

California's draconian Three Strikes law does not adequately differentiate between "serious" and "violent" crimes, so a person may wind up doing life for stealing a lawn mower from an open and unoccupied garage. A man who stole a pack of cigarettes was sentenced to seven years. The theft of a bicycle resulted in a sentence of 14 years. The cost of keeping someone in prison in California is about $20,000 a year. Multiply that by 25 years and it costs a minimum of half a million dollars to incarcerate each non-violent offender under this law.

The California Department of Corrections (CDoC) predicts it will need an additional $6 billion a year if "three strikes" remains the law. Between 1852 and 1984, California built 12 prisons. Between 1984 and 1994, it built 16 additional prisons, costing $5 billion. The CDoC predicts that by the year 2003, the state will need 41 more prisons at a cost of $10 billion.

There are more than 150,000 in California prisons (1997) and it's predicted that their numbers will double to 300,000 by 2006. By that time, California will imprison more than seven times as many of its citizens as it did in 1980. The number of prison guards in California has tripled, from 7,570 in 1984 to over 22,547 in 1994.

The basic concept behind "three strikes" was a good one. So good, in fact, that most states already had similar laws on the books, but without the catchy name. They were called "habitual criminal" or "repeat offender" laws.

Mike Reynolds, the "father" of the California three strikes legislation, conceived it after the brutal slaying of his 18 year old daughter outside a restaurant where she had just dined with friends. Sorrowing people are often urged to divert their grief into some positive channel and work to change the system, rather than act out their emotions in violence. And this is what Mr. Reynolds did: he took steps to change the system.

Unfortunately, it didn't work out exactly as he had envisioned it. While a large number of violent, predatory criminals have been taken out of commission, and this is laudable, prisons have also been filled to beyond their capacity with people guilty of nothing more serious than minor, non-violent property or drug offenses. Some judges and prosecutors have gone overboard in their quest to "make an example" of these offenders, so that just as many people are receiving draconian sentences for possession of marijuana or writing a bad check, as for rape or aggravated assault.

Reynolds applauds the Supreme Court decision which allows serious and violent felonies committed by 16- and 17-year-olds to be counted as strikes. If this were not so, Reynolds asserts, youthful offenders could have their slates wiped clean when they reach 18, regardless of how vicious their crimes. His only regret, he says, is that the age limit for counting strikes was not lowered to 14.

Statistics produced by the Criminal Justice Consortium show that as of January 31, 1997 there were 2,900 prisoners in

California sentenced for three strikes cases, of whom 41 were women. Blacks represented 43% and Hispanics 27%, both grossly over-represented. The number of second strike cases is astounding: nearly 24,000, 37% black and 33% Hispanic. Only 35% of the 3rd strike and 17% of the 2nd strike cases involved crimes against persons. All the rest were relatively minor property and drug crimes including burglary, petty theft with a prior, vehicle theft, marijuana and other drugs.

The American Civil Liberties Union (ACLU) has published a list of 10 reasons, here condensed and paraphrased, to oppose "Three Strikes":

1. Most states already had habitual offender laws, and Three Strikes is "overkill."
2. The law is not a deterrent because most violent crimes are not premeditated.
3. It could lead to more violence if a criminal facing a mandatory life sentence decided to resist arrest or kill a police officer or witnesses rather than go to prison.
4. The law will clog the courts.
5. Discretion in sentencing is taken away from judges. Limiting the possibility of parole fails to consider that some prisoners can be rehabilitated.
6. The cost of imprisoning three-time losers for life is prohibitively high. The cost of incarceration for younger prisoners is about $20,000 a year, but this rises to $60,000 for prisoners over the age of 60.
7. The law has a disproportionate impact on members of minorities, a result of the "war on drugs." Drug use among Blacks and Whites is said to be comparable, but more Blacks than whites are arrested and convicted for drug charges.
8. Life sentences will be imposed on offenders whose crimes do not warrant such harsh punishment.
9. The punishment does not fit the crime. The first two felonies must be "violent," but the third can be any felony. There is a risk that people could be given mandatory life sentences without parole for relatively minor non-violent crimes such as prostitution or shoplifting.

10. The Three Strikes law is not a valid response to crime because it focuses on the offender after the crime has been committed. Instead, the ACLU urges crime prevention by elimination of the conditions that cause crime, such as illiteracy, lack of jobs, poverty and lack of hope. Three Strikes was a good idea that went a little too far. With some fine tuning, and combined with programs of crime prevention, it could yet become an effective tool in crime management.

*   *   *

It isn't just a question of our moral obligation to help steer kids and their families in a better direction. There are practical considerations, including lower cost, that argue powerfully for placing more emphasis on early intervention and prevention, than the back-loaded system of retribution and punishment we now have in place.

Fresno Bee Editorial, July10, 1997

Violent crime has declined 4.6 percent in states that don't have Three Strikes, as opposed to 1.7 percent in those states that do. Violent crime in California, which has the most stringent Three Strikes law, has dropped 4.2 percent, which is below the national 4.6 percent average. Various studies have concluded that Three Strikes is not an effective deterrent and has had no significant impact on crime.

FAMM

PART TWO
INSIDERS

The Bullet Never Stops

Challenged by his friends, or the lack of none.
A young man trying to belong, was given a deadly gun.
With this gun no one will ever fuck over you again.
What are you waiting for, it's either you or him.
One shot through the heart and a tragedy unfolds.
He never thought with just one shot, how far that bullet would go.
A young man lying lifeless on the ground, that much he surely knew.
Not knowing it also pierced his mother's heart, and his father's too.
Even brothers and sisters would feel the pain, a family torn in two.
As the bullet found each heart, and passed its way on through.
What would it take to make you see, it's never a One-On-One.
So many lives feel the hurt and pain, when the bullet leaves the gun.
And don't even try to justify the wrong that has been done.
By closing your eyes and trying to believe it was only a One-On-One.
For it won't be long before you see, the journey's just begun.
You have a mother and a father too, and a family who loves you so.
Each of them will feel the hurt and pain, the deeper the bullet goes.
You started this in foolishness, in anger or in fun.
And you see the bullet make its rounds, all the damage that its done.
Then you will feel it rip into the heart of the one that has fired the gun.
A young man lying lifeless on the ground, two families dying slow.
What would it take to make you see, how far a bullet goes?
Just ask anyone around me now, we're surely the ones who know.
Would you listen to us, as we await our fate?
San Quentin, Death Row.

I know not whether laws be right
Or whether laws be wrong;
All that we know who lie in gaol
Is that the wall is strong
And each day is like a year,
A year whose days are long.
Oscar Wilde, *Ballad of Reading Gaol*

THE FUTILITY OF PUNISHMENT

Punishment serves no useful purpose. In fact, it has the opposite of the desired effect. When society punishes criminals for their actions, it doesn't stop or deter crime. Instead, it causes them to commit the same crimes again and again.

John M. Fisher, LCSW, a marriage and family counselor specializing in interpersonal communications, says the answer is to teach people to change their behavior through the creation of positive feelings of personal worth. Once the individual learns to express anger and other emotions in a positive way, he or she will no longer feel the need to act out by committing violent acts.

People act as a result of their feelings, Fisher says. When we punish someone, we try to change their behavior by creating "feelings of obedience."

Threats create fear. Blame creates guilt. Condemnation creates shame. Restriction creates feelings of powerlessness. Removal of privileges creates feelings of loss and disappointment. These tactics work only with people of high self-esteem, people who feel a sense of pride, security, power and worth; they don't want the negative feelings to continue.

But when we punish people of low self-esteem, the opposite happens. These people already have entrenched feelings of fear, guilt, shame, worthlessness and powerlessness. To punish them only reinforces what they already believe about themselves through their own victimization: "I don't matter" (worthlessness); "It's my fault" (guilt); "I'm not good enough" (inadequacy); and "The world is out to get me" (fear). Out of these feelings comes anger.

The acts for which they are being punished sprang forth from anger. Because they don't have other ways to express their anger, they re-commit the same offenses, only the next time with more sophistication.

How can we stop the cycle of recidivism? Through personal power and discipline, Fisher says. The root word of discipline is "disciple", a person who follows a teacher. To discipline means to teach, not to punish. Discipline attempts to alter people's behavior through the creation of new feelings of bondedness, personal worth and empowerment.

To create feelings of:
* bondedness - listen
* trust - honestly display feelings, especially anger
* security - make agreements, then follow through on them
* empowerment - invite the person to join in problem solving.

We commit violence out of a positive intent, the attempt to gain for ourselves a sense of power and control over our environment, a sense of worth, and a sense of connectedness. All these are basic needs common to all people. Violence and punishment only create an illusion of power, worth and bondedness, but fail to accomplish anything beneficial.

*   *   *

A partial list of rules and regulations published by San Quentin (CA) prison in 1891 (paraphrased) includes:

RULES

* No profane or disrespectful language permitted
* Possession of a weapon shall be punished by flogging
* Prisoners must recognize officers by rising, uncovering (removing their hat), and saluting
* Clothing issue will be two shirts, two pairs of pantaloons, two pairs of shoes, two hats, and four pairs of socks. As a special reward for diligent labor and good conduct a reasonable amount of underwear will be issued.
* One plug of tobacco and one pint of coal oil will be issued every week.
* Prisoners are required to bathe and be shaved once a week unless excused by a physician.
* Prisoners are not allowed to wear their pantaloons while in bed.
* If any prisoner shall attempt to induce a fellow prisoner to debase himself as a bardash [engage in sexual activity] he shall be reported to the Director with the recommendation that he be flogged.

THE FINE ART OF DOUBLESPEAK

Incredible advances have been made in modern penology as evidenced by the updated politically correct lexicon now in use. In a remarkable demonstration of Doublespeak, Oldspeak has been amazingly transformed into Newspeak.

OLD SPEAK- Death Row
NEWSPEAK- Capital sentences unit, Unit for condemned clients

OLD SPEAK- Executioner
NEWSPEAK- Lethal injection technician

OLD SPEAK- Goon Squad
NEWSPEAK- Cell extraction team, Special Services Unit, SSU, Execution
             strap down team

OLD SPEAK- Prison
NEWSPEAK- Correctional facility;   Therapeutic correctional community;
             Rehabilitation center

OLD SPEAK- Prisoner
NEWSPEAK- Client

OLD SPEAK- Prison guard
NEWSPEAK- Correctional officer, counselor

OLD SPEAK- Reform School, Juvenile Hall
NEWSPEAK- Youth Development Center, Youth Authority, School.

OLD SPEAK- Solitary Confinement, the Hole
NEWSPEAK- Adjustment center, Seclusion, Meditation facility, Individual
             behavioral adjustment unit, Secure housing unit (SHU),
             Administrative segregation (Ad Seg), private attitude
             adjustment unit

OLD SPEAK- Warden
NEW SPEAK- Institutional Superintendent

                    *   *   *

LOSS AND GRIEF

When their men go to prison, women experience loss of financial and emotional support, personal privacy and their reputation in the community. They are faced with raising their children alone, according to an article by Susan Hoffman Fishman (*Journal of Personnel and Guidance*, vol. 59 no. 6, February 1981). Ms. Fishman, who was then executive director of Women in Crisis, refers to prisoners as "he" and spouses as "she" because male prisoners outnumber females.

Prisoners who maintain family ties have a better chance of not recidivating. Family members, however, are often unable to give the inmate the support he needs because of their own problems related to the incarceration. The family and inmate can expect to encounter several crisis periods.

The first is when the man is arrested. The family may believe he is innocent. They have little or no understanding of how the system works. Because of the time between arrest and sentencing they may spend a year or more in "limbo."

The next crisis is the day of sentencing. No matter how well prepared they think they are, most are really unprepared and express symptoms of shock in court. The spouse will have many questions: where is the prison, when can she visit, can she bring the children and so on.

After incarceration is the next crisis: financial problems, grief, contradictory feelings of wanting to defend him and feeling anger toward him for what happened. Women will have to cope with telling the children where their father is, and the children will exhibit symptoms of distress such as eating disorders, bed wetting and clinging. The desire to maintain the relationship is offset by the distance to the prison and the cost of getting there.

The final crisis comes at the time of release when both inmate and family may have expectations for the future and for each other that are entirely unrealistic. It may be hard for her to trust him: if he wants to "go out with the boys" she may fear he is using drugs or committing another crime. The woman may have become independent and successful at running the household alone. Now she has to turn over the reins of control to the man and resume her former role of passive dependency.

Don't expect the transition to be smooth, and you won't be disappointed.

     *   *   *

SEEK AND YE SHALL FIND (MAYBE)

Counties, cities, all states but one, and the Federal prison system can tell you if a specific individual is imprisoned in their jurisdiction. Some have an "Inmate Locator Service." Others provide this information through their Records Department.

Before you call, you need to have certain information:
* inmate's name, including middle name
* date of birth
* social security number
* prison, jail or booking number, if you know it.

These phone numbers are accurate as of October, 1997. The Federal system has one central number for all Federal prison facilities. There is no national clearinghouse for cities, counties and states,

ALABAMA (Records Department)	334-240-9500
ALASKA (Classification Office)	907-269-7426
ARIZONA (Prisoner Locator Service)	1-900-226-8682
ARKANSAS (Records Office)	501-247-2600
CALIFORNIA	916-445-6713
COLORADO	719-540-4781
CONNECTICUT	860-692-7480
DELAWARE	302-739-2091
FLORIDA ("Option 1" on touch tone phone)	904-488-5021
GEORGIA	404-656-4569
HAWAII (Inmate Location Information)	808-587-1288
IDAHO	208-334-3120
ILLINOIS (ext. 2008)	217-522-2666
INDIANA (ask for Mr. Holdeman)	317-232-5772
IOWA (ask for Eileen)	515-281-4816
KANSAS (Records Department)	913-296-3317
KENTUCKY	502-564-2433
LOUISIANA	504-342-6649
MAINE	207-287-4360
MARYLAND (or 410-764-4110)	410-764-4109
MASSACHUSETTS	617-727-7299

MINNESOTA	612-642-0322
MISSISSIPPI Female inmates	601-932-2880
Male inmates	601-745-6611
MISSOURI	573-751-8488
MONTANA	406-444-9521
NEBRASKA (ext. 5661)	402-471-2654
NEVADA	702-887-3285
NEW HAMPSHIRE	603-271-1823
NEW JERSEY	609-298-9077
NEW MEXICO	505-827-8676
NEW YORK (State)	518-457-5000
NORTH CAROLINA	919-716-3200
NORTH DAKOTA	701-328-6122
OHIO	614-752-1076
OKLAHOMA	405-425-2624
OREGON	503-945-9090
PENNSYLVANIA	717-730-2721
RHODE ISLAND	401-464-3900
SOUTH CAROLINA	803-896-8531
SOUTH DAKOTA	605-773-3478
TENNESSEE	615-741-2773
TEXAS	409-295-6371
UTAH	801-265-5525
VERMONT	802-241-2276
VIRGINIA	804-674-3111
WASHINGTON (State)	360-753-1598
WEST VIRGINIA (Records-ext. 42)	304-558-2037
WISCONSIN	608-266-2097
* WYOMING (Department of Corrections number)	307-777-7405

* Wyoming has a Confidentiality Law Statute which prohibits releasing names of inmates. Corrections staff say if you want to locate a prisoner in Wyoming, go to the court where he was convicted, look up the transcript in the court archives, and get an order from the judge who sentenced him. In all other states and jurisdictions,this information is non-confidential public record

OTHER JURISDICTIONS

FEDERAL BUREAU OF PRISONS (all federal prisons)	202-307-3126
COOK COUNTY, Illinois (Chicago)	1-800-425-5245
DISTRICT OF COLUMBIA (Washington DC Jail)	202-673-8270
LOS ANGELES (city and county)	213-780-2600
NEW YORK CITY (all five boroughs)	212-487-7145

Write me a letter,
Send it by mail,
Send it in care of
The Birmingham Jail
"Down in the Valley"

LETTER WRITING & OTHER FORMS OF COMMUNICATION

Letters are very important to inmates; they help them to remain connected to family and friends in the free world. When someone you care about is incarcerated, you will probably want to write to him in between phone calls and visits. Or, you may want to write to a prison pen-pal, but first you'll have to get acquainted.

GUIDELINES FOR WRITING TO INMATES

* CENSORSHIP. All mail, incoming and outgoing, is censored. There are a few exceptions, and sometimes an occasional letter is overlooked by the censor, but don't count on it. DO NOT JOKE ABOUT TABOO TOPICS. You wouldn't risk joking about a bomb or a hijacking at an airport, would you? In your letters, don't comment or joke about escapes, drugs or contraband. Censors tend to be literal minded and take such jokes seriously. They have no sense of humor.
* DON'T ASK, DON'T TELL, in the context of letter writing, means DO NOT ask about the crime the person is convicted of, or whether or not he is guilty. Attorneys caution that

communications about the crime may be used against the inmate in his appeal process. Anyway, it's bad prison manners to ask this question.

* LOVE AND SEX. Some inmates are very lonely and so are some of the people who write to them. DO NOT GET ROMANTICALLY INVOLVED with someone you have just recently met by mail. Write love letters to your spouse or honey if you like, but with a new friend, avoid remarks of a romantic or sexual nature. Sometimes romantic overtures from a pen-pal are genuine, sometimes they are made for the purpose of exploitation. Sometimes the person is in prison because they never learned to handle relationships appropriately. The best way to avoid a problem is - JUST SAY NO.

* MONEY. Most inmates are broke. Death row inmates in all states except Tennessee and Texas are not allowed to work at all, so they have no way of earning money. General population prisoners who work may earn as little as four cents an hour. Most inmates have pride and don't ask for money from someone they've just met. Others think the world owes them a living, and they don't hesitate to exploit the gullible. Use your judgment. If you want to send a small money order ($5 or $10 or whatever you can comfortably afford) for Christmas or a birthday, that's okay. If you want to enclose a booklet of stamps in your letter, that's okay, too, if stamps are permitted. Some institutions allow stamps to be sent in, others don't. But if the inmate asks you for $1,000 because his mother needs an operation, DON'T BE A SUCKER AND DON'T BE TAKEN ADVANTAGE OF. You can be sure it's a set up.

A woman told us this story:
My daughter, a high school senior, was dating a college boy whose family was very well off. We were neighbors. The young man, whom she had known since third grade, was sentenced to Federal prison for a very serious crime. He wrote her pathetic letters in which he begged for money to pay his lawyers. She sent him her life savings of $2,000. Our family tried to tell her this was a hustle, that this amount wouldn't be

enough to pay for lawyers, but would buy a lot of drugs. We told her that either his family would have paid the lawyers, or he would have been represented by the Public Defender. She didn't listen. She sent him the money, and that was the last time she ever heard from him.

*   *   *

* BOOKS OR MAGAZINES MAY NOT be sent by you to most prisons. You can give magazine subscriptions to an inmate, as long as magazines are sent directly from the source. Books may be sent directly from the store or publisher. Nudes of either sex, pornography and sexually explicit materials are not permitted. Also forbidden by some institutions are publications considered a security risk, such as those that advocate anarchy or rioting, or tell how to make home-made bombs. You may be permitted to donate books to the prison library, as long as they are not designated for any specific prisoner.

* CARTOONS, NEWSPAPER CLIPPINGS, pictures cut from magazines and advertisements are enjoyed by inmates. Find out first if they are permitted.

* POSTCARDS, PHOTOS and colorful greeting cards are usually permitted. Inmates enjoy pictures of scenic places, a sunset or the beach. Novelty greeting cards such as those that play a musical tune are usually not permitted (contraband could be concealed inside the mechanism). Send a photo of yourself on regular or Xerox photo paper, NO POLAROIDS, and NO NUDES OR X-RATED pictures.

* WHAT YOU CAN WRITE ABOUT is yourself, job, hobbies, family, pets, vacation, travel, that new restaurant you ate at, your new computer with all the bells and whistles, your impacted wisdom tooth, a flat tire, a movie or TV show you love or hate, books you have read. You might think inmates would resent hearing about these things, but most say they enjoy the vicarious experience of a trip to the beach or mountains. It helps them keep in touch with the realities of the free world. Some inmates seem especially to enjoy hearing about your humorous misadventures.

* SETTING LIMITS ON HOW OFTEN TO WRITE. Some inmates are emotionally needy and have nothing else to do but write. Some will write daily or even several times a day. Set limits. Tell him it's best if each writes only in response to the other's letters, so that each of you will be writing no more than about two letters a month. Avoid burnout.

PROBLEM SOLVING

* SELF HELP. When the incarcerated person has a problem with administration, encourage him to do everything possible to rectify the situation himself: ask for a hearing or submit a grievance, depending on institutional procedures.
* DECISIONS, DECISIONS. Once you have collected all the facts about what happened, you and the inmate must decide together if it's worth making an issue of. Is the problem important enough, or is it petty? Is it worth hassling over some minor inconvenience? Does the inmate want you to act on his behalf? If you take action, will that change anything, or will it just create more trouble and confusion? Be aware that you and the prisoner may be harassed because of your intervention. Is it worth it? You have to decide.
* RETALIATION. Be aware that there may be retaliation if you or the inmate register a complaint. An inmate may be threatened, transferred, given "diesel therapy" or thrown in the hole because he or someone else stood up for their rights.
* DOCUMENTATION. When working on a problem, document everything. Write down what happened. Don't rely on your memory. Keep a copy of all letters you send and receive. Take notes of phone calls including date and time, the person you spoke with, and what was said.
* FACTS. Keep a written record including what happened, when it happened (date and time), where it happened, who was involved, who were witnesses, what people said or did. Write all this down as soon as possible after the incident, before you forget something important.

* FREEDOM OF INFORMATION ACT (FOIA) can be used to request documents from any government department or agency. When writing your FOIA request, be specific about the documents you want. List the date of the document, who wrote it, what it was about, to whom it was written, and any other useful information that will aid in identifying it. If certain records are confidential, you may need to get the inmate's written authorization to obtain them. The government bureau has the right to charge you for copying, usually about 20 cents a page. They may also charge you an hourly fee if getting the documents together is time consuming. They may refuse to send you the documents for some reason. If this is the case, you do have the right to appeal, but this can be expensive and may take a long time.
* ANGER. If you are angry, calm down before you phone or write. Don't express your anger to the person in authority you are contacting. Never make any kind of threats.
* WRITE, PHONE or IN PERSON. How do you want to handle this? How urgent is the problem, and what do you want to accomplish? Before taking any action, think hard about what you want to accomplish, what you want the person to do for you. Is it within that person's power to give you what you want?

    Consider writing if:
* you write well or can get someone to help you write
* you get angry easily
* travel is difficult or expensive
* you don't want to directly confront the person involved
* you want a written record
* it's not an emergency.

    Consider phoning if:
* you talk well on the phone
* you do not write very well
* you are able to stay calm and not get angry when upset
* you don't need a written record of the transaction
* you can afford the phone call

* the situation is urgent.
    Consider discussing the problem in person if:
* you do not write very well
* you are able to stay calm even when upset
* you are already at the institution anyway
* a written record is not important
* the matter is urgent.

TIPS FOR WRITING LETTERS TO PUBLIC OFFICIALS

Sometimes, you'll need to write to public officials about your loved one's case or some problem. You might even need to conduct a letter writing campaign on behalf of your loved one.

When you write to a public official and request a favor, such as asking him to look into someone's case, remember YOU ARE IN THE POSITION OF A BEGGAR! The public official holds all the power. He has something you want. He has the power to give it to you if he wants to, but has no duty or obligation to do so. HE OWES YOU NOTHING. Just because you voted for him and pay his salary doesn't mean he's going to grant your wishes. Yes, maybe he should, but that doesn't mean he will. His purpose in life isn't to grant wishes to constituents like you, as though he were your Fairy Godfather; his only interest is in getting re-elected.

The only (legal) way to win him over is to be both COURTEOUS, even to the point of being obsequious, and PERSISTENT, even if it means becoming a pest. You may not feel inclined to be polite when you're feeling angry and desperate. You may want to express your feelings in the strongest possible terms. If your goal is to vent your rage, then go ahead. It won't solve your problem, but it might help you to feel better temporarily. So if you have a burning desire to express yourself, better call a talk show or go to a therapist. But if your goal is to get the politician to give you whatever it is he has that you want, you have to be POLITE. Do it. You may be amazed at the outcome!

WHAT NOT TO WRITE

* DON'T BE HOSTILE, BELLIGERENT OR CONFRONTATIONAL.
* NO DEMANDS, THREATS, SARCASM, INSULTS, NAME CALLING, WISECRACKS, WHINING, or VAGUE, MEANINGLESS DIATRIBE.

THE "WRITE" WAY

* BE POLITE. Call the person by name and title. Spell the name correctly.
* CONVEY THE MESSAGE THAT YOU WANT TO ESTABLISH DIALOGUE. Point out that you and the official are both on the same side, you have a mutual problem, and you would like to work cooperatively with him to solve it in a way that benefits everyone concerned.
* BE HUMBLE. Say "I have a problem and I hope you can help"
* TELL HIM WHO YOU ARE AND WHY YOU CARE.
* TELL HIM WHAT THE PROBLEM IS.
* STICK TO THE POINT.
* INCLUDE ALL RELEVANT INFORMATION. Your name, address and phone number. The name, DOC number and address of the prisoner. The name, address and phone number of the inmate's family, if this is relevant. Case numbers, docket numbers, the name and location of the court, names and addresses of attorneys, judges, witnesses.
* PUT IT IN THE FORM OF AN INQUIRY OR REQUEST, NOT A DEMAND.
* EXPLAIN EXACTLY WHAT YOU WANT FROM HIM.
* BE BRIEF - ONLY ONE PAGE. Don't omit anything important, just say it succinctly and don't repeat yourself.
* DOCUMENTS. Send a copy of any relevant documents.
* SEND A COPY of the letter to the boss of the person you're writing to if he doesn't answer within a month.
* THANK HIM PROFUSELY.
* SIGN OFF COURTEOUSLY.

TIPS ON PHONING

When phoning about your problem, follow these suggestions:
* Have all facts written down in front of you
* Stay calm, do not shout, call names or make threats
* Do not call near the end of the work shift when staff are ready to go home
* Be brief
* Listen carefully. Take notes. Get the name of the person you spoke with and write down what was said
* Do not call too often and become a nuisance
* Explain clearly what you want done
* If the person says they will do something, ask when
* Agree on who will call next, and when.

TIPS ON PERSONAL CONTACT MEETING

When you decide to have a personal meeting, do this:
* Stay calm. If you are feeling very angry or emotional, postpone the meeting until you have calmed down
* Make sure you are talking with the right person. If you're not sure, ask who is the best person to help with your type of problem
* Make an appointment if possible
* Have all facts and records handy
* Be brief
* Listen carefully, take notes
* Tell the person exactly what you want him to do
* Ask when it will be done
* Arrange for follow-up.

FOLLOW UP

If the situation is an emergency, you may reasonably expect an answer within hours or days. If you don't hear anything, try and contact the person again. If that's not possible, contact the person's boss.

If the situation is not an emergency, it's reasonable to wait as much as a month for a response. Contact the person again and politely remind him of the problem. Ask what has been done. Keep a record of all contacts and follow-ups. Note the date, time, whom you spoke with, what was said.

If you still get no action, continue calling and writing to persons higher up the chain of command. You may have to contact your legislators or the media if all else fails. (Some of the foregoing tips were adapted from "Advocating with the Incarcerated in Michigan", Spring 1996 Revised, a publication of the American Friends Service Committee and MI-CURE).

FINDING SOLUTIONS FOR PROBLEMS

A prison belongs to the people of the state, and your tax dollars pay for it. As a taxpayer, you may believe you have the right to demand service or an explanation, like you do from the street cleaning department where you live. Well, you're WRONG.

Prison is a closed system, a bureaucracy that runs itself by its own rules. Some of the things they do, or the way they do things may seem to you to be stupid, absurd, illegal, unconstitutional, counterproductive, nonsensical, immoral, inconsistent or incomprehensible, and they probably are all of those things. So what? They have all the power and you have none. It won't do you any good to scream and demand your rights, so don't waste your energy and make a fool of yourself. Instead, start with the person in charge of whatever the problem is. If that person does not respond to your polite request, go to the next person higher up. Keep on going up until you get the desired response.

Sometimes it's necessary to start at the top. Try to avoid doing this unless a life is in danger, such as an impending execution, a life threatening sickness like a heart attack, or serious abuses like beatings by the guards. In these circumstances, DON'T FOOL AROUND. GO STRAIGHT TO THE TOP. Call or write the president, governor, mayor, police chief and anyone else you can think of. Call the media and arrange a press conference. Start a letter writing campaign. Call upon every organization you can think of that might have some influence. Have a parade or demonstration in front of the prison, city hall or the state capitol. Invite the media.

WHOM TO PHONE OR WRITE TO

GO TO THE TOP is the advice often given, but something is left out. The top of what? Go to the top of whoever is directly responsible for correcting the problem or dealing with the issue, or go to that person's boss. If your problem is the food, go to the head of the dietary department, not the President of the United States.

TYPE OF PROBLEM AND WHOM TO CONTACT

* Impending execution
    President, Governor, Supreme Court, Senator, the Pope, Representative, Pardon Board, Assemblyman, Media
* Abuse or mistreatment by prison staff
    Warden, Head of Dept. of Corrections, Chaplain, Governor, State Attorney General, Media
* Forfeiture of good time
    Warden, Parole board
* Abuse by police
    Police chief, Internal Affairs, State Attorney General, Media
* Parole, length of sentence
    Counselor, Parole Board chairman, Warden, Governor
* Personal crisis, inmate or family
    Counselor, Chaplain, Unit Coordinator, Lieutenant or Captain, Warden
* Visiting snafu
    Visiting Sergeant, Lieutenant or Captain; Associate Warden
* Package or mail mix-up
    Mail room supervisor
* Property
    Property Room supervisor, Asst. Warden
* Transfer
    Warden, Asst. Warden, Transfer officer

* Outstanding warrants
  Records Department
* Grievance
  Grievance officer
* Medical crisis
  Physician, Warden, Inmate's attorney

Depending on the nature of the emergency or problem, a polite letter or phone call to the inmate's counselor, associate warden or warden often will bring results. Always keep in mind that if you antagonize the staff, they may retaliate by punishing the inmate. This is exactly what you DON'T want to happen.

If it's a genuine emergency and you can't seem to get any action, ask the inmate's lawyer to phone the warden. This often gets rapid results. But don't abuse this practice, or you will become known as a troublemaker, and the inmate may be punished for your actions.

HOW TO CONDUCT A LETTER WRITING CAMPAIGN

Letter writing campaigns have been used very successfully for decades by human rights groups such as Amnesty International. When they learn of abuses, hundreds of Amnesty members write polite letters to the heads of governments and heads of departments. They very clearly, briefly and politely describe the problem and state what they would like the official to do about it. When these officials realize the world is watching them, very often they change the way they do things. Don't abuse or overdo this tactic, or it will lose its effectiveness. All the suggestions in the section about letter writing apply. Here are the steps:

* DETERMINE EXACTLY WHAT THE PROBLEM IS. Write and rewrite it until you can express it as clearly as possible in one sentence.
* FIGURE OUT EXACTLY WHAT IT IS THAT YOU WANT THEM TO DO, THEN SAY SO.

* DECIDE WHO SHOULD RECEIVE THE LETTER(S). Go over the foregoing list. Ask around. Has anyone you know had a similar problem? Whom did they write to? Names and addresses of public officials can be found in the front of the phone book, and sometimes in a local newspaper. Or you can phone the state capitol or department you're targeting, and obtain the names and addresses of key people.
* WRITE THE LETTER. Make it clear, concise and polite. Rewrite and edit it until it's perfect. One page only.
* INCLUDE ALL IMPORTANT INFORMATION: your name, address and phone number; the name, address and phone number of each letter writer; the name, number and institution of the inmate.
* ASK FRIENDS, FAMILY, NEIGHBORS, CO-WORKERS, MEMBERS OF YOUR CHURCH AND SUPPORT GROUP to join with you in this project.
* OFFER THEM CHOICES. Tell them they can use a photocopy of the letter you wrote, copy it by hand, or write their own letter using the facts in yours as a guide.
* PHOTOCOPY THE LETTER. Leave blank spaces so each letter writer can put in his return address and name of the addressee. Each public official should receive between five and 20 letters, each one from a different person. Multiply the number of officials by the number of letter writers. In a recent successful campaign we sent about 400 letters to 15 different officials, from about 25 or 30 different letter writers.
* GET BUSINESS SIZE ENVELOPES AND STAMPS. Address the envelopes to the various officials and stamp them ahead of time. Leave a blank space so each writer can put his return address on the outside.
* HAVE A MAILING PARTY. Get everyone together around the kitchen table. Form an assembly line. Sign the letters, stuff and seal them.
* ENCLOSE COPIES of supporting documents, if needed. If the entire package is more than one ounce, or about five pages, use a large manila envelope. This will require extra postage.

* ENCLOSE A POST CARD FOR A REPLY if a reply is requested. Not all such letters need a reply. If yours does, enclose a post card already addressed to you. On the back of the post card, give several choices for the recipient to fill in or check off.
* LETTER WRITING IS COST EFFECTIVE BUT NOT CHEAP. The cost for mailing 400 letters was 400 stamps at 32 cents each ($128); 400 photocopies at 5 cents each ($20); 400 envelopes at 2 cents each ($8), a total of $156. It was money well spent, because the desired result was achieved.

Ask each family member or friend to contribute $5 or $10 to the cause. It's not always necessary to send such a large number of letters, but in this particular case, it did succeed.

No man can put a chain around the ankle of his fellow man without finding the other end fastened around his own neck.
                                            Frederick Douglass, 1883

BOTH SIDES OF THE LAW

Excerpts from a dialogue with Michael Marcum, who has been on both sides of the law. At age 19 Michael killed his abusive father. He was sentenced to seven years in prison. Now he is Assistant Sheriff in charge of San Francisco's seven city-county jails. As a convicted ex-felon, he can never be a sworn police officer or carry a gun.

Prison culture is the antithesis of everything we claim to value in this society. It has two different but similar impacts both on prisoners and on staff. First, the prisoners have internalized they're losers. They've broken the law, their lives are out of control and now they're coming into an institution that represents the second most extreme sanction the constitution allows us to take against a citizen, which is deprivation of their liberty.

Prisoners have a tendency to blame everybody else for what has happened to them. This isn't to say they don't have racism, poverty and unequal opportunity in their lives. It's just that finger-pointing is their way of dealing with what got them jailed. When they come to an institution which is out of control and has no rational response to their plight, it encourages them to continue to point the finger and not take their situation seriously.

Once inside, prisoners immediately know if staff aren't playing by the rules. Everyone has fashioned their own way of surviving, including staff. Prison culture is also the ganging up, the romanticization of being a con and a tough guy. Everyone needs integrity and pride, and that's one way prisoners see their identity. All this convict stuff comes out of a need to fashion a different set of rules and ethics. Parallel to that, staff does the same thing.

The other part of institutionalization is the myth that we coddle prisoners. Anyone who has had their freedom taken away, whether in a concentration camp, jail or prison, knows it is no longer a human experience. Your dignity is gone. People believe that television sets, recreation or education is coddling. It isn't. It's just one way to control the population.

Ninety-five percent of the prisoners are going to get out sooner or later. The longer they're in, the worse they become. I certainly wouldn't want someone who had served a 25 year sentence paroling next to my family. It's too difficult for them to make the transition.

This is what I'd tell a new prisoner: When I went to prison I thought I could trust the staff, but I was wrong. Now I'd tell them to trust staff until they learn otherwise. Avail yourself of every opportunity the institution offers. Anything so that you leave a paper trail of your life, like getting a GED or a college diploma. Don't keep your eyes focused on how you're going to survive. That's important, but watch out for what you're going to do when you get out.

Maintain contact with everybody and don't get resentful if 90 percent of them disappear. It's usually women, wives and mothers, who stick around. In my case, because of shame and embarrassment, I cut everyone loose. I could never explain the reality of prison to them. I did reunite with most of them after I got out.

I would encourage people to do everything to maintain their relationships. Time outside moves much faster than time inside. Prisoners have difficulty understanding why someone isn't writing to them every day. It drives them nuts and they sometimes take it personally. They forget the burden of what it's like taking care of kids or working full time.

I would tell a mother to become known to the system. Write letters, call, introduce yourself to the warden, counselor, director of the DOC, parole board and staff, so they know your child has someone on the outside. It's sad, but it does make a difference on how your child will be treated, how seriously they are given consideration for various programs.

Counter the bitterness and finger-pointing. Don't fan the flames from other family members. You can fight for fair and just treatment for your son, but be careful he doesn't make that the center of his existence. You can also encourage him to take the opportunity to better himself and to be accountable for what brought him to prison. It's a delicate balance and it takes a lot of juggling to do both simultaneously.

When he is to be released, don't let your excitement get in the way of understanding how critical and volatile coming out of a brutal environment can be. The problems are going to be multiple and they could last a year or more. He will have adjustment problems. He may feel skeptical about how much you love him. You need to be cautious, and if you suspect he's getting high, confront him about his behavior. Don't let it get out of hand, because he could go back for that behavior. Very few people go through a smooth transition, it just doesn't happen.

On "60 Minutes" I talked about doing another crime in order to go back. Nobody wants to be in prison. They want a different life, but they don't know how to get it. I didn't want to go back because prison was wonderful. In fact, it was horrible. But I felt like I was excluded from society. I didn't have the acceptance or the self esteem to make it on the outside. I felt anger and discomfort and I was unable to adjust to a free society. There are few transitional programs, and everyone coming out needs them. You cannot walk out of jail and into your old neighborhood and think everything is going to be great, so you panic. The institution, because it's a brutal rigid place, encourages people to fail by destroying their ability to make it in the free world. That's why people go back.

I was a middle class college kid who killed my abusive father. I wasn't a street thug or gang member with a criminal history. But my background became irrelevant. There are a lot of middle class people who wind up inside. But I was just another convict, and that stunned me. I was uncomfortable with everybody. I was forced to confront my own racism, homophobia and everything else to understand the people inside. I found they wanted the same thing I wanted, to make it out of there.

In my case, if a gun had not been readily available, things might have been different. I certainly couldn't have beaten my father to death. Also, the gun was identified with his terrorizing of me. My sentence wasn't rational. My father's abuse was not an excuse, but mitigation.

The fact that I survived is not because of our system but in spite of it. I wasn't handed this job, I had to work for it. I was locked out of law enforcement for years. Without Sheriff Hongisto I would never have been hired.

People think that once you've gone off the edge you have

no right to go back into society. But if the purpose of the criminal justice system is to correct you, then we should welcome ex-inmates who've changed their behavior back into society so they can be productive. We have every right to hold them accountable for acting badly, but you've got to treat them as people or you're not going to recognize the change in them. We use programs in prison, not as a privilege, but as a way to make the correctional system work. Arguing over rehabilitation or punishment leaves out the hysteria of retribution, and that's the emotion that runs the system today. It keeps us from playing by the rules, and I think we need to acknowledge this anger; talk about it in a constructive way.

I don't consider the death penalty a deterrent. I've never met a convict or ex-offender who has ever been deterred by the death penalty or by the existence of prisons. It's the last thing on their minds. Ninety percent of the people who end up inside or get the electric chair never consider the business of punishment. You have dysfunctional people coming into the system that's supposed to represent a functional society. Once they see how dysfunctional the system is, all it does is further their belief that "oh well, this is the only way to live." The death penalty says the same thing. We say we revere life and then we take the life of a human being. It tells people that there is no sacredness about human life. No matter how emotional it is, we cannot lower ourselves to that level.

They call my jail the "glamour slammer" and I hear about "Club Fed." I've been in a hundred or more institutions across the country and there is no "Club Fed." If there was, and if my tax money was supporting it the same way it's supporting San Quentin, I'd rather have the person coming out of "Club Fed" into my neighborhood. He'd probably have the social skills, the education and the respect for the standards of property and politeness that I do. I also think we can improve conditions inside the prisons so we don't have these "pit bulls" coming out.

To the question of do we have innocent people in prison, there are a couple of issues here: the issue of prisons and incarceration as a response, and the good and bad of our court and criminal justice system. Yes, there are innocent people inside. Most people in prison do not belong there. We have other sanctions that would be much better for both the person and the community. But it's common for people to say they're innocent. They may be guilty of something else other than what they're in prison for, but they still need to claim innocence.

There are parents who claim their son is innocent, that

his attorney didn't do anything for him. That part of the system needs to be changed. Every person should have a competent defense. What you're liable to get can be unbelievable in terms of training, funding, motivation and investigations. There is no consistency in defense and there is only a small percentage of people who can afford a good private attorney. Look at the prison population and look at their attorneys. Most were public defenders, and that's not to say public defenders aren't good, it's just that they don't have the same resources as the district attorney or a private attorney.

Regarding the fee cap on defense spending, it's the wrong people setting rules and making assessments. We owe it to ourselves as a society that human life cannot be capped by money.

In two states, Texas and Tennessee, death row prisoners work and make money. Other states don't. There are statutes, regulations, DOC policy, and the "get tough on crime" people who won't allow this. Looking at restorative justice, it's a progressive idea to allow people on death row or doing life to be able to make money to create resources. If people can make money, and do something positive with it, whether it's with their families, or victims, it makes sense.

As for the new system where prisoners are charged room and board, the incarcerated population is broke. That's the reason they're incarcerated, because they can't pay fines. Most don't have jobs or decent places to live. If we don't have jobs for them in here, how are they going to pay room and board?

People complain that prisoners sit around all day and look at TV, but if there are no programs, what are they supposed to do? Unless we have gainful employment or programs or both, there is nothing for the prisoner to do but lie around. Sheriff Arpaio in Maricopa (AZ) County has prisoners work in chain gangs without pay and that's all going to come back to haunt him one day. He's probably losing all his staff support because they're scared to death they're going to get hurt. You can't maintain an institution like that without giving people some kind of human outlet. It's going to explode. We ran institutions like that for years. We had brutal riots and people were killed. We found substance abuse problems, psychotic breaks and stress disabilities with staff, not to mention what we created among the prisoners. Arpaio's time will come soon. I'd love to see a wide open inspection of that place.

Three strikes is ludicrous. Not only is it unjust and unfair, it's gimmicky. We're getting a lot of minor offenders who have no right being in prison for 25 years. Unfortunately, it gives the public this false impression we are doing something about crime. If anything, we are getting the prisoners angrier because of the injustice of their sentence. They go over the edge. Three strikes is an embarrassment and it makes for unsafe institutions. People with a three strikes case will avoid plea bargains and this puts a heavy burden on our court systems.

People who are incarcerated move further away from mainstream society. Our institutions and the criminal justice response to their activity forces them to deteriorate. Robbers graduate to strong armed robbery, not because of a lack of punishment, but because they weren't able to make it in our society as a petty thief.

In terms of the families of the offenders, get them to stay involved not just in the lives of their loved ones but in the system. Also, get involved in the "other side," victims' organizations, people who are pushing for stricter laws. It's important to join those groups and get dialogue going.

*   *   *

Attitudes commonly found among offenders include hostility, rationalization, and victimization. Imprisoned criminals are often impulsive, seek immediate gratification, act without thinking of consequences, do not deal effectively with problems or with other people, rationalize thier behavior, and blame others for thier actions. They see themselves as victims and society as the "criminal."

Cognitive Skills Training is now being used widely in Canadian prisons, and is beginning to be used in a few American prisons as well. The program teaches prisoners to think of the consequences before they act, manage their anger, and make effective decisions. The recidivism rate for inmates who have attended the program are 20 to 30 percent lower than for those who did not.

Knight-Ridder Newspapers

*   *   *

Fear motivates our crime laws and politicians pander to this fear. What triggers this emotion is the media. More citizens are afraid of being carjacked than of getting arrested.

Wendy Kaminer, *It's All the Rage: Crime and Culture.*

THE POKEY PERSPECTIVE

Excerpts from a dialogue with a registered nurse who comes from an upper middle class background. She has worked for five years at a county jail:

It's a county seat so it's a crossroads for county, state and federal prisoners. Federal prisoners are mixed in with the general population, not segregated, but they get the better housing of what's available. Federal prisoners get everything there is to be had, nobody stands in the way of that. If they decide they need to see the doctor on a daily basis, they'll get that. If the prisoner decides he needs special shoes or special medical treatment, he gets it. It's a county facility, but they get paid for housing federal prisoners, so it's held to a strict standard. Not the whole jail but just the part for federal prisoners. If there's overcrowding, the federal prisoners don't get crowded so they're given preferential treatment. So there is a little "Club Fed" there. They can see doctors or attorneys whenever they want, special clothing, shoes, eyeglasses, hearing aids, special privileges, law library. But not better food. There's only one quality of food and you'll find maggots in all of it.

In the old jails, prisoners raised the vegetables on the farm, they had a bakery and worked in the kitchen. That was good food, well done. It was not subject to the kind of ugliness of this plasticized giant corporation thing that feeds them now. They don't have the farm anymore.

They get a bag lunch, "green baloney." In the jail, they eat in their cells, not in a mess hall. A general rule is, don't move a prisoner if you don't have to, for security. You take the food to the inmate, the medicine to the patient, the books to the cell. For security and economics you move them as little as possible. Every time you open that door the risk of an incident goes up.

Most of the inmates who have been in prisons before are always glad to get the hell out of jail and into prison, because prisons have more things to do, more work, more activities, more recreation.

Some of them, when they're incarcerated is the only time in their lives when they have a predictable three square meals a day, a cot, people who are not going to knife them in the night. Well, at least the percentage of that is down. It's almost like they have come back to the womb because they don't have to take care of daily living requirements. It's all done for them. Prison is still prison and being incarcerated is still a punishment, but for some of them, their lives in the free world are so bleak, prison or jail is an improvement. This doesn't mean prison is a country club, it just means their free world life is even worse, and believe me, prison is no picnic.

I think in the case of a life sentence without possibility of parole, another alternative should be to offer the convicted person an option of assisted suicide. I personally would fly into a snarling rage if someone decides my death has to be prolonged because of some half-assed law.

Certain people need to be kept out of the herd. Sex offenders should only get one strike. I think the three strikes law is unrealistic and costly. The system is screwed up. Some maniac who rapes and mutilates a girl will get out in three years. Some jerk who smokes a joint will get life. It doesn't make any sense. Three strikes won't work and we can't afford it.

I think it's a sin that the state will use all this costly technology to execute a prisoner, but will deny euthanasia to a patient who's suffering from some horrible terminal disease because it's against the law. I'm not asking for Club Fed and I'm not asking for kid gloves, but I am saying we have a responsibility to meet basic human needs, and that doesn't mean frills.

Our prisoner population at the county jail is about 3,000. It makes no sense to leave 3,000 able bodied young men idle for 24 hours a day. I believe there are better places to spend our money. We would better utilize our resources to allow those people to work 40 hours a week just like you and I do, and earn the roof over their heads. I think it's a reasonable approach.

We charge them room and board here, and I think that's okay. But the problem is, most of them are indigent and can't pay. There ought to be some form of appropriate workplace education. Education and job training are not frills. If we had secure workplaces, even lifers could get job training and move up within their own system. They would have some control. If there was a sort of sliding scale where prisoners could move up in terms of responsibility, life style, privileges, behavior, then you've taken some of the hopelessness away. We treat dogs better than we treat prisoners.

Corrections is a growth industry. It's the will of the state now that we lock up everybody with a parking ticket, so to speak. If we as a nation decide we have to lock everybody up then we as a nation need to handle it in a humane way. Even child molesters and sexual predators very often are intelligent, well educated and could do something useful in prison. There are so many needs in this society that poor people can't meet, and these needs could be met by prisoners. All prisoners are not stupid or lazy, but even those who are, there are a lot of jobs they could do, like cleaning up by the roadsides.

The vast majority of prisoners are people who live at ground zero. That's all they've got. We've had four generations of the same family incarcerated at one time for things like armed robbery, burglary. There is no shame. This lifestyle is the family business, how they earn their living. It's a way of life. People like that, they have a certain interest in their family members, mostly because they have nothing else to do. But are they affectionate? No. Would they step in front of a bullet for a family member? No. They're just not as evolved as the rest of us.

From my observation, most of the guards have come out of the same strata of society as the very lower part of the lower class, the Archie Bunkers of the world. The state prison guards make very good money, but the guards at the county jails make the minimum. The benefits are the best most of them ever had, but they are not very good. The inmates have better medical coverage and better TVs. The guards make zip. They belong to a union. Their life and their life expectations are not much different from that of the prisoners, so it's from this middle group that you get the horror stories. Not all guards, but that's who you've got, the lower middle class.

Some of the inmates have a "black belt" in malingering. They can manipulate so security is compromised. If they can con you into thinking they need to go to the county hospital, you've got to go through the building and through the yard. That's an escape risk. They get medicines they don't need, then buy and sell them. It becomes commerce.

Those who are "holding/waiting" and those who have been sentenced for some misdemeanor are treated the same, except holding/waiting's can't be trustys. There are TVs and a reasonable library. I'm against weight rooms. I can tell which ones are going to prison soon because they're the ones buffed up so no one will challenge them when they get there. Some of these guys are in and out like a revolving door. It's like, "Oh, hi, you were here for Thanksgiving and now you're here for Easter.

Did you have a good winter?" Those people don't need to be made stronger. They do have a basketball court up on the roof of the county jail so they do get out in the air sometimes.

There's a laundry where the trustys work. They do all their laundry for them. They get two jumpsuits and three changes of underwear. They don't get to keep their own clothing like in prison. It's all county issue. They can't even have their own shoes. But they can have court clothes, which are stored down in the clothing room. In the morning they bring the clothes up to them.

Women prisoners are different from men. Women tend to complain more so they take more medical staff time, which is also true in the free world. Women go to the doctor more and are more in tune with their health. Men avoid the doctor, but women try suicide more often than men. When women fight, cat fights are not as likely to involve shanks and shivs. It's just bitchiness, not weapons, as a rule. I never saw a female inmate seriously hurt by another female. In a county jail one floor is for females only and the rest is for men. The attitude of the correctional staff towards the women is a hell of a lot more negative and more condemning than towards the men, regardless of what they were accused of.

There's very little privacy. When women have their period they get their pads or tampons from us but they get no privacy when it comes to using the toilet. That would be a problem to me. I would die. These ladies come from a different paradigm. They don't come from the same place as we do. For the most part they've never known that kind of privacy. Most of the women I took care of were "working girls" (prostitutes). All that stuff about modesty and privacy just isn't there. They are different from us. Most are involved with drugs or are being manipulated by their men, like to drive a getaway car. Not usually violent crimes. One woman assisted her boyfriend in beating her two-year-old to death. I was enraged and sickened by what she had done.

If a woman talks about her crime at all, it wasn't her fault, he made her do it. That is a common theme throughout the prison population. The SOB made me shoot him, if he had just given me his money I wouldn't have had to shoot him, it's his fault. It's always somebody's fault. This particular woman who helped her boy friend kill her baby, she professed to speak no English, but I didn't believe her. It was hard to read her because she was from Mexico, and they are different from Chicanos.

The difference is that American born people are raised with the belief that things can change, that we can make our lives better if we work hard, that there will be some kind of equality, and that we are entitled to certain basic things. None of those things are true for the folks from Mexico unless they are in the top eight percent. You and I don't expect to have our babies at home alone while trying to take care of the last three that were born. They are hopeless, they have a hopeless helplessness, therefore they don't accept responsibility for their actions.

With men hopelessness brings on aggression; with women, passivity. Mexican national men are very submissive to everybody in an American prison, and try to fade into the woodwork. Now our white trailer park trash don't do any fading. They have the attitude of tough, you can't push me around, bitch, that kind of thing.

You are alone in the exam room with this patient. There's no guard, there's no panic button, so you have to be careful. An older man, maybe 65, I don't know what he was in for, he was on the exam table and was complaining of sinusitis. I was up close and he said something risque, suggestive, so I just put the instrument down and stepped back and said "Mr. Smith, you have to understand that what you said was inappropriate." He said "I'm very sorry." I took care of him a number of times and never had any trouble again. For the most part the inmates are not abusive. If they start to be I say "I'm really sorry about your sore throat. Guard, take him away." If he comes back later and acts like a gentleman, that's fine. I take care of him.

Body cavity searches don't happen real often in jail. You've got different kinds of prisoners. Federal, who may have done anything. City, county, state, some in jail for a misdemeanor, a lot of dui's [driving under the influence], some sentenced and waiting to be transferred to state prisons. They could wait up to a year or two if they don't have beds at the prison. Some are awaiting trial.

This is the basic problem for jail being an unmanageable place. There's too damn much going on, not enough technology, not enough staff. All the various rules, regs and guidelines, so the jail is constantly in violation, always with the feds, usually with the state. Always 10 or 20 percent over capacity, so they spew out 300 people.

Child abusers are kept in ad seg [administrative segregation] for their own protection. They can request that. I took care of rapists in the general population but not child rapists. We had one old guy, like 80 or 90 years old, for child molestation.

The problem of three strikes is that it doesn't really deal with the real career criminal. They go after someone who committed two or three crimes 20 or 30 or even more years apart but not in between, but it does nothing about the day to day career criminal.

If they implement a death penalty for so-called drug kingpins they will wind up executing the street dealer but not the international smuggler, the CIA operative behind it or the corporate businessman who financed the whole deal.

In terms of sexual crimes, we need a whole lot of work. Instead of having professionals draw up the parameters, you have politicians making the rules, who may have good intentions but are not knowledgeable.

I would tell a new prisoner mind your own business, don't volunteer for anything, don't make eye contact with anyone unless you must to take care of your needs. That's where the challenges happen and that's where the submission happens, among both inmates and guards. Be very careful about eye contact. Keep your mouth shut and do what you're told, don't look at a guard in a contemptuous manner. Don't be a do-gooder, don't intervene in people's squabbles. If there's a fight, go to the farthest corner of the room, sit down and stay out of it.

Police could try and plant an informer in your cell, so if a new cellmate wants you to confide in him, don't do it. Don't confide and don't accept confidences. Breathe in and breathe out until the time goes by then get the hell out of there.

They have to buy their personal stuff from commissary, shampoo and the like. But the women get their Kotex pads from us. I used to think it unfair when they started charging $3 in the jails and $5 in the prisons to go to sick call, but it's one of the ways prisoners use to get out of their cells to pass messages or just to break the boredom. They use the medical visit for a lot of things not having to do with their health needs.

You do an assessment carefully and simply to look for malingering. The flip side is that real illnesses often get overlooked. Some prisoners write 20 requests a day to go to the infirmary for eyes burning, constipation, itching, and when you finally get to that person there's nothing wrong, he was just bored. So the next time I see his requests I'm going to disregard them because he's like the boy who cried wolf. So I would advise an inmate not to abuse the system. They have to convince the guard they're sick before medical staff is called.

There's an organization of correctional health care workers and I think that's really going to improve the quality of medical staff people who show up in corrections. Right now there's a lot of people working in corrections medicine who couldn't make it in other areas of practice, so they wind up down there. Standards and criteria are being developed and written down, and that will make a difference. Some old time correctional nurses say "I could never work on the outside because you have to listen to their complaints." This made my blood run cold. Some of the nurses and docs who come to correctional medicine don't speak good English, lack basic skills, or have some sort of cloud hanging over them professionally. That helps create the Nurse Ratchet stereotype. And the power thing. Some are there for reasons of power, not cure. That's alive and well in the correctional world.

In the jail system they use the LVNs (Licensed Vocational/Practical Nurses) badly. They give them horrendous amounts of work for half the pay RNs get, and they do the grunt work. In the prison system the MTAs (Medical Technical Assistants) are on the LVN level, but are the first line person who makes the initial assessment. Sometimes LVNs wind up in that slot in the jail, but not usually. The LVNs and MTAs are required to make judgments beyond their scope of ability and practice. RNs are not allowed to make a diagnosis, it's beyond our scope of practice. So they give a six week training course to a guy who used to be a bus driver, and it's perfectly legal for him to make a diagnosis that an RN isn't allowed to make.

*   *   *

California Department of Corrections recently announced they will limit medical care for prisoners to what is "medically necessary." A doctor, nurse or medical technician (MTA) must decide what is medically necessary before an inmate can be treated.

Services included are those that will save the life of an imate, prevent serious illness or disability, or lessen severe pain. Also included are certain diagnostic tests such as lab tests, x-rays and EKGs.

Treatment will not be provided for any illness that will get better on its own such as colds and flu, and conditions that do not respond to treatment such as wide spread cancer.

All drugs used for treatment will be generic, not brand names.

Jails have no apologists, they are universally recognized to be hellish places.

Jessica Mitford

BIG CITY JAILS

Excerpts from a dialogue with a social worker at a big city jail:

The difference between men and women in jail is that most of the women are mothers. Women worry about their children and that complicates the time they do. Women also have fewer reserves than men. They relate to each other and treat each other like family.

The average woman in jail has a fifth grade education, she's a housewife with limited social experience. She has not traveled extensively and has few expectations in life. Most of the women are on drugs. If they've had a violent offense, it's often against the abusive man in their lives.

Some of the women get into lesbian relationships for survival, and some of those relationships continue even after prison. Forming unions or strong bonds protects them from each other and against the establishment.

When a woman goes to jail, the jail becomes her whole family. For men in jail or prison, their women stick around and visit. They stay in the relationship. Men, on the other hand, leave when a woman goes to jail or prison. They don't stick around and care for the kids. A woman's most serious problems are economical and child care. If her sentence is long, her problems only get worse.

There is no privacy for women on the inside. Every thing she does, dress, shower, sleep, go to the bathroom, is all done under the watchful eyes of the guards. She's never alone and there's no way to get away from that fact.

If a man goes to jail, even if he is the kindest man in the world, he soon gets involved in the way things are done in prison culture. He becomes mean. He tries to control her because he can't control his world. When he finally gets out, he's a different person.

Prison often begins the cycle of abuse for a couple. He's now a convict and he treats her as if it's her fault he's locked up. The system, in the way it creates violence, encourages this behavior. It's a rare man who waits for his woman.

Of all the people I've met, only about two percent say they're guilty. Eight percent say they did it for someone else. Innocence is different. If you get the feeling the person is telling the truth, and you see it in how they carry themselves, they get respect from others. Have dignity; it also gets you respect.

If you're a big fish on the outside, you need to learn how to be a little fish on the inside. Learn who's in control. Don't mate yourself to that person, but take the time to get to know them. Gain their respect.

If you don't have a lot of money, quit smoking. There are few resources on the inside and jobs are scarce. Most women do odd jobs such as ironing, writing letters, nails or hair, and they read to others who can't read.

Medical care where I work is good quality, and women are treated at County Hospital for illness or injury. If you have an acknowledged health problem, you won't be put into a cell alone. If something happens to you while in your cell, yell and do what you can to get someone's attention. We have a nurse who makes rounds to see how the inmates feel.

In our society, women are told they aren't worth much. Men are the priority. Most women have no medical care in prison and that's why. With our gender role stereotypes, men in prison are men in prison. Women in prison are "sluts and deserve to be there."

The city has made a concerted effort to do a good job with its inmates. We have a very progressive sheriff. I've found that in some cases I'm more afraid of the deputies than I am of the inmates. Some deputies should be in prison themselves.

Working at the jail cannot be just a job. You are not turning out parts for some factory. You may affect someone in a good or bad way. It's always personal. Jail can be such a toxic experience. If someone gets out and then goes back, a little piece of yourself says, "you're a flop."

If I were in charge of the system, I'd make sure no one was ever released unless they could read. I'd have jobs and therapy waiting. On the inside, I'd have counseling and employment training, along with Alcoholics Anonymous and Narcotics Anonymous. I'd teach women how to get control in their lives.

African-Americans, the biggest population in jail or prison, are a very religious people. I'd also teach them to take control of their lives, but until we change the economy in this world there will always be prisons.

RECEPTION AND DIAGNOSTIC CENTER

A new inmate said:
The reality of going to prison finally hit when I found myself seated on the bus on my way to the reception center. My hands were cuffed behind my back, my legs shackled to the metal bars of the bus seat. On my lap, in a brown paper bag, sat my lunch. The significance of that moment, knowing I couldn't move my hands or feet, much less eat the lunch they had given me, sent shivers of foreboding down my spine. As I glanced around the bus, I could see the worried and fearful expressions on the other guys sitting near me. I knew then that prison was going to be one of the worst experiences of my life.

Before he goes to the prison where he will remain the inmate first goes to a reception center.

One inmate described the reception center process this way: "In the case of new recruits, fish, this is the training ground for what is to come. A sort of pre-prison atmosphere camouflaged in diagnostic jargon. It's cold, bleak, and uncaring. Most new guys are frightened, and they should be."

First the inmate is classified. This will be completed before he is shipped out. During classification, a printout of the inmate's criminal history is run through a local, state and federal computer criminal data base. This checks for any records of local jail time and any prior prison commitments.

Next, a needs assessment is used to determine whether the inmate is suicidal, or if he has a fear of or problems with other inmates. In Tennessee, the diagnostic tool is called the Decision Tree. It's a set of questions with Yes and No answers. This tags the inmate for special considerations. Some questions are used to determine if:
* The inmate is suicidal
* He has had any problems in the past, or current problems with another inmate
* He is an escape risk
* He has a prior or current assault history
* Homosexuality
* Disciplinary problems in the past
* Pending charges against him.
* Past convictions
* Warrants
* Family ties
* Employment history
* Educational level

After testing, an inmate may be placed in protective custody or lockdown for:
* Current or multiple escape history
* Assaultive behavior
* Active parole/probation status
* Homosexuality
* Disciplinary action.

California Department of Corrections (CDoC) uses a scorecard and considers various factors before classifying an inmate.

Security levels are for Level One (Minimum) 0 to 18 points; Level Two (Medium) 19 to 27 points; Level Three (Medium) 28 to 51 points; Level Four (Maximum) 52 points and above.

Two points may be added to the scorecard if the prisoner is under the age of 26; has not been married or in a common-law relationship for at least a year before the term started; failed to graduate from high school or have a recognized trade; was not employed for at least six months, and, for men, had no military training.

Special case factors such as medical problems or restrictions, work skills, gang affiliations and enemy situations are added to the point system to determine where an inmate is placed.

At the reception center, the inmate is interviewed by counselors, therapists, social workers and others. He undergoes a battery of psycho-social, educational and work-related tests. These tests determine where he will be housed and what programs he will be eligible for or will be required to participate in. For example, if the inmate cannot read, he may be assigned to an educational counselor for further testing.

Not every reception center has the staff or facilities to accomplish this. According to a recent news program, funding for education, vocational training and therapeutic intervention have come under the scrutiny of penny-wise and pound-foolish politicians, and voters who are frustrated with the rising crime rate. Even though these programs work as rehabilitative measures for outgoing inmates, they will be the first eliminated.

Inmates are also required to go through a medical examination. If he has medical problems that keep him from actively working or pursuing work, he will be classified or tagged for special consideration. After all tests have been completed, the inmate is assigned a level. This entire testing process can take anywhere from six weeks to six months.

Periodic reviews during the inmate's commitment can change the level he is on or his custody status. If a Level One inmate gets into a fight, or is written up for other violations, his level may change to a higher custody level.

From a correctional officer's point of view, this classification process offers opportunities to help the inmate by determining what he will need for a successful stay in prison. This means that if an inmate is classified as a level one, nonviolent drug abuser, he may be placed into Alcoholics Anonymous or Narcotics Anonymous (alcohol or drug programs). If his work history includes janitorial or automotive experience, he may be placed in one of those work-related fields during his commitment. If he has a history of assaultive behavior, the testing process will indicate he must be supervised more strictly than a Level One. This is for his protection, as well as that of other inmates.

During the reception stay, the inmate is introduced to regulations, guidelines and rules of conduct for inmates.

"Prisons reinforce a criminal subculture," a correctional officer in Northern California said, "by herding massive groups of testosterone-laden offenders together in a small area. To survive, a new inmate must learn the rules of conduct. These rules are often totally opposite those of the free-world, and when meshed with free-world thinking, create conflict."

An old prison hand sees it this way:
The reception center is where fish learn the cockeyed confusion of prison policy from administration versus the strict set of rules made up by the inmates. Prison policy is supposed to be for everyone, but it's not. The guards change the rules anytime they want whenever it suits them. Inmate rules rarely change. Our life depends on it. This is why the reception center is so important to fish. They learn never to depend on a rule made by "the man" (administration). It's like smoke drifting in the air. Here one minute, gone the next.

In prison, cons have good values, but they're criminal values. The newer guys entering prison nowadays don't have those same values. They don't have compassion for their compadres. All they think about is who can take down who or who hassles who for what. I'm glad I'm out. I wouldn't want to be in prison today.
Danny "Red Hog" Martin, *Committing Journalism.*
*   *   *

The man or woman who one day discovers they have been accused of a crime begins the tortuous journey into hell. Attorneys are expensive, the court process confusing, sentencing is based on a rigid and arbitrary set of rules and imprisonment is sheer terror, but what happens to their family and loved ones often goes unnoticed.

Lenore B., Social Worker

PRISON CULTURE AND MORES

A young inmate explained a situation at the reception center:

The only thing lower than a snitch is a prison thief. After I arrived at the reception center, I began hearing about a thief stealing smokes and other stuff. At first, we thought it was one of the new recruits. Every time a batch came in, something disappeared. One day, someone saw an old timer, a guy who's been waiting for quite a while to transfer, sifting through his stuff.

Later, I found out what happened to him. The leader from each ethnic group chose two men to represent their race. They all cornered the thief in the shower and knocked him around. Put some sense into the idiot so he won't get killed later. It's important for each group to be represented. That way, the thief can't claim it was a racial incident.

One of the worst things that can happen to you in prison or jail is to be labeled a snitch. This is telling on someone to the authorities or to a rival gang, selling them out down the river. It can be deadly.

Another rule of etiquette: Don't ask, don't tell. If you're curious about what your pen-pal or friend did to get himself locked up, refrain from asking.

Advice from a public defender:

A new fish will sink or swim in the prison culture. The prison culture has its own rules, norms and language. Basic rules are, do your own time, don't talk to others about your case, and don't accept gifts from strangers who might turn you out as a punk in return.

*   *   *

Cons don't understand people like Ted Bundy or Charles Manson.
They just don't fit into the scheme of prison life.
Death row inmate

RACIAL ISSUES

A young inmate told us:
One of the most stringent rules is "having heart". It means you stand up for your race. You don't back down from a fight, because it would signify a defeat for your race.

The important part for a fish to know is if you are Black, Hispanic, White or whatever, and you are hassled by someone of another race, you must stand up to them. If you don't, you disgrace your entire race. It's looked upon as humiliating the whole race. Both sides will think you are nothing but a coward.

You don't knowingly take a drag off of a cigarette from someone of another race, or drink from a water fountain after someone from another race has drunk. You can't play cards alone with a group from another race and don't be overly friendly. You can talk to, but not walk alone with, someone of another race. Most ethnic groups are tight. The Hispanics follow their gang affiliations. When a gang member arrives, he finds his gang as soon as possible. It's survival.

GANGS

"Blood in, blood out," is what prisoners and ex-cons say about gangs. You have to shed blood, your own or someone else's, to qualify for membership. If you want to resign, your blood will be shed by others. Corrections officials we talked to have varying opinions about how prevalent and how powerful prison gangs are.

Those gangs that originated within the prisons were first organized along racial and geographic lines ("homeboys") in the 1950s and 1960s. Their purpose was for "securing the main line," prison slang for mutual aid and protection. One of the most notorious is the so-called Mexican Mafia, called Eme (pronounced "em-may"). According to prison officials the gangs, once only used for mutual protection, have branched out and now include drug smuggling and extortion.

Street gangs, on the other hand, are carried into prisons when their members are incarcerated. Street gang members continue their affiliation inside, and carry on their feuds with members of rival street gangs.

California prison authorities say that out of more than 150,000 prisoners in 1997, they have identified only 400 as official gang members, and another 430 as affiliates or "wannabees." However, Corey Weinstein M.D. says in his opinion that is a low estimate. Dr. Weinstein believes that 50% of the security housing unit (SHU) is labeled as gang affiliated. Of course, being labeled as gang affiliated does not necessarily mean that label is correct.

Even though so few are officially recognized as gang members, several thousand others in California prisons are kept segregated because of mere suspicion of gang activities.

Devan Hawkins, a correctional counselor at Pelican Bay [CA] State Prison, and a recognized expert on prison gangs, says gang members make up less than one percent of the prison population, yet are responsible for 85 percent of the criminal activity that occurs inside the prisons.

In addition, that small number, Hawkins says, are a disruptive influence outside as well. They have a dreaded reputation and are known for following through on threats. Prison gang members, Hawkins asserts, are able to conduct criminal activity on the streets even though they are locked down in tight security. Using the mail, they direct friends, relatives and their gang members in the free world to make "hits" and perform other criminal acts, such as robberies and assaults, on their behalf.

Defense lawyers and criminal rights activists say these claims are greatly exaggerated by prison authorities. They assert gangs are far less of a threat than authorities claim.

A young gang member told us about his life. Two of his brothers were in prison. A third brother had been murdered. They had been abandoned by their father, and their mother was an alcoholic.

"In a way, I wanted to [go to prison]. All the other guys who'd done time, when they came back, they got a lot of respect.

And I wanted that. When [you've been] locked up . . . everyone wants to be the first to be seen with you. You come back from prison and you're a hero," he said.

*   *   *

TALKIN' THE TALK

The language of prison, like all living languages, is constantly changing. Some of these words are local or regional, others are universal, and some may be out-dated.

AB: Aryan Brotherhood, a white supremacist prison gang.
Ace Boon Coon: Best friend.
Ace-Duce: Best friend.
Adjustment Center (AC): euphemism for disciplinary solitary confinement, "the hole."
Ad Seg: Administrative Segregation, a controlled unit or "prison within a prison" where inmates are placed for institutional security or misconduct
All day: life sentence.
Attitude: display of hostility or contempt.
AW: Aryan Warrior (see AB); Associate Warden.
Badge: guard.
Banger: knife.
Beef: infraction
Big House: prison.
Billys: White men.
Blanket party: throwing a blanket over a prisoner so he can't identify attackers, then pummeling or raping him.
Blind: blind spot where officers can't see what's going on.
Bonaroos: best clothes.
Boneyard: area reserved for conjugal or family visits.
Boss: guard.
Brick: carton of cigarettes.
Broadway: the first floor of a cell block where inmates can walk and mingle.
Bubble: plexiglass enclosed guard station
Bug: crazy person
Bull: Guard
Bunkie: person with whom prisoner shares double bunk bed.
Burn rubber: Get lost, get outta here.
Bus therapy: also called Diesel therapy, a practice used in both Federal and state prison systems of endlessly transferring inmates by bus from one facility to another for the purpose of effectively rendering them

incommunicado for long periods of time.

Buster: what Southern Mexicans call Northern Mexicans

C-file: each prisoner's central file.

Cadillac: the best food, job, etc.

Call (call out): mail call, sick call, when these events take place

Camp: minimum security facility

Car (in the car): a (usually influential) group of friends; a group of officers who unofficially but effectively control a particular prison

Carnal: Homeboy (Mexican).

Case: see Beef (infraction)

Case Manager (counselor): staff member who prepares classification reports

Cap: the amount of marijuana that fits into a Chapstick cap.

Catch a beef: to be charged with an infraction.

Catcher: the passive or submissive sexual partner. See "pitcher."

Cellie: cell mate.

Chalk: see Pruno.

Check: a group beating given to an inmate, an initiation

Cheese Eater: informer, snitch (q.v.)

Chester: child molester.

Chrono: notes made in C-file documenting medical orders, disciplinary problems etc.

Clavo: stash.

Click up: to join a gang.

Commissary (Canteen): the place to buy cigarettes, candy and other items; the money with which to buy them.

Con: short for "convict"; also, to use deception

Convict: an old timer of dignity and honor, usually respected by both inmates and prison staff.

Convict Bogey: an inmate who escapes, then preys upon citizens or communities

Corner: people a prisoner hangs out with.

Counselor: see Case Manager.

Count: prisoners are not only counted to make sure no one is missing, they are identified by name, number and cell. All activities stop until the count is cleared, three or more times each day.

Cut-up: suicide.

Date: release date.

Diesel therapy: see Bus therapy.

Dig this out: check this out.

Dime: ten (years, dollars worth of drugs etc.)

Dis: disrespect

DOC: Department of Corrections

Drop a dime: to inform or snitch on someone.

Dog: homeboy or friend.

Do your own time: mind your own business, don't ask questions

Ducat: scrip used to obtain photos or withdrawals for canteen; passes for movement within the prison.

Dump truck: a lawyer who sells out his client.

Eme, el eme: ("emmay") Spanish letter "M", refers to so called "Mexican Mafia."

EPRD: earliest possible release date.

Easy time: to adjust to prison life.

Featherwood: a peckerwood's (q.v.) woman.

Feed the warden: to defecate.

Fish, fish cop: a new inmate; a new guard.

Fish bundle: the initial clothing issue, one of everything.

Fish line: a line or string used to pull items or kites (q.v.) from one cell to another.

Flavors: brand name cigarettes brought in from the free world

Free pass: allowed to get away with something by prison staff, avoid catching a beef

Freeway: see Broadway.

Free world: the world outside of prison.

Galboy: effeminate homosexual consensual sex partner

Gassing: to throw urine or feces on a guard

Germs: cigarettes

Getting Rec: harming someone for no reason

Gladiator fight: fight between prisoners set up by guards for entertainment of guards

Good time: time by which sentence is reduced for work or good behavior

Goon squad: security squad of officers that handles riots, disturbances, executions etc.

Green: money, marijuana

Groupie: women (occasionally men) who choose to limit their relationships to prisoners, often to the exclusion of other people, activities or interests.

Hack: guard

Hard time: having difficulty serving one's sentence

Heart: strong convictions, loyalty to one's "corner" (q.v.)

Herb: a weakling

Hit a lick: come into some money

Hole: disciplinary solitary confinement (as opposed to single cell occupancy)

Home boy, homie, homes: a prisoner from one's neighborhood, home town, gang etc.

Hooch: see Pruno.

Hook-up: a lie told by an officer to get an inmate into trouble.

House: cell.

Hurry up and wait: rush to be on time to a mandatory "call," (q.v.), then stand around and wait

Hustle: pull the wool over someone's eyes, take advantage of, borrow

Ink: tattoos.

Inside: in prison.

IWF: Inmate Welfare Fund, money obtained from surcharge on canteen, supposed to be used for athletic equipment etc., but sometimes misappropriated by administration

Jacket: C-file.

Jail: city or county lockup where detainees who can't afford to post bail are held awaiting trial, and those convicted of misdemeanors serve sentences of less than one year. Because of prison (q.v.) overcrowding, some jails rent out space for the housing of state prisoners

Jailhouse lawyer: self-taught, assists other prisoners in filing suits; sometimes called "lay advocates"

Jailin': the lifestyle of "groupies" (q.v.) whose principal occupation is visiting at every possible opportunity

Jeff: joke, play

Jody: the free world lover of a wife or girl friend

Keester: (n.) the rectum; (v.) to hide contraband therein

Kit: drug paraphernalia

Kite: note, letter, message passed to a prisoner.

K-9 (canine): correctional officer

Lame: someone who doesn't fit in, an outcast, oddball

Laying the track: having sex

Leg rider: brown-noser

Life on the installment plan, doing: refers to a chronic recidivist whose long stretches of prison time are interspersed with only brief sojourns in the free world

Line: mainline, general (prison) population

Lockdown: confinement to cells, particularly during an emergency or time of unrest

LWOP: life (sentence) without possibility of parole

Man, the Man: guard or person in authority

Missive: letter, correspondence

MTA: medical technician

Monster: HIV, AIDS

Mule: visitor or guard who smuggles drugs into prison

Nickel: five (of anything), five year sentence

Nut-up: go crazy

On the books: amount of money in prisoner's trust fund account.

On the bricks: the outside, the streets.

Pass: see "ducat"

Passenger: someone who is in the "car" (q.v.)

Pay rent: paying "protection" in money, goods or services to an inmate or gang to avoid being harmed

Peckerwood: white prisoner

PC: protective custody

Peel [his] cap: hit someone in the head.

Phone's off the hook: a guard is listening

PHU: protective housing unit

Pile: weights

Pitcher: sexually aggressive or dominant sexual partner (see "catcher")

Playing on ass: gambling without money

Pod: housing unit in newer jails and prisons, in which cells are arranged in a circle around a central bubble, sometimes with a central communal area or dayroom

Postal: crazy

Potty watch: instituted to look for the emergence from the rectum of contraband, such as drugs, inmate is suspected of ingesting

Press your bunk, punk: Lie down on your bed and be quiet

Priors: prior arrests, convictions or prison terms

Prison: state or federal institution housing those convicted of felonies with sentences greater than one year

Pruno: prison made contraband fermented alcohol, made with yeast or bread, sugar, fruit or fruit juice

Pull a card: find out about a prisoner

Punk: passive homosexual partner

Put on Front Street: openly defy a guard

Put your pen to the wind: go ahead and write a disciplinary report or grievance

Raisin Jack: see "pruno"

Rag: bandanna

Range: tier, cell block

Rappie: charge partner, co-defendant in the same crime

Rat, Rat jacket: a known snitch or informant.

RB: rich bitch

Rest your neck: shut up, be quiet

Ride out: transfer to another prison

Ride the rack: sitting or lying on a bunk or bed

Road dogs: prisoners who walk together on the exercise yard

Roll in: arrive

Roll out: depart

Rustler: predator

Safe: vagina, when used to hide contraband

Salami slicing: asking for favors

Schooled: has learned the facts of prison life

Senseless count: census count

Shakedown: search or "toss" of cell or work station. Prisoners' property is often lost or destroyed.

Shank: home made weapon

Short, to get short: approach release or execution date

Shot: disciplinary write-up.

SHU: security housing unit, characterized by isolation and sensory deprivation

Skinner: sex offender

Slam down: lockdown, send to the "hole"

Snitch: informant, rat

Spread your hustle: don't always borrow from the same people

Spun out: crazy, stupid, idiotic

SSU: Special services unit, euphemism for the goon squad, cell extraction team or execution strap-down team

Stash: stockpile of contraband

Stinger: immersion heater to heat water, may be store-bought or home made by rigging electrical wires

Street: free world

Sympathy play: telling a sad story to gain special favors

Tack: tattoo

Tack head: a prisoner's woman

Tailor made: packaged cigarette

Tally water: inhaled intoxicant (i.e., glue)

Tat: tattoo

Texas Syndicate: a prison gang

That's dead: No.

That's straight: that's good

Ticket: transfer order, disciplinary report

Tier: cell block, usually in older institutions, in which cells are laid out in long rows

Tip: prison gang

Tipped up: member of the AB (q.v.)

Traffic ticket: minor offense

Transpack: pack belongings for a transfer

Tree jumper: rapist

Trusty (plural: trustys): a prisoner whose trustworthiness has earned him special privileges and a good prison job. (Often mis-spelled "trustee," which means a member of a corporation's board of directors.)

Turnkey: guard

Turn out: rape an inmate, make him into a punk

Violate, violation: parole revocation

Walk(ed) out: to be escorted to the gate

Wood: white prisoner

What is the difference between the grief of a mother who loses her
son to murder and the grief of a mother who loses her son to a murder
conviction, or life without parole? How do we rate their sorrows and
relative claims of compassion.

Wendy Kaminer, *It's All the Rage: Crime and Culture*

You have to keep your stamina, your awareness and mental capacity.
Try to hold onto your family and friends, if you have any. That's a
lot of pressure, a continuous struggle. You never know if you're
going to make it.

"Jazz"

RELATIONSHIPS AND MARRIAGE
A TOUCHY TOPIC

Good touch? Bad touch? It all depends on who's doing
the touching, their intent, and the reaction of the person being
touched. You could say it's a touchy topic.

In Calistoga, the "mud bath capital" of California, a
professional masseur at a resort had this to say:
In my family touching was a part of life. It meant we
shared love. Whenever my father put his arm around me and
said, "Great job, Son," I knew he was proud of me. Today, there's
paranoia about "good touch, bad touch." We are afraid of
connecting by way of skin to skin contact, afraid we will be
accused of unwelcome sexual intent.

The masseur had worked as a counselor at a group home
to pay his way through massage school. The boys always asked
why he'd do something as stupid as pampering others for a living.
"They had never been touched, never hugged," he said. "Their
parents would hit on them, spank them, or just plain ignore them.
Not once had they ever been patted on the back and praised for
something they had done right."

*   *   *

In central California, a male substitute teacher was on trial for allegedly molesting female students. Previously, he had allegedly touched two girls on the shoulder. According to the principal, "his touch made the girls feel uncomfortable." When asked why he hadn't reported the episode to the police, the principal said he "didn't think it was that important." He did, however, not hire the teacher again as a substitute.

A grandfather asked, "Should I hug Jennifer?" his granddaughter. "With all the messages about perverts and little children on TV, I feel like a suspect in a bad B-movie if I even want to hug her at all."

*   *   *

"When a man or woman steps behind bars, the world they once inhabited ceases to exist for them. If, in the free world, the inmate used touch to show his affection or approval to others, that gesture will soon be crushed on the inside. We don't like it when someone tries to pat us on the back. What if they have a knife?" explained a forty-two-year-old inmate.

"In here, this is an oppressive, nervous atmosphere and touching someone, unless in a fight, means submission or sex. That's bad, too. Either way creates stress for the population. You on the outside need to understand that if your loved one is hesitant to touch you, it isn't because they don't want to, it's because they've forgotten how."

*   *   *

On a hot afternoon, a woman was having trouble walking up the steep hill to the prison parking lot. Wiping the sweat off her face, she muttered, "This is difficult to talk about. I visited my son today. An officer, who must have seen the terror in my face, asked if it was my first time. When I said yes, he handed me a book of rules, smiled and asked if he could answer any of my questions. I had only one. Can I hug my son?

"He laughed and said. 'Of course you can. We make it a policy for mothers to have two or three hugs per visit'."

The woman said, "That guard made me feel so much better about being here. When my son came in, he first checked in with someone at the desk, then came over and gave me a big bear hug. I can't tell you how relieved I was."

For those who have a touchy-feely style, hugs are paramount. In the case of your own loved one, if in doubt, ask. They will know. The prison has specific rules about what type of physical contact is allowed. It's up to you to honor both their rules and the inmate's wishes.

*   *   *

A correctional officer at the visiting center at Sierra Conservation Center in Jamestown, California told us:
The usual visiting rules regarding touch and hugging are: a hug at the beginning of the visit and one at the end. Touching is restricted in most prisons. Some prisons may be more lenient than others. Sometimes they let you hold hands. Follow the rules to the letter and don't deviate from them. If you do, you could get your loved one in trouble, and you could be banned from visiting.

*   *   *

Those who say all prisoners are murderers, rapists and child molesters, haven't been to prison lately. Most of the inmates I see are non-violent, first-time offenders. They are drug abusers, not drug king pins. They are parents, husbands and wives, they're our children. Murderers, rapists and child molesters make up only a tiny portion of the prison population, so why are all prisoners always described this way?
Raphaella, wife of a prison inmate.

BALL AND CHAIN

One morning while we sat in the waiting room at a Northern California prison, a group of thirty or forty women came in. They were chatting with each other and seemed in high spirits. One woman, JoEllen, chose to talk to us about the upcoming event:
The women who marry prisoners are a diverse lot. Most of us know exactly what we are getting into. In the eyes of

society, he's scum. He's a low life criminal in prison and society doesn't believe prisoners should have the right to marry.

I fell in love with my husband before he went to prison. He had a good job, health benefits, retirement, the whole works. One day, he made a bad decision, not a criminal one. Now he has a criminal history and he lost his job. Of course, he'll have to start all over again. Both us of will.

She described the wedding ceremony:

We arrived around nine A.M. and signed in. Since the wait is usually an hour or two, the women begin the transformation from street clothes to bride. Some dressed in pants and T-shirts. Others wore filmy pastel gowns. We still had to adhere to the dress code. All of us had to go through a security device to check for weapons or other metal objects.

We were all nervous wrecks. Some wanted to up-chuck on the spot. One had a migraine, and one who was pregnant visited the restroom every ten minutes. Most of us were accompanied by family or friends. We sat on hard wooden benches in the hallway, chatting among ourselves, twirling our hair or twisting Kleenex up into little balls. Only twenty could enter the main visiting area to get married at one time. That left the other sixteen of us outside to wait another hour.

When the time came for us to go though the metal detector, everyone got up, hugged the strangers who had become friends, and wished them well. In the midst of razor-wire and realism, we women had bonded. We were entering into a relationship with a man who had broken the law. His label of felon would soon be ours, too.

The wedding itself took only ten minutes. We said our vows, gave each other a ring, then had a Polaroid taken. After that, we sat while the others got married. That was our honeymoon. Jack couldn't wear his ring when he returned to his cell. I had to mail it to him later.

The wedding was a pleasant civil ceremony. Those who wanted a religious blessing would have to wait until the inmate is out, unless a minister who already has visiting permission attends the wedding and gives an unofficial blessing.

We watched as the women lined up to go through the metal detector. Although they had chosen to marry prisoners, they still seemed full of hope. We wished them luck. They were going to need it.

One new wife of a prisoner explained how she handled intimacy:

For me, the biggest turn on is emotional intimacy. Sharing your innermost thoughts and feelings, helping each other understand who or what you're all about. Paying attention to the little things, learning how far you can go with each other. I've accepted him for who he is and I haven't tried to change him.

Thinking you can change someone is really not accepting who they are in the first place. Understand that in any relationship there are ups and downs. Don't be the "thought police" or therapist. Learn to roll with the punches and evolve as he does. If he comes to the door with boxing gloves on, don't get offended or put yours on. Something has happened. Get him to talk about it. If he abuses you verbally, be firm. Don't take it. Threaten to leave immediately.

All marriages and intimate relationships require work and commitment. Maintaining a marriage or other close relationship with someone in prison is hard work and requires a heroic degree of devotion. If you were already married or engaged to the person before he went to prison . . . If you recently met someone already in prison and are thinking of developing a romantic relationship . . . If you're thinking of divorcing your spouse who's in prison . . . you need to seriously consider these issues:

* you may be his only contact in the free world
* what is he getting from the relationship?
* what are you getting from the relationship?
* are you willing to "do time" along with your loved one and be faithful long after the newness wears off?
* do you think you're going to "save" or "rescue" the loved one?
* does feeling needed make you feel important?
* what do you really know about each other?
* how does the crime he's incarcerated for affect the relationship or your feelings?
* what do your family and friends think of the relationship?
* is he using you, making inordinate demands for money or contraband?
* what will it be like when he is released from prison?

* what are your goals for the future?
* how will you cope with his mood swings?
      While pondering these imponderables, you should: talk, write, visit and get to know each other:
* go slowly; you have plenty of time
* read books on relationships
* talk to a clergy person or marriage counselor
* engage in honest communication with your loved one
* avoid illicit sexual intimacy such as in the visiting room
* learn to say "No" when appropriate
* learn to deal with issues of dependency and control
* don't get pressured into doing anything that makes you feel uncomfortable or is against the law, such as drug smuggling
   If your child is in prison:
* don't blame yourself; it's not your fault
* don't abandon him. A parent's love should be unconditional (in most cases). You can still love your child though you don't condone the crime of which he has been convicted
* don't be pressured into spoiling him by providing money you can't afford because you feel responsible
* try to be honest with yourself and with him about your feelings. It's not unusual to feel various combinations of love, hate, anger, fear, resentment, shame, guilt . . . you name it
* be helpful to your child's attorney and investigator who are working on the appeal or some other aspect of the case.

                  *   *   *

He loves me? He loves me not. He loves me? He loves me not. He loves me?
                     Barbara, wife of a man in prison

A MOVING EXPERIENCE

      When someone you love goes to prison, your first instinct may be to move and live near the prison.
      DON'T do it.
      At least, don't do it before giving it serious thought and talking it over with family members and other trusted advisors. If you live

in a state with only one or two prisons, it might not be unwise. If you live in a state like California, with 32 prisons and more being built every day, or if your loved one is in the federal system, moving is probably a bad idea. Chances are, he will be transferred to another prison at a great distance even before you unpack.

Sometimes people want to move near the prison because:
* they cannot bear being apart
* he has a lot of time to serve or is on death row
* they can't afford to travel to make visits
* they have no strong ties to where they live now.

Before moving, think about these factors:
* can I afford to move (moving is expensive)
* do I have people in the new town who will help me
* will it disrupt the lives of the children if we move
* what will be my source of income in the new place
* can I find a job there
* what about child care
* when is the best time to move (most people choose summer when the kids are out of school).

If you do decide to move, make sure you're not just "taking the geographic cure." If your misery is inside of you, it will go right along with you wherever you go.

*   *   *

> Going to court has nothing to do with innocence or guilt, it has everything to do with checkbook justice.
> Mother of son in prison

A CHILD'S EYE VIEW

If your loved one who goes to prison has children, you have to face the reality of telling the children what's going on. DO NOT LIE TO THEM OR IGNORE THE SUBJECT. Children are not stupid. They know something's terribly wrong in the family. You may think they don't know about it, but neighbor children will taunt them: "Your daddy's in jail." If it's a high profile case, and the child is old enough to read or look at the TV news, he or she knows, whether you admit it or not.

Children will be afraid, confused, angry and sad. They will even feel guilty. Children often believe that when something happens, it is their fault. The child may think Daddy or Mom went away because the child wet his bed or didn't drink her milk. Children worry a lot, too: "If Mom's not here, who will take care of me?"

Tell the child age-appropriate truth: Dad did something wrong, and had to go away for a while for "time out." He will be home again. It's not your fault. Grandma, or Aunt Ruth, will take care of you. We will take you to visit Dad.

If the child is old enough, encourage him to write, send photos and drawings, copies of report cards and awards, and allow the child to talk to Mom when she phones.

Several books are available to help children:

* My Mother and I Are Growing Strong, Inez Maury, New Seed Press, POB 9488, Berkeley CA 94707, bilingual Spanish and English. Price: $6.95 + $2.00 postage, total $8.95.
* Joey's Visit, The Family Matters Prison Program, Cornell Cooperative Extension, 1050 West Genesee, Syracuse NY 13204 Price: $2.00.

Imprisoned and rendered powerless and without any choice or control in the things that affect him, his personal desires and feelings regarded with gracious indifference, and treated as a child at best and an animal at worst by those having control of his life, the existence of a prisoner is one of acute deprivation and insignificance.

Wilbert Rideau, a lifer at Louisiana State Prison, Angola

INSIDE THE WALLS
PRISONERS RIGHTS

The Supreme Court has said that prisoners do not forfeit all Constitutional rights. But they fail to specify what rights prisoners do have, saying instead that a prisoner retains all rights of an ordinary citizen except those expressly taken from him by law. This statement does not really enumerate which rights are taken away, or which rights are retained. This is apparently left up to local courts and/or prison administrations to determine on an individual case by case basis.

It's clear that the right to travel at will is taken away from prisoners because by definition they are confined. Some rights generally held to be available to prisoners include, among others:
* First Amendment rights to free speech and religious practice
* Eighth Amendment right to be free from cruel and inhumane punishment
* the right to petition the courts for relief when rights are violated.
* prisoners in Massachusetts, Maine and Vermont retain the right to vote.

Even some of these rights are being chipped away. The right to free speech has been curtailed by the refusal of Corrections Departments in some states to allow prisoners to be interviewed by journalists. The right to practice one's religion is sometimes curtailed for reasons of "security."

Early in our country's history, prisons were little more than snake pits in which torture, harsh discipline, filth, brutality, mind-deadening labor and isolation were the norm. The prevailing thought 200 years ago was the Calvinist belief that all people are born "evil," some more so than others, and the only way to change them was by the infliction of brutal punishments.

In the last century, reformers saw that these methods did not work. They developed an opposite theory, that people are born "good" and do bad things because of social conditions such as poverty, alcoholism and abuse. These reformers attempted to bring about change in criminals by rehabilitation. Unfortunately, this method didn't work either because it failed to address the social conditions that caused at least some crime. The rehabilitation method utilized strict and compulsory religiosity, and was doomed to failure.

Present day penology has given lip service to some notions of rehabilitation and prisoners' rights. In the 1960s prisoners for the first time sought and obtained legal relief from the courts for abuses. Subsequently, prisons offered at least a few programs of education, job training and alcohol and drug rehabilitation.

Now in the '90s, with the "get tough on crime" attitude that prevails, which is generally interpreted to mean "be cruel to inmates," most of these programs have been dropped. They have been replaced by isolation in Secure Housing Units (SHU) and the return of abuses like the chain gang, the electric stun belt and "gladiator fights" allegedly staged between prisoners by guards at places like California's Corcoran State Prison.

When conditions get bad enough, prisoners sometimes riot, as they did at Attica, or they file law suits for judicial relief. Unfortunately for prisoners, the courts, the prison administration and the general public view such law suits as "frivolous." In addition, people persist in the false beliefs that prisons are "country clubs" and prisoners live a life of comfort and ease in luxurious surroundings.

In the free world, persons accused of crimes have the right to a lawyer, and evidence of guilt must be "beyond a reasonable doubt." This is not the case in prison. Inmates may be charged with relatively minor offenses such as gambling, disrespect or manufacture of pruno, or serious offenses such as assault, battery or even homicide. Generally, prisoners in these circumstances do not have the right to an attorney, and a conviction can be upheld as long as there is "some" evidence of guilt.

Prison staff generally cover for each other. The cop's "code of silence" applies. At trial, staff may "forget" details beneficial to the inmate. Those who violate the code of silence risk hostility from other prison staff.

Prisons are still brutal places, and prisoners are still brutalized, as in the past. Such rights as they have are given or taken away at the whim of whoever is in power.

SHOWERS AND BATHS

The Penal Code says inmates are allowed to shower or bathe when they arrive at their new home, at least every other day thereafter, and more often if possible. The regulation actually says "shower or bathe," although nobody we know has ever seen a bath tub in a prison. What they don't tell you is there is no overabundance of hot water, either. In some prisons, showers automatically shut off after five minutes.

A death row inmate told us how he does it. His first few years on the row, he just washed one section of his body at a time. By week's end, everything had at least a passing acquaintance with soap and water.

Then they were issued five-gallon plastic buckets with the wire bails removed. These all-purpose containers, which had previously held detergent or paint, get plenty of use. Turned upside down, they can be sat upon. Upright, they are used for laundry, sponge baths and making pruno (q.v.).

So now when it's his turn to shower, he gets completely soaped up in his cell, soaks his feet in the bucket, then runs to the shower where he spends the whole five minutes rinsing off.

RELIGION

"CONGRESS SHALL MAKE NO LAW RESPECTING ESTABLISHMENT OF RELIGION OR PROHIBITING THE FREE EXERCISE THEREOF."

That's what the First Amendment to the United States Constitution says. But what does it mean for prisoners? Considering that sages, philosophers and the Supreme Court can't agree on the meaning of the Constitution even for free citizens, it's no wonder that confusion exists regarding how prisoners may exercise their right to practice their religious beliefs.

In America's first penitentiaries, in the 1700s, it was mandatory that all prisoners practice the Protestant faith. So much for the First Amendment. Where have we come since then? Are prison officials required to accommodate religious practices, and if so, do they favor some religions over others?

In the 1960s courts began to hear complaints that Black Muslims were not allowed to practice their religion in prison. In 1964 a Buddhist prisoner in Texas made a similar claim. The Supreme Court held that the free exercise of religion is a right retained by all prisoners, not only those who profess conventional or traditional beliefs. The Supreme Court did not address the issue of religion in prison again until 1987. In the interim, lower courts put forth a variety of contradictory opinions.

What it amounts to is this: it's a standoff. A prisoner has the right to practice his religion. The prison authorities have the right to limit or prohibit any activity, religious or otherwise, which could interfere with security. If prison officials ban a religious practice, they are supposed, in theory, to ask if there is a bona fide security issue, and if the prisoner has available an alternative way to practice his religion.

In one case (Fromer) a district court clearly favored the rights of the institution. When the court ruled that the state cannot prevent him from praying in private, what it really was saying was that there was no compelling need to permit the inmate to attend group services. Another court leaned more toward prisoner rights when it told prison officials to ask "does the ban make sense?"

Courts have ruled that it is not illegal for prisons to hire chaplains, but prison employees, including chaplains, may not proselytize or evangelize prisoners in an attempt to convert them to a particular faith.

Court rulings raise more questions than answers:

* If a prisoner has a belief, does that belief constitute a religion? (It depends on whether the belief is secular, moral or theological in nature.)
* Do adherents to unfamiliar faiths have the same rights as adherents to conventional or organized churches? (Probably.)
* Does the inmate have to demonstrate he is sincere in his beliefs in order to be allowed to practice the religion? (Not necessarily.)
* If an individual does not steadfastly adhere to every single tenet of his religion, does that disqualify him as a member of that religion? (No, because nobody is perfect.)

Prisoners whose religion requires them to wear a hat or cap may be allowed to do so. Some prison authorities have ruled that wearing caps constitutes a danger to security. Others have said that Jews cannot wear a yarmulke (skullcap) because it compromises security, but it's okay for them to wear a baseball cap. When the authors questioned a warden to clarify this policy, he was unable to explain how a skull cap would interfere with security. However, he did repeat the words "security issue" and "a matter of security" a number of times, without further elaboration.

Growing beards or long hair, or wearing hair in dreadlocks have all been held to be a security risk. Contraband could be hidden in a hairdo or beard. If a prisoner escapes he could shave his beard, changing his appearance. Yet some prisons do permit beards and dreadlocks, so the definition of "security" remains vague, nebulous and arbitrary.

The right to a religious diet has been a source of litigation.

Jews and Muslims are prohibited from eating pork. Most prisons allow them to have a protein pork substitute but this is not required by law. In one case (Kahane) a court ruled the prisoner should be provided with a "diet sufficient to sustain good health without violating the Jewish dietary laws." If the cost of providing the diet is extravagant, the diet may be denied. However, prisoners may purchase provisions at their own expense to accommodate their religious dietary needs. An inmate who works in the kitchen may not be punished for refusing to touch a food he is forbidden to eat, such as pork.

Religious services are believed to have rehabilitative value, so are generally encouraged. If no chaplain employed by the prison is available, volunteer chaplains from the community are allowed to conduct services. In some cases, inmate chaplain assistants are allowed to officiate at services if no one else is available. However, prisoners housed in secure housing units (SHU), protective custody or death row do not have the right to attend services with the general population, nor to have group services in their own unit. However, they do have a right to be visited by a chaplain.

Sometimes converts change their name to reflect their new beliefs. Some prisons permit this, while others insist the prisoner retain the name he had when he arrived at the prison. Some prisons will adjust the official records by adding A.K.A. (also known as) and the new name to the old name. Courts have ruled that a prisoner cannot be denied mail delivery or visits just because the mail is addressed to, or the visitor asks for him by, the new name.

It has generally been held that prisoners can possess religious literature and publications such as the Bible or Koran. However, the Satanic Bible may be excluded because a court ruled it might incite its readers to murder or rape.

The prison has the right to ban religious medals or rosary beads if they are thought to be a threat to security, for example if they can be turned into a weapon. Candles may be forbidden because of fire hazard. Practitioners of Santeria are not allowed to possess live chickens or knives to accommodate rituals that include the sacrifice of the fowl.

Inmates whose Sabbath is other than Sunday may be barred from attending religious services on those days if it interferes with their work schedule or the "orderly functioning" of the institution. Prisoners cannot be forced to accept medical treatment which interferes with their religion. For example, a Jehovah's Witness cannot be compelled to accept a blood transfusion. If an inmate objects to a medical test or inoculation for an infectious disease for religious reasons, he may be segregated until he consents to the procedure. This is for the protection of both inmates and staff, to prevent the spread of disease.

> A paradox definitely exists: inmates are said to have a Constitutional right to practice the religion of their choice; the institution has the right to control the nature and extent of that practice, and to prohibit anything that might even remotely infringe upon the security of the institution.

*   *   *

The most singular circumstance inmates face is they've got all this time, they want to do something with that time, and they don't know what to do with it. So they start looking at their lives, and they look for something that will help them understand or cope with what's going on.

John Auer, United Methodist pastor

CHAPLAIN

Most jails and prisons have at least one paid chaplain on staff. In addition, religious services are sometimes conducted by volunteer free world clergy. If no chaplain is available, inmate chaplain assistants may be permitted to conduct some services.

Some denominations have an Office of Detention Ministry that oversees chaplains of that particular faith.

Some staff chaplains are ordained priests, ministers and rabbis. Others are non-ordained church laymen and women who are part of an organization within the denomination, such as Catholic nuns or religious brothers. Many Catholic deacons also serve as chaplains. Deacons are ordained, but are not priests, which means they can conduct some services, such as baptisms and marriages, but cannot hear Confessions or say Mass.

Volunteer clergy or laity from the free world also serve as part-time chaplains. Eucharistic Ministers bring Communion to the inmates, and others come in to teach religious education classes or Bible studies. Inmate chaplain assistants may conduct services and Bible studies in the absence of a chaplain, but have no official standing with prison administration.

Many inmates have told us they "don't trust" the chaplain who's on the prison payroll. They say their perception of these chaplains is that they are, first of all, prison staff members, and only secondarily are they clergy. The prisoners believe the chaplain's allegiance is to the administration, not to the inmates. Chaplains we have talked to about this say that while they feel a loyalty to their employer, which is the state, and to the hierarchy of their denomination, they would never, under any circumstances, reveal anything an inmate told them in confidence.

This is a particularly hot issue with Catholics. An important part of the Catholic religion is the sacrament of Reconciliation (sometimes called Confession or Penance), which includes confession of one's sins to a priest, a promise to try to avoid these sins in the future, and the recitation of certain prayers. Sacramental Confessions may be told only to a priest, and priests are bound by a very strict rule, called the "Seal of the Confessional," never to reveal what is told to them during religious Confessions. The authors know of no documented case of a priest ever breaking this vow, while there are several cases in Catholic lore of priests who were willing to die rather than break the "seal." Still, many prisoners say they will never trust a clergy person who's on the prison payroll.

The "paranoia," if that's indeed what it is, of many prisoners was fueled by an egregious violation of the sanctity of Confession that happened in 1996 in a Lane County, Oregon, jail. An inmate who was awaiting trial asked to have a Catholic priest come in from the outside to hear his religious Confession. Entirely without the knowledge or complicity of the priest, the sheriff bugged the private room in which the priest and inmate met, and tape recorded their conversation. The prosecutor who ordered the sheriff to install the listening device has been quoted as saying "I was wrong to authorize the taping. There are some things that are legal and ethical, but are simply not right."

When this violation was made public, a judge ordered the tape to be destroyed. However, the damage was done, and for many prisoners it just served to reinforce their fears.

We spoke with a Catholic nun who has served for many years as staff chaplain in federal and state prisons, as well as one of the nation's largest county jail systems. In the Catholic church, she said, the position of prison chaplain has traditionally been reserved for priests. Since there is now a shortage of priests, with not enough of them to fill the needs of parishes nationwide, the hierarchy presently permits nuns, religious brothers and deacons to serve as prison chaplains.

Whatever his denomination, the staff chaplain's responsibilities are both religious and administrative. Religious duties include conducting services and Bible studies, performing baptisms and marriage ceremonies, and helping prisoners deal with family and personal problems.

Administratively, he supervises and schedules assistant and volunteer chaplains and inmate chaplain assistants, schedules services and use of the chapel, attends meetings and has responsibility for departmental budgeting.

*　　　　*　　　　*

All of us clergy are called directly by God
John Auer

A MAN OF GOD

Excerpts from a dialogue with Rev. JOHN AUER, a United Methodist pastor, human rights activist and death penalty opponent:

I have visited parishioners in prison, and I have a dear friend who's doing federal time.

A young man I visited not long ago, the son of a parishioner but not a church member himself, enjoyed reading his Bible. He asked me to send more spiritual and political reading matter. He had never taken time to reflect before he went to prison.

As for jailhouse conversions, I think there's a tendency to want to get on the right side of something, but I'd discount some of them. Some persons, when they go to prison, take a new direction in their life; not just a religious conversion but a change in their life.

I would tell a new prisoner to take advantage of everything available, and take advantage of whatever people are available in the prison. Don't be alone on this journey. Reach out to people.

Some people say they are Christians, but they also say they believe in "an eye for an eye." Trying to maintain a commitment to the radical character of Jesus is difficult on a lot of issues. I don't know if the death penalty, in and of itself, is any more revealing about a person's struggle or inability to be fully Christian than a lot of other issues that might have to do with war, economics, the way we treat children.

What engages me is how much time biblical people spent in prison. Jesus was executed. Paul was in and out of prison. Jesus never claimed to have committed a political act, but he was willing to be identified with people who were being executed for political activity.

My approach would be to help people demystify the whole experience of being in prison. Some people I've grown up idolizing, like Daniel Berrigan and Dorothy Day, have been in and out of prison all their lives. Prison is one more venue in which we give witness. I don't want people to be so narrowly focused on the eye for an eye.

A writer named Lakoff says there's a fundamental world view difference between conservatives and liberals. Conservatives essentially believe there has to be an authoritarian government. Whether it's in the family or in the work place, there has to be somebody at the top setting some sort of absolute rules. Liberals are a lot more interpersonal, interrelational. It's not just that people are vengeful or blood thirsty. It's their whole way of seeing the world and their relationships.

For me, theologically, the death penalty comes down to this: is anybody beyond redemption? Is anybody beyond the reach of the holy spirit? Who am I to define who is and who isn't? I got called for jury duty on a capital case. The lawyers asked me where I stood on the death penalty. I refused to say I was absolutely against it, but they dismissed me anyway.

Conservatives are Liberals who've been mugged.
Liberals are Conservatives who've been arrested.
Anonymous

*   *   *

After watching a bowl of white rice wiggle off my plate one night, I decided to limit my intake of prison food to what I got in my package or what I could easily identify as peanut butter.
Prison inmate

FOOD AND DIET

Inmates' diet is regulated by law and, in its written version, differs only slightly from one institution to another. In actuality the quality and quantity of food differs greatly. Some meets the legal requirements and some doesn't, but none exceeds what is specified by law. Inmates complain their food is tasteless, starchy and doesn't always meet minimum sanitation standards, although some laughingly refer to maggots as "extra protein." One universal complaint is the almost total absence of fresh fruits and vegetables.

Most prisoners eat in a cafeteria or mess hall. Those in special segregation units (SHU), death row or on lockdown are given trays in their cells.

Food is supposed to be served three times in 24 hours, with no more than 14 hours between the evening meal and the next day's breakfast. Depending on the institution, either one or two of those meals should be hot. Regulations don't stipulate what temperature constitutes "hot," so often "hot" means "lukewarm." The cold meal, usually lunch, generally consists of a "green" bologna or peanut butter sandwich, dispensed in a brown bag along with breakfast. Inmates are allowed 15 minutes to eat their meals in the dining hall unless a physician orders more time be allotted.

The diet is based on the routine daily allowances (RDA) of the National Academy of Sciences, and lists specified amounts from each of the four food groups - protein, milk, fruits and vegetables, and grains, for a total of 1,800 calories a day. Adjustments are made for juveniles, pregnant or lactating females, and those requiring special diets for medical reasons, such as diabetics. Allowances are also made for religious dietary requirements. Whenever pork is on the menu, an alternative source of protein and/or additional vegetables are supposed to be provided. Prisoners say this doesn't usually happen.

There's a regulation that states "food shall not be withheld nor standard menu varied as a disciplinary sanction for any inmate." Notwithstanding that rule, the same document (Title 15: California Code of Regulations) gives a recipe for a "disciplinary isolation diet," which is to be served twice in 24 hours, along with two slices of whole wheat bread and a quart of water each time.

This culinary concoction, sometimes called "disciplinary meatloaf" or "jail biscuit" consists of:

2 oz. powdered milk	3 1/2 oz. raw grated potato
3 1/2 oz. grated carrots	1 oz. tomato puree
2 oz. oil	1/4 tsp. salt
1 egg	1 oz. whole wheat flour
1 Tbsp. chopped onion	5 oz cooked red beans
1 Tbsp. chili powder	3 1/2 oz. chopped cabbage

and 5 1/2 oz. lean ground beef or turkey, shaped into a loaf and baked at 350-375 degrees for 50-70 minutes. Some inmates swear this is better than the usual mealtime offerings.

A few prisons have been experimenting with contracting out food services. Frozen meals, which inmates say are like a cross between TV dinners and airline meals, are brought in by a catering firm. They are then re-thermed, a euphemism for "heated," in microwave ovens on each unit.

Prisoners say that when the caterers are trying to sell their product to the system, they provide free sample meals for a week. The guys love them. Beef Stroganoff, burgundy beef, chicken cacciatore, and the list goes on. Once a particular company is awarded the contract, the food reverts to "cardboard and gravy, with or without maggots."

In general, prisoners who have experienced it both ways prefer food cooked on the premises by inmate kitchen staff. Old time convicts who remember "the good old days" when prisons had farms say present day rations can't compare with the fresh produce formerly grown on the grounds. Prisons that contract out food service say it's more cost effective that way. Some prisoners have wondered who, if anyone, gets a kickback from the purveyor of frozen dinners.

Canteen Corporation Of North Carolina is one supplier of such treats. Kansas prisoners say the company is "starving" them and serving "shit" for food. Prisoners held demonstrations and were placed on lockdown. The governor called for an "investigation" (of whom? the food company or the prisoners?), the prisoners remain on lockdown as of this writing, and the company still provides the "food."

If all else fails, there's always Vita-Pro. This powdered soybean meat substitute was first tried out in Texas. When prisoners there refused to eat it, some enterprising Texas prison system officials packaged it up and foisted it off on the Louisiana prison system at $4.10 a pound, only slightly higher than the price of a good filet mignon. They stopped serving the stuff in Louisiana after more than 100 inmates filed grievances complaining, among other ailments, of skin rashes and intractable diarrhea attributable to the synthetic foodstuff. Meanwhile, some Texas prison officials were charged with conflict of interest for purchasing $33 million worth of the product outright without competitive bidding.

The only food I trusted in prison was peanut butter. At least I think it was peanut butter. All the other stuff they called food tasted rancid and looked as if it had come over on the Mayflower.
Prison inmate

HAUTE CUISINE IN THE HOOSEGOW

Prison food falls far short of haute cuisine. The ubiquitous "green baloney, maggots and gravy" just doesn't do it for most folks. Prisoners whose good behavior has earned them privileges have devised some ingenious recipes to supplement or substitute for prison fare. Prisoners who are considered "dangerous" are not permitted the privilege of cooking.

"Groceries" are obtained from Commissary, or are sent in the gift boxes some prisoners receive periodically. They lean heavily to quick-cooking pasta, instant rice, powdered mashed potatoes, canned meats, summer sausage, cheese and seasonings. Cooking utensils generally consist of a large plastic bowl or two, one or more "stingers" (immersion heaters that boil water in a cup), or a "hot pot." The intended use for hot pots is to boil water for tea or coffee, but they are used just as often for heating canned chili and similar treats.

These recipes are favorites of a woman on death row, who inherited her love of pasta from her Italian mother.

Pasta recipe number one:

2 cups uncooked pasta - any kind
1 package Knorr pasta mix - any flavor - mixed with milk
1 can Spam or chicken
1 teaspoon garlic powder
2 tablespoons cheese - any kind
Jalapeno peppers to taste
Cook pasta, drain, combine with all other ingredients.

Pasta recipe number two:

2 cups uncooked pasta - any kind
1 can clams
1 tablespoon garlic salt
1 teaspoon garlic powder   1 Tablespoon soy sauce
Cook pasta, drain, combine with all other ingredients.

Pasta recipe number three:

2 packages sun dried tomatoes, flaked
4 or 5 cups water
1 package Italian tomato sauce flavoring
1 can tomato paste
1 small summer sausage chopped or torn apart
2 tablespoons sugar
1 tablespoon garlic powder
1/2 teaspoon black pepper

Cook tomatoes until skin is soft. Do not drain tomatoes; liquid is part of sauce. Add tomato paste and all other ingredients. Use with any type of pasta desired.

CLAM CHOWDER, an old bank robber's favorite:

1 envelope (4 serving size) instant mashed potatoes or garlic mashed potatoes
1 or 2 cans clams, with juice
4 to 6 cups boiling water (in plastic bowl)
Dried onion flakes, garlic powder, salt and pepper to taste
1 chicken bouillon cube (omit added salt if too salty)
Dash of Tabasco sauce (if available)
Milk and margarine saved from meal tray (if available)

Combine potatoes with boiling water and stir until well mixed. Add other ingredients, milk last. Makes about 4 cups

For this culinary delight you need access to an iron (the kind you iron clothes with.)

GRILLED CHEESE SANDWICH

2 or more slices bread   Sliced cheese
Sliced canned ham or Spam, if desired.

Save a wrapper with "foil" inside, from potato chips or Doritos. Open carefully so it doesn't tear. Assemble sandwich, carefully place inside wrapper. Wrap in two thicknesses of towel. Place on hard surface and "iron" at medium setting until done, about 5 minutes each side. If towel starts to smolder, it's too hot.

Many prisoners have sent us a variety of recipes for Pruno, the infamous institutional hooch. They all call for canned fruit or fruit juice, sugar and bread (for its yeast content), in assorted quantities. Combine ingredients, stash in a container in a warm, dark place, and wait a few days until bubbles appear in the liquid.

Jessica Mitford, an investigative reporter, was denied permission to visit an inmate because, said the warden, "the inmate might make defamatory remarks about the institution." Mitford wrote ". . . prison walls are meant to keep the . . . investigator out."

WHAT FIRST AMENDMENT?

"We don't want prisoners becoming celebrities and heroes," as well as the ubiquitous "security" excuse were reasons given by the California DoC for banning media representatives from interviewing specific prisoners. While unable to specify exactly how interviews would compromise security, DOC officials added that the ban would stop prisoners from "receiving the attention they crave" and from propagating their "sociopathic philosophies."

Not to worry, prison officials reassured us. Reporters could still make guided tours of the prisons during which they could talk with prisoners randomly selected by prison staff.

The taxpayers who are in effect the "owners" of the world's largest prison system should have the right to learn the truth about what goes on inside "their" prisons. Prisoners should have the right to go public when abuses, which are increasing exponentially, occur.

A bill to rescind the ban was passed in the California Senate by a margin of 22-8 and has gone to the Assembly for consideration. Senator Ross Johnson said "This bill is worthy of our support for one reason: a free, democratic society does not have anything to fear from a free, unfettered press."

Several respected journalists have suggested that it's a "coincidence" that the ban coincides with negative publicity about alleged barbaric abuses at Pelican Bay State Prison, and staged "cock fights" or "gladiator fights" allegedly at Corcoran State Prison for the entertainment of guards.

Interviews with prisoners have been routine in most other states and in the federal prison system, where they have caused no administrative or security problems. However, since the California ban, the Federal Bureau of Prisons and the states of Pennsylvania, Illinois, Indiana, Missouri, Rhode Island and

Virginia have imposed similar bans.

Journalists say these bans not only violate the prisoners' First Amendment right to free speech, but "interfere with [journalists] ability to make a living and [their] duty to bear witness to public life."

The Supreme Court in 1987 (Turner v. Safley) upheld the right of prison officials to limit contact between inmates and the media, but only on two conditions:
* if the ban is the result of legitimate security concerns
* and if the inmate is permitted to communicate by means of
    uncensored letters.

Of course, it's the people who run the prison who decide what's a "legitimate security concern," and what mail should be censored.

SECURITY

Security is regarded by prison and jail staff as their most important concern. Security includes preventing escape, preventing prisoners from injuring themselves or others, control of unauthorized visitors and exclusion of contraband. Some principles of security are universal, while others are somewhat arbitrary and limited to one or a few institutions.

Common security measures include walls, fences, some of which are electrified, razor wire and guard towers. "Sally ports" ("sally" comes from a French word that means "to leave") are encountered at all facilities. Upon entering or leaving prison gates, or a particular area within the prison, staff, visitors and prisoners alike step through a door or gate into a small enclosure. The gate behind is closed and locked electronically by a guard before the gate in front is opened in the same manner.

Upon entering and leaving, visitors have to show a pass and photo ID, and their hands are stamped with ink that glows under ultraviolet light. In some institutions, visitors are required to show their pass and ID when they go to and from the visitors' bathroom.

Guards, prison staff, and in some institutions, inmates, all wear photo ID badges.

When prisoners are moved from one area of the prison to another, or when they go to court, they are sometimes made to wait in holding cells or pens. These are uncomfortable small cages. For example, when a prisoner is brought to the medical clinic, he may have to wait in a holding pen until being seen by the doctor.

THE COUNT

The Count is a sacred ritual performed three or more times daily in every prison and jail, usually at about the hours when guards change shifts. At least one count will generally fall at the beginning of, or during, visiting hours. All other activities within the institution come to a halt during Count, which can take an hour or more each time.

The obvious need for the count is to make sure no one has escaped or otherwise disappeared. At count time, each prisoner must return to his cell, place of work or other designated area, to be counted. They don't just count bodies; each individual is identified by name and number. They have to be in the place they're supposed to be, and not walking from one location to another.

When the count in each area is correct, the guard phones or radios a central office. When every unit reports the count is correct, they announce "THE COUNT IS CLEAR." Sometimes a bell is rung. Until they CLEAR THE COUNT, other activities may not resume.

If the inmate is somewhere he is supposed to be, but not in the cell during count, he is "out counted". Some places "out count" to the visiting room; others don't. If visitors arrive shortly before or during Count, they will have to wait until the count is cleared before visiting.

During night count, when inmates are asleep, guards don't want to see just a bulge beneath the covers when they look inside the cells. They have to "see flesh." Most inmates get in the habit of sleeping with a hand, foot or face sticking out of the covers, so that they will not be awakened.

Some inmates complain the guards deliberately shine their flashlights directly into the sleeping inmates' eyes, waking them up unnecessarily "just to be mean."

CONTRABAND

Contraband is anything "the man" says it is, and things can be added to the list at any time. Drugs, alcohol, condoms, weapons or anything that can be turned into a weapon, or anything that can facilitate an escape, are all on the list. Even some things that seem innocent are contraband, because they can be turned into something else. Necessity being the mother of invention, inmates display amazing creativity in this regard.

It's obvious that guns, knives, mace spray and booze are prohibited. Less obvious are screwdrivers, other tools and rolled coins, which can be used for stabbing or head-bonking. Some chocolate candies with cherries inside contain alcohol, and are prohibited, as are cakes soaked in rum.

Maps and cash money can facilitate an escape, and are therefore contraband. One inmate sent away for a science fiction novel about life on an imaginary planet. The book contained a map of a fictional city. An overzealous guard cut the map out of the book; he said he had no way of knowing the place wasn't real, and anyway, a rule's a rule. The inmate appealed. It took six months, but he eventually got his map back.

Some institutions allow postage stamps to be sent in by mail, and others don't, for a variety of reasons. The most common reason is because inmates claim stamps were stolen by mail room staff, and the prison authorities don't want the hassle of responding to charges of theft. If someone sends stamps when they shouldn't, the mail room just sends them back with an explanatory note.

An inmate's sister sent him some stamps. That particular prison does not prohibit stamps being sent in. In fact, stamps are on the printed list of permitted items. Nevertheless, the stamps were returned to the sister with a letter stating she would be barred from visiting if she attempted to send in contraband (stamps) again. The inmate was written up for possession of contraband, even though the stamps never reached him, and he was threatened with loss of privileges.

Inmate and sister both appealed directly to the warden. Postage stamps were allowed, he said, but stamp *collections* were not. The mail room staff apparently didn't know the difference between a book of ordinary postage stamps and a stamp collection.

It's generally agreed that more drugs are smuggled by guards and prison staff than by visitors. Some visitors have devised clever gimmicks, though. They arrange with the prisoner to wear sports shoes identical to the visitor's. The visitor conceals drugs in a hollow spot inside the shoes. During the visit inmate and visitor switch shoes, and voila...

Sometimes visitors are allowed to bring food into minimum security prisons, but when your man's in max, what's a girl to do? Some women say visitor searches are so superficial at "their" prisons that they have smuggled in an entire Thanksgiving dinner, bundled in plastic cling wrap and tucked inside their bras. Kept it warm, too.

The mother of a death row inmate wrote to us:

Sometimes you have to wonder whether the people who make and enforce the rules are crazy or just plain mean. I work in a pharmacy. Various stock items come in boxes of all sizes, which we throw into the trash after they are emptied. The boxes naturally have the name and address of the pharmacy on them, for delivery purposes. I asked my boss if I could take an empty box, because it was exactly the right size to send my son his quarterly package. The prison is very strict that the box be exactly a certain size. I sent my son the things on the list, and the mail room officer let him have everything in the box. He also told my son he could keep the box to store his possessions in. About a month later, the guards came and tossed my son's cell, confiscated all his belongings, wrote him up for "Possession of contraband pornography, and receiving stolen goods." When he got out of the hole, after a month, my son filed a grievance and asked for a hearing. This is what they told him: the so-called "stolen goods" was the box. It had the name of the pharmacy on it, so it must have been stolen from there. And the pornography? On the box it said "Contents: Kotex female sanitary napkins." This is what the lunatics said was pornography. It would be funny if it wasn't so stupid. You can't give my son back a month of his life, though, not to mention all his stuff they threw away.

SEARCHES

"Assume the position. Bend over, lift 'em, spread 'em, squat, cough five times." With these magic words, presumably any "buried treasure" in an inmate's possession will be revealed.

Prisoners undergo a strip search before and after every visit, and at any other time they are suspected of concealing contraband. They remove all clothing, spread their arms and legs and bend over at the waist so that all possible hiding places can be inspected. In a body cavity search, all anatomical openings are searched manually by medical personnel wearing latex gloves.

Inmates are subject to searches at any time. Whenever guards feel like it, some prisoners say. Guards periodically "toss" their cells to look for contraband.

Some prisons don't allow inmates to use the toilet at all during visits. In those that do, inmates and visitors have separate bathrooms. If the inmate needs to use the facilities, he or she is escorted by a guard and observed visually at all times.

Visitors' cars can be searched when entering or exiting the prison grounds. Bags, packages, suitcases or containers of any kind can also be searched. When exiting the gate, visitors may be asked to open the car trunk to ascertain no one is hiding in it.

Visitors walk through a metal detector, unless they have a medical condition that makes this unsafe (heart pacemakers, for example). Visitors may also be asked to submit to a pat-down search, fully clothed, but may not be made to undergo a strip search or body cavity search without a court order.

A lawyer who went to Centinela Prison, Imperial, California was denied a contact visit with his client because the attorney refused to allow guards to remove and dismantle his

$21,000 artificial leg. The lawyer offered to submit to a pat-down and a thorough visual search of the leg. He even offered to undergo a strip search if necessary. Not good enough, said the guards. They wanted to take the leg completely apart. The attorney refused, so he and his client had to talk through a plexiglass barrier.

A California appeals court later ruled the guards were not within their rights. The court said the lawyer should not have been ordered to remove the prosthesis.

A former prosecutor who was jailed for some minor offense enjoyed just one visit with his family. After experiencing the strip search, he told them not to bother coming back. He said he'd rather do his time without seeing any visitors than submit to the humiliation and degradation of strip searches.

PHYSICAL RESTRAINT DEVICES

Physical restraints are commonly used to promote security. They include:
* handcuffs
* disposable plastic "Flex" cuffs
* waist chains to which handcuffs are attached
* leather waist belts to which handcuffs are attached
* leg irons, often called shackles or "ankle bracelets"
* Black Box

In many prisons, trustys and minimum security prisoners are allowed to move about to authorized destinations within the prison without physical restraints. Medium and maximum security and death row prisoners are not moved unless they are handcuffed, and in some institutions, shackled. This is the generic term for various combinations of waist and leg chains and/or cuffs. Most institutions have a policy that all prisoners traveling outside the prison, such as going to court, are cuffed and shackled, and many are forced to endure the Black Box as well.

What most prisoners say they hate worse than anything is the Black Box, which fits over handcuffs to make them "escape proof." Unfortunately the device holds wrists and arms in a rigid and unnatural position, causing numbness, swollen hands and wrists, nerve damage, scarring and intense pain. When traveling outside the prison, inmates may have their hands and arms immobilized for hours on end inside the Black Box, even when they find it necessary to scratch an itch or use the toilet.

For a prisoner who is violent or "acting out," sturdy chairs like the "Pro-Straint" are becoming popular. The unruly prisoner is strapped into a heavy oak chair which is bolted to the floor.

Stun guns and electric stun belts that emit a jolt of 50,000 volts are being used with increasing frequency. While staff regard these devices as state-of-the-art security technology, various human rights organizations regard them, as well as restraint chairs, as instruments of torture, and want to have them outlawed.

PACKAGES

Some inmates are allowed to receive a package four times a year, others less often than that, a few not at all. It depends on their security and privilege level, determined by behavior. Box size is subject to restrictions of weight and dimensions. Rules are usually inflexible: no exceptions are made, no special privileges given.

DO NOT send a package unless the inmate requests it, or unless you ask first. The first package to arrive counts as *"the package"* for that time period. If your small package arrives before the big one sent by family or other friends, the big one will be sent back.

DO NOT BE MANIPULATED INTO SENDING DRUGS, ALCOHOL OR OTHER CONTRABAND, such as cash money or maps, which could be used in an escape attempt.

There are very strict rules as to what may be sent, so ask first. Some institutions allow items to come directly from a mail order catalog, but ask about this first, so that the mail order item does not count as "the package." Books sent from a book store or publisher, or magazine subscriptions sent to the inmate from the source, generally do not count as part of the package, but ask first.

The institution will send you a list of allowable items, which differ from one prison to another. Generally, you may not send things that are available in canteen, or things that could be turned into weapons, such as glass or metal.

Things you *may* be allowed to enclose in the package:

PERSONAL GROOMING items such as shampoo, deodorant or cream rinse in transparent plastic bottles, not containing alcohol. Complexion soaps, make-up, perfume, shaving supplies may be permitted. Feminine hygiene products.

FOODS like cheese spreads, cookies, candy, beef jerky, Vienna sausages or summer sausage. All foods must be in factory sealed boxes or containers and not contain alcohol.

HOME MADE GOODIES such as cookies or candy are NOT allowed.

MEDICINES of over the counter variety like Aspirin, laxatives, sinus pills or eye drops.

CLOTHING on the approved list. They may permit bras, but without under-wires. Pants may not have pockets. There may be restrictions as to color and type of clothing. Shoes may or may not be allowed.

WRITING MATERIALS or boxes of greeting cards the inmate can send to family and friends.

BOOKS, MUSIC TAPES or CDs. Some prisons allow them, others don't. Find out first.

SMALL ELECTRICAL APPLIANCES such as hair dryers, hot pots, electric fans or heaters, radios, TVs and typewriters. Ask first.

ART AND HOBBY SUPPLIES such as paints, needlework kits, embroidery thread or model airplane kits may be included in the package to some institutions. In others, these must be purchased through the prison hobby shop.

JEWELRY and RELIGIOUS ITEMS such as medals, rosary beads, rings, watches or earrings.

          *   *   *

Some institutions have installed contraband-detecting

"scanners." Before they were even hooked up, rumor mongers spread horror stories of disfiguring burns, miscarriages, deformed babies and radiation sickness. A woman claimed an officer made crude remarks after viewing someone's tampon. Nobody said they actually witnessed or experienced these events, but each "heard it from a reliable source."

A Lieutenant in charge of the visiting room said he would not permit his pregnant staff to sit in front of the machine if he thought it would make them "glow in the dark." He told us the machine was not an x-ray, but an "ultrasound." He said you'd get more radiation from your TV or microwave.

A 1990 report from U.S. Occupation Health and Safety Administration (OSHA) says "there is no consensus on the potential hazard of exposure to [this] radiation."

Literature dated October 1997, provided by the manufacturer of the Secure 1000 Personnel Scanning System, says it is cleared by the Food and Drug Administration (FDA). It can detect narcotics as well as wooden, glass and plastic objects. A standard three second exposure can view the body's surface, but not the interior of the body. Each scan cycle produces three micro-Rems of x-ray radiation, comparable to radiation exposure all persons experience naturally in a five minute exposure to air and soil, and is said to be safe for children and pregnant women.

*   *   *

The money in the inmate welfare fund goes for important things like a pizza party for the guards, flowers for the administration parking lot and two spider plants for the warden's secretary. The inmates have been asking for basketball equipment for a year now. Admin' says they don't have the money, yet I work in the office and I see where that money goes.

Inmate in East Coast prison

INMATE WELFARE FUND (IWF)

Another way of labeling the Inmate Welfare Fund could be "The Unsolved Mystery of the Disappearing Money." In just about all prisons this "fund" conceals an acceptable and perfectly legal way of exploiting prisoners.

Upon arrival at the prison, new inmates are required to sign a form allowing all money they receive to be placed in a trust fund, and all money they spend to come out of that same fund. Refusal to sign means they cannot receive money from outside sources, and they waive the privilege of purchasing from canteen.

All interest earned on their money in the trust fund goes into the Inmate Welfare Fund (IWF). So does the surcharge, usually 10 percent, on canteen purchases. If a prisoner has more money than an allowable maximum in his trust account, the surplus also goes into the IWF, never to be seen again. The mystery is, where does it go from there?

Some goes to purchase things like TVs for common areas and athletic equipment. However, some accounting sources claim that only a small portion of the IWF money goes for these amenities, and the balance is unaccounted for.

Jessica Mitford, in her 1973 book *Kind and Usual Punishment*, says "The Inmate Welfare Fund is an accounting fiction, a convenient source of petty cash to be dipped into at will by the administration . . . it's an extortion racket, an illegal use of prisoners' money."

In Kansas, the fund is called the IBF, Inmate Benefit Fund, which suggests it was intended to benefit inmates. It is their money. Kansas inmates filed a class action suit. The court ruled the state had the right to spend the $1 million generated yearly by prisoner phone calls on various projects such as a victim notification fund. There was no requirement to spend any of the money on prisoners.

MONEY

In prison, MONEY is contraband, because it can be used to facilitate an escape and to buy drugs.

Prisoners' funds are kept in individual trust accounts. They may make withdrawals for commissary/canteen purchases.

These withdrawals are not in cash; they are deducted from the account. The prisoner may have a check mailed from his trust fund to a store to purchase an approved item, such as clothing from a catalog. Some institutions charge a fee of several dollars for these checks.

Checks or money orders may be mailed to the prison to be deposited in the trust account. It's better to send a cashier's check or postal money order; personal checks won't be credited until they clear. Some institutions refuse to accept any personal checks.

If the institution has vending machines in the visiting room, visitors may purchase snacks. The amount of money each adult visitor can bring in varies from place to place, and depends on the cost of machine items. In general it's an amount that allows a reasonable number of purchases from the machines for two people. Purchases must be made by the visitor as prisoners are not allowed to handle money.

Vending machines in different prisons may accept cash, plastic debit cards you can purchase at the front office, (similar to ATM cards), or tokens. One large prison has finally found a good use for those Susan B. Anthony "silver" dollar coins everyone hated because they look like quarters: you exchange your "green" (paper) money for them and use them in the vending machines.

PERSONAL PROPERTY

Personal property, both state issued and privately owned "stuff," including clothing, may not exceed six cubic feet. Every now and then, a property officer comes along with a six cubic foot box. Whatever doesn't fit into the box has to be sent home or thrown out.

Most inmates accumulate far more than this amount and get away with it for long periods of time. However, they are always subject to the regulation being strictly enforced at the will or whim of the administration.

In addition to the six cubic feet, some institutions may allow a TV or radio, CD player, typewriter, electric heater, electric fan or "hot pot" to boil water for coffee. These may or may not be counted as part of the six cubic feet, depending on institutional policies.

Prisoners are also allowed a box of legal documents pertaining to their case or appeal, and these are not counted as part of the allotment. Some institutions also allow a box of hobby-craft supplies that doesn't have to be included as part of the allowance.

*   *   *

We are not allowed to take home any personal property that has been left to us by former prisoners. We must designate a new owner for that property before we are released. I was given a radio and a fan from a guy I knew at mainline. When I was to be paroled, I gave both to a guy I knew and liked at camp.
                              Inmate at Baseline, CA

The first rule of brutish tyrants everywhere: create confusion and uncertainty. What is acceptable today must be forbidden tomorrow.
Benita Eisler

VISITING

Visiting between prisoners and their families and loved ones has been proven to be a stabilizing influence. Visits are critical in maintaining family unity and the prisoner's connections with the community, and help him readjust to the free world upon release.

Visits are encouraged to further institutional goals, not for some altruistic "be kind to prisoners" motive. Prisoners are kept in line by using visits as one of several forms of leverage. They are more likely to behave better when they can look forward to a contact visit, and are less likely to break rules if it means having to give up a visit. While prison administrators give lip service to this concept, it's paradoxical that little is done to make visiting pleasant, convenient, or even, in some cases possible.

California, in an effort to show state officials are "tough on crime," has seriously challenged visiting for many classifications of prisoners. Prison visits in California are no longer a statutory right (Section 2601, Section 1, Penal Code), but are now an Administrative Privilege to be meted out by the Department of Corrections at its whim.

Whether visits are a right or a privilege is often debated by prisoners' rights advocates, legal authorities and prison administrators. Some legal experts say that if a right to visit exists at all, and they're not sure it does, it extends only to non-contact visits, in which a barrier such as a plexiglass window stands between inmate and visitor, and they talk by telephone. Contact visits, they say, are definitely a privilege and not a right.

Whenever we visit someone in prison, what we find most frustrating is waiting in line for hours to get in, then having the visit cut short because there are more visitors than there are places to accommodate them. Prisoners and jailers alike say this is the result of prison overcrowding. The number of prisoners has doubled in recent years, but the visiting areas have not been enlarged accordingly. And it will only get worse.

CONTACT VISITS, where visitor and inmate may briefly hug, kiss, embrace or hold hands at the beginning and end of the visit are earned by good behavior. This privilege can be revoked at any time, and staff is not required to state a reason.

The priorities of the institution are to maintain security, safety, order and necessary institutional routines.

SECURITY of the prison includes preventing escapes and excluding contraband.

SAFETY means the safety of the guards and staff comes first. Prisoners and visitors can fend for themselves in an emergency situation. Hostages get no special consideration.

ORDER means, among other things, preventing sexual intercourse, although prisoners and their visitors have been known to display amazing ingenuity in this regard. Many babies have been conceived in prison visiting rooms. Please don't ask how. Use your imagination.

INSTITUTIONAL ROUTINE means THE COUNT (q.v.) takes precedence over all other activities, including visiting.

The comfort and convenience of visitors and inmates are not institutional priorities, and are not a right to which you are entitled.

Rules predominate. They are used to maintain control and keep the place running smoothly and efficiently. Some rules are necessary and logical; others are unnecessary and arbitrary. Nonetheless, they are THE RULES, and they SHALL be obeyed. By everyone.

A crucial fact for the prison visitor to keep in mind is: THE STAFF IS IN CHARGE. The prison belongs to the staff, and they wield absolute power. So, if you are unhappy with a rule, you may want to beg, cajole, grovel, implore or beseech. But you don't have any rights in there, so DO NOT try to achieve your goal by DEMANDING, THREATENING, ARGUING or NAME DROPPING. It won't work, and your loved one may have to pay later for your indiscretion. Retaliation is alive and well in prisons.

"I'm a taxpaying citizen, and I know my rights," shrieked a woman who wanted to visit her boyfriend. She was told by the guard she could not visit because she was wearing inappropriate attire: short shorts and a sleeveless top with plunging neckline. She was undeterred.

"I demand to see the warden right now. Don't you know who I am?" she ranted. "Well, for your information, my uncle is Judge [So-and-So], and I'll have your job. If you don't let me in, I'll sue you and I'll own this place."

The guards were not impressed. The woman was "walked out" (forcibly escorted from the premises), and barred from visiting for 90 days. If she came back before then, she was told, she would be arrested for trespassing.

If she had kept her cool and politely asked what she could do to resolve the problem, the guard would probably have told her where she could borrow slacks and an overblouse to cover or replace the offending garments. Various prisoner's rights organizations have a small office or trailer near the front entrance of many (but not all) prisons. They keep a supply of donated clothing visitors may borrow for this purpose.

VISITING APPROVAL

Before you plan to visit, you need to obtain a VISITING APPROVAL FORM from the inmate. Fill this out completely and TELL THE TRUTH. They really do check everything, so if you have ever been arrested, say so. Then mail it back to the institution. Follow all instructions on the form. It's not unusual to wait as long as 90 days before you are notified whether or not you have been granted approval. If you are not approved, the institution will inform you of the reason(s). They will also inform you of the procedure to appeal this ruling.

In some states, if you are a convicted felon, you may not enter the prison grounds without the expressed permission of the warden.

Some institutions may have a procedure to allow for special or emergency visits, such as when a visitor travels from a foreign country, or there has been a death in the family. Phone the prison and ask for the VISITING OFFICE, and they will let you know what special arrangements may be available. But don't count on any special consideration; it's rarely given.

VISITING RULES

Some institutions will include a copy of visiting rules when they send your LETTER OF APPROVAL. If they don't, then phone them before the planned visit. Find out the regulations regarding clothing you may wear, what you may bring, and the visiting days and hours. They vary from place to place, even within the same state, and sometimes even within the same institution for different classifications of prisoners. In some institutions, prisoners are limited to one or two one-hour visits a week or month. In others, they may visit all day on every visiting day.

When you visit, it's a good idea, though not required, that you carry a copy of your approval letter and the visiting rules with you. That way, if there's any confusion, you have supporting documentation.

VISITING CLOTHING

Permissible clothing varies from one institution to another. In general, women are told not to wear tops that are sleeveless or that reveal any part of the breasts. Tanktops and sheer or see-through clothing is not permitted for either sex. If shorts are worn, they should be of the Bermuda length, no more than two inches above the knee. Very short mini-skirts are not allowed.

Some places prohibit tee shirts with printed messages or logos. Others prohibit plain tee shirts without printed designs. Anything of a style or design that could possibly be mistaken for gang attire is forbidden. Women are required to wear panties and bras, and a slip if they wear a dress or skirt. Some places want visitors to wear socks or stockings, even with sandals. Shoes are required for all visitors, no thongs or shower shoes. Generally, leotards, tights, revealing, form-fitting or provocative attire are banned. Modesty is the rule.

Some prisons don't permit colors that could be confused with the inmates' or guards' uniforms, or gang colors. Forbidden colors, in some places, may include red, blue, black, tan, khaki, orange, green and camouflage. Others prohibit denim of any color.

> "Lavender taffeta should be a safe bet," commented the mother of a prisoner. "And don't wear a lot of bobby pins or hair pins. They'll set off the metal detector, and you'll have to disassemble your hair-do."

PROCESSING VISITORS

You will be asked to fill out a form with the inmate's name and number, and your name. Be sure you know the correct spelling of his name, and the inmate's number. Some Hispanic people have two surnames (Luis Garcia Lopez). Be sure which of the two names is entered in the records. Also be sure to know the middle initial, if any. Common names (John Smith) are differentiated by the middle initial.

You will go through a metal detector. Artificial body parts (knee or hip prostheses) will cause the metal detector to alarm. Some heart pacemakers can be caused to malfunction when they pass through the detector. If you have any of these devices, bring a letter from your doctor, and you will be permitted to go through a different entrance. If you use a cane or walker, phone ahead and ask if you can bring them, or if they can loan you one.

While in the visiting room, you may be instructed to sit down at all times, unless you are walking to or from the rest room or vending machine. That's so the guards can constantly watch what's going on. If several people stand up and stand still, guards will assume they are intentionally forming a visual barrier to conceal some illicit activity, such as sexual contact or the use of drugs. Keep your hands visible at all times; if hands are concealed, guards assume some monkey business is in the works.

WHAT TO BRING FOR YOURSELF

TRANSPARENT COLORLESS PLASTIC BAG, either zippered make up type, or a kitchen food storage kind that zips shut, to carry your money and ID in.

PICTURE ID (driver's license, passport, military ID)

MONEY in the amount and denominations allowed by the institution, to buy snacks, if permitted. Find out the specifics before you go. Most prisons let you bring only unrolled coins (rolls of coins can be used as a weapon), or $1 or $5 bills (larger bills could be concealed and used in an escape). Others sell you debit cards or "ducats" (prison scrip). Some use tokens or special coins, like the Susan B. Anthony "silver" dollars, for vending machines.

HANDKERCHIEF or TISSUES. Some institutions don't allow tissues because they say they could be impregnated with LSD. Others don't allow handkerchiefs for the same reason.

CAR KEY. Some institutions allow only one car key, because an entire key ring could be used as a weapon.

PRESCRIPTION MEDICATION. You may be allowed to bring in one dose of a prescription medicine if it needs to be taken during the visit. It should be in a correctly labeled pharmacy bottle, and you may also need to bring a note or prescription from the doctor.

Everything else will have to be locked in your car. Some prisons have lockers for visitors, but these are scarce. Don't bring large sums of money, expensive jewelry, cameras or anything beyond the bare minimum. Beepers and cell phones are definitely not allowed.

While cameras are not allowed, most prisons sell "photo ducats" for anywhere from $1 to $3 each. You give the ducat to the person in charge of pictures inside the visiting area, and he will take a Polaroid photo. If permitted, bring photos (not Polaroid) to share with the inmate.

An exception to the rule about not bringing a whole lot of unnecessary, extra stuff is this: it's a good idea to bring a change of clothing that's different from what you're wearing. That way, if the guards disapprove some article of your clothing, you can make a quick change.

BE EARLY OR AT LEAST ON TIME. The visiting area is usually crowded, and the processing is time-consuming, so get there early. Visitor processing may take up to three or four hours at some prisons. Before your first visit, phone the Visiting Office and ask what time they recommend you arrive. If you arrive during THE COUNT, you will not be admitted, and will have to wait until THE COUNT has been completed. This can take up to two additional hours.

It's a paradox. Most prisoners don't get any visits at all, yet the visiting area is almost always crowded. That's because more and more people are being imprisoned and the prisons are overcrowded, but they haven't increased the visiting facilities to keep up with the expanded prison population. Visiting areas are generally filled to capacity, and very noisy.

TERMINATION OF VISITS by guards can be for any reason or no reason. Visits can be cut short because of overcrowding, to allow other visitors to enter, or for other reasons such as security.

CHILDREN. Institutions have various rules regarding children. If you bring your minor child, you may be asked to provide a birth certificate. If you bring a minor child not your own, you may be required to have notarized consent from a parent or guardian. If you bring the inmate's child, there may be a special procedure to follow. Some institutions may permit small children to sit on the inmate's lap. It is generally up to the visitor to discipline children; inmates are not allowed to spank children or otherwise use physical discipline, or even to raise their voice to discipline.

WHAT TO BRING FOR BABY. It varies from place to

place, but generally you can bring in enough to care for the baby during the visit: one or two diapers, a blanket, a jar of baby food, one or two bottles, a pacifier.

WHAT ELSE TO BRING. Some minimum security institutions allow you to bring in a picnic lunch or hot dogs for grilling. Again, the rules are strict. They may prohibit glass or knives, and most will permit only foods in factory sealed packaging.

FAMILY/CONJUGAL VISITS are a privilege for the chosen few, intended to solidify family unity. Frequently they may include parents and children of the inmate. Only a legal spouse is allowed to come for family visits, not boy or girl friends. The visits are held in a trailer or small apartment on prison grounds, and may last about 48 hours. The inmate checks in periodically with staff. The prison may supply bedding, but family members have to bring all food, beverages, and paper products.

IT'S AGAINST THE LAW to assist an inmate to escape. It's also illegal to bring into the prison grounds any contraband, weapon, gun, knife, explosive, tear gas, alcohol or illicit drug; don't even have these in your car. Maps are considered contraband (they could be used in an escape) and so are condoms (illicit sex), except during family visits.

HOSTAGES. If you are taken hostage during a riot or other similar situation, you're on your own. The authorities will not recognize hostages for bargaining purposes, and will not take action for your safety, protection or release.

UNDER THE INFLUENCE. Visitors who are under the influence of alcohol or drugs will have their visit denied or terminated, and may be barred from future visits for a period of time.

WHAT TO BRING FOR THE INMATE

Some jails (city or county), but not prisons (state or Federal) may allow you to bring in small sums of money for the prisoner. Again, the rules vary. They may permit the prisoner to have the money, or it may be placed in his trust account.

You may be allowed to bring photos to share, but you have to take these home with you. Polaroids are not allowed because contraband could be hidden inside the many layers of paper and cardboard.

Some institutions may allow you to bring in one or two unopened packages of cigarettes. Even if the inmate you are visiting doesn't smoke, he may request cigarettes. In prison they are a form of currency that can be bartered for candy, snacks, reading material or personal services such as a haircut.

THE RIGHT TO REFUSE VISITS

One of the few absolute rights prisoners have is the right to refuse any visit. It doesn't matter who you are or what their reason is. They can just refuse. Some women inmates will refuse visits during their menstrual periods; it causes them embarrassment to remove their clothing and undergo a strip or body cavity search at that time.

HOSPITAL

If your loved one is in the prison hospital or infirmary you may be allowed to visit. If your loved one is at an "outside" community hospital, you will probably not be allowed to visit unless he is in critical condition. Before attempting a hospital visit, call the warden's office or the visiting office and find out what the rules are.

Excerpts from a dialogue with the mother of a lifer :

I'm terribly hurt by so-called friends or relatives who don't want to write or visit my son. Even his own brothers and sisters, except for one, don't visit. They are selfish, thinking of their own feelings. They will say "we have nothing to talk about" or "we have nothing in common" or "I feel funny talking to him" or "I don't like prisons."

Well, nobody likes prisons, least of all them who's got to live there all their natural life. But you go, not because you like it, it's not fun, but because it's the right thing to do. When you needed him, he was there for you. Now he needs you, you gotta be there for him. That's all there is to it.

Like some lady told me, when she was real sick in the hospital, her husband didn't visit her even once because he said

he didn't like the smell of hospitals. Now isn't that just too bad.
Poor fella. He should of visited her because she needed him
and it was the right thing to do, and she was there for him when
he needed her.

And it's the same with visiting the prison. I don't like
going there, but I don't care about what I like because my son
needs me. He needs contact with the world. And what do we
talk about? Anything and everything. And we laugh a lot. A
whole lot. So I would tell them that don't want to visit, try it
once anyway, you might be surprised. And it's the right thing to
do. He's your brother.

Excerpts from a dialogue with a visitor:

The doors open at 7:30 A. M. If you're lucky, you'll get
to the visiting room by 9:30, if the lines are not too long. Many
visitors don't know the regulations, especially during the first
visit. They wear the wrong clothes, the wrong colors, or women
wear wires in their bras, causing the metal detector to go off,
and they are sent back. They lose the visit because of
inappropriate clothing.

If the visitor wants to get food from the vending machine,
the inmate is not allowed to stand in line with her, so precious
visiting time is lost. You are only allowed to hold hands. If you
touch the shoulder of the inmate or put your arm up over the
back of the chair, your visit will be terminated.

There's an old guard, a vicious, sadistic man who keeps
the visiting room like a concentration camp. Women visitors
are afraid of his comments, and he treats visitors like they were
tough criminals. Women are afraid to complain about him for
fear their visits will be canceled. Life is miserable under the
supervision of this man. He is a racist and constantly picks on
people he doesn't think should be together. Children are afraid
of him.

Excerpts from a dialogue with the mother of a death
row inmate:

My son has been on death row for a year. Last week
they had the first execution since he's been there. My family
and I, and the families of a lot of the men on the row, and some
abolitionists, and a couple of nuns, we all held a vigil in front of
the prison on execution night. There were FBI men there, and
they took pictures of all of us, and wrote down our car license

numbers. Now, this was a quiet and peaceful vigil on our part. The only yelling and rock-throwing was being done by the lynch mob.

The guards in the visiting room all know our family, they recognize us. They know we have to drive 200 miles every time we visit. Well, this last visit, the week after the execution, they let us in for ten minutes and then they threw us out. They have the right to do that if you're causing a fuss, or if the visiting room is over crowded, they send people out so others can come in. But the visiting room was half empty that day. Everyone who was at the vigil was thrown out after ten minutes. People who were not at the vigil were allowed to stay. They intentionally singled us out. I was going to say something to the guard, but my son begged me not to. He said they'd only take it out on him later if I did.

Excerpts from the writings of a prisoner at an east-coast prison:

My family and I decided we needed a visit. In September, I requested, and the prison administration approved in writing, a "special visit" for October 2. I do not need to tell you how poor my family is or how hard they worked on two jobs to pay for the trip from the country where they live. It took months to save enough money. It costs thousands, even with modest accommodations.

The day before the visit I was suddenly moved to another prison. One can only assume the move was an administrative attempt to demoralize my family. All prisons in this state are governed by one man, and he approved the October 2 visit at the prison where I was. The prison where they sent me had no approval for my family to visit. By the time they go through the approval routine again, my family will have to be back home or lose their jobs.

It was no coincidence that at about the same time I was being moved, my family was boarding a plane bound for the United States. Now, I am approximately 170 miles away from where they expected to find me. It is not like the prison administrators had forgotten that they had approved the visit. They did not even have the courtesy to let the family know that I would not be present.

When you wonder why so many families forsake so many men, women and children in U. S. prisons, and why so many prisoners walk out of prison angry and full of rage, just remember what you have read here.

BAH, HUMBUG!

Holidays and birthdays are stressful in the best of times. When someone you love is in prison, these events cause even more stress than usual. You miss the presence of your loved one, and he misses the family. Each of you may have a different way of dealing with being apart. You may want to inflict artificial cheer on him, while he may not be in a festive mood. You may want to celebrate. He may want to crawl onto his bunk, pull the blanket over his head and mutter "Bah, humbug."

If that's how he feels, so be it. Respect his wishes. If he wants to receive packages, greeting cards and visits, go all out to the extent that you're able and permitted. But if he asks you not to visit or send anything, honor those requests, too. Prisoners are allowed to make very few decisions. Respect him for the adult he is and let him make those decisions he is permitted to make.

In either case, be honest and talk about how you feel. Tell each other how you spent the day. Send photos. Plan to talk on the phone on the holiday. You can share your feelings about the day without insisting he feel the same emotions you may be experiencing. You shouldn't try to dictate how someone else feels, and you have no right to dictate what they do.

Try to keep holidays up-beat and special for the children, even if the adults don't much feel like celebrating. If you're sad, let the kids know why you're sad, but don't deprive them of Santa or the Easter Bunny because of the adults' agenda.

Whether or not you are able to visit the prison on the holiday, you might want to get together with other families who have loved ones in prison. Have a pot-luck and make it a festive occasion for the youngsters. You will be with people who know how you feel and will help you cope.

At a support group meeting, the mother of a 40-year-old son who was "doing life on the installment plan" said she was going to "make him celebrate Christmas," even though he said he didn't want to. She wanted to send him cards and gifts to "make him cheer up."

"I'm his mother. Isn't it my job to make him happy?"

"He's an adult," a woman told her. "It's nobody's job to make someone else happy. It can't be done. When are you going to let him grow up and start doing what he wants? It's his life, whether you like it or not. If he wants to be unhappy, that's his problem."

"But what if he changes his mind and it's too late to send a package?"

"Well," another woman said, "wouldn't that be just too bad. He'd have to learn to live with the consequences of the choices he makes."

"Something he should have learned about 39 and a half years ago," another woman chimed in. "Maybe that'll do you both some good."

THEY SAY TALK IS CHEAP...

. . . but they lie. Talk is not cheap. Just ask anyone who receives collect phone calls from someone in prison. One mother in our support group, whose son is imprisoned in a distant state, says her phone bills run $400 a month for collect calls. This is partly her fault as she never refuses a call, even if there are several in one day. Many families say about $50 a month is a realistic figure to budget for prison collect calls.

Forty-nine states plus federal jurisdictions permit prisoners to make phone calls. The one exception is Texas, where phone calls are considered a privilege, not a right. Texas allows only one five-minute call every 90 days for "good behavior." Texas inmates nearly had prison officials convinced to permit phone calls, especially when they told them the state could pocket about $30 million a year in kickbacks from the phone company. Victims rights activists put the kibosh on the plan when they claimed prisoners would use the phones to commit new crimes. They were not swayed by the fact that inmates in other states rarely misuse phones for this purpose.

Most phone calls from prison are collect, as prisoners have

no access to cash. At least one state, Tennessee, allows prisoners to deposit funds in a telephone debit account, so they can pay for their outgoing calls if they have money on the books. A few jails allow detainees who have not yet been convicted of any crime to retain pocket change for phone calls, but this is not a common practice.

Each state contracts with the long distance carrier of its choice, and the prisoners have no option but to use the contracted company. Prison phone calls are charged at a higher rate per minute than the going price for free world collect calls, plus a surcharge of about $3 per call. Some charge even if there is no answer or the line is busy.

The calls are automatically cut off after a certain number of minutes, usually 15 or 30. Some institutions allow unlimited phone access, others limit inmates to as little as one 15-minute call a week or a month.

From some prisons, at the beginning of the collect call, a mechanical voice says "This call is from ———— at a State Prison." The prisoner fills in his name. The voice tells you to press a certain button to accept the call, and a different button to refuse it. This is not unreasonable.

But some phone companies have a mechanical voice that interrupts your call every few seconds, repeating "This call originated from a state prison," as if you didn't already know this. During those interruptions, it's impossible for caller and listener to hear each other. Questioned about this, phone company and prison executives said it's for "security." However, when pressed for details, no one was able to explain exactly how this improves security.

A few years ago, inmates at Angola, Louisiana's maximum security prison, complained of terrible phone service. Neither party could hear the other because of static and faulty equipment, and the overcharges were outrageous. An inmate delegation obtained permission from administration to boycott the phones. They convinced all the general population prisoners to join the boycott. Death row prisoners were not asked to give up their phone calls because of their unique circumstances. After a few months, during which both the state and the phone company felt the pinch in their pocketbooks, they acquiesced to the prisoners' demands: lower prices and improved sound quality.

The profit from these calls, and from various legal kickbacks, goes into the prison General Fund, not the Inmate Welfare Fund.

An article in the St. Petersburg (FL) Times suggests one way to find out if you're being ripped off. Arrange with the prisoner to phone you at a specific day and hour. Time the call, and write down when it started and ended. Have somebody else go to a pay phone as near to the prison as possible, and place a collect call to you on the same day and near the same time. Write down the times that call started and ended. When the bill arrives, compare the charges.

If you are being overbilled on prison calls, write to the state attorney general, the public utilities commission and other officials such as your representative, senator, the department of corrections and the long distance company.

* * *

I'm attracted to the danger of him, the way he manipulates me and how easily he pushes my erotic buttons. The thrill of sitting next to him, knowing who he is and what he's done, is dark and tantalizing. I take that feeling home to my safe and sane husband and use it when we make love.

Death Row Groupie

GROUPIES AND OTHER LOVERS

"Marlene," an elementary school teacher and self-proclaimed "prison groupie," developed these definitions during her more than ten year tenure as the latter. She declined to say which category she fits into. She calls this her "groupie taxonomy":

There are all kinds. Most are women. A few are men, too. There's a hierarchy. Some old men adopt a woman prisoner and become her sugar daddy. He will give her a place to stay when she gets out, money, even buy her a car. Some dykes will do the same. Money, a place to live, anything she wants. Jewelry. Oh well, it takes all kinds.

Of the women, and these are not necessarily groupies, first come those who had a relationship with the man in the free world. They are the ones who "stand by their man." If they weren't already married before, they will marry him in prison, to get conjugal visits. I can see marrying someone who'll eventually get out, but a lifer or a man on death row? Never! Not for me.

Then come the romantics who meet a man and grow to love him, and would probably have fallen for him in the free world. Sometimes even women lawyers or prison staff will do this. Some of these women care about the specific individual, not the mystique of being involved with a convict. Sometimes he's a great guy, but others are real jerks. You know what I'm sayin'? How can they know what he's really like. Some are just fascinated by his prisoner status, like it makes him glamorous or sexy.

Next come the lonely and pathetic women who can't deal with a real relationship for one reason or another, so they invent a fantasy love affair with someone who'll never get out, like a lifer or someone on the [death] row. It's all very melodramatic and they can whine about how unfair it is. That's the key word: "unfair." Everything's always "unfair." They are like free-world women who are attracted only to married men or priests, because they're unavailable. Same sickness. They place ads, and answer ads, in the agony columns that cater to prison romances. If they ever got their claws into a real live man they wouldn't know what to do with him.

There are the really dumb ones who let themselves be conned by cons. They turn all their money over to the guy, work two jobs to support his [drug] habit, smuggle in contraband, sneak sex in the visiting room, and sometimes help him escape. Then they get dumped and still can't figure out they done been had.

Stupidest of all are those who need to get a life. Call them "co-dependents" or whatever name you choose, or call it an addictive relationship, but their problem is, they need to get a life. I think they're sick. They have no life apart from the prisoner, but if they had a man in the free world, they'd be the same way about him. All they talk about is The Relationship, like it's something sacred and unique. And they talk about him like he's their god. "Oh, he's just so wonderful, he's so fine." They don't care about their kids, their jobs, nothing else. They don't want to travel or have a hobby or go to church. They just sit by the phone and are afraid to step outside in case he might call, like God forbid he might never call back. Like, if the line is busy,

"Who the hell were you talking to?" They wait for the mail every day in case there might be a letter. Let him dictate from long distance every move they make, what they wear, where they go. I tell you, they don't [go to the bathroom] unless he says to.

At the bottom of the food chain are the women who imagine they have fallen in love with a notorious serial killer or serial rapist. They admire and idolize these scum, get the guy's name tattooed on their [private parts], and would gladly kill or die for him. You know, like they'd drink the poisoned Kool-Aid for him. Yes, they really would. Really. As far as I'm concerned, these women are nuttier than the maniacs they're in love with. They're like a fan club, only worse. If these guys get out and they kill her, or force her to do a crime . . . these women deserve whatever they get. They're fruit cakes and they deserve each other. Two of a kind. I've been with cons, but never like that.

> He makes me feel things I've never felt in years. He never touches me except with words. He exposes my desires and I imagine what it would be like to make love to him. I walk into the room and he's in control. He's interested in me, what I do, how I feel, and he makes it seem as if everything I say is vitally important. How many men in the free world do that?
>
> Death Row Groupie

What prisons represent to me is the destruction of what it is to be human beings.

                              Death row inmate

HEALTH CARE

Excerpts from a dialogue with COREY WEINSTEIN M. D., who identifies himself as a prison abolitionist. He'd like all prisons to be shut down except for the minimum necessary to contain "the dangerous few," individuals who definitely need to be contained, who need to be protected from their own impulses as much as we need to be protected from them. Dr. Weinstein is part of California Prison Focus (CPF), a nonprofit organization that works with and on behalf of prisoners in California's control units. CPF is an independent citizens' group that responds to prisoners' complaints of brutality and lack of medical care. He visits prisons regularly as a medical consultant to Legal Services for Prisoners with Children to investigate conditions of medical care. He is a physician in private practice in San Francisco, CA.

The prison system is terribly malicious in petty and significant ways. Someone in prison may be targeted by the system if he has made any complaints, called the counselor, opposed the guards or has in any way made waves. This malice isn't understood by the families and often not by the prisoner. What you need to know is that it exists and your loved one will probably not tell you if he has been targeted. Prisoners want to protect their families from the horrors inside, the inner games and conflicts that happen every day. My advice, if you want to advocate for your loved one, is to be very careful and don't blame yourself if your advocacy doesn't work. Any attempt to help a prisoner must be directed to the appropriate person, accompanied by clear and specific written complaints. Send copies to the warden, your state representitive and, if need be, the media. (See Communication section).

Health care is not available to every prisoner. Hurdles to obtaining it are numerous. In California, the inmate must first contact the MTA (Medical Technical Assistant) whose skill level is that of an LVN (Licensed Vocational Nurse). MTAs are the first line of contact with the patient, which means they must perform triage functions, making a preliminary diagnosis and deciding how serious the illness may be. This is beyond their training and should be done by an R. N. or M. D. MTA's are often called on in urgent situations to make clinical decisions in terms of evaluations and treatment far beyond their ability.

MTA's get their medical training in the corrections department, not at a medical facility. They are members of the correctional officers union and they are viewed by the prisoners as guards, not as medical professionals. Their basic function, and how they perceive themselves, is custody, not health care. I've seen MTAs blame the inmates for getting sick, saying they are faking their illness to get out of work, so they deny medical care. Inmates have passed out on the floor, had heart attacks that go unrecognized for days despite complaints, and some have died. Often it's the line guard who knows that prisoner and who gets care for him, not the MTA.

California has been found to be out of compliance with the Constitution in its medical care for prisoners. We have a law suit against the state over how inadequate medical care for women prisoners is.

The second hurdle is money. There is a $5 co-payment for sick calls. The supposed reason for co-pay is so inmates won't abuse the system. Administration wants to stop inmates from trying to get pills or get off work

If a prisoner doesn't have money on the books to pay his $5 co-pay, he has to file for indigency status each time he needs to see a doctor. This takes four to six weeks to be approved. Even if the inmate is seriously ill, he still has to wait for approval before he can get medical care.

A family who is poor sends a little money to the inmate and that money is confiscated for restitution. It might be better to be totally indigent. Prisoners who have plenty of money will have care. Those in the middle are out of luck.

Most prisons do not have specialty clinics for illnesses like diabetes, hypertension, heart disease, TB, or hepatitis. Each state may have one or two facilities that specialize in serious or contagious diseases such as HIV, but those get filled fast.

Another problem is that prisons are unable to recruit and hold qualified medical personnel. They often have physicians who are relatively impaired, for example by alcoholism, who've lost their license elsewhere or are under the supervision of the court or medical board. Care for prisoners with serious, long-term and complex illnesses is entirely substandard, superficial and below what they would get in an ordinary county hospital.

To be fair, the medical staff is confronted with an onslaught of "cons" and they have to be intuitive to figure out what's going on. Staff cannot treat everyone with sympathy. They must know the tricks prisoners play, and they must know the prisoner before making that decision. Staff have to develop the skill to determine who's malingering, therefore the "malingering antenna" is always up.

It's more difficult for death row prisoners to get medical care. Physicians often look at release dates when deciding whether to give care. The feeling is, why get this guy well if he's going to die or be released soon.

As opposed to the state prison system, the San Francisco county jail system has two good things going for it: it has a committed staff who love their work and are interested in being correctional health care providers. They have an excellent quality of people from the top right on down through the nurses, social workers, and HIV team. They also have a smaller, more manageable system.

Bureaucratic administration decisions within the Department of Corrections (DOC) are difficult to litigate, and resist any advocacy attempt from outside. Declarations are good, and every family member should know the formal way of writing a legal declaration. It begins with, this is who I am, this is what my connection to the problem is and this is my testimony. Keep it short.

For instance, if you can't obtain the inmate's medical records, you can write a declaration saying, "I certify that my husband has had three heart attacks and he has not received proper medication or attention." The prisoner can attach it to his grievance. All declarations are legal documents so what you say is under penalty of perjury. Tell the truth because these documents are submitted to court as evidence.

Wives and mothers are the usual advocates. If a prisoner had a family physician on the outside, a family member could get a letter from the physician with a summary of the person's complaints. They can send this to the Chief Medical Officer of every prison the inmate goes to. This is effective because it's collegial, non-judgemental and non-adversarial. The staff physician gets the feeling there's a connection between this prisoner and some other life on the outside.

Unfortunately, most prisoners have never had a family physician. Another way to do it is to get their medical records from whomever they were treated by on the outside. The problem here is that medical personnel are sometimes reluctant to give this information out.

My advice to new prisoners is to obtain all medical records and keep them in his cell. Send copies to his family, so that if his cell gets rousted and everything he owns gets thrown away, he'll have copies somewhere.

If he has a medical problem that may need attention in the near future, he should begin the process now. Get a sick call slip, map out his schedule and keep a calendar to know how much time has passed since he sent that slip in. He has to be totally responsible for obtaining the care he needs.

If he is diabetic and he knows he needs certain tests done, try to build rapport with the medical staff, ask questions, don't make complaints about what he didn't get. Tell the doctor he's interested in taking care of himself.

I always advise people to be very respectful and not to get emotional in all conversations with prison staff and in the letters they write. Don't direct your anger at the doctor. Take it to the legislature. Choose your fights. Go after the most important issues, not the trivial ones.

Form groups, help each other, vent to each other. Families call us, vent to us over the phone. They're so angry, it's hopeless. But in their own communities, they can share their concerns in a more productive way.

PRISON HEALTH CARE?

"Prisons have become a refuge for several doctors with troubled pasts," according to the Prison Legal News: "One doctor had his medical license revoked by the state of Michigan for sexually abusing six patients. When he moved to Texas in 1990, he was placed on probation by the board of Medical Examiners, and ordered to undergo psychiatric treatment. He was also given a job as a psychiatrist for inmates at the state Pack and Ferguson prison units. Five of the other cited doctors are practicing with restrictions ordered by the Texas Board of Medical Examiners, with three others on probation. Since prisoners have no choice in who their medical provider is, an incompetent doctor could mean a death sentence," says Marta Glass, a nurse and prisoner rights advocate with Citizens United for the Rehabilitation of Errants (CURE). "I think the amount of tax money we're paying to provide for these doctors dictates that we provide good medical care. Salaries of the eight cited doctors range from $111,000 to $130,000 annually."

According to Corey Weinstein M.D.:

The criminal prosecution and detention system continues to grow at a rapid pace in the USA. More than one million women and men are locked up with increasingly longer sentences and harsher conditions. While the incarcerated population as a whole grew by 250% between 1980 and 1993, the number of drug offenders locked up increased by 900%. The racially discriminatory police investigation and arrest of petty drug users and dealers has further filled our prisons with people of color.

Poverty, psychiatric illness and mental disability are being criminalized as the homeless, disturbed and mentally challenged are swept off the streets into the prosecution and detention system. Jails are bursting at the seams as the social and treatment support of these populations decreases.

The Fire Inside, Newsletter of the CA Coalition for Women Prisoners says:

. . . medical care is practically non-existent in prison, turning a two year sentence into a death penalty, since some prisoners contract tuberculosis while in prison and die from lack of treatment for it. We call for compassionate release of terminally ill women. Right now, the only ones even considered for release are AIDS infected women who have white blood [cell] counts so low that the prison itself does not want to deal with them.

Last year, the parole board refused to release a comatose prisoner who spent the last six months of his life under armed guard at Marin General Hospital. This travesty cost state taxpayers nearly $1 million. Albert Brown, the prisoner, finally died chained to his hospital bed because of the parole board's insistence that he was still dangerous, even though he was in a vegetative state.

Over the past month, six women have died at [women's prisons in Chowchilla, CA]. The infirmary . . . is filled with seriously ill women and to make matters worse, Governor Pete Wilson has just vetoed the compassionate release bill for terminally ill prisoners.

On April 4, 1995, a class action lawsuit was filed on behalf of women in California's state prisons. This lawsuit has uncovered a startling pattern of medical neglect and abuse of women who are either pregnant, have a chronic illness like asthma or diabetes, or have a terminal illness like AIDS or cancer. The lawyers have been working overtime to bring these cases to light but women are still dying:

* a woman dies at Valley State Prison for Women from kidney failure after repeatedly seeking medical attention for several months.
* a woman who was denied compassionate release died at Central California Women's Facility because she didn't meet the criteria
* a woman who was never recommended for compassionate release, died a painful death from AIDs- related complications."

*   *   *

"Many states have either a legislated mechanism or an internal department of corrections procedure for the early release of dying prisoners. Often, the process is labeled 'medical parole,' involving the overview of the state parole board. Occasionally, the courts have the final word. Sometimes individual cases go directly to the governor for clemency action," according to Judy Greenspan, HIV/AIDS in Prison Project, Catholic Charities, Oakland, California.

Advocates and activists have to fight for each individual early release. The prison system is more than reluctant to part with even the most seriously ill or disabled prisoner. The worst is New York, which has the largest population of prisoners with full-blown AIDS. Medical parole in New York and other places is a political issue rather than a medical decision.

In California the procedure is long, cumbersome and without realistic time limits. Prisoners must first be designated terminally ill, with six months to live, by the prison doctor. The prisoner's counselor and the prison warden must concur. The application goes to CDoC Director, who must also sign. The application must then go to the parole board and/or the sentencing judge.

One man lived only two weeks after his release. A woman lived only two months. Each prisoner owed their eventual release to public pressure and high-profile media exposure.

*   *   *

"Your son can die for all I care," an enraged physician told her. The doctor was furious because the mother had publicly criticized the lack of care her son received.

Janette Sherlock, mother of former inmate Dwayne Sherlock, tells in the February 1997 issue of Prison Life magazine, how she had to fight to save her son' s life:

I knew Dwayne would die unless I got him out of there. He was covered with bed sores, his feet were so swollen they burst open and were stuck to the bed. He was forced to lie for days in dirty diapers, he was dehydrated; he had liver and kidney failure, pneumonia and a blood infection. And no one was doing anything.

Dying of AIDS, Dwayne was thrown in the hole in retaliation for his mother's efforts on his behalf. He was being fed Vita-Pro, a soybean meat substitute that caused diarrhea even in healthy prisoners. In someone afflicted with AIDS, Vita-Pro can cause death from dehydration and gastrointestinal bleeding.

When he was near death, Dwayne was brought to the prison ward of a public hospital. He received no treatment, yet his mother was forbidden to bathe, or even to touch him. She fought "the system," and eventually her efforts were rewarded. He was transferred to the civilian side of the same hospital where he was adequately cared for. She then fought for and obtained a compassionate release. He was transferred to a free world hospice, where his condition improved significantly. He eventually was well enough to leave the hospice and now lives in a halfway house. While still a sick man, he is now "living with AIDS" instead of "dying from AIDS."

AIDS is a leading cause of death among prisoners. According to the U. S. Bureau of Justice statistics, only four states - Texas, New York, Florida and California - house more than half of the nation's HIV/AIDS infected inmates.

A class action lawsuit [Shumate v. Wilson] has been filed on behalf of women prisoners in California who have been denied adequate medical care. Despite the filing, prisoners continue to describe incidents of mistreatment and neglect.

With the pace of executions quickening and the total number of executions rising, I fear it's only a matter of time before we learn we've executed the wrong man.

Alex Kozinski, a Federal Appellate Judge and a proponent of capital punishment, in *Esquire* magazine.

Prison: The ultimate oppression of humanity
Lance Lindsey, 1996

THE VALUE OF EDUCATION

Excerpts from a dialogue with Lance Lindsey, who is executive director of Death Penalty Focus of California, a statewide anti-death penalty organization. He's worked in juvenile delinquency and prevention programs, and has been a teacher in a maximum security prison and in county jails:

Illiteracy among inmates is massive. Around 80 percent are educationally disadvantaged. Their reading level is significantly below their chronological age. Learning handicaps prevent them from doing simple computations or reading simple text. Some have developmental disabilities. Others have normal or high intelligence, but their basic reading and computation skills are low. These difficulties keep them from participating in a mainstream world. They can't fill out work applications, read a bus schedule or write letters.

The percentage of incarcerated illiterates far exceeds that in the free world. The vast majority of inmates are not only educationally handicapped, but also indigent. Use of drugs, violence, an inability to succeed in school as well as an inability to exist in mainstream communities, are the primary reasons they are incarcerated.

As human animals we need to feel a sense of accomplishment in our lives. If you don't have normal avenues by way of work or socialized activities, there will be unsocialized activities like criminal behavior.

A person with absolutely nothing to lose is the most dangerous person on this planet. They have no fear of losing a family member, a support system, skills or opportunities for jobs, because they've never had those in the first place.

Having worked in both jails and prisons, I learned that the incarcerated people arrive with their whole mind-set based on a survivor mentality. From birth on, their life is a perpetual war. If we can excuse the Viet Nam vet for going crazy and shooting up the post office, we can certainly look at these individuals who have come from violent homes and neighborhoods. The crimes they've grown up with are often no different from the crimes they commit.

It's interesting why we don't want to connect these horrible deeds with the whole fabric of the prisoner's life. I've heard people call up radio stations and say they want these criminals tortured or used in medical experiments before they're executed. This says more about who we are as human beings, than who they are as inmates.

We put grieving crime victims on a jury and we know they're not going to judge the defendant fairly, yet our system is coming closer to being controlled by the anguish and grief of a family wronged. In addition, it's a requirement to be in favor of the death penalty in order to sit on a death penalty case. What we have is not justice, but a criminal justice system that generates a lynch mob mentality.

In many jail programs prisoners are taught how to read. It's voluntary. In a class I taught, for example, I had two serial killers who took this opportunity very seriously. However, we had all these children-type books to teach these guys to read with and they resented it. So I threw the books out and taught the class reading based on their street language. The guys were thrilled to see their world spelled out, which encouraged them further to learn. It gave them hope.

In both jails and prison the inmates can, of course, be very manipulative. They want to control everything. They're desperate because the system makes them desperate. We don't give them any skills that will be useful when they get out. This goal of punishment in our society seems to be to exterminate any vestige of humanity an inmate might have or, in the case of state-sanctioned killing, to exterminate them all together.

I am often asked if there are any "country club" prisons where prisoners get masters degrees at public expense. In most prisons, inmates have absolutely no opportunity to do or accomplish anything. Still, I believe the public should want inmates to get an education, even at public expense while inside, because they're going to get another kind of learning to go with it, and that's the knowledge of how to continue predatory behavior. Getting an education helps them bring something positive back into the community and it keeps them from going back to prison at taxpayers' expense. It's a no brainer. There are various studies that show the recidivism rate to be much lower for those who get an education than those who don't.

To do his or her time in a more productive way, a prisoner can take advantage of the few programs that are offered, even if they're not very good. It gets him or her out of their cell and provides an opportunity to meet others who are trying to better themselves. It puts them in a more positive environment. I'd also advise prisoners to stay aloof, not to get involved with gangs, if possible. I know it's hard because of the pressure, but you can regulate the degree of your involvement. When I worked at the state pen in Arizona, I saw young kids who had been busted for a few joints placed in with hardened criminals. These guys were scared to death and they had to figure out a way to survive or they'd die. I'd tell them about AA, religious groups, chapel, NA, and encourage them to get involved in the more productive "gangs."

I'd also say to stay in touch with the outside. The tendency is to withdraw and go into a shell, but don't. You need to stay in touch with your family and friends. Inside, the most important thing is mail call or getting packages sent in. The whole day is centered around it. Even if you think everyone hates you, it's still important to stay in touch.

There's a huge grieving component to being in prison for the person inside as well as for the family. Incarceration represents a kind of "personal death." You are now suddenly cut off from everything you've ever known. Look at the five stages of dying Elizabeth Kubler-Ross wrote about: Anger, Shock and Disbelief, Denial, Bargaining, Acceptance. Prisoners go through these steps, too.

I'd advise the family to be supportive and keep the connection open. The prisoner wants to lock everybody's heart, mind and soul away, as well as his own. That's why communication is so vitally important.

Parents and friends need to come forward and say "I'm here for you. I'm not judging you by this one act, you're more of a person than that." I'd also get the family to get more of their friends involved. Letters heal.

If the inmate doesn't want to celebrate Christmas or his or her birthday, don't force him. You can write a letter and say "I'm thinking about you."

I knew one man on death row who would say things like, "if my team wins the world series, I'll die a happy man." It's called decathecting, withdrawing. His relative wanted to know what she could do to address this. I told her that she should say, "I refuse to talk in terms of when you might be executed. I don't recognize the authority of the state to kill you, so I don't want to talk in terms of what may happen ultimately. Let's talk in terms of where you are now and how I can help you."

Dealing with someone on death row requires an open and sympathetic attitude, as well as sensitive honesty. St. Thomas More said being aware of your impending demise tends to focus the mind, or words to that effect, and that's a good thing, because we are not that far from going ourselves.

I know of a group called "Fight Crime: Invest in Kids." It's supported by Marc Klass, Polly Klass's father. They advocate putting more money into head start and after school programs that will help children and stop crime in the future.

> The criminal justice system isn't the most effective way to reduce crime. It's like fighting a deadly disease by building more cemeteries. If we put the money into schools that we now spend on the death penalty, we wouldn't need the death penalty.
> Lance Lindsey

---

                    *   *   *

Current prison policies are mean-spirited and politically motivated. There's no question that they're going to have a negative impact on long term public safety for all Americans. Prisoners are being released more bitter and enraged than ever.

Donna Hamm, Middle Ground Prison Reform.

JUDGE NOT

Judge Sol Wachtler, former Chief Judge of New York State, served 15 months in federal prison for stalking a former mistress. He knew he had a bipolar mental disorder (manic depressive), but chose to medicate himself with Halcion, a depressant, and Tenuate, an amphetamine, rather than obtain suitable prescriptions from a medical doctor.

"I did a wrong thing. I don't expect anyone to forgive me. I can't forgive myself," he said. Even though they knew he had been a judge, most prisoners treated him well.

"A lot of people, when they go to prison, their families abandon them, and when they get out they have nothing." His family supported and visited him, and he has reconciled with them.

"I was frightened. I was scared to death," Wachtler said in a television interview. "The strip search was a humiliating experience. You go through this exercise where you're bending and doing a pirouette, and doing all the gyrations in front of a group of people who are looking at every orifice, every crevice in your body.

"Look how far I've fallen. Look what's happened to me. What happened to my life?"

When he went to prison, he was found to be mentally ill. He was housed in solitary confinement in what inmates call the "loony bin." Of this experience he said "The first night was incredible because of the noises. This was not only the hole, this was the hole that was attached to the mental health unit, so there were people there suffering from certain aberrations, screaming, barking like dogs, yelling constantly . . . "It is certainly a long way from Club Fed . . . I have been in prison for only two days and I cannot endure it. If death is the only way out, I want to die. This is one of the reasons they don't provide you methods to kill yourself when you're in solitary, because you can't conceive of having to endure this any longer," he wrote in his journal.

Two months after he arrived in prison he was assaulted by another prisoner, who slammed him against a wall as they waited in line for medication. Two days later he was stabbed, he believes by the same prisoner.

"I was lying on my side, half asleep, half not, and suddenly felt two very sharp punches in my back. I saw a shadowy figure, and I shouted for the guard. The guard came in and my back was bleeding. There were two wounds, not into the chest cavity, as they were stopped by bone. It took stitches [to close] each one. At first they said I did it to myself, but after a while they came to the conclusion that it was physically impossible. I could not have done it."

He describes how prisoners make homemade liquor: "You take a bottle of water and fill it half with sugar. You steal packets of sugar out of the dining room. And you take a roll and tighten it up and roll it into a tight ball. It has enough yeast to start the fermentation process. Then you get a rubber glove from the medical room and put it on top of the bottle. The fermentation causes the glove to expand. When all five fingers are up, you know there's been enough fermentation to make wine."

About imprisonment, Wachtler says "For every 100,000 people in our population we have 500 behind bars, compared to England which has 97, Japan which has 45. We have 500 because any time someone does something which offends our sensitivity, we put them in prison. Some 70 percent of the prison population now are first time drug offenders, not kingpins, and yet we put them away for very long periods of time because of the sentencing guidelines, so that I was with drug offenders who were going to be there for 10, 20, 30 years, and it was absurd. Mandatory sentencing guidelines only invite injustice.

"Some guards are very decent. Most of them are not. Most feel their role is to punish you. They don't recognize the fact that being in prison is punishment enough. They browbeat you. We're not talking about having compassion for the inmate. He committed a crime and he's being punished for it. Don't give him any frills and don't give him any extras and don't give him any love or affection. But recognize his humanity. Treat him like a person. Recognize the fact that if you don't, when he comes out he's not going to be a person."

He concluded, "I can't remember meeting anyone in prison who would say honestly that his sentence was fair."

After the Madness: A Judge's Memoir, is a book Judge Wachtler wrote to "give some degree of humanity to people in prison."

*   *   *

The vilest deeds, like poison weeds
Bloom well in prison air;
It is only what is good in Man
That wastes and withers there;
Oscar Wilde, *The Ballad of Reading Gaol*

A MAN CONSUMED

Excerpts from a dialogue with a former professional counselor who served 20 months for drug possession:

In prison, everybody gives you advice. Senior inmates take it upon themselves to educate you: don't talk to guards, don't associate with people from other races, don't eat after people from other races, keep to yourself, don't borrow, don't get in debt using drugs, don't snitch. Associating with guards can set you up for a violent attack. You have to stand up for yourself if you are attacked. There's also a lot of advice about don't submit grievances because guards will retaliate. Cut everyone loose back home, give up your wife or girl friend, it's easier that way. Totally adapt to this universe and just cut everything else loose.

My advice is ignore a lot of the advice. Try to blend in and not be offensive to anyone so you don't become the victim of guards or inmates. Preserve your personal integrity.

It's impossible to judge who's safe to affiliate with. You can find sanctuary by affiliating with people from your home town. Territorial issues are real big, so hang out with your home boys and you'll get some protection.

I was in 20 months. It was my first arrest and first conviction. I was 40, old for a first timer, and scared shitless. For those who have never had any integrity, the habitual criminals, there's no effort at rehabilitation. There's little effort at any type of training or internalization of any standards that would be of value to society. Clerks are good to affiliate with. They tend to be more educated and less violence-prone. Go slow and do not appear to need people too much or you will project your neediness and someone will make use of you in some way.

Be cautious of the person who is overly eager to be friendly. Ask yourself what's in it for them. There are some people in there who are honest, and you check their references, you ask people about them the same as you do in the free world.

If you get into trouble, lock up in the hole. It's kind of humiliating, but it's better than getting killed, so put yourself into protective custody (PC).

When someone gives you something, ask what am I expected to give back? If you accept something it needs to be clearly understood that you'll repay it in commissary draw by such and such a date, and make damn sure that you have it to give back. Make sure the transaction is done in front of witnesses so you're not set up so you owe more than you should. People are very dishonest in there and a $2 debt can become as important as a $2,000 debt on the outside.

Use the time to find yourself, look at your life. The whole point is to come back to this life, not to remain an inmate, but to become a social being again. Don't lower yourself to the level of sexual bestiality or whatever goes on in there, or six guys beating up on one guy. Make every effort to make the time meaningful with reading and whatever else you can do.

A prison counselor said to me there's three prison types: the rule breakers, the offenders and the monsters, and it's a matter of degree. The rule breakers are the ones with things like dui's (driving under the influence) or half gram possession busts, they are real naive. Like I was so naive I was going around saying hi to people, and you're not supposed to do that. The monsters are just the monsters, the beasts who are very far gone.

A common ploy authority uses to get its way is, if you're an intelligent inmate and you write a few articulate grievances, you've got problems. Once they realize you can read and understand the rule book, you're dangerous because you can quote the law to them and your intelligence and your grasp may exceed that of many of the guards. They label you a manipulator.

Part of the philosophy of cutting the world loose is to become passive. You always hear there's nothing you can do about it, you can't change it, other people have tried. They arrest you and tear you from your life. They tear you from everything you hold dear, then expose you to the type of authority that is corrupt, that you can't respect. This promotes bitterness and alienation and animosity, and this is part of the reason prisons turn out criminals in the revolving door.

SUDDEN MURDERER

Excerpts from correspondence with a man who's serving a life sentence for what he calls "sudden murder":

I exclude from my definition of "sudden murderers" those who were dysfunctional and into a criminal life-style prior to their commission of a murder.

"Sudden murder" is committed during a quarrel or in the heat of passion. Finding one's wife in bed with someone else, a fight in a bar, an argument that gets out of hand are things that lead to the phenomenon of "sudden murder" in a person who is not a criminal, who has never committed a crime before. This description is similar to the legal definition of Voluntary Manslaughter.

Most are naive about the legal system, since they have had no prior contact with it. "Sudden murderers" are disoriented, frightened, and find themselves in a totally alien environment. They often make the mistake of being talkative, which makes them fair game for jail house snitches and informants who want to win points with the D.A.

The amazing thing is that when a convicted felon is testifying for the prosecution, his eyesight is 20-20, his memory is perfect and his word is golden truth. Anyone testifying for the defense, felon or not, is portrayed as crazy liars. People who find themselves in deep legal trouble need to know that silence is golden. Everything they say will be used against them, whether they really said it or not. They naively believe truth and justice will triumph, the guilty will be punished and the innocent will be set free.

In my case, every time I was placed in a holding cell or transported to court, the list of witnesses for the D.A. grew. I said nothing. I was smart enough not to talk about my case in any way, shape or form. Nevertheless, I was said to have "confessed" to several different snitches.

"Sudden murderers" come from every socioeconomic and ethnic background. Many have been functional members of society. Many are veterans who served in Vietnam, Korea and WW II. We are on the whole what people would call "average" or "normal." The most outstanding feature of the "sudden murderer" is his age at incarceration, usually much older than the late teens and early twenties who come into prison for the first time. All can read and write at a level far above what the Department of Corrections calls "normal."

The average citizen tossed into jail is in for a rough time. The poor guy who is middle class, without any legal connections, is preyed upon by lawyers, inmates and everyone else. Lawyers take all your money, then advise you to accept a plea bargain, which only benefits the D.A. Judges accept them because of the overcrowding of the system.

You can tell who's new, coming to prison for the first time, and who's coming back to the familiar routine. The new fish are lost, looking around, hardly able to understand what is being said. They are herded like cattle. When they are issued a mattress, you can tell the new fish because they find the filthy mattresses disgusting. The old timers don't pay attention to the filth, they take it for granted.

Prisoners become enthralled by their captivity. It becomes second nature for a man to lick the boot that stands on his neck. They call this the Stockholm Syndrome, where the hostage begins to believe his captor is "God."

Most "sudden murderers" can read and write and have a good work ethic, and are valuable for those traits. We are more similar to the staff than to our fellow inmates. By choice, some of us become career clerks in prison and are said to have "juice" with the staff.

Prisoners look for ways to buy or steal extra food. Guys who work in the kitchen see food the rest of us never do. But a clerk with "juice" can sometimes get extra food or other perks.

*   *   *

Something was dead in each of us
And what was dead was hope.
Oscar Wilde, *Ballad of Reading Gaol*

LIFE WITHOUT

Excerpts from correspondence with Lane Nelson, a native Californian who's doing life for second degree murder (which carries a mandatory sentence of life-without-parole) at the Louisiana State Prison (Angola) and is a staff writer for *The Angolite* magazine:

It's their ball, their bat and their playing field. One of the tricks of retaining your sanity in prison is, don't sweat the small stuff.

The despairing situation in my life at Angola, as well as

that of so many others, is the life sentence without parole. Every morning I wake up no closer to another chance at freedom than the day I was arrested in 1981. However, I don't let the despair dictate my peace and purpose in life. I pursue constructive things that will help me grow as a person and give my life meaning. Drugs, alcohol and irresponsibility are the main reasons I'm here. You don't embrace what has tried to kill you. You eliminate it, which I have done.

I'm thankful for the accomplishments I've made in prison, but that can never take the place of my strong desire to again be free, to have a second chance at life, and to experience that life as the person I now am; not taking for granted those small things in life that can bring so much happiness.

I stay on a positive path through strength and spiritual awareness simply because I made a choice years ago to live this way, in or out of prison.

I keep hope alive in my heart that one day I will be free, and I think most lifers do the same thing. No matter how unrealistic, how manufactured that hope may be, it is hope that gives strength to make it through each day, each year. There may come a time when I do feel it will be best that I banish all hope and resign myself to growing old and dying in prison, but I'm not at that point yet.

If a new prisoner asked my advice I'd tell him to do his own time and no one else's, mind his own business, pick wisely a few people to associate with, and to educate himself. Involve himself in inmate clubs and organizations. Just because he's in prison his life doesn't stop. Each day that passes is a day that he will not get back, so he should make each day count for something positive. If you just learn one new word a day, that's better than not learning anything. I'd also tell him it's his life and he needs to live it like he wants. I don't know if I have the right to tell him not to do drugs if that's really what he wants as a means of "escape." I'd tell him not to "cry" all the time, not tears, but complaints. Don't be a chronic complainer.

The best way to avoid violence in prison, to avoid becoming preyed upon, is to stay away from situations that cause violence such as drugs, gambling and homosexuality. In prison, homosexuality is different from on the street. In prison, sex is a master/slave-control thing. Another way to avoid violence is simply to be a man. This means to give respect where respect is due, and to mind your own business.

A newcomer should not trust other prisoners who are

too eager to be his friend, nor trust the prisoner who wants to do favors for him. There's the old prison parable about the fresh fish who comes in from his first day at work and finds a carton of smokes on his bunk. He's thrilled and puffs like a train. All the while, a seasoned con is watching for him to smoke the last of the cigarettes. When he does, the con comes up and wants his carton of smokes back, plus an extra one for interest. The newcomer doesn't have any money, so the next best thing (or the best thing for the old con) is the newcomer's ass. Time and observation are the best indicators of who to trust.

I'd say to a wife, mother or friend, just love him, encourage him, but don't partake of the pity-party he might want to throw for himself now and then. Financial support for a prisoner is good and makes his time a little easier, but not a lot. Most prisoners are in prison because they were irresponsible on the streets. They need to learn responsibility, and one way is by being forced to manage their own small incomes properly.

I don't think the issue is, how can the wife or mother make the prisoner's time more bearable. The question is, how can the prisoner decrease the wife's or mother's heartache and fear over the situation. A prisoner's time is going to be what he makes of it, regardless of the outside support or lack thereof. On the other hand, the wife/mother have to suffer, to some extent, the imprisonment of her husband/son. The prisoner can make a lighter load for his loved ones in the free world by not being demanding on them, by not "crying" to them all the time about wanting to be free, by not calling them all the time and running their phone bill sky high, by writing them regularly and sharing positive conversation.

Why, if a prisoner truly loves a woman, would he want to subject her to his imprisonment? For a woman to fall in love with an inmate, or a man to fall in love with a female inmate, part of that person's life is being imprisoned. Is it for selfish reasons that the inmate allows his lover to continue the intimate relationship? Or is it just that his need to love and be loved in that special way overwhelms all other negative factors? Probably it is a driving need propelled by loneliness.

A study conducted ten years ago by the Angolite revealed that 80 percent of the prison population at Angola did not receive regular visits. While some of that 80 percent received one or two holiday visits a year, many received none at all. Being from out of state, with my parents deceased and my only sister disowning me, I have received very few visits over the last 16 years of my incarceration. I, like many prisoners, find that the torment of loneliness is something to be grappled with on a daily basis. And the torment increases over the years. The longer a person stays in prison, the more he/she is shut out of the minds of others in the free world. If visits were regular at the beginning of the incarceration, they get less and less as the years drag on. Mail gets lighter and lighter. Loneliness gets stronger and stronger. Of all the "enemies" I must wrestle with in prison (the dim hope for a bright future, the lack of privacy, the nitpicking rules and regulations, and the ever-present reality that I took a life and ruined my own in the process), none carries the weight loneliness does.

There's a mean spirit sweeping the country that affects our nation's prisons. They have taken away cable TV and are trimming down the iron piles, and some of our clubs and groups are being eliminated. We have to pay for medical care and medication, and that's a lot of money when you make between four and 20 cents an hour. This is all because of the political tough-talk rhetoric from politicians who have never even seen the inside of a prison. Well, no, there's a deeper meaning to it. America has always been a warring nation, has always had to have an enemy to vent its hatred and anger at. Today we have no enemy, no Communists to curse, no Nazi nation to destroy, no Vietnam war to fight (for or against). So America has turned inside herself to focus its hatred and anger on prisoners.

*   *   *

Jails and prisons are designed to break human beings, to convert the population into specimens in a zoo, obedient to our keepers but dangerous to each other.
                         Angela Davis, 1974

WOMEN IN PRISON

Women are the fastest-growing category of prisoners nationwide. This is a result of a shift in criminal justice policy, not from a change in women's crimes.

The increase suggests women are treated more harshly than men and are given longer sentences for nonviolent property offenses such as shoplifting, check forgery, welfare fraud and drug violations. The percentage of women in state prisons for violent offenses has declined.

Most of those convicted of serious offenses had been involved in abusive relationships and had lashed back at the batterer. Most women convicted of murder or manslaughter killed the man who had repeatedly and violently abused them.

A drug addicted woman who killed her abusive lover in 1992 and spent four and a half years behind bars is a classic example of women who go to prison for violent crimes. The product of alcoholic parents, she lived in poverty all her life. Her father began raping her when she turned seven. He gave her alcohol and drugs so she would submit to his attacks. She grew up addicted, and turned to prostitution to support her habit. A succession of abusive men entered her life until the last one broke her nose and knocked out all her teeth. The day before she killed him, he hit her twice and shot at her but missed. The next day he began beating her again. He reached for the gun, but she got it first.

In 1996, the California Supreme Court ruled unanimously that battered women who kill their abusers can plead self defense. They overturned this woman's conviction and she is now free. Prior to the ruling, the best a woman could hope for from the battered woman defense was a manslaughter verdict instead of murder. In California, the new ruling allows for the option of acquittal. In contrast, Alabama sent Maxine Walker, a battered woman who was for years assaulted by her abusive boyfriend, to death row for his murder. Her court-appointed lawyer presented no defense and called no witnesses at her trial. If a man killed under similar circumstances, it would most likely be regarded as self-defense.

"It is impossible to think that a man who lived through what [one] woman lived through would have been seen as a criminal. A man held at knife point, beaten with fists, kicked, pistol whipped, tied up and left for hours to listen to his children in the next room being beaten, and then released to be brutally sodomized, would not have been arrested on murder charges if he finally got free long enough to shoot the perpetrator. He would more likely be given praise and viewed as a hero defending his life and the lives of his children. But, [this woman] is still serving time on second degree murder charge," Dana Ryan writes in *The Fire Inside*, a newsletter of the California Coalition for Women Prisoners.

"Why is a woman in such circumstances subjected to arrest and convicted of murder, when a man would be acting in self-defense?", Ryan asks.

"Of course, the answer is the double standard."

This double standard has permeated male-female relations since the beginning of time. Ann Jones, in her book *Women Who Kill*, points out that women receive fewer death sentences than men for comparable crimes. However, Jones asserts, women receive tougher sentences in numbers of years than men do for comparable crimes.

Because more women than men live in poverty or live with abusive mates, and because of tougher drug laws with longer mandatory sentences, and because of social circumstances that keep women from achieving financial and social equity with men, the number of women behind bars will continue to increase. Women in prison generally have a limited education, poor employment skills and histories of drug abuse. They are often single parents who have sole responsibility for their children. Prior to a mother's arrest, the family typically survives on less than $500 per month.

Seventy-five percent of women in prison are mothers, most with two or more children. On average, 165,000 children daily are affected by their mother's incarceration. In Los Angeles County about 70 women each year give birth while incarcerated. They are taken to the County Hospital where they are chained to the bed while in labor. The mother can keep her baby for 48 hours before the child is turned over to relatives, foster care or an adoption agency. Two New York institutions, Riker's Island and Bedford Hills, and one in Nebraska, allow women to keep their babies for one year. In Nebraska, the women's older children are allowed to sleep over at the prison several nights each month. In Russia, inmate mothers give birth in a maternity ward and see their children daily in a child care center until the infant is two years old. Prison officials in Russia are now considering raising this age to three years old, according to Prison Legal News.

In U.S. prisons, pregnant inmates are usually taken to community hospitals to deliver. Within two or three days, the baby is taken away and the mother is returned to prison. The bonding between mother and child is broken. Most women won't see their child again for years, if ever. The care of those infants is sometimes given to those least able to care for them properly, like elderly grandparents, or a husband who himself may have serious problems with drugs and alcohol.

Disruption of family life due to parental incarceration is an increasingly serious issue in America. Between one and two million children have at least one parent in prison at any given time.

Frieda Watson lives on a dairy farm near the Corona, California, Institute for Women. Frieda agreed to take care of babies born to mothers behind bars. She looks after them until the mother is released. She also makes daily trips to the prison, often waiting for hours before she can take the baby in to see its mother. Frieda has eight children of her own, with five still at home. She also helps her husband on the farm. Over the years, Frieda has taken care of 120 babies and most of them stay at least three to six months.

Several states have laws that can terminate parental rights of prisoners. They include Alabama, Arizona, California, Colorado, Georgia, Idaho, Kansas, Louisiana, Mississippi, Missouri, Montana, Nevada, New Hampshire, New Mexico, New York, Oklahoma, Oregon, Rhode Island, Wisconsin and Wyoming.

California is home to the world's largest women's prison, Central California Women's Facility (CCWF) at Chowchilla. About 4,000 women are housed there, including eight who are on Death Row.

There's no doubt that women prisoners are neglected and mistreated. Their medical needs are ignored. CCWF does not have a gynecologist on staff. Women prisoners report that when they have gynecological examinations, they are often observed by male guards. They are strip searched by male guards, and forced to listen to vulgar and sexist comments about their bodies.

Young, first-time, non-violent women offenders are often targeted by guards as easy prey. Women complain of sexual abuse, rape, invasion of privacy and sexual slavery by staff. Sometimes guards have permitted inmates from nearby institutions to rape women prisoners. In California, Alabama, Michigan, New York and other states, female inmates have filed suits alleging that sexual abuse is constant. Women say correctional officers often taunt them with sexual innuendoes while they are dressing, showering or being searched.

Women inmates have sued federal prison authorities in California alleging guards took money from male inmates and "sold" the women as "sex slaves." In a similar east-coast case, a woman prisoner says she was raped by guards and male inmates. When she reported the incidents, she was punished by being thrown in the hole for having "consensual sex."

Women who have had years of abuse at home find it difficult to seek relief from abuse in prison. Some claim the abuse and sexual slavery by guards gives them special considerations such as canteen privileges, extra visiting time and protection against more violent inmates. For them, the cycle of abuse never ends.

*   *   *

Even in murder, women demand more foreplay.
Ann Rule

A mother may be guilty, but a child is always innocent. Children born to inmates, however, are punished in one way or another, whether by staying with their mothers in prison, as is customary in many countries, or by being estranged from them, sent to live with relatives or foster parents, as is usually the case here.
Claudia Glenn Dowling, *Women Behind Bars*.

A freeworld person was touring a men's prison. He saw a prisoner lying on the grass eating oysters. He was appalled. He said he wished he could lie on the grass all day eating oysters. How sad a life that freeworld person must have, to envy a prisoner who was lying on unkept grass, surrounded by razor wire, eating mollusks out of a can, that cost him $2.65 from the canteen, with a plastic fork. If that's not a life to envy, I don't know what is. Whenever you envy a prisoner, go look up the word "choice" in the dictionary.

Mickey Dee

In Xanadu, Did Kubla Khan
A stately pleasure dome decree . . .
Samuel Taylor Coleridge

THE TRUTH ABOUT "COUNTRY CLUB" PRISONS

"Attica" is a word that says volumes: the name of a dilapidated prison in upstate New York where the mother of all prison riots, once described as the worst in U. S. history, erupted on September 9, 1971. Prisoners took 50 correctional officers and civilian employees as hostages.

Negotiations lasted four days. Finally, the prison was stormed by New York State Police and National Guardsmen. The rescue operation lasted only minutes. When it was over, there were 43 dead: 11 hostages and 32 inmates. About 80 inmates were injured.

Attica inmates were forced to work 12 hours a day in temperatures over 100 degrees. They were allowed one shower a week and one roll of toilet paper every five weeks. Housed in cells infested with rats and cockroaches, and fed rotten food contaminated with maggots, they also complained of overcrowding, racism on the part of the administration, and generally poor sanitation conditions. Reporters described the rioting prisoners as attempting to present their demands by the only means available to them. Violence escalated when police and national guard troops called off negotiations and rampaged. After the Attica riot was quelled, and an investigatory commission reported the prisoners demands were justified, Governor Nelson Rockefeller allocated $3 million to improve conditions. The money was spent thusly: hiring more guards and clerical help; security equipment, including metal detectors and gas masks; office equipment.

This is what the prisoners got: two showers a week, and an unlimited supply of toilet paper.

Other riots in New Mexico, Folsom Prison in California, and many other institutions invariably present the same complaints and demands: edible food and tolerable living conditions.

Pleasant Valley State Prison in Coalinga, California, open about one year, has had numerous reported incidents of shots fired at unarmed prisoners, several of whom were wounded.

Three inmates at the Washington Correction Center for Women are crammed into cells they say are "too small for two women," and the levels of stress and irritation are very high. Also, because of the overcrowding, guards are often unable to "see flesh" during nighttime counts. As a result the women are awakened several times nightly and have become sleep deprived.

Overcrowding and other conditions at the Pierce County Jail (Tacoma, WA) were the subject of a lawsuit that was settled in 1996. Improvements ordered by the court included limiting the jail population to 772, and providing beds that are safe and "suicide resistant" by not having an anchor point from which prisoners can hang themselves. In addition, no prisoner is to be bedded on a floor mattress for more than 72 hours, and not at all if a medical condition makes that unadvisable. Prisoners are to be given access to religious services, health care and outdoor exercise.

Joe Arpaio of Maricopa County (AZ) bills himself as the "meanest sheriff in America." He dresses inmates in pink underwear, and houses them in a tent city in the blistering Arizona heat. Toilet facilities are 12 "porta-potties" to accommodate 800 detainees. When inmates rioted and set fire to the tents, complaining about bad food, inadequate medical care, the unendurable heat and brutality by the guards, Arpaio said "This isn't a hotel." He added "nothing will change" including the chain gangs.

Chain gangs? Yes, chain gangs. For both men and women. In the broiling Arizona heat where summer temperatures sometimes hit 130 degrees.

The city of Ephrata (WA) has also erected a year-round tent jail to house 60 prisoners, but the conditions are more humane than at Arpaio's place. Ephrata's military surplus tents are both heated and waterproof.

The chain gang still thrives in Alabama, in spite of erroneous reports that the practice has been discontinued. Alabama prisoners report that chain gang inmates are not allowed visits, canteen privileges, medical care, television, or any type of recreational or educational programs to which all other prisoners in the state have access.

In addition, Alabama has instituted the "hitching post," where inmates are chained to a fence for hours or days at a time. While on the "hitching post" they are not given food or water, and are not permitted to use the toilet, forcing them to soil their pants when answering nature's call.

In the progressive state of Wisconsin, not only are chain gangs now permitted by gubernatorial decree, but chain gang prisoners are required to wear electrical stun belts while "workin' on the chain."

Inmates are often transported by private conveyance companies which contract with prisons. In April 1997 six prisoners, who were handcuffed and shackled, burned to death. The van in which they were riding, operated by a Memphis contractor, burst into flames on a Tennessee highway. The prisoners were locked in a wire cage in the van and could not get out. Guards said there was a fire extinguisher on board, but they were unable to reach it because of heat and flames.

Georgia prison inmates have long complained about guard brutality. Recently several guards, a counselor, a prison librarian and a lieutenant in charge of the riot squad have given sworn depositions in which they support the prisoners' claims of abuse.

A group of correctional officers at California's Corcoran

State Prison were suspended for up to 180 days for abusing prisoners. In July, 1997 the State Personnel Board revoked those suspensions and reinstated the officers. The guards, the Board said, "did not know the amount of force they used was excessive."

The abuses included "routine and systematic violent attacks on prisoners," such as "gladiator fights," in which prisoners are made to fight, sometimes to the death, for the entertainment of guards; "greet the bus," in which guards assault and beat newly arriving prisoners; and using selected inmates for "target practice."

The California Department of Corrections "is well known for its abuse of prisoners, and is notorious for its physical beatings and psychic assaults" says Corey Weinstein M.D. of California Prison Focus. In January, 1995 the CDoC was ruled "deliberately cruel and malicious" for its activities at Pelican Bay State Prison [Madrid v. Gomez].

Ongoing hostility between African-American and Hispanic inmates at California's New Folsom Prison, near Sacramento, escalated into a 31 minute race riot in October, 1996. About 50 inmates were treated for injuries, including those decontaminated for pepper gas spray. Ten inmates were hospitalized and one died. Fifteen officers were injured, four of whom required hospitalization. As many as 200 inmates may have been involved, and 56 inmate-made weapons were recovered, including "shanks" made from sharpened toothbrush handles.

Folsom prisoners were not allowed to write or phone their families for ten days to let them know if they were alive. Several women who called the prison to ask if there was a list of injured men say they were laughed at by guards.

All of the foregoing abuses are fact, not fiction. They all happened, and are still happening, in our prisons and jails today. All of the cases are well documented by reliable authorities.

> I always say to the people who claim they didn't know what they did was against the law, "Ignorance is no excuse." Therefore, when an officer of the law claims he didn't know the force was excessive, he is still responsible for his actions and he should receive the penalty gracefully.
>
> JPD, Los Angeles cop

Prisons are institutions that should mete out punishment. But wouldn't it benefit all of us if prisoners were taught a trade so they could earn an honest living when released? Extremely harsh treatment doesn't make people behave better. It makes them meaner.

Ann Landers

THEN WHY DO THE MYTHS OF COUNTRY CLUB PRISONS PERSIST?

In the opinion of the authors, the media and the "get tough on crime" politicians are responsible. The politicians take advantage of the public's fear of crime in order to win votes. The media publishes politicians anti-criminal rhetoric and the "country club" fables prominently, and without substantiation, as though they were solid facts, while giving minimal space and prominence to documented stories of abuses such as those described here.

Mobsters in a New York federal prison had the run of the place, according to a New York Times report. Eleven correctional officers were arrested after they were caught taking bribes of from $100 to $1,000 for allowing the organized crime members to order out for Italian food, view secret documents and conduct secret meetings. If convicted on bribery charges the officers each could face 15 years in prison and a $250,000 fine.

It's the general nature of people to try and get away with whatever they can. If some prisoners get away with inappropriate activities, they are certainly responsible for their own behavior. But equally responsible are guards and prison administrators who don't run a tight ship. This doesn't mean brutalizing inmates, but it does mean making and enforcing strict but reasonable rules of conduct.

In Fresno in 1996, several radio stations broadcast diatribes on talk shows by persons who claimed to be correctional officers at nearby prisons, of which there are an overabundance in the area. They told bizarre tales of prisoners phoning out for pizza, and having wild and crazy pizza parties at which "dancing girls" performed. By the time the story made the rounds, "dancing girls" were upgraded to "prostitutes." While it's undoubtedly true that there are some prostitutes in prison, they were definitely not brought there to entertain the other inmates. All these amenities were supposedly paid for by the prisons, out of taxpayers' money. These stories were repeated many times on various programs. When the author (MT) phoned the radio station to explain the facts of the situation, she was called a liar, plain and simple, and cut off the air.

What the author said was also plain and simple: let's imagine for a moment, for the sake of discussion, that the tales of pizza parties and dancing girls are true. If the people in charge of the prisons didn't want to authorize these activities, all they would have to do would be to say "No" and lock everyone down. That's all it would take!

Here are some facts which illustrate the absurdity of these claims.
* prisoners can only make collect phone calls, and no pizza parlor we've ever heard of accepts collect calls
* prisoners don't have access to cash or credit cards with which to pay for the pizza
* prisons are out in the boondocks. What pizza parlor would deliver 15 or 20 miles outside of town?
* if, by some miracle, a prisoner actually managed to order a pizza, why didn't the guard at the main gate simply turn the delivery person away?

Here's what actually happened that gave rise to the legendary "pizza parties" story: on special occasions once or twice a year, coinciding with a special holiday or high school (GED) graduation, prisoners are allowed to order pizza, hamburgers or chicken from outside establishments. This is an undisputed fact.

A guard starts the ball rolling by taking orders, usually about three months in advance of the event. The guard who does this does so voluntarily, to raise money for charity. The prisoners don't compel the guard to do this against his wishes.

Prisoners, with jailhouse irony, call these occasions "catered banquets." The profits from the sale are donated to some charity in the name of the correctional officers union. Only prisoners who have earned the privilege by good behavior, and who have money in the bank, are allowed to participate.

The officer who takes the orders receives payment from the inmates in the form of vouchers which allows money to be withdrawn from their trust accounts, as prisoners are not allowed to possess cash money. The officer negotiates a price with the restaurant, which may be discounted below retail. The prisoners pay a surcharge, usually ten percent, and the difference is donated to charity. Traditionally, the guards' treat is paid for by the prisoners. No public funds are involved. And there are no dancing girls, (or boys, for that matter.)

At the height of the nonsense about "pizza parties at the country club," a local newspaper published an article by a local resident who had never seen the inside of a prison and had no qualifications that would make her an authority on the subject. Without checking the accuracy of the allegations, the newspaper nevertheless printed the following fallacies as facts:

*   each new prisoner, upon entering prison, is given a complete set of law books (most lawyers can't afford these, and have to use a law library; most prison law libraries have books that are damaged and out of date)
*   specific days each week are designated for pizza, fried chicken and other delights, and each prisoner places his order from a menu (not true)
*   each inmate is given free college education (not true, but some prisons do have classes to teach illiterates how to read and write)
*   each inmate who enters prison is given his own computer (she neglected to mention if they get to keep it and take it home when released)
*   each inmate is given a color TV; if there are two inmates in a cell, there are two TV sets (not true; some prisoners are allowed to purchase radios and TVs through the prison at greatly inflated prices out of their own funds)
*   all of the foregoing luxuries and amenities are paid for by the taxpayers (absolutely false)

* inmates are allowed to practice their religion (true, under certain conditions and restrictions, a First Amendment guarantee.)
* inmates are paid holiday pay and other bonuses for their work, and are entitled to workers' compensation (not true; they average four cents per hour in pay and get no benefits whatsoever)
* if an inmate goes to an outside hospital he is given the luxury of a private room (true, but this is for security reasons)
* because prisons are so luxurious, people are committing crimes in order to be admitted to them, and as a result prison populations are expected to double in the next decade (it's true that prison populations may double in the next decade, but this is because of increasing population and laws like "three strikes").

The author (MT) sent the newspaper editor a long rebuttal to the absurd claims made by this woman, which after two years still remains unanswered and unpublished.

The following was published on the Internet by "Dan", who claims to be a correctional officer:

Inmates have it way too easy in prison. If it were up to me they would be locked down for 24 hours a day. They would be allowed showers and recreation on a merit basis. Maybe then the dumbasses would keep their stupid ass out of trouble and make themselves useful to society. When they get it so easy in prison, why would they want to leave? All they do is get out and take care of some business and then get caught doing something so that they can go back to three hots and a cot. The only way to stop this trend is to make prison hell. They wouldn't be able to riot because they would be locked up.

This is the kind of ridiculous simplethink that has gotten the country into the mess it's in. The causes of crime are many and varied: poverty, drugs, greed, passion, illiteracy, culture, revenge, to name only a few. If the only cause of crime was that prisons were so luxurious that people commit crimes to get into them, then the cure would be as simplistic as the alleged cause: do away with all prisons. If there were no prisons, people would not commit crimes in order to gain entrance into them.

Gee, why didn't we think of that?

        *   *   *

The degree of civilization in a society can be judged by examining its prisons.
Fyodor Dostoevsky

Excerpts from a dialogue with a man who's been doing life on the installment plan off and on for about 30 years:

I've been in a few joints, more than a few. Sure, they're country clubs, all right. Cells are six by eight feet, with a triple decker bunk, a toilet and a small sink that only spouts cold water. Three guy packed like sardines into a cell, only enough floor space for one to stand up at a time. If one guy wants to take a piss, the other two gotta ride their racks. No wonder people get violent. About every coupla weeks the man gives you clean towels that they wash in the laundry. You have to wash your personal laundry, socks and underwear, in that little sink, with no place to hang them dry. I've been in dorms with 60 men jammed into a room no bigger that 30 feet by 28, bunks stacked three high, and only two pissers for 60 men. No privacy, no place to store your things. Some guys will store their belongings on the bunk and sleep on the floor underneath it. In a cell or dorm, each man has about 14 or 15 square feet of floor space and most of that's taken up by the bunk. If these places are so luxurious and they say people commit crimes just so they can go to prison and enjoy all the comforts of home, if that's true, then how do you explain people who escape? If people want to get inside because it's so great, then the ones who try to escape must of gone postal (crazy).

*   *   *

The cost of liberty is less than the cost of repression.
W.E.B. DuBois

WHAT PRICE FREEDOM?

Michael Tonry, Professor of law, University of Minnesota says:

The money spent building and running prisons to house non-violent offenders offers a new twist to the aphorism "spend it now or spend it later."

We are spending unnecessary billions now, to no lasting effect, and will have to spend massive amounts later to address not only the social and economic causes of crime, but to correct the damage caused by unnecessary incarceration, with its side effects of blighted lives, broken families and disrupted careers.

*   *   *

Taxpayers have been sentenced to pay for a brand-new, empty prison in Taft, a small agricultural town in California's San Joaquin Valley. Because of political fighting between the government and private industry, the prison has been held hostage, keeping the entire $75 million state-of-the-art, low-to medium-security complex deserted. Costs of construction, maintenance and security soak the taxpayers to the tune of $105,000 per month, since the facility was completed in 1996.

*   *   *

From Laugh Lines: "The Iowa State Penitentiary has decided to charge each inmate $5 a month for a 7-by-8-foot cell with a bunk, small toilet, table and stool. The good news for the prisoners is that if they don't pay the rent, they get evicted."

*   *   *

OVERCROWDING AND RELEASE

Because of overcrowding, many prisons and jails release prisoners early, before their sentences are completed. There has been much public outrage at the early release of violent, predatory criminals in this program, especially when inmates serving mandatory minimum sentences for minor nonviolent property and drug crimes cannot legally be released. This practice has been the subject of lawsuits in Florida.

A federal civil rights lawsuit has been filed against the sheriff of Los Angeles County, alleging defendants are not released promptly when criminal charges are dismissed.

*   *   *

Prisons are a recession-proof industry. Prisons will always be a business.
Reed Smith, Wackenhut Warden

PRIVATE PRISONS

Wackenhut, a private security company, is just one of several in the business of private, for-profit, prisons. The other industry leader is Corrections Corporation of America.

Texas Governor George W. Bush says such prisons are

not suitable for housing violent prisoners. He cited a series of escapes from a San Antonio facility. Private prisons are generally limited to housing Level I and Level II inmates, Bush said.

Warden Cloyd Schuler of a Wackenhut prison said escapes and riots will occur at both government and privately run prisons. The only difference between the two, Schuler asserted, is that private prisons "manage their money better."

Private prisons housed 77,584 felons in 1996. In 1997, the number was up to 111,588. A University of Florida study predicts that number will rise to 276,455 by 2001.

A videotape has surfaced of a private prison in Texas showing guards kicking inmates in the groin, sicking dogs on them and shocking them with stun guns. The FBI has started an investigation into possible civil rights violations.

Amazingly, this tape was shot by a Brazoria County [Texas] sheriff's deputy for training purposes. The tape showed a dog attacking at least two inmates, one of whom screamed in pain as he was bitten on the leg. It also showed a stun gun being used on at least one inmate, deputies in riot gear dragging an inmate with a broken ankle by his arms, and at least one prisoner kicked in the crotch while crawling. The taping of the alleged assaults happened after a jailer said he smelled marijuana in a prisoner housing area.

Charles Wagner, chief deputy at the jail, said "I grant you that the film depicts a lot of unprofessional actions, [but] there's not any real brutality."

Missouri, which contracted with Texas to house 415 inmates at the Brazoria County Detention Center in Angleton, has terminated the contract.

MARIONIZATION

The Federal penitentiary at Marion, Illinois is said to be the most secure in the country, if not the world. It is the prototype for Pelican Bay (California) and other super-max facilities, which are supposedly reserved for the most violent felons who are believed to be a danger to the community and at risk for escape attempts.

Inmates are kept in secure housing units (SHU) for 23 hours a day. Meals are delivered to their individual cells, so they have virtually no human contact and suffer ongoing sensory deprivation. They are let out of their cells, chained, for a half hour once or twice a week to shower.

Many prisons using this model have no windows, so inmates may go for years without seeing natural daylight, the earth or sky, or even enjoying a breath of fresh air. The creation of prisons of this type is called "Marionization."

REHABILITATION

A group of New Jersey senior citizens has developed a volunteer prisoner rehabilitation project which has been in operation for over two years. Members of the American Association of Retired Persons (AARP) chapter teach weekly classes in music, sewing, job application and interviewing skills at the Middlesex County Adult Correction Center in North Brunswick, New Jersey. About 85 percent of the inmates are eligible for the program, based on their behavior.

Warden Rudolph Johnson, who has worked at the prison for 28 years, says attending the classes gives inmates a "sense of hope, and may help them to stay straight once they are released."

Across the river in New York, a state official espouses the opposite viewpoint. "Prison is for punishment," says Chris Chichester, the Empire State's budget chief. "New York is not in the business of rewarding those who commit crimes with a subsidized education." As a result of this attitude, a successful rehabilitative program is being phased out.

At New York's Sing Sing prison, a group of convicts was studying for a Master's degree in theology in a tuition-free program offered by the New York Theological Seminary. Graduates of the program have only a five percent recidivism rate compared with 42 percent in New York and 35 percent nationwide. Upon release, graduates agree to return to their home communities to work with at-risk populations.

But the program, though successful, is being dumped because prisoners can no longer obtain the prerequisite Bachelor's degree. "It's a bone-headed idea," says the Rev. George Webber, program director.

New "get tough on crime" policies have made prisoners ineligible for tuition grants for college courses. Many inmates have a desire to do the right thing and improve themselves so they can enter mainstream society when released from prison. Policies like this only serve to release felons who are angry and frustrated. They have not learned usable job skills in prison, so they are no more capable of earning an honest living than they were when they were first sent to prison. This punitive and non-progressive attitude is retributive, not rehabilitative, and serves no useful purpose.

*   *   *

> Prisoners must totally adapt to this universe. They are reborn in here, in a negative sense.
> Death row inmate

INSTITUTIONALIZATION

"It's easy to make a free man a slave. It's darn near impossible to make a slave a free man." We don't remember who said it, but it's been proven to be true. Put a person into an environment where, for years on end, he is forced to be passive, and passivity becomes imprinted upon the spirit. Tell him he may never open a door, under pain of punishment, but wait for it to be opened for him. Tell him he may not make any decision, no matter how small, but must eat, sleep, dress and use the toilet only when, where and how instructed to do so.

A friend, who was once a successful professional woman, is hoping for release soon, after 15 years. She said "You'll have to re-socialize me. I need lessons on crossing the streets, handling money, grocery shopping. I'm scared to go out there. Sometimes I'd almost rather stay in here."

When people like these commit another crime, and a few

do, in order to violate their parole and go back to prison, the "Tough on Crime Club" says it's because prisons are "country clubs" and need to be made even more horrific so nobody will want to return. They've got it all wrong. Those who want to go back to prison don't feel that way because prison is so luxurious. They need to go back because it feels safe, it's familiar; the place into which they have been thrust is worse, and they don't know how to function in the free world.

A very graphic portrayal of this is seen in the movie "The Shawshank Redemption." An old convict who is entirely institutionalized is released. He has no place to go, nothing to do and nobody to do it with, and he ends up committing suicide.

While it's financially disastrous to keep these old men and women in prison forever, it's morally catastrophic to just turn them loose and wave good-bye to them at the prison gates. If we're going to imprison people until they are no longer capable of functioning as adults, then we owe it to them and to society to provide for their basic needs, perhaps in government-run nursing homes similar to those operated by the Veterans' Administration.

Some jurisdictions have recognized the need. Alabama opened a 250-bed geriatric prison on 1991. Pennsylvania has opened a prison hospital that will house about 1,300 inmates, 375 of whom will be geriatric. Louisiana is in the process of developing a geriatric inmate facility.

What do you suppose happens when you take someone who:
* had a problem with immaturity, irresponsibility or indecisiveness in the first place
* which contributed to why he landed in prison in the second place
* then you take away any remaining vestiges of decision making power and responsibility, making him totally passive and submissive for many years, until he's incapable of taking even a drink of water without permission
* then one magic day you shove him out through the gates with nothing but the clothes on his back?

*   *   *

Prison menopause is what happens to longtime lifers who have been stripped of hope. Lifers initially have to come to terms with the probability that they may suffer the ultimate rejection, death in prison. What keeps them going through the wasted days and lonely nights is hope of redemption through eventual release. As the years pass and their youth slips away, irreplaceable loved ones die, the system ignores their sporadic pleas for release and they enter middle age. At some point between the twentieth and thirtieth years of their continuous confinement, lifers lose momentum. The wall is too strong. Their spirit dies and they become the living dead.

Douglas Dennis, *The Wall is Strong: The Living Dead.*

AGING PRISONERS

Forget the morality or necessity of keeping an 80-year-old in prison until he dies. Those issues aside, the cost is astronomical. It costs about $20,000 a year to imprison someone under the age of 40. Between 40 and 54, the cost rises to $22,000 yearly. For inmates 55 and older the cost skyrockets to a whopping $69,000 per annum.

The cost hike is almost entirely attributable to increased medical costs. Old people need eyeglasses, hearing aids, dentures, kidney dialysis, medications and surgery. As they become enfeebled, they need around-the-clock nursing care and aid in the normal activities of daily living, like eating, bathing and toileting, requiring the assistance of health care aides.

Prisoners don't age well. They start to have problems in their 40's and 50's that people in the free world don't start getting until they're 60 or 70. This is because many have not had regular health care, compounded by abuse of alcohol and drugs, and the added scourges of AIDS and TB.

In 1995, there were about 55,000 prisoners nationwide over the age of 50. Their number is estimated to exceed 125,000 by the year 2,000, but that estimate is low, as it was determined before the three-strikes legislation went into effect.

It's well established by criminologists that most crimes of violence and most property crimes are committed by people under age 25. By the time most offenders reach the age of 40 they are either dead or have mellowed out. Most but not all.

There will always be a certain number, estimated by some experts at about ten percent of the so-called "criminal" population, who will always need to be kept locked up until they die, for the protection of society. These include sexual predators, psychopaths and those whose violence is uncontrollable.

It's a paradox lacking in common sense that young criminals, the most likely to recidivate (they have a 70 percent re-arrest rate) are released early because of prison overcrowding. Yet prisoners over 60 who have terminal illnesses and are no threat to anyone, are routinely denied compassionate early release.

The problem today is that with three-strikes and other habitual offender laws, people are being sentenced to life, effectively to die in prison, for relatively minor non-violent crimes like drug possession, writing bad checks and theft.

It was sheer folly to have five thousand men caged inside dormitories and cells all day with nothing to do but get into trouble. Donald A. Cabana, *Death at Midnight: the Confession of an Executioner*

Inmates have nothing but time on their hands. With political posturing on both sides of the congressional [aisle] screaming for a decrease in funding for education, work and recreational outlets, inmates will devise their own entertainment.
Tony Lesce, *The Big House: How American Prisons Work.*

TREATMENT OF PRISONERS

Politicians equate "getting tough on crime" with "getting tough on prisoners." The "no frills" policies they promote reduce or eliminate educational and rehabilitation programs for prisoners. Politicians claim that such programs are "coddling" prisoners, and are turning prisons into "resorts."

Violence and recidivism are significantly reduced when inmates are treated with fairness and respect, and are provided with basic education and usable skills. Various studies over long periods of time have shown that education at the basic level, and especially at the college level, reduces the rates of criminal behavior and recidivism substantially. In spite of these facts, Pell grants (government tuition grants to prisoners) have been entirely eliminated, and educational programs in prisons have been drastically reduced.

Legislators claimed giving Pell grants to prisoners was "unfair" to citizens. They overlooked the fact that no Pell grant was ever denied to a free world citizen in favor of a prisoner, because the grants were awarded on a merit basis. Less than one percent of all Pell grants went to prisoners during the 1993-94 award year. Since the elimination of Pell grants for inmates, prison college programs have virtually disappeared. Prison violence has increased in direct correlation to cuts in educational and vocational programs.

California courts have ruled that prisoners do not deserve the minimum wage. AB 344, passed by the California Assembly, guts basic education and vocational training classes, while it requires convicts to work 40 hours a week. Out of that pay would come room and board for their upkeep in prison, restitution and family support. The bill does not explain how inmates would accomplish this on prison wages of 40 cents to 90 cents a day. (Yes, a day, not an hour.)

In their frenzy to show how tough on crime they are, politicians try to outdo each other with meanness. They complain that prisons are "country clubs where inmates lounge around watching cable TV at taxpayer expense," and urge the introduction of chain gangs and "hard labor, breaking rocks into gravel."

Prisons should be "a tour through the circles of hell," Massachusetts Governor William F. Weld has been quoted as saying, "where inmates should learn only the joys of busting rocks."

Prison officials meanwhile say prisoners work at prison maintenance, laundry and kitchen chores, but there are not enough meaningful jobs to employ all prisoners. Wardens know the realities of prison life. They realize meaningful work, not breaking rocks, is the way to go, yet the politicians continue to make their unsupported claims. And, the DOC adds, there is no cable TV in California prisons. And the prisoners who have TVs purchase them from their own funds. They are not a gift from the taxpayers.

Dennis Luther, retired warden of McKean Federal Correctional Institution in Bradford, Pennsylvania, has demonstrated that the opposite approach can be the most cost effective and successful. McKean, described as one of the most highly successful medium-security prisons in the U.S., is noted for smooth operations and low rates of recidivism. The cost of running McKean was approximately two-thirds less per prisoner than any other U. S. prison during Luther's tenure. Also during his term there were no escapes, no homicides and just nine assaults in six years. Most prisons have that many assaults in a *day*.

"If you want people to behave responsibly, and treat you with respect, then you have to treat them that way," says Warden Luther, whose policy of unconditional respect for inmates was visible on plaques throughout the prison.

A few of Luther's aphorisms include:

* Inmates are sent to prison as punishment and not for punishment.
* Correctional workers have a responsibility to ensure that inmates are returned to the community no more angry or hostile then when they were committed.
* Inmates are entitled to a safe and humane environment while in prison.
* You must believe in man's capacity to change his behavior.
* Normalize the environment to the extent possible by providing programs, amenities and services. The denial of such must be related to maintaining order and security rather then punishment.
* Most inmates will respond favorably to a clean and esthetically pleasing physical environment and will not vandalize or destroy it.

"Providing long term goals," Luther says, "helps [prisoners] to stay sane and makes them less prone to violence. It also makes the entire prison easier and less expensive to manage." A prisoner serving a life term at a New Jersey institution put it this way: "You create Spartan conditions, you're gonna get gladiators."

*   *   *

> No prison administrator faces a greater adversary than inmates who have nothing to do.
>   Donald Cabana

When a work program was introduced at a prison he administered, Cabana said, "The majority of prisoners just wanted to do their time and get back home as quickly as possible, and a lot of them actually preferred working to sitting around and doing nothing. One old con who proclaimed the virtues of the work program put it succinctly: 'By the time these boys work all day in the fields, they're too tired to fight and fuck at night. It's got so a fella can actually get some sleep up in them camps now'."

           *   *   *

California Assemblyman Robert Prenter Jr., a member of the "tough on crime" faction, urges that prisoners be put to work breaking rocks into gravel. He says hard labor in prisons would deter prisoners from reoffending.

"They should certainly do something in their cells besides watching cable television at taxpayer expense, working out on weights or playing basketball, and having a life of leisure with three square meals a day," Prenter said, adding that "Inmates should be required to perform 40 hours a week of strenuous manual labor."

Prenter was unaware that cable TV is not available for California inmates, and in states where cable TV is available, it was pointed out that the prisoners pay for it, according to a Corcoran State Prison spokesperson.

At Corcoran, more than half of the nearly 5,000 inmates already work at janitorial, kitchen, groundskeeping, prison dairy industry or cleanup jobs. Those who do not work are in administrative segregation and maximum security, because they are considered too dangerous to be allowed to work. The only others who do not work are new arrivals awaiting job assignments.

The subject of work in prison is controversial. Prisoners too violent to work are locked down. Others work running and maintaining the prison, but there are not enough of those jobs to go around. Some prison industries, like making license plates for the state, don't teach the inmate a usable skill that will enable them to work after release.

Some states welcome private industries to use prison facilities at no cost, and to hire prisoners at low wages, without benefits. Some prisoners claim they are very happy with this arrangement. They have no living expenses, so they can earn enough money to help support their families and still have enough left over for Canteen.

Some prison rights activists believe this is a form of "slave labor." They allege that the industries have laid off free world employees in order to hire prisoners, and when the prisoners doing the work are released, there won't be jobs for them to go to in the free world.

Only two states, Tennessee and Texas, allow death row inmates to work.

*   *   *

Inmates working in the California Joint Venture Program receive minimum wage, $4.25 per hour, minus the 80 percent that is garnished for various prison expenses, such as restitution, room and board, and the inmate welfare fund, which does absolutely nothing for inmates. "It is cheap labor, not social responsibility that fuels the rise of for-profit prison labor. They get cheap labor, undercutting the competition which has to pay full costs to their employees. Unfair advantage, it further undercuts an already deteriorating wage market," says Christian Parenti, *Making Prisons Pay*.

*   *   *

An inmate at California Conservation Corps:
Without an education or work experience, the ability of a former inmate to assimilate into the community is greatly jeopardized. In California, all correctional camps are run by the Department of Forestry. Only level one inmates with three years or less, and those who aren't an escape risk, can go. Those eligible can be at camp for three years. Classes in fire training and conservation, lasting for a week, are held at the main prison. You learn the 10 basic fire conditions, fire safety standards, weather conditions and how to protect yourself. You also must go through physical training and be physically fit. We have one week of actual fire training. We learn how to use the tools of the trade, deploy fire shelter and control burns. After that, we are sent to camp.

If you come in with special skills such as mechanic or maintenance you are accepted into that line at camp. When you arrive, you do odd jobs until you are assigned into a crew. Work crews go out into the community to clean up schools, cut trails, cut fire wood, shore up damaged roads. Fire crews fight fires.

California Department of Forestry personnel do not like California Department of Corrections personnel. For some reason they don't get along well.

Some inmates don't make it at camp. They want to lie around all day. They don't want to work. Some deal in contraband. Most camps don't have the time to deal with drug or alcohol abuse problems. Those with a history of substance abuse aren't accepted. Camps are a privilege, not a right. Most of us stay out of trouble by doing our job. We know the other option is going back to a cell.

Inside, when there is not much to do, you might try to find yourself, look at your life and see why you ended up in prison.
Death row inmate
*   *   *

TORTURE

An electric "stun belt," in use since 1994, delivers a 50,000 volt, three to four milliamp electric shock to the wearer's left kidney. It causes excruciatingly painful muscle contractions which result in severe cramping, collapse of the entire body and total loss of bowel and bladder control. Victims are knocked unconscious to the floor, where they shake uncontrollably and remain totally incapacitated for about 15 minutes. The devices are known to cause irregular heart beats, epileptic seizures and cardiac arrest in susceptible individuals.

Powered by a nine-volt battery and activated by a remote control in the hands of guards, from up to 300 feet away, the device produces "continuous stun power" for eight seconds. The blast is advertised as "devastating."

No, it isn't an imaginary contraption used in a horror movie. It's real. It's manufactured by StunTech Inc. of Cleveland, is available for $600, and is in use in our burgeoning prison industry.

Colorado, Wisconsin, 16 other states and Federal jurisdictions use the belts to control violent or dangerous prisoners when they are being transported, or during court appearances. The Wisconsin legislature has approved the device for use on prison work crews, and plans to use it on chain gangs in the near future.

The belts have been accidentally activated, shocking prisoners who had done nothing to prompt its use. In one case, a prisoner was shocked and incapacitated while talking to his lawyer during a break in court proceedings.

Correctional officers learning to use the gizmo are required as part of their training to use it on each other. A Texas officer who endured two "stun gun" shocks died of a heart attack shortly after the second shock. The manufacturer adamantly denies the belt could cause fatalities, and denies there could be any connection between the use of the device and the officer's death.

> Any act by which severe pain or suffering, whether physical or mental, is intentionally inflicted on a person for such purposes as obtaining information or a confession, punishing him for an act he has committed or is suspected of having committed, intimidating or coercing him when such pain or suffering is inflicted by or at the instigation of or with the consent of or acquiescence of a public official, is the definition of Torture.
> The United Nations Convention Against Torture

William Schulz, U. S. director of Amnesty International, accused 27 American companies of exporting torture equipment, including shock batons, stun guns, stun belts, electronic riot shields and thumb cuffs, to countries known for their abuses of human rights. Schulz denounced the U. S. Commerce Department for permitting such sales.

American legislators loudly and publicly criticize governments that use instruments of torture sold to them by U. S. manufacturers. The ultimate hypocrisy: they remain silent about the use of these same devices on American prisoners in American prisons at American taxpayers' expense.

Amnesty International is conducting a petition

campaign urging President Clinton to ban the export of electric shock equipment to other countries, and to suspend the use of such devices in this country until their safety is proved by medical testing. Amnesty does not believe that companies that make shock batons, stun belts and similar products have performed proper testing. Amnesty believes the use of such devices is a form of torture, is cruel and degrading punishment, and can cause permanent physical and mental damage.

A visiting British human rights activist was invited to speak to an American senior citizens' church group about stun belts and other forms of torture. He was booed by the audience, who told him that "criminals deserve to suffer" for their crimes.

Later that evening the Britisher said: "You Yanks are a strange lot. You insist upon your personal rights and freedoms, and complain against human rights violations in other countries. Yet many of you think it's jolly good fun to torture and inflict pain on your fellow Yanks. You are like naughty school boys who enjoy torturing insects by pulling off their wings, only instead of insects, you get your pleasure by torturing prisoners."

EXPERIMENTS

At various times throughout our history, prisoners in many state and federal institutions have been used as guinea pigs in medical experiments. Some have been infected with diseases, others have been used to try out new and unproven drugs. The practice is believed by some to continue today, but, if so, is a closely guarded secret. Prisoners selected for these studies are volunteers who are lured into participating by promises of a small stipend, about $1 a day, early release or special privileges including conjugal visits or furloughs. They are required to sign a waiver by which they give up the right to sue or receive compensation for injuries, damages or death resulting from the experiments.

The World Medical Association proposed in 1961 that prisoners should not be used for medical experiments because they were captives and therefore lacking in control over their circumstances. American physicians vetoed the measure. One researcher was quoted as saying that using prisoners was "cheaper than [using] chimpanzees."

Ironically, 15 German doctors were convicted in 1947 at the Nuremberg war crimes trials for using concentration camp inmates for human experimentation. Seven of the doctors were subsequently hanged, the others imprisoned. In their defense, the German physicians pointed out that American doctors were conducting experiments on prisoners with impunity.

FRIVOLOUS LAWSUITS

Corrections officials say they are "swamped" with grievances, most of them frivolous, like the complaint by a prisoner that the peanut butter he received from canteen was the wrong kind, chunky instead of smooth. As a result, corrections officials have increased, from six months to one year, the amount of time they allow themselves in which to respond to inmate complaints.

Prisoners and prisoner rights advocates say officials greatly exaggerate the number and frivolousness of complaints.

Most, they say, are of a serious nature, such as inadequate medical care or sexual abuse by guards. It isn't realistic, advocates say, to expect a prisoner to wait a year for resolution of a grievance regarding a medical issue.

Chief Judge Jon O. Newman, Second Circuit Court of Appeals, wrote an article in "The Corrections Professional" condemning the effort by the National Association of Attorneys General to enact legislation eliminating a prisoner's access to the courts.

Judge Newman wrote "The facts of the 'peanut butter' lawsuit are: The inmate ordered two jars of peanut butter from the canteen. When both jars arrived, one was the wrong kind. A correctional officer offered to exchange the jar and assured the inmate that the correct kind of peanut butter would be sent to him the next day. That night, the inmate was transferred to another facility, but his trust fund account was still charged $2.50 for that second jar of peanut butter, which he never received. The inmate sued the state, not because it gave him the wrong peanut butter, but because, at the rate of pay he made, four cents an hour, it would take nearly 62 hours of work to pay for another jar of peanut butter."

Paul Wright, an inmate in Washington State, writes for *Prison Legal News* that there are hundreds of meritorious lawsuits filed by prisoners.

"A federal court in California condemned a massive pattern of brutality at Pelican Bay State Prison which included shooting of unarmed prisoners, one prisoner being boiled alive, placing naked prisoners in wire mesh cages outdoors in freezing weather, nonexistent medical and mental health care, hog-tying prisoners in their cells for hours on end and more. The court held that the pervasive pattern of brutality was known and condoned by high ranking California DOC officials." [Madrid v. Gomez, 899 F. Supp. 1146 (ND CA 1995].

This suit was hardly frivolous.

Five Sacramento CA County sheriff deputies conducted mock executions of inmates at the downtown jail. Selected inmates were seated and strapped in to the "pro-straint" chair which is designed to immobilize unruly inmates who may be a danger to themselves or others.

Once secured, the officers informed the inmates they were going to be electrocuted. Inmate Carmelo Marrero died from the abuse he received in the chair, which prompted a federal civil rights investigation. A Sacramento County Supervisor said "All I know is that to the extent that this occurred, the deputies were supposedly joking. It was just a prank."

Tell that to the the day care provider, arrested for drunken driving, who was confined in the chair for five hours. She reported that while restrained, and with a towel over her head, deputies pulled her hair and ripped her blouse. She said, "I was a piece of meat in the middle of everybody else's joke. They were [using us] for their experiments."

Aimee Fisher, so-called "Long Island Lolita," is serving

a sentence in up-state New York for attempted murder of the wife
of paramour Joey Buttafuoco. Aimee and her mother have filed
a Federal Civil Rights lawsuit against the New York State
Department of Corrections, alleging her civil rights were violated
when male guards allegedly raped her six times and allegedly
urinated in her food.

               *   *   *

> The prison-industrial complex, the second largest industry in the
> United States after the military-industrial complex, poses one of the
> greatest threats to our freedom as a people that we have ever faced.
> We are becoming a nation of prison guards.
> Marguerite Hiken, formerly of National Lawyer's Guild
> Prison Law Project

JAILHOUSE LAWYERS

Jailhouse lawyers are loosely defined as those inmates
who do their own legal work, or who help others, according to
Rose Braz, spokeswoman for the National Lawyers Guild Prison
Law Project. There are many ways an inmate can become a
jailhouse lawyer: correspondence courses, self study, or working
in the prison law library, to name a few. Some have received
certificates from educational programs, but most have not.

A great amount of their legal work involves challenging
their convictions and the conditions of their confinement.
Prisoners are not permitted to "run a business," Braz says, but in
some institutions are permitted to charge small sums for their
services on behalf of other prisoners.

"Get tough on crime" policies make it difficult for inmates
to help others with their legal work in some prisons, Braz says.
Prisons design internal rules that make it a violation of institutional
policy for an inmate to have in his possession legal documents
belonging to another inmate.

The Prison Law Project publishes a Legal Journal "on no
regular schedule," Braz says, in which prisoners' most frequently

asked legal questions are answered. The Project receives large volumes of mail and cannot answer all letters individually. If an inmate writes with a specific question, the Project will mail him a copy of an article on the subject.

"Prisons have become a gulag," Marguerite Hiken, formerly of the Prison Law Project says. "Jailhouse lawyers are one of the last hopes for prisoners on the inside. One of the greatest fears we have right now is that the doors of justice are being closed to all prisoners, with no remedies available to them, because of new laws such as the Anti-Terrorism Act of April 26, 1996," Hiken concluded.

The National Lawyer's Guild Prison Law Project is located at 558 Capp Street, San Francisco CA 94110. They do not publish their phone number because they are unable to accept collect phone calls from prisoners.

*   *   *

The truth of the matter is that the sexual violence, the turning out of youngsters and the enslavement and abuse of weaker prisoners is primarily the product of criminally-corrupt heterosexual males, the "studs."
Wilbert Rideau, Prison: *The Sexual Jungle*.

STOP PRISONER RAPE

New inmates worry about rape and violence in prison. Parents and loved ones often say their number one fear is rape. Old timers, those who have been in the system for years, say the act of rape isn't as common on the inside as we on the outside believe. Most say rape occurs more often in jails than in prisons.

An older convict who feels responsible for the younger, less experienced, men in his yard said:

I've been on the inside, off and on, for twenty years. Now I'm on death row. In that time, I've only seen four sexual assaults. Two went willingly, one was brutal and the last one killed his attacker. I don't mean to sound like it isn't a big thing, because it can be. What we older cons do is organize protection for the younger, more vulnerable inmates. If one comes to my yard, I make sure he's not hassled. The other cons do the same.

We don't want kids in our care messed up.

Stop Prisoner Rape (SPR) is a non-profit organization dedicated to combating the rape of prisoners. They offer assistance to survivors of jailhouse rape. The former president, Stephen Donaldson, a survivor of jail gang-rape, spent five years in federal prison for protesting the war in Indochina. He recently died from HIV contracted from that assault, so his sentence, in essence, was death.

SPR takes the position that rape is mentacide, the killing of the mind and spirit. They conduct education about protective custody, legal rights and remedies, AIDS and rape trauma guidelines. Part of their informational package includes an article from the *Journal of Sex Research on Sexual Coercion Reported by Men and Women in Prison*. They also carry a cassette called *Becoming a Survivor*.

If your loved one is the victim of assault, discuss the problem. Assault is not the same as submitting. Parents and loved ones can offer support and can contact SPR and other victim assistance programs on behalf of the inmate.

Parents and loved ones of prison inmates may contact SPR at 333 North Ave 61 #4 Los Angeles, CA 90042. The web address is www.spr.org. Pamphlet costs are nominal or free.

     *   *   *

A former correctional officer says on the Internet:

Sex is very available in prison. Rape is, perhaps more so than in the free world, an act of dominance and violence. Prisoners segregate along racial lines. Rape happens . . . but is not the crisis some claim.

     *   *   *

The transgendered (sex-change) population is at great risk in prison. I worked with a female to male transgendered person who had completed all of the hormone therapy, plus I had him in 3 years of sexological therapy when he was arrested. He didn't have a penis yet, but for all purposes he was male. They placed him in jail with men who took advantage of him, then put him into a woman's prison where he didn't belong either. His life was pure hell. He's never gotten over it and he's been out for years.

Jackie Davison Ph.D., Sexologist

PROTECTIVE CUSTODY

Violence in prison is always just one heart beat away. The possibility of violence is greater between two individuals, as a rule, than among groups where it might lead to a riot.

The duty of prison officials to protect prisoners from harm extends to not allowing known enemies on the yard at the same time.

Prisoners who believe they are in danger may ask to be placed in protective custody in a Protective Housing Unit (PHU). Some institutions will try to avert this potential problem by moving the inmate to another facility.

Protective custody or PC units are called a "prison within a prison." Prisoners are confined to these sanctuaries by prison administrators or at the prisoner's own request when there is reason to believe the individual would be safer in this environment. According to The Angolite (July/August 1989) housed there are those described in prison jargon as "snitches [informers], queers, punks, rats, faggots and gal-boys", child molesters, as well as former cops and prosecutors.

*   *   *

SEX OFFENDERS AND THEIR FAMILIES

Donald Moser Ph.D., author of *Macho Men, Machismo, and Sexuality*, writes:

Traditional culture defines masculinity into a gender hierarchy of superior male, inferior female social categories. Men who display strong masculine aggressive tendencies in erotic and sexual behavior with their partners, often are viewed as heroic and lustful. This belief is common throughout the world. It has been documented by historians as a universal maneuver of war, where the conquerors use domination and rape over the captives (usually women).

*   *   *

Society values aggressive men and passive women. Role reversals often end up in social suicide with men being labeled "pansies" and women "ball breakers." Movies which include hair-raising episodes of violence and television with its sexually saturated soaps, all pander to this maleness stereotype. So, when a man sexually violates a woman against her will or dominates a child, he is following his forefathers in an age-old tradition. That it's wrong doesn't occur to him until the law shows up on his doorstep.

*   *   *

An open letter from an adult sex offender to young people with a history of offending:
. . . I was 16, very confused, and about to start my addictive behavior which included molesting kids from as young as one and one-half years to around ten. I didn't understand that I was doing this destructive behavior because I was afraid of adults and didn't know how to become one. I looked at myself as a monster that no one who really knew me would want to know, so it seemed easier to "hide out" and get my unconditional loving from other children. That was the emphasis, not the sex, but being loved and belonging to someone specially.

*   *   *

President Clinton signed the sexual predator "Megan's" law in 1997, ordering sexually violent offenders to register their address, place of employment and other demographic information with local law enforcement. According to proponents of this law, sexual abusers will be easily identifiable and law enforcement will be able to nab any perpetrator who is out on the prowl. Critics, such as the ACLU, say this law violates the offender's right to privacy and punishes him after he has served his sentence. Researchers say sex offenders are the most difficult to treat, yet a few men have been treated successfully and now live among us as non-offenders.

One California town has taken the aggressive approach. They "sweep" the streets at night with city police, county sheriffs and state and county parole agents, checking to see if sex offenders are living where they say they are. According to the newspaper, this cadre of lawmen muscles its way into homes and disrupts the lives of many non-sex-offender parolees trying to keep clean. Admittedly, they do occasionally find drugs, guns and other contraband. In some cases, they also find that the registered offender has disappeared.

Should we go overboard with the militant posse approach, or should we sit back and wait for the next child to be victimized? Do the rights of one outweigh the safety of many? That's the question that is difficult to answer.

California Governor Pete Wilson signed a bill making California the first state in the nation to require repeat molesters of children under age 13 to undergo chemical castration. Offenders will receive injections of the testosterone-inhibiting hormone Depo-Provera (medroxprogesterone acetate) one week prior to parole and weekly thereafter during parole, up to a maximum of three years. When the drug is discontinued, the sex drive reportedly returns.

Proponents of the procedure say such treatments have significantly reduced child molestation by ex-convicts in Denmark. Critics say the treatment could be effective for offenders who have abnormal sex cravings, but would not affect those motivated by anger or hostility. The California Psychiatric Association says the primary problem of most such offenders is not an overactive sex drive but their appetite for violence.

California law requires that DNA specimens be taken from all newly incarcerated sex offenders and other violent felons. A previous law required DNA sampling before an inmate was released from prison. This policy effectively eliminated those sentenced to life or death who might be responsible for unsolved crimes. The intent of the new law is to help solve existing and future crimes.

*   *   *

The mother of a sex offender wrote this letter:
My son tried to be honest when he got out of prison. He had a great deal of treatment in there and he was determined not to re-offend. But when he applied for jobs and checked the box that he had been in prison he was out of there in a second. No one wanted to hire an ex-con, especially a sex offender. The only jobs he could get were taking the census and delivering papers. Both put him right into homes where young children were. He had to quit both jobs. He also had no housing available

to him except a Christian halfway house that booted him out
when he was job hunting and could not get back there three
times a day for prayers. And they wouldn't let him use the
telephone to receive calls. It was a catch-22. He had several
close calls in those years before he moved to where his family
could at least give him a bed. The system seems set up to let
ex-offenders trip and fall back into those old patterns. I call this
"social recidivism." We blame it all on the repeat offender, but
how badly do we really want to prevent more abuse?

> Denial is typical in sex offenders. Family members should not turn
> their back on the inmate who is a sex offender, but I would like to see
> them be firm and not let the inmate get the family caught up in doing
> the inmate's time. I believe everyone should be accountable for their
> own actions, but you see families saving their children all the time.
> Jackie Davison Ph.D., Sexologist.

*   *   *

> Each narrow cell in which we dwell
> Is a foul and dark latrine.
> And the fetid breath of living Death
> Chokes up each grated screen.
> The brackish water that we drink
> Creeps with a loathsome slime,
> And the bitter bread they weigh in scales
> Is full of chalk and lime.
> And never a human voice comes near
> To speak a gentle word;
> And the eye that watches through the door
> Is pitiless and hard;
> And by all forgot, we rot and rot,
> With soul and body marred.
> Oscar Wilde, *Ballad of Reading Gaol*

IF THE SHU FITS

Welcome to Hell.

Hell isn't fire and brimstone. Hell is cold and damp and
mildew. The chilly wetness makes your bones ache. The smell
of mold and seawater permeates your lungs. When you're in
Hell, you never can get warm enough, your clothes never feel

quite dry. The fog rolls in, and you can't see beyond your nose. You hear waves sloshing noisily against the pier. You want to step onto the ferry boat that will carry you to the mainland, but you can't see the gangway. You're afraid if you miss your footing you'll wind up in the freezing water of the Bay. The fog lifts, and you're taunted by the lights of one of the most beautiful cities in the world, so close it seems you could reach out and touch them, yet so far away.

If you're ever in San Francisco, don't leave without visiting America's own Devil's Island. The Rock. Go to Fisherman's Wharf and catch the launch that'll take you there for a guided tour. It's well worth the few dollars. Movies don't do it justice. You'll have to see it for yourself. Tiny, windowless cells, four by eight feet. Solitary confinement cells, dungeons with no light, stinking of rot and mold. A cavernous open shower room that reminds you of pictures you've seen of Auschwitz. You'll shudder. But you're not fated to remain there forever. You'll get to go home on the next boat.

Be sure and dress warmly.

"Alcatraz" is synonymous with "hell" in the world of prisons. Immortalized in books and films, it's a rotting monument to the absurd and outdated penological theory that abuse is the magic potion that turns bad people into good people. Early in the 20th century Alcatraz was a military prison. From 1933 to 1963, it was a Federal maximum security prison for the so-called "worst of the worst" lawbreakers.

The island has no natural water supply. It was closed down in 1963 when it became too expensive to import thousands of gallons of water each day from the mainland in barges. In 1973 the U. S. Park Service reopened it as a museum.

Mother of all prisons, Alcatraz sits on a tiny island in San Francisco bay. Alcatraz, in Spanish, means "pelican," the big sea bird "whose beak can hold more than his belly can." Is it only a coincidence, or did the humorless bureaucrats display a sense of subtle jocularity when they named California's newer, more modern version of Hell "Pelican Bay?"

Opened in 1989, Pelican Bay, in the northernmost corner of California, is home to the infamous Security Housing Unit (SHU). It houses over 1,000 male prisoners who are said to be the "worst troublemakers" and gang members in California. The men are kept in windowless cells for 23 hours a day, and never see the sun. According to California Prison Focus, an advocacy group, "there is no education, no job training, no work, no religious services, no hobby materials. No communal activities of any kind are allowed. All meals are eaten "in-cell." If a prisoner has money, he can purchase a radio or TV through a CDoC approved vendor at an inflated price. Those who can't afford these distractions can go slowly insane while counting the cracks in the ceiling.

In fact, many SHU inmates are not the incorrigibles the DoC claims they are. Many are mentally ill and are there because they were acting out. They would be in mental hospitals if such institutions still existed. Others are there for filing meritorious lawsuits or grievances against the system.

Even though Alcatraz had a rule against talking, the inmates had jobs and had contact with other human beings. Not so in the SHU. While the SHU in a modern prison is clean and supposedly free of vermin, some might prefer Alcatraz where it was dirty and cold, but inmates were not subject to total isolation.

Prison Life Magazine has received complaints from inmates who say cells at Pelican Bay are kept at a constant temperature of 90 to 95 degrees, so that prisoners will not have the energy to cause trouble. (The authors have not independently verified these reports.)

Two other California prisons also have SHU units: Corcoran State Prison for men and Valley State Prison (VSP) for women. It has been alleged that guards at Corcoran set up "gladiator fights' between prisoners from rival gangs, and that guards call beating prisoners "baton practice."

Women at VSP say male guards observe them while they are using the toilet and undergoing gynecological examinations. Some guards harass the women by making sexual comments.

The women are afraid to strike back physically or verbally

for fear of repercussions; they could be subject to prosecution in an outside court, even be tagged with another "strike," for defending themselves against a predatory guard.

The federal prison system is often ridiculed for what detractors call "luxury prisons" or "Club Fed," but you don't hear them complain about the federal "supermax" joints at Marion, Illinois and Florence, Arizona. There, in addition to the other luxuries, comforts and amenities they enjoy, inmates get to languish in cells that are completely soundproof, designed, no doubt, to drive them loco even quicker than the ordinary SHU.

Louisiana's Angola Penitentiary, made famous in the book and film *Dead Man Walking*, boasts a Controlled Cell Restriction (CCR) unit where cells are six by nine feet. Several CCR inmates have been kept in total isolation in that unit for upwards of 20 years. Like inmates in all the SHU units, they can't mingle with each other or with the prison's general population, and they don't have jobs, classes or religious services. According to The Angolite magazine (January/February 1995) "They leave the tier only after being secured with enough shackles and chains to sink a ship."

Corey Weinstein M. D., a San Francisco physician and prisoner rights advocate (See chapter on Medical Care) says:

Sooner or later, all will experience the "SHU Syndrome," a very predictable set of symptoms of mental and emotional breakdown that begin to occur in anyone who's held in long term solitary confinement with isolation, sensory deprivation and the absence of human contact. Whether or not they're with one other person in the cell, whether or not they have a TV, turns out to be fairly irrelevant, although for those who are housed in single cells without a TV or radio this happens much more quickly.

They begin to have a kind of mental breakdown that involves dissociation from reality and a sense of paranoia and distrust, worry about ordinary details that other people don't worry about. They begin to go buggy, they see little black spots on the wall, they see movements out of the corner of their eyes, their mind begins to create images of motion for them. Ordinary little stimuli like the clanging of the doors closing and opening, the turning off or on of the air conditioners, little clicks on the speaker intercom system, become of immense importance and difficult to endure. In their minds, those sounds seem like screeching. They can go on to hallucinations and delusions, outbursts of anger and violence. One of the most common delusions is that the guards are out to attack them, that the staff is out to get them. The guards pick up on this, some of it is fairly obvious, some is observable, and they will taunt the guys. I know prisoners who were just endlessly taunted by guards. One fellow had 10 years of "good [behavior] time" in the SHU, and only one rules violation against him, and they won't let him out. They know he's spoken about his food and he's convinced that they tamper with his food. So now the guards will give him his lunch sandwich when they bring his breakfast, and they'll actually wet the sandwich in some way and wet the cookie, and they'll giggle when they leave his cell and mutter under their breath "another semen sandwich" or "another semen cookie." That's the level at which the guards begin to stir all of this up within the prisoners. The guards have the same mentality as a school yard bully."

*   *   *

A Vietnam veteran compared his time in the SHU with his time as a prisoner of war (POW). In the Viet Cong prison camp where he was held for six months, the filth and isolation were unbearable. When he returned home from that war, he heard words like "atrocities" and "war crimes" directed at the POW camps.

Then he committed an armed robbery, and "went off the deep end" while in prison, so he wound up spending the last four years of his sentence in the SHU, heavily dosed with psychotropic medications. The isolation, he said, drove him "even crazier than [he] already was." When the day came for his release, without any transition or preparation, guards from the SHU drove him, shackled, to the bus depot in town. There they unchained him, dropped him off, handed him a bus ticket to the city where he was convicted, and drove off.

"I had no money, no medicine, jack shit is what I had. I got off the bus, walked into the first bar I came to, had a beer, pretended I had a gun, and tried to rob the place." Now he's in jail awaiting trial. "Another statistic is what I am," he said. "Another f—ing statistic."

For he to whom a watcher's doom
Is given as his task,
Must set a lock upon his lips
And make his face a mask,
Or else he might be moved and
try To comfort or console.
Oscar Wilde, *Ballad of Reading Gaol*

KEEPERS OF THE CAGED

Excerpts from a dialogue with Ben Aronoff, a former correctional officer at San Quentin State Prison in California:

I went to the academy for seven weeks. I had virtually no weapons training. I was handed a gun and told to shoot.

In training there's little sleep, strenuous calisthenics at 5 A.M. for an hour, running two and a half miles, close-order drill, and classes where, if you fell asleep, you were required to do 30 push ups as punishment and didn't get to go home on the weekend. If your tie clasp wasn't shiny or your shoes weren't spit shined you were disciplined. Back at the prison you see riots and people getting shot and stabbed. What flashed through my mind was, I'm glad my tie clasp is shiny and my shoes are spit-shined.

So most guards cop an attitude. Some of them are very bright, others not so bright. The ones not so bright quickly develop this power thing because they've found power for the first time in their lives.

Prison is a microcosm, a concentrated example of everybody in the world. If you lie to a prisoner, you're labeled a liar and 7,000 prisoners know it. If you transfer to another prison, this label follows you.

I became a guard for the money. Power trips and dedication went away quickly, the money lived on. There is an 80 percent staff turnover at San Quentin. Very few guards make the decision to get out, the system makes that decision for them.

In the beginning you're told to "treat the prisoner with dignity." This is part of the brainwashing. What makes the guards quit is the blood and guts they see. They say, the hell with my pension, this is not for me.

Virtually every prisoner and guard has the we-they mentality. Us against them. It's the most destructive part of institutionalism. I know guards who are absolutely wonderful people, whom the prisoners would give their own lives to save theirs. But guards have to do this we-they separation. When you have to shoot somebody, it can't be your friend. Like the enemy in war are "gooks," the prisoners are "assholes." Prison will bring out the best and worst in you.

The first week I arrived at the prison there was a riot. One guard, a woman, was running up and down the gun rail shouting "I shot them all." She was like an animal. It was the scariest thing to watch. I felt the adrenaline flowing and I was ready to shoot someone. The other guards said to get ready and there we were, ten guys ready to shoot this one prisoner. It was like mob behavior. Nazi Germany was the same way. All these nice guys leave their families and go murder people, then go home to their families.

Can an inmate trust a guard? Sometimes. And guards can trust inmates, sometimes.

I don't believe rape is as prevalent as people think. Everyone is afraid of it. It exists. Prisoners say it's not as big an issue as what people say on the outside. To be protected you either pay someone and they'll protect you, or you submit to somebody and become his punk, then nobody will touch you.

Every prisoner will take advantage as far as we let them. It's part of their survival ritual. If they ask you for something and you do it, they'll ask for more.

Indigent prisoners can do art in the hobby program, which tends to be the center of the drug trade, to get money for canteen.

Prisoners get good money for paintings. If you have no artistic talent, it's worth a try to develop it, or else come up with some sort of hustle. Perform services: laundry, tailoring, hair cuts, read letters for those who are illiterate. If you have any skill or power it will be exploited, willingly or unwillingly. For instance, when some notorious killer gets his hair cut, other inmates gather up the clippings and sell them. There's a big market for that.

The biggest obstacle to survival is the unknown, believing something is going to happen because someone says it's going to happen. That's very frustrating for a prisoner. The best thing to do is to study something, learn a trade, not with the idea of making money, but to transcend the prison experience.

One ex-prisoner said prison was the best time of his life because he used the time to learn about himself. Now he feels better than he did before prison. It's what you make of it.

When I worked at San Quentin, I participated in the Warden's tours. The first stop was the gas chamber. It was a joke because nobody used it for 25 years. The death row inmates didn't think it would happen to them. Then one day, I was told Bob [Robert Alton] Harris was going to be the first to go. Is this really going to happen? I remember seeing the straps and the chair and the reality that somebody would be sitting there.

To psych yourself up for an execution, you either say yes or no. I was glad I was there for Bill [Bonin]. He asked me to be there. I didn't want to see it, but I wanted to be there for him. There were 50 witnesses. Forty-five of them were hoping he'd choke and puke and scream and yell, and five of us were friends. He needed us there. I went through changes and came out of it more spiritually oriented. This guy murdered [people], but I felt like, because he's going to die, I wanted to make sure the forty-five witnesses and their negative energy were as far away from him as possible. I wanted him to feel my love. This was after I no longer worked there.

They say the execution is painless. Bill asked that he be able to see us and we be able to see him, but by the time they opened the curtain, it seemed as though he was already dead.

Why did I go to the execution? How do you explain this person who was the horrible killer of 14 people versus the nice, sweet guy I got to know? Jekyll and Hyde. As a kid he was nearly drowned in a toilet, starved, raped and tortured. He spent time in foster home after foster home, abandoned, always a little weird. Then he went to Viet Nam and they told him to kill and he killed. They gave him a medal for it. Then he came back to the states and killed some more.

I never looked at him as a saint. I looked at him as what he wanted to be for those last two months. He wanted to be a person who spoke and taught the truth. He put everyone at ease. He learned how to read and write in prison and became a beautiful artist. He was there 14 years. He grew up there. Just before he died, he said, "the animal is no longer here. The person they are executing is someone else."

The executioner knows exactly what he is doing. The most

bizarre thing is that they're killing this guy. We think lethal injection is so sweet, so simple, because you go to sleep, but you die.

If you have the opportunity to be with a friend [at his execution] do not pass it up. It is absolutely the most special thing you will ever experience. It's sad, tragic, brutal and terrifying, on your part as well as his. It's going to happen whether you're there or not, so you might as well go as a friend. If you feel guilty about the morbid curiosity, well of course it's there, it's the experience, but it's also the ultimate gift you can give to this person and he can give to you.

Since the executions have resumed, it's amazing how close we all have become. Before an execution, it's very tense. Some prisoners say how much they hate the guy and "I can't wait until he dies." Prisoners feel a lot a rage at executions. The whole prison is locked down. The prisoners are so tuned in to the negativity, they'll stop what they're doing and say, "something just went down." Then a moment later the whistles blow, and they know it happened. It's a collective consciousness. They say they hate the person before he dies, but after it's all over they say how much they miss him.

Death row inmates form close relationships, like a family. Some child molesters and sex criminals are real intellectuals. Some of the older convicts command a certain dignity, a respect they get from other people. A convict is a righteous guy, as opposed to just an inmate. These ancient convicts with long white hair were transferred from "citizen's row" to another prison seven years ago. I knew this old man who was going to be paroled after 61 years. He had no home to go to and they had to send him out and then he died.

Are there any innocent men on death row? I don't know. Of all the guys who've claimed innocence, I believe only one and he's not on death row. That was Geronimo Pratt. What is common is that one guy will be convicted of murdering five people and he might be innocent of that, but the other guys who were with him testified against him and now he's on death row and they're out. That happens a lot. Jailhouse snitches are 99 percent liars. They will testify against you and they'll walk and you'll burn. Ultimately, they'll try anything to get out because who wants to be in prison.

Women who are prison or death row groupies, those who want to see the notorious killers and those who make a life of being groupies, serve a purpose for the prisoners, and I'm glad they're there. It adds a dimension to their lives and to the lives of the prisoners. They don't see the guy they're visiting as a scumbag. If you seek the good in people, you'll certainly find it.

Some people know they're being manipulated, but it fulfills a need so they willingly allow it to happen. It's a numbers game. If a prisoner asks ten people for something, one will give it to him, so they ask everyone. Never do or give them anything that's illegal or they could own you.

What makes a parolee fail is his expectations. I met one guy at the gate. I took him out for breakfast. He couldn't eat or sleep because it was too quiet. Then I took him to the beach and he panicked. He had become agoraphobic. He'd been inside 17 years.

When a prisoner gets out, the state is supposed to give him $200. One hundred at the gate and the other $100 at the parole office. Either you leave wearing prison blues or somebody gives you clothing. They walk you to the gate and don't give you a ride into town. If there's nobody to meet you, you're screwed. In order to survive, you might have to knock over a store and go back to prison. If we really want a solution to all of this, we don't have to spend millions to execute someone, we must spend the money on rehabilitation. Also drug and alcohol rehab a good two years before they get out is essential. I've read thousands of files and drugs are the cause of almost every incarceration.

The advice I have for a new prisoner is, you've got to deal with being in custody and deal with inmates at the same time. Inmates dealing with custody adhere to the rules, but understand beforehand that 98 percent of the rules are worthless, are incredibly paranoid and serve no useful purpose. They are totally arbitrary. If you try to analyze them, you'll go nuts. Everyone worries about homosexuality, but it's the rules that will drive you crazy.

Don't break the rules, but if you do, don't get caught. The prisoners mostly respect cop killers, but the guards hate them. Everybody hates child molesters.

My advice to a new guard is to do the same: follow the rules. I can't stress enough how guards and inmates are the same. Those prisoners are our family. They are not the enemy. They may want you to think they are, but get beyond that.

Family and loved ones should always be there for the prisoner. Help them get through their incarceration, help them know they have a family, write letters, send packages, make no excuses for anything. Get the rest of the family to understand that this person is still a member of the family and he has a sickness that needs to be cured. Use love to cure him.

I think three strikes is the crowning blow. It's an indication that our society isn't willing to look at crime as a sickness. It's all about revenge. It's the most costly waste of taxpayers' money and it serves no purpose.

Anything that isn't curative is sick. That's why I'm against the death penalty. If it did any good, I'd pull the switch myself, but it doesn't. The cost, the amount of time, the torture we go through as a society is ridiculous.

When I took my civil service interview the examiner asked me why I wanted to be a prison guard. I said because I love my fellow man. He said, "Don't you ever say that again if you want to work for the CDC."

*   *   *

Excerpts from a dialogue with Corey Weinstein, M.D.:

Many of the state employees making over $100,000 a year are prison guards. If a riot occurs on a holiday weekend, and the guards have to work, they get their regular pay plus double time for hazard pay, plus double time for holiday pay. Sometimes the guards create these circumstances, especially in the high security units, for their own aggrandizement and for the money. Those guards are the worst of the worst.

Some guards, not all, are playing their own inner game. They're the best, most efficient gang in the whole correctional system. The job calls for people who are more likely to be abusive and sadistic. Even guards who don't have those tendencies are drawn into it by other guards who teach them how to behave. Cruelty toward those who are perceived to be inferior and those who are helpless is common. Guards also have long memories. If a prisoner gets into a fight with the guard, the prisoner usually forgets about it, but if the guard is injured, he doesn't want to forget.

The routine and systematic violent attacks on prisoners at Corcoran Prison by guards have had two forms. Each is dramatic, committed by many guards, and known at the highest levels within the California Department of Corrections. The two methods are known as "greet the bus" and "gladiator fights."

"Greet the bus" has been carried out many times by guards at Corcoran State Prison. Prisoners arriving from other prisons in California are greeted at the bus and are assaulted and intimidated by guards before being processed.

"Gladiator fights" have been conducted by guards over

an eight year period between 1988 and 1996. Every day one or two prisoners were assigned by staff to the small yards of the super maximum SHU. Waiting inside were rival gang members. Bets were placed by guards on the outcome of the fights and viewed on videotapes. Hundreds of prisoners were involved. Some were seriously injured, and seven were killed by guard gunfire.

So vicious have been the assaults against prisoners that the Justice Department of the United States is investigating Corcoran State Prison, and considering indictments against staff. A few guards have been fired and others disciplined by the CDoC in direct contradiction of its usual code of silence in its good old boy network.

*   *   *

Excerpts from a dialogue with Jim Allen, a former California prison guard trainee who now volunteers to help restore an old army base in the San Francisco Bay area, where he was stationed in the late 1960s, to its original condition:

I went into it for the money. I wanted to be a counselor, get into something where I could help someone. The guards I knew wanted to help the prisoners, they wanted to treat them lawfully, but the reality gets to you quickly.

In training, I heard that prisoners will get bleach and put it around the light bulb socket. When the guard screws the bulb in, it would blow up in their face.

I was in the mess hall with one or two other guards while the prisoners ate. We had to monitor the whole group of 75 prisoners by ourselves. We couldn't show too much force. It seemed like they could take over an area without any trouble.

We had to go into the shower area and observe everyone to insure no weapons were being brought in. Cons can be very resourceful.

I remember one time we had to escort a known snitch through the other prisoners. I was amazed at how much he was hated. A person who snitches, or tells on another prisoner, becomes known real fast.

We couldn't carry weapons. They were not allowed inside the prison walls. Scatterguns could be used in the yard. What I noticed was the guards were always looking around, and that told me that the job was very stressful. You can't believe how much noise there is inside and how it makes you feel when you're working.

*   *   *

Excerpts from a dialogue with Michael Marcum, Assistant

Sheriff, San Francisco County:

This line of work does not attract brutal, dysfunctional people. When I interview people who come into this department, they say they want to work with inmates, make a difference in their community, feel like they're part of law enforcement and criminal justice. After a year, two or maybe five, you interview these same people again and find their commitment gone. It's been destroyed by the institution they've been hired to run.

Staff, like the convicts, wind up relying on each other. They start cutting off all their friends because outsiders don't understand how horrible, how irrational the inside is. Staff take an oath of office but somehow it goes out the window. They realize how hypocritical it is and how it doesn't fit the institution they're mandated to run, so they come up with an oath identical to the inmates', which is "don't snitch."

The green or blue code among staff means they don't snitch on each other. These are people who are supposed to be the epitome of our constitution, of our laws. The prisoner sees this and it further verifies his belief that the whole system is wrong. The two behaviors between prisoners and staff feed on each other. It's insane.

All our resources are going to the prison system. These are resources that could be going to other institutions like schools, foster care and families. The tragedy is that we have this knee jerk reaction to lock more people up and this only guarantees that we have to build more prisons. How many lives [staff and inmate] are we going to waste this way?

*   *   *

Wilbert Rideau, author of *Prison: The Sexual Jungle* is a lifer at Louisiana State Prison (Angola) and editor of the award-winning Angolite magazine:

The deprivation of basic human needs imposed upon prisoners, and the violence resulting from it has created a horrible situation in the nation's jails and prisons, one that adds an extra dimension to the punishment of an offender, one that it can be reasonably assumed no sentencing judge intended. It would be easy for one to blame the whole affair on prisoners, using the violent situation as proof that they're criminals or animals, and justification for the present penal practices. But the prisoners didn't create the situation. Their behavior merely reflects the response of desperate men, locked in a cruel and abnormal situation, exercising the only avenues left to them, to cling to the very normal need to feel strong, masculine and worthwhile, to "normality," trying desperately not to lose touch with the "real" world by creating an artificial one patterned after the one they left behind. The violence, the murders, the suicides, and the human debris left in the wake of their effort, is the cost.

> The true source of evil is us.
> Frank Black, *Millennium*

*   *   *

> If you cram people into prison, create forced idleness without the supervision that is needed, you can expect the situation to get out of hand. It's an unbelievable burden on corrections staff to manage people in inhuman conditions.
> Stephen Bright, Executive Director, The Human Rights Organization

PRISON GUARD PROMO
[California Correctional Peace Officers Association]

A video infomercial, paid for by the California Correctional Peace Officers Association (CCPOA), was shown on television touting "The Toughest Beat" in California. CCPOA wanted the public to know how difficult and dangerous their job is. The video was teeming with hyperbole and exaggerations, which left people in other law enforcement occupations fighting mad.

The video began with statements from several Folsom prison guards:

We deal with murderers, rapists, child molesters, robbers, armed robbers, drug dealers, thieves, grand theft auto, you name it, we have it.

In response to the video, another California prison guard adds his two cents:

What isn't said is that we also deal with first time, non-violent offenders who are incarcerated together with violent offenders. These first time offenders often had jobs on the outside and families who cared about them, and they are more than likely responsible citizens who got caught doing whatever they were doing. There is a good probability that the crime they committed was victimless and they would not have done it a second time, if they had understood the consequences. Some of these first timers are severely damaged by their prison time. They lose hope of ever having a job again and they feel heavy remorse for their actions. Some even contemplate suicide.

        *   *   *

On the video, Jan Miller, representing the Doris Tate Crime Victims Bureau, describes her visit to a prison:

I was amazed at the freedom with which these prisoners just get to walk around in and out of their cells, just sitting around outside, playing cards, basically doing nothing, and I guess I resented that because I have to go to work every day. I run a business, and here they are like they were sitting on a college campus and it was break time and I was frustrated by that and I hate it. I'd like to change all that.

The facts are that prison jobs are few and far between, therefore many inmates don't have the opportunity to work. Because of cost cutting and political posturing concerning so-called "country club" prisons, large chunks of work, educational and recreational programs have been cut to the bone. This leaves the inmates with nothing better to do with their time except play cards, run scams on each other and riot.

Michael Quinlan, former director of the Federal Bureau of Prisons (FBOP), believes that work programs are "absolutely the most important ingredient in managing a safe and secure institution to keep inmates productively occupied, either in work, education, drug treatment or structured recreation."

Quinlan also believes that work programs prepare inmates for reentry into society . An FBOP study found that inmates who worked on the inside were less likely to cause problems in prison or to be rearrested after release than inmates who were not involved in prison work programs.

        *   *   *

"Unlike other law enforcement professionals, correctional peace officers deal with violent felons every minute of every day," a prison guard says on the video.

"You deal with 100% certified felons every day," says Don Novey, CCPOA President.

A 25 year veteran of the Los Angeles Police Department responds:
This statement surely negates the violence police officers face every day. Prison guards deal with felons, that's their job. If they don't like it, they can go into a business where the climate is less violent. Police officers face uncertainty. They never know when a suicidal man with an AK 47 is lurking behind a wall waiting to blow them away. Each traffic stop contains an element of potential violence, each domestic scene can turn deadly.
     I'm a police officer in Southern California. I know what I'm getting into and I prepare for it each afternoon before going to work. To imply, like the guard stated, that I don't face violent felons every minute of every day, is preposterous. I'm the one who arrests the violent felons. I take the chance of getting axed from so many people, it boggles my mind, yet I still go to work, and I don't make videos for television complaining about my job. Then again, some areas of law enforcement hire from the shallow end of the gene pool, making sure there is a degree of unpleasantness and hostility in their job.

              *   *   *

On video, Jan Miller states:
Most prisoners are con men and they got there because of what they are. The officers are dressed impeccably, hair is cut and they live by a set of rules, where the prisoners do anything they damn well please, their hair is any way they want it to be and they dress like a bunch of slobs, and I feel that we have the wrong people following rules. The prisoners should have their hair shaved, wear a certain set of clothes and act in a specific manner.

A former guard at San Quentin State Prison replies to Jan Miller:
I'm not sure where this woman got her information, but as a former prison guard, I know that prisoners wear the clothing the state provides. Some inmates wear clothing and shoes that are way too small for them, or too large. In the winter, some don't have coats. The state doesn't allow gang style clothing, meaning If an inmate wants pants three sizes to big, we don't allow it.
     Each inmate arrives with his own hairstyle. That doesn't

mean they have it their way. It means we allow them to wear that hairstyle as leverage to control their behavior. If an inmate hides contraband inside braids or long hair, then that inmate has his hair cut or shaved.

The statement about most inmates being con-men is true, and yet not all con-men are inmates. It depends on where you put your emphasis. This woman's use of the media to publicly lump all inmates as con-men, especially when she doesn't know them personally, is pure meanness. Why waste time and energy to devalue a group of incarcerated men, unless it's politically motivated to create an atmosphere of hatred? It's like saying all immigrants are a lazy bunch of ingrates. That way, simple-minded people watching the video will say "ah-ha, I knew they were nothing but a bunch of lazy, no-good, con-men."

*   *   *

On video, Nina Solarno, Assistant DA, Sacramento, CA County, states:

I went on a walk through this one prison. Prisoners were yelling and spitting and they do things like that, living a life of luxury while the officers have to support their families. I don't think the general public knows that.

A prison guard responds to Ms. Solarno:

The general public isn't aware of what goes on behind prison walls because in California the media isn't allowed to interview inmates. Most knowledge about prison life comes from fictionalized movies or television. It's usually a violent depiction of prison life or prisoners, like notorious mafia leaders, who run the prison their way. Other information about prison life is mostly exaggeration. The truth is somewhere in between.

I've been a prison guard for thirty years. I've worked in nine different institutions in four different states. Some positions were in level three and four, which is hard core, others were in levels one to three, which is minimum to medium. Every institution is different, but I've never seen a luxury prison. In fact, I'd love to know the specific circumstances this woman uses to justify her identifying a prisoner as having a "life of luxury."

Level four, protective custody and the SHU (security housing unit), mostly house violent offenders. I believe this is the level Ms. Solarno is referring too. Some men on this level are vicious. Others have had the rotten luck to be labeled gang members or homosexual, even if they're not. Not all of them belong there.

The "luxury" is that each man is locked up 23 hours a day, seven days a week. He eats, sleeps and showers in his cell. He has, maybe, one hour four or five days a week for recreation and even then, he is alone. That, to me, isn't luxury. That's hell.

As for yelling and spitting, if all I had to do was ride the rack (lie in bed) every single monotonous day, I'd be real creative in finding ways to get back at my jailers. The D.A. should know that.

*   *   *

Four Folsom State prison guards in the video say:

"Over the past ten years inmates have gotten more violent, less caring, no remorse."

"This kind of inmate is predatory, always on the hunt, tightly gang structured."

"A lot of these guys aren't here because of first offenses, they're here because they're habitual criminals."

"This element, it's their lifestyle and it has been since they're young."

Retired San Quentin guard responds to forgoing statements:

These statements imply that all prison inmates are extremely violent, predatory, gang oriented hunters who've been born and raised for prison. Some are and some are not. The inmates who are most violent are housed on level four, maximum security.

I'd like to see a representative of the prison say it like it really is, "over the past ten years, some inmates housed in maximum security have gotten more violent, less caring, and feel no remorse. Some of them are predatory, always on the hunt for weaker, non-violent inmates. Some belong to gangs where they find comfort and security from other gangs. Some are on maximum because they have criminal records dating back to when they were children. Some, but not all, cannot be rehabilitated, and need to be locked up forever. Others are highly rehabilitatable, and could be released on parole.

*   *   *

Video statements:

We're concerned about diseases. Some of the prisons are old. They don't have air conditioning. We're not talking about a comfort zone here. Leslie Price, correctional officer.

Diseases can ruin a career and can kill us. Don Novey, CCPOA.

Retired San Quentin Guard responds:

Not to mention the inmates who cannot go home after an eight hour shift. They are forced to breathe diseased air seven days a week, twenty-four hours a day. Without proper ventilation or air conditioning, warm, moist air acts as an incubator, hatching new diseases.

Inmates do not have medical insurance, nor do they have a medicine chest. If disease-laden air can kill a guard, think about what it can do to an inmate. First, he gets sick. Since he is indigent, he cannot afford to pay the $5 fee for a medical visit, so he suffers. The disease spreads to his cell mate who is being paroled in a month. The cell mate spreads the disease to others before he is paroled, then he goes home and gives the disease to his wife and kids. The wife carries it to work and the kids share it with their classmates. Soon an entire population is infected. Stephen King couldn't have invented a better horror story.

Politicians concerned with public safety should stop wearing blinders. Violence and crime are small potatoes when you consider how quickly disease can spread without medical intervention. Treating an inmate like a human being, with consideration for those he will come in contact with once paroled, should be paramount to running a prison system.

Dispensing justice maliciously, degrading the inmate's humanity and forcing him to live with filth and disease, only enrages him and diminishes his sense of self, and that self will one day live in our community.

*   *   *

More statements from the video:

California Governor Pete Wilson says "We have over 2000 assaults a year on staff."

Statements from various prison guards:

"Assaults on officers are escalating."

"There are five attacks every day."

"One out of 15 officers are attacked each day."

"The 1980's was the bloodiest decade in history at Folsom. There were the Black-Hispanic wars, the Father's Day massacre."

"In 1985 Hal Birchfield, a prison guard, was stabbed at San Quentin. He was also stabbed four years earlier. That year, 99 other staff were stabbed. In August 1996, a female officer was stabbed at the Youth Authority ."

> Don Novey, President, CCPOA, says "I'm proud
> to be a part of the legislation that is cost cutting the
> expenses to help protect the public interest."

Social worker from the California Youth Authority, responds:

As of April 13, 1997, there were 150,016 men and women
in 24 California State prisons, filled 150% to 200% over capacity.
Human beings are locked up behind bars like sardines. They
eat and live in tightly compacted surroundings, often without air
conditioning, proper ventilation or sanitation. Each man's stink
and disease is another one's air. The only view some have of
the outside world is through three electrically charged fences,
topped with razor wire, twenty feet high, that surround the entire
prison. That's enough to make a sane man psychotic.

Educational opportunities have been reduced or
eliminated and there isn't enough prison work for everyone. Hard
nosed politicians, intent on appearing tough on crime, have
passed legislation to eliminate recreation and family visiting.

The only thing left for an inmate to do is sit and smolder.
Is it any wonder there are 2,000 assaults on staff each year or
that assaults are escalating?

According to [Steven] Donziger in *The Real War on Crime*,
the absolute number of assaults has gone up, but the
rate has gone down because of the increased number of prisoners.

If Mr. Novey is proud to be part of legislation that is cost
cutting expenses in prison to help protect public interest, he is
dead wrong. Education, work experience and technical training
have all been proven to lower crime rates and recidivism.
Reducing or eliminating these programs only produces a need
for more prisons, thus ensuring job security for prison guards.
Abandoning recreational opportunities while exploiting the
inmates for poorly paid slave labor creates an atmosphere of
hostility and rage.

With this cost cutting, what Mr. Novey and the status-
seeking politicians have accomplished is the release back into
our society of a group of angry, uneducated, unskilled,
unsocialized men and women, who cannot survive on the
outside, so they are rearrested and sent back to prison.

This, of course, cements job security for prison
administration, prison guards and law enforcement. By 2006, the
prison population in California is expected to increase to 242,000.

If they continue to build new prisons at the present rate, every school child and every college student will be stuffed inside antiquated buildings and read from outdated school books. Social programs will be non-existent, battered women will die, rape victims will not have counseling, juvenile programs will wither away and the streets we drive on will fall into disrepair, all to pay for more prisons.

Inside prison walls, more non-violent men and women will be raped, assaulted, murdered, executed and driven insane. Guards will die by the droves.

We don't live in a vacuum, we interact with our environment. The violence and rage on the inside will rapidly spread to those of us on the outside, poisoning our minds and bodies. Unless we stop the madness now, society as we know it will no longer exist. I sure don't want to be around when that happens.

*   *   *

The California Correctional Peace Officer's Association (CCPOA) is at odds with the California Department of Corrections bureaucracy. A union lobbyist says reforms are needed to bring the profession into the 20th century.

The CCPOA endorses proposed legislation that would increase officers basic training from six to nine weeks and supervisor's training from two weeks to three. Other provisions of the bill include psychological screening for guard candidates and a limit of four years for wardens to serve at each institution

The DoC says these issues should be determined by the Department, not by the Legislature. The guards' union is adamant that these changes are necessary to enable them to do their job more efficiently.

I had chest pains, but when I went to the doctor for a checkup, I got the feeling that he was telling me, well heck, lady, you're standing on your own two feet, what more do you want.

Mother of a death row inmate

THERAPEUTIC INTERVENTION

Sheila, a social worker at a mental health clinic told us:

As a therapist, I see the terrible complications families face when a loved one is arrested or incarcerated. Many times the free person loses his job. They are often without the money to continue living in their house, so they sell or move to a less expensive area. Food and comfort items such as gas and electricity, phone and after school events become a luxury, the car disintegrates.

Family relationships with others in society, whether it's with relatives, friends or a minister, become strained, if not completely severed. Often, one or more family members breaks down emotionally and needs professional help. That's where I come in.

Many of the clients I see are professionals. Most have college degrees and few have friends or relatives who have ever been arrested. For them, arrest is social and economic destruction, yet more professionals than ever are getting arrested now. According to some families, the arrest was for minor violations. The one arrested didn't know or comprehend the law. Over 3,000 new laws have been passed in the last few years, and I can easily understand their confusion.

Most violations are what I call low-to mid-level non-violent crimes. This includes office theft, embezzlement, sexual and emotional harassment, drugs and alcohol, traffic infractions, and minor aggressive behavior. Some even include wrongful arrests.

In order to understand how healthy individuals can zoom, with bullet speed, into mental illness after they or a loved one is arrested, you have to hear their stories.

I see an elderly, disabled woman who was driven to her doctor's office by her son. As he wheeled her toward the front door, the police showed up and arrested him. They left the woman on the doorstep, and only told her that her son had been accused of multiple murders. She went into shock and had to be hospitalized.

One evening while barbecuing hot dogs for his daughter's party, a man was dragged out of his own back yard and beaten to a pulp by police. His wife and children watched helplessly as he was arrested. Evidently, a malicious neighbor had called 911 and reported the father was beating his children. Six people who had been at the party witnessed the officers' assault. They all told the cops no one had been beaten, but the officers continued to bully the man, until suddenly, one cop grabbed him and pulled him out the front gate. This father sustained serious head injuries and two broken ribs. Yet, according to one police officer late that night, there wasn't enough evidence to hold him. He was released before being booked. That way the family had to pay the medical bills. The police only have to pay if the person is in custody.

My ten o'clock [appointment] is a woman who was arrested as she fixed dinner. Her husband had to explain to their three young children that Mommie was going to jail. She had taken six cases of soft drinks from the office supply room without telling the unit supply clerk. Even though she had asked the boss and been given permission to remove the soft drinks, that order never made it down to the supply person. The unit clerk called to report the theft, saying the young mother had been seen near the storeroom at the time. Instead of investigating the situation, a warrant was issued for the woman's arrest. She was carted away in handcuffs, booked into the county jail and strip searched before going to her cell. The judge said there wasn't enough evidence to hold her, and let her go.

A sixty-four-year-old man sued his employer for age discrimination when they fired him. He'd been with the company for over thirty-three years. To avoid defending the lawsuit, this multi-million dollar corporation accused the older man of stealing industrial technology. Without the big bucks to fight the company, the man lost his lawsuit and his home. Just before he committed suicide, his wife died from a heart attack because they no longer had the medical insurance from his job. My client's attorney told me that had the man chosen to live, he would have faced fifteen years in prison for stealing secret plans and selling them to competitors. This was the most trumped up charge I ever heard, yet it was one man against the mob.

I could go on and on, but I won't. None of the people I've mentioned ever entertained thoughts of going to jail or having a loved one arrested. It would have been beyond their worst nightmare. Each considered himself an upstanding, law-abiding citizen. They took pride in their homes, families and jobs.

The kinds of mental problems people face are numerous. Most often I see what is called Post Traumatic Stress Disorder (PTSD).

According to the DSM (Diagnostic and Statistical Manual of Mental Disorders), PTSD is where "the person has experienced an event that is outside the range of usual human experience and that would be markedly distressing to almost anyone."

Ways this disorder presents itself:
* Thinking about the traumatic event when you don't want to
* Nightmares about the event
* A sense that the event is happening again and again, reliving the experience in flashbacks
* Intense feelings when confronted by other events that resemble the event
* Continued refusal to talk about the event, avoiding thoughts and feelings about what happened or talking about it continuously
* Not able to remember anything about the event
* A feeling of being apart from others
* Unable to show or express feelings to those you love.
    Symptoms include:
* Difficulty falling or staying asleep
* Irritability or outbursts of anger
* Inability to concentrate
* Constantly on the alert
* Jumpy
* Overreacting when faced with a similar event.

Other mental problems experienced are mood disorders such as anxiety. These symptoms include: feeling shaky, tension with sore muscles, restlessness and fatigue, shortness of breath, sweating, clammy hands, nausea, diarrhea, trouble swallowing, feeling keyed up, and trouble falling and staying asleep. Depression includes: poor appetite, low energy or feeling tired all the time, low self-esteem, poor concentration, a feeling of hopelessness, and excessive daytime sleeping.

Children often react by expressing a fear of being lost and never reunited with the jailed parent. They act out by being defiant and angry. They worry about the absent parent, thinking the parent may be dead or dying. Sometimes children play act the event of the arrest over and over. They have nightmares and are often afraid to go to sleep. Most will have an unusually great fear of the police.

Teens may run away from home, blame themselves for the arrest, attempt suicide or become overly anxious or depressed; or they may lie, steal, break into neighbor's houses or nearby businesses, start fights, and in some cases they can become physically or verbally cruel. They will taunt authority and when asked about the event, say they hate the police and if given the chance would physically harm an officer.

According to recent statistics, children of incarcerated parents have a 60 percent higher chance of being incarcerated than their counterparts who have never had a parent arrested.

What this tells me is that we as a society must slow the burgeoning prison population by attending to what is wrong with how people are viewed as criminals and incarcerated as such. When innocent people are jailed on a neighbor's whim or accused of a non-crime such as defending their home, the aftershocks are tremendous. The family suffers in lost wages, excessive attorney fees, terror and guilt over the arrest, mental problems which call for therapeutic intervention and in extreme cases, hospitalization.

Society suffers by footing the bill for incarceration that isn't needed, hospital and therapy bills, a smaller tax base and in extreme cases, a new criminal element derived from childhood trauma.

I don't believe we as a society can continue this way without serious threat to our future. With the government asking for new laws which call for longer sentences and new prisons to be built, those future inmates will not come from the current adult population. They will come from our children and our grandchildren.

If prisons become our biggest industry, as they have in California, then the fallout from lost souls, broken families and discarded humanity will become our downfall. I am only one therapist. I don't think there are enough therapists for a crisis like that.

When I asked my family doctor if he could refer me to a psychologist, he wanted to know why. I explained about my son's trial and how difficult it was for me to attend every day, plus go to work at night. "Don't go," he said. "You don't understand," I said, "I want to go because he's my son and it's important for me to be there." The doctor said, "Well, if you were the victim of a crime, I'd surely understand the need for a psychologist. But since you're the mother of a criminal, I just don't see why you feel you need to seek the help of a professional."

                    Sixty-seven year old mother

STRESS MANAGEMENT

At a county mental health clinic, a social worker explains how she helps clients overcome stress related hardships:

The function of managing stress begins with the acknowledgment that something isn't quite right. Either your behavior is off kilter or you suddenly develop an illness that doesn't go away. Either way, your life has changed for the worse.

The goal of stress management is to achieve a balance between the individual's ability to handle stress and the amount of stress they face in their life situations. This balance can be achieved in one of many ways: by changing the stressful situation and diffusing its control over the individual, or if you can't change the stressful situation, you can change how the individual reacts to it by empowering him with stress reducing-techniques.

When someone is facing a prison sentence or a family member has been arrested, nothing can be changed except the way the individual reacts to the situation. The person who was arrested cannot change enough to stop the prison sentence, and the family member cannot change what has already happened. Therefore I work on the individual's reaction and coping mechanisms.

I teach people how to relax during the stressful situation. When people experience stress, their body tenses. When the stress is removed, the tension is gone. People who are forced into stressful situations, or those who must cope with massive amounts of stress daily, face potentially life-threatening problems if that stress isn't reduced or eliminated.

                    *   *   *

A client at the clinic explained how she and her therapist

worked on pain control:

> I started to have headaches every day. Some days they were so bad I couldn't work. My doctor said the pain could be from the tension of not knowing the outcome of my court case. The threat of going to jail made me extremely nervous. He sent me to a woman who specialized in relaxation therapy. I learned to identify the signs of tension, the areas in my body where this tension hit and how to relax those muscles. For instance, most of my tension built up in the back of my neck. The therapist would instruct me to sit comfortably and fold my hands in my lap. Then I'd think to myself, "relax." After that, I go through each section of my body and tell it to relax. It took almost six weeks, but now all I have to do is tell my neck to relax and my headaches are gone.

*   *   *

A therapist told us how she helped an older woman:

> A female client, age 73, is facing ten years in prison for drug possession. One of her grandson's friends, unbeknownst to her, had concealed marijuana among her tomato plants.
>
> The narcotics squad was notified and the woman was arrested. It was her first time. In jail, she experienced a mild heart attack. So far, the prosecutor has refused to drop the charges. While she is out on bail, I am trying to teach her coping skills so she can learn to relax during those anxiety-producing moments in court. First, I have her sit in a chair and relax. I then begin the progressive relaxation techniques. This is where each muscle group is identified and then tensed for thirty seconds. Once she feels the tension, she is asked to relax that muscle. We do this for the entire body. She learns that when she relaxes that muscle, tension is gone. Once I have her completely relaxed, I tell her to imagine a real-life scene in the courtroom. Then, I have her go through each muscle group again, tensing and relaxing, until she is only using the relax command. When the time comes for her court appearance, she will have several relaxation commands available to use when she begins to feel tense.

*   *   *

A mother whose son is behind bars for nine years for his third DUI (driving under the influence of alcohol):

When my blood pressure shot up to 240/180, my doctor told me to begin walking. I started with one block, now I walk three miles a day. When I went to visit my son in prison, he was amazed at how healthy I looked. He finally confessed that my poor health was getting him down. He had carried the guilt of his arrest and my failing health as a sword, hacking away at his self-esteem and hindering any progress he might have made in the prison programs. Now, he has the incentive to help himself. He's joined Alcoholics Anonymous and is going to sign up for trade school. By helping myself first, I'm more able to help him.

*   *   *

Some people are able to handle their stress by developing a more healthy lifestyle. Aerobic exercises, like walking or riding a bike, can help reduce stress-induced illnesses such as heart disease, respiratory disease and arthritis. Exercise lowers the heart rate, increases stamina by pushing more oxygen into the heart, and keeps the joints and bones limber.

Martha L., R.N

*   *   *

Wife of a man doing three years for possession of drugs:
After walking, gardening is my favorite way to manage the pain of having my husband in prison. I use flowers and plants to ease my depression. When he gets out, he'll see that I've planted a new herb garden.

*   *   *

Sister of man in prison for possession of drugs:
Developing better eating habits will help your body resist disease. Less fat and sugar, more fruits, vegetables and grains. Use less alcohol and stop smoking.

*   *   *

The more physically fit you are the better able you will become at handling stressful life events and warding off illness.

Eleanor D., wife of death row inmate

Twenty-eight year old man who spent six months in jail for traffic tickets:
Jail food is the most unhealthy gunk I've ever tasted. Green meat is not a myth. It exists, along with thick, pasty

peanut butter. Even the Army fed me better. All that high fat gave me gall-bladder disease and rickety bones. After I got out of jail, I sloughed off my dislike of exercise and started riding a bike. I also became a vegetarian. My blood pressure went down and I feel a lot better. Even my bones don't creak anymore.

*   *   *

Married man who did three years in state prison for credit card theft:

In prison, cigarettes are money. I could get anything I needed by handing out smokes. Most of the time I used them to barter. By the time I got out, I had stopped smoking altogether. I feel better and I'm not so nervous. Now, every time my parole agent hassles me in some way, I can handle it without flying off the hook.

*   *   *

Sometimes the entire family breaks down. A Marriage and family therapist gave us examples of how to keep the family together and stress free:

The best way for a family to reduce the amount of stress it experiences is to sit down with each other and talk about it:
* pick a time when everyone can be together
* make sure there are no distractions. Unplug the phone and don't answer the doorbell
* have rules such as no blaming and no interrupting. Each one has his say without a lecture from someone else. Absolutely no confrontations
* each should be encouraged to speak openly and honestly about their feelings
* participants are urged to give their undivided attention
* a pledge that everything said is confidential and not to be shared with others.

These rules instill a sense of safety, where family members can speak about their pain without fear of ridicule. If the family is unable to comply or is resistant to discussing the problems, a therapist or mediator can be called in. Do so only with every member's permission.

*   *   *

Sometimes I have to be five places at the same time.
Mother working on her son's appeal.

GOING NUTS BY THE NUMBERS

In the early '70s behavioral scientists began to study and understand the effects of stress, which was defined as "physical, mental or emotional tension caused by change." The scientists found that "good" stress (a change for the better) causes as much tension as "bad" stress (change for the worse).

Dr. Thomas Holmes of the University of Washington School of Medicine prioritized life events in order of their ability to produce stress, and awarded point values to each. Death of a spouse ranked number one, and was given a value of 100 points. Getting a parking ticket ranked number 45, and was given 11 points on a scale of one to 100.

Dr. Holmes did not list every conceivable life event, but determined that similar events would earn similar point scores. He did not specifically list things like being arrested and going to prison, but it's easy to plug those events into the list.

Stressful events amounting to about 200 points in any one 12 month period represent a degree of disruption most people cannot manage, Holmes said, and will cause severe physical and mental illness within a year. People who experience 300 points in a year's time can die from the stress. The study concluded that people who suffer a major loss or disruption in their lives, such as the death of a spouse, their home burning down, job loss or bankruptcy often undergo as many as 500 points or "life change units." Many people who attain such high scores become gravely ill and some die prematurely.

These are the point values Dr. Holmes determined:

Event	Points
* Death of a spouse	100
* Divorce	73
* Marital separation	65
* Jail term	63
* Loss of job	47

* Change in finances   38
* Change in line of work   36
* Change in number of arguments with spouse   35
* High mortgage payment   31
* Foreclosure of mortgage or loan   30
* Change in job responsibilities   29
* Trouble with in-laws   29
* Change in living conditions   25
* Change in personal habits   24
* Trouble with boss   23
* Change in work hours or conditions   20
* Change in residence   20
* Change in recreation   19
* Change in church activities   19
* Change in social activities   18
* Change in sleeping habits   16
* Change in number of family gatherings   15
* Change in eating habits   15
* Holidays, Vacations, Birthdays etc.   13

How many points would you give the events in your life since your loved one was arrested and incarcerated?

* Arrest   ____
* Sitting in jail and knowing you're innocent   ____
* Sitting in jail and knowing you're guilty   ____
* Police brutality   ____
* Trying to raise bail money   ____
* Seeing a loved one shackled   ____
* Finding a lawyer   ____
* Finding the money to pay lawyers   ____
* Being told the situation looks pretty bad   ____
* Too upset to go to work   ____
* Loss of job   ____
* Loss of loved one's job   ____
* Loss of income   ____
* Hounded by bill collectors   ____
* Children taunted at school   ____
* Seeing your/his picture in the paper   ____
* Hounded by media   ____
* Attitude of family and (former) friends   ____
* Disfellowshipped from your church   ____
* Teenage daughter attempts suicide   ____
* Eviction from, or foreclosure on, home   ____

* Move in with in-laws   ____
* Move in with your relatives   ____
* Attend trial day after day   ____
* Hear guilty verdict, sentence pronounced   ____
* Visit prison   ____
* Plan to move near prison falls through   ____
* He writes from prison, asks for divorce   ____
* Pre-teen son wants to join a gang   ____
* Not allowed to visit when he's sick   ____
* Constant worry, feelings of anger, grief, despair,
  hopelessness, fear, shame, guilt, "going crazy" etc.   ____
* _____   ____
* _____   ____

           YOUR TOTAL   ____

We have not conducted a scientific study, but we did give our modified version of the "Holmes test" to a few willing subjects, and this is what we found:

Person/Event	Points
* Mother of man on death row for murder she believes he didn't commit	874
* Wife of man sentenced to 10 years for insurance fraud	568
* Teenage girl, father convicted of attempted murder	562
* Sister of man who got 7 years for growing pot	441
* Brother of serial rapist	392

How does your score compare to theirs?

*   *   *

If we don't organize to resist injustice, then injustice will ultimately visit us all.

Dorsey Nunn, KNow INjustice

SUPPORT GROUP

You feel like you're going crazy. You can't eat, can't sleep, your hands shake all the time and you've developed chronic diarrhea. You can't stop crying. You sit and stare into space all day long. Your memory is shot, you can't even decide what to have for lunch, you're not paying as much attention to the kids as you used to, and you're totally neglecting the house. You're afraid to look in the mirror; you look like you've been through a war, you've lost ten pounds, have bags under your eyes and your hair just hangs there. Whenever a car door slams or the phone rings, you get heart palpitations, like you did that night when the police came bursting in. You wish you were dead.

Family, (former) friends, co-workers and neighbors are no help. They just don't get it. Ever since your husband (son, brother, boy friend) went to prison, people avoid you. Hardly anyone phones or visits. If you run into them at the supermarket, they pretend not to notice you. If you greet them, they are in a terrible hurry to catch a plane and don't have time to chat. The people where you used to go to church aren't much help, either. They want nothing to do with sinners!

Those who do phone, mostly your mother and your sister, never ask how you're doing, or how your husband (son, boyfriend) is doing. Instead, they just dish out free advice: "Dump the bum and get on with your life." "You're not really going to visit him in that disgusting place, are you?" "He got what was coming to him. Divorce the jerk." "Don't waste your tears, you're better off without him." "Straighten up and straighten out, or you'll never find a new man." (What makes them think you're looking for one?)

You can't go it alone any more. People who haven't been through it just don't know what it's like. You need to be with people who are experiencing the same problems and emotions you are. Where will you find them?

You need a support group!

There may already be one in your area. Check out the various organizations that help prisoners and their families (see Appendix). If there's no support group near you, START ONE. It's easier than you think, and will do two important things for you:
* provide you with the support you need from new friends who've been there, done that
* keep you so busy you won't have time to be miserable.

Here's what to do:

* Think up a name for your group. It should tell exactly what the group is. "Support Group for Families and Friends of Prisoners" isn't cute, but doesn't leave any doubt what it's about.

* Make a flyer. If you don't have a computer or typewriter, do it by hand. Give the name of the group, the time of the first meeting (4 to 6 weeks away), the place where the meeting will be held, your name, and a phone number to contact. Depending on the circumstances, you might not want to use your home address. Instead, you might want to use a post office box or message service.

* Make about 500 copies of the flyer. Some photocopy places will do large orders for two or three cents a copy.

* If you don't have a telephone answering machine, try and buy or borrow one. You'll need it.

* Plan to have the meeting at a church hall or some other public place, not at your home. A restaurant, or even a homeless shelter, might let you borrow a room. In summer, a park can be a good daytime meeting place.

* Send flyers, with a cover letter, to all newspapers, radio and TV stations in your area and within a 50 mile radius. Send a separate flyer to the news editor, and one to the community calendar, at each media outlet. You can get the names and addresses of out-of-town newspapers and radio/TV stations from phone books, which are available at your local public library.

* Phone the news editors at all media outlets, tell them what you're planning and ask to be interviewed.

* Phone local area talk show hosts and ask to appear on their programs.

* Prepare in advance what you want to say in an interview. Ask the interviewer to agree in advance that he won't verbally "beat you up" on the show. If they do, you have the right to get up and leave. Tell the interviewer that most prisoners are not violent "monsters." The majority have committed non-violent

crimes related to drugs or theft. Point out that you are not seeking "sympathy" for prisoners (that part can come later). Explain that family members of prisoners have committed no crime, and are merely seeking to provide each other with emotional support and companionship.

* PRACTICE WHAT YOU ARE GOING TO SAY SO THAT YOU DO NOT SOUND ANGRY. DO NOT SAY ANYTHING NEGATIVE ABOUT THE POLICE OR JUSTICE SYSTEM. REMEMBER, YOU ARE LOOKING TO START A SUPPORT GROUP, NOT A WAR!

* Send flyers to criminal defense lawyers, and ask them to hand them out to the families of their clients. Look in the yellow pages of your phone book under "attorneys."

* Send flyers to the Public Defender's office, too.

* Watch your local newspaper for ideas. If someone is on trial or has been sentenced, contact the family. If you don't know their address, send a letter to their lawyer and ask him to forward it. Or go to the court house to their trial.

* Read the "Letters to the Editor" column. If someone writes about a family member being in prison, write them a letter telling about the support group. If you don't have their address, mail it to the newspaper and ask them to forward it.

* Phone the editor of your local paper. Ask if you can write a brief article about the support group, or write a "letter to the editor" telling about it.

* Ask churches to put your flyer on their bulletin boards and put a write-up in the church bulletin or newsletter.

* Put a flyer on bulletin boards in the court house lobby and cafeteria.

* Stand in front of the court house and hand out flyers.

* Go to nearby prisons and jails on visiting days. Hand out flyers to the visitors. Ask the guard if you can put one on the bulletin board.

* Some organizations have a guest house or hospitality house near some prisons. If there is one near you, ask them to distribute flyers for you.

* Visit colleges and universities in your area. Go to the offices of the departments of psychology, sociology, social work and criminology. Ask them to post your flyer on a bulletin board, or leave a few on a table.
* Ask the professors in those departments if they will give you a few minutes of class time to talk about the group.
* Tell your loved one in prison about it. He may want to pass the word to any home boys in his pod, and they can pass the word to their families.
* Don't expect miracles. If you give out several hundred flyers, you might get one or two people at your meeting. But don't give up - THEY WILL COME.
* After the first meeting, keep generating publicity. Hand out business cards or flyers wherever you go. Make phone calls. After the first few who join, new members will come from word of mouth. Old members will bring new ones.

                    *   *   *

"It has been my experience," the organizer of a support group said, "that those who've had the most success dealing with the courts, the attorneys and the criminal justice system, exhibit specific attributes:
* Each takes a proactive stance
* They obtain and read the trial transcripts
* They discuss the case with the attorney and keep up with all new developments
* They educate themselves about laws
* They keep family and friends apprised of each segment of the case. They know they must keep information confidential. (Suspicion and paranoia are two of those prominent features families of inmates develop during the trial)
* They search for or develop a support system where they can openly discuss their feelings. This includes a support group of peers, a prisoner's rights group, family support group or organizations which deal with prisoners and their families
* They ask for support and assistance when going to court

* They prioritize their activities so that all non-essential activities are relegated to a back burner during the trial
* They educate themselves on prison administration, prison law and prison rules
* They keep an active and intimate relationship going with their spouse and children
* They take time out to "smell the roses" along the way
* They know good mental and physical health are important if they want to be of any help to their loved one.

*   *   *

Juliette Trainor, RX Justice says:

Don't stuff it, watch out for health and stress overload. There is a need to react and a need to stop and regroup. It's the healing process. Support groups need to be prison centered and knowledgeable about prison services. They need to know and understand the process of day to day existence for prisoners and moment to moment emotions. There is no room for power trips, queendoms or fiefdoms. Support groups need to network with other groups, put all jealousy aside, and keep their professionalism at all times. It is this moral and ethical attitude that will facilitate healing.

The gut-wrencher in all of this is that I feel so totally betrayed by a justice system I used to believe in. Now, every waking hour is taken up with thoughts of revenge. If I can't clear these caustic thoughts out of my head, then I'm probably destined for a life of hate.
42-year-old parolee

WHEN THE GATES OF HELL FINALLY OPEN

After a few years inside, the prisoner has forgotten the basics of everyday living, and no attempt is made to prepare him for reentry. Opening a door, which is forbidden in prison, crossing a street, taking a bus, driving a car, banking, shopping for groceries all are foreign to the parolee.

One man, accustomed to standing passively in front of a door until a guard opened it, said when first paroled:

If someone didn't tell me to go and eat, I'd probably stay in this [motel] room until I starved; and if the place caught on fire, I'd probably burn to death before it would occur to me to open the door and walk out.

They give you "gate money," anything from $20 to $100 depending on the state, and they shove you out the gate with a cardboard box that holds everything you own in the world. If you have nobody to pick you up at the gate, or if no bus stops there, you start walking.

If you're lucky to make it that far, you take a bus to whatever town you're paroled to. The bus ticket has taken all your gate money. Now you're supposed to find a job and a place to stay. How you're supposed to do this with no money is beyond me. Unless you have family or friends in the free world to help you get yourself together, you will wind up going back. There's no choice.

*   *   *

"I'm more afraid of getting out than I am of staying in," we were told by an inmate who had served 11 years. "I don't remember how to cross a street or open a door, let alone drive a car or go grocery shopping. I'm scared."

             *   *   *

Many inmates had trouble accepting responsibility or behaving responsibly before they went to prison, which may have helped them to get there in the first place. While in prison they are infantilized, deprived of every vestige of adulthood. Prison is an environment of enforced helplessness and powerlessness. Prisoners are not encouraged to make decisions. They are told when to eat, what to wear, where and when to sit or stand. Making choices is not an option.

If they're lucky, some may be given an opportunity for making the transition back into the free world. They may be given a furlough to find a job and readjust, or paroled to a halfway house where they can slowly become accustomed to freedom.

Others may have had the opportunity while in prison to learn responsibility, get an education or work at a prison job that enabled them to grow.

But most will just one day be thrust out the gates and sent on their way with no money, no job, no prospects, no place to go, nothing to do and nobody to do it with. Their chances of success in the free world are very slim. The least likely to succeed are those who have been housed in a prison mental facility. When their time is served, out they go. When the last dose of medicine wears off, watch out world!

When your loved one comes home, you will feel overjoyed. Then reality will set in. You are used to running the house and disciplining the kids a certain way. Now he may want to take over those responsibilities. He may go a little wild squandering money, start issuing orders like a drill sergeant or be a totally passive couch potato. You may feel like strangers at first, and will have adjustments to make in your sexual relationship.

There will be many other adjustments to be made, too. You don't want him to hang out with his old friends. They helped him get into trouble in the first place. He doesn't want you to hang around with your new friends. He doesn't know who they are and doesn't trust them.

Worst case scenario: the relationship that survived years of incarceration may not survive in the free world. In order to help it survive, you might try these suggestions made by couples who were successful in maintaining their relationship:

* Communicate throughout the prison experience about your day to day lives, about goals and expectations for the future
* meet him at the prison gate if at all possible
* take it slow and easy
* don't make demands
* don't have expectations
* give him a chance to readjust
* don't nag
* give him the opportunity to gradually resume making decisions and taking on responsibilities at his own pace
* remember that you both have changed
* try to remain optimistic
* think about attending a support group or family counseling to help you over the hump
* don't make any hasty decisions about important issues such as buying or selling a house, divorce, having another baby, or moving to another area. Whatever it is, it will keep.

You will probably worry about your loved one getting into trouble again and going back to prison. If this does happen, remember it is not your fault and not your responsibility. Be strong and compassionate at the same time. You both have to adjust.

Sitting behind bars for five years makes a man forget who he is. He can't go to the bathroom or open a door to the outside without someone threatening him. No wonder when he goes home he just sits on his ass. He's scared to death to make a move.

Ex-con on parole

*   *   *

Prison teaches a person to lie in order to open the door. It turns people into dependents, then turns them lose without anything and says to be independent.

Danny "Red Hog" Martin, *Committing Journalism*

PAROLE SNAFU

The mother of a prison inmate told us about a problem that almost cost her son his freedom:

One week before my son was to be released from prison, he was detained for outstanding warrants. These warrants originated from the same charges that put him in prison in the first place. My son's crime spanned two different counties and each had it's own record division.

When he was first arrested, my son went to court in one county to stand trial on both county's charges. What he didn't know was that the other county hadn't bothered to take those charges off its records. Hence the outstanding warrants.

After we found out about the warrants, I spoke to a public defender. She told me to make a copy of my son's trial transcripts and take them to the District Attorney's Office. I made sure the D.A. knew this was a "double jeopardy" situation and that my son was now sitting in jail waiting for the outcome. The D.A. told me it could take up to six weeks for a new trial. I went ballistic inside, but outwardly maintained my dignity. Meanwhile, my son, who already had a job waiting and a new wife at home, sat in jail, helpless to do anything. He was depressed and suicidal.

I gathered all of my wits and hit the public defender's office again. She understood what was a stake. She called the D.A. and they met. Since I already had the arrest records and court transcripts, neither department had to spend valuable time to send away for them. This helped tremendously.

Court was set for the end of the week. By then, my son had spent an additional seven days behind bars, and he had lost his new job. All of this foul-up could have been averted by having a records check done at least six months before the parole date. That way, there won't be any horrendous surprises.

    *   *   *

About six months before your loved one is due to be paroled, ask him to obtain two forms from his counselor. In California, those are Penal Code 1381 and Vehicle Code 41500. Other states use different, but similar, forms.

P.C. 1381 gives permission to search for any outstanding warrants. V.C. 41500 searches the Department of Motor Vehicles for any outstanding warrants or tickets. In California, anyone who has spent time in prison can send the vehicle code form to the DMV. It will then erase all prior tickets and failures to appear. It may take a few months, but afterwards, he will have a clean slate as far as tickets are concerned. If he didn't do this while in prison, he can ask his parole agent for the form once he is paroled. Doing this can prevent a snafu.

A California law enacted in 1988 allows the governor to overrule the parole board and cancel scheduled releases of murderers convicted prior to 1988. In theory the law is said to be "neutral" because the governor can review both grants and denials of parole. Effectively, however, the governor has never invoked this law to review a parole denial.

In 1996, Governor Pete Wilson signed legislation preventing murderers from earning "good time" credit that would reduce their sentence for good behavior or time worked in prison.

Parolees are required to sign a "conditions of parole" form. Refusal to sign will cause the parole to be rescinded. Conditions of parole generally relate to the past crime or to possible future crimes. The person can be forbidden to work at certain jobs or from associating with certain people. It can require narcotics testing or participation in rehabilitation programs such as Alcoholics Anonymous (AA).

Parole may be revoked if the parolee commits a new crime or a parole violation such as drinking alcoholic beverages. If the person is found not guilty of a new criminal charge, parole may still be revoked. It has been ruled that such revocation does not constitute double jeopardy.

*   *   *

One young woman told us her experiences with parole:

Having my husband, Ethan, home from prison for our first anniversary was very important to me. We were childhood sweethearts and we had gotten married while he was in prison.

When Ethan called, I thought he was being paroled early, but what he said chilled me to the bone. "I can't come home," he said. "They won't let me parole in that county."

The crime was committed 250 miles away from our home. The law stated that he had to be paroled to the county where the crime occurred. Because we lived in a county with a high parolee count, Ethan was denied permission to transfer there. Even though that count changed daily, the parole agents refused his request.

Ethan was arrested on suspicion of drunk driving. When the police pulled him over, they rammed his truck with their car. Ethan, seeing that his truck was about to be hit, cranked the wheel and tried to move out of the way. Unfortunately, he moved into the path of a second police car. He was traveling less than five miles per hour.

The prosecutor charged him with felony evasion, and assault against a peace officer with a deadly weapon. There was no evidence of drunk driving and the medical records supported this. Those charges were dropped. Nevertheless, the courts sentenced him to three years in prison for the evasion and assault.

When he was finally paroled, I met him at the gate. Since there had been a mix up in his parole date, his gate money wasn't there. I wondered what others guys did in this situation. Did they have to knock over a grocery store in order to eat?

We arrived at his new home town two hours later, an hour before the scheduled meeting with his parole agent, so we took a tour of the area. It was the largest town in the entire county, but it looked small and bleak. It didn't have much in the way of apartments or jobs. His parole agent told us, "This is a small town. We don't have facilities for single men, and jobs are scarce. Across the street is the homeless shelter. You can stay there a couple of nights. After that you're on your own."

I was devastated. "But how," I asked, "is he going to survive. He didn't get his gate money. How will he eat?"

"The shelter serves dinner. He can eat there," the agent said.

We were in a dilemma. I owned a house and a car, and Ethan had a job waiting for him in our home town. Here, he had nothing. "If this is the best this town can offer," Ethan said, "can you help me transfer to my home town?"

"Sorry," the parole agent said. "I've been told they won't have you up there because you assaulted an officer."

"I've never assaulted anyone," Ethan shouted.

The agent glanced at the transcripts and smiled. "I know, but according to those guys up north, you're a vicious criminal."

I was astounded. "But he's never been in trouble with the law before. How can he be labeled a vicious criminal if all he's ever done is swerve to avoid hitting a police car?"

"I understand, but they don't. If he has relatives near by, I may be able to let him stay there."

Ethan's mother lived in another county twenty-five miles away. He had been visiting her when he was arrested. The parole agent worked with us and got Ethan transferred to her house. His gate money arrived six weeks later. If his mother hadn't lived nearby, Ethan would not have had a place to live or food to eat. The day after he moved, he got a job.

I went back to my house, called the Department of Corrections and asked who was in charge of parole. They gave me names of the people to talk to. I gathered all of our friends together and we sent 86 letters to the Parole Board, The Director of the Department of Corrections, the Board of Prison Terms, the Parole and Community Services Division, several prisoner's rights groups and to my U. S. Senator. For a variety of reasons, they all refused to help. It seemed as if the whole parole system was designed to set the parolee up for failure.

Meanwhile, Ethan had to take two hours off work every week to travel to his parole agent's office in the next county. This was beginning to upset his employer. I spent a ton of money on travel to see him, and soon I became pregnant. Now, more than ever, I wanted my husband living with me.

I found the parole code in the law library and thought it might help. In the Penal Code Book: "the period immediately following incarceration is critical to successful reintegration of the offender into society and to positive citizenship."

Ethan's parole was not designed for a successful reintegration.

According to the code book:
* an inmate may be returned to another county if that would be in the best interests of the public and of the parolee
* The verified existence of a work offer, or an educational or vocational training program
* The last legal residence of the inmate was in another county
* The existence of family in another county with whom the inmate has maintained strong ties and whose support would increase the chance that the inmate's parole would be successfully completed.

In Ethan's best interest, according to the code, he should be moved. The verified existence of work, and the existence of family in another county fit our situation. I used those facts in a letter to my senator to argue for Ethan's transfer.

The Director of Corrections responded to the senator's inquiry by saying "the wife and child are being supported by General Assistance and have no other means of support. Additionally, Parolee Calder would also be supported by public assistance if he were allowed to transfer. Based on that, parolee Calder does not meet the criteria for transfer and his request has been denied."

I was on public assistance, but I also had a part-time job and I was in college full time. To deny my husband a transfer on the possibility that he might receive public assistance is like shooting a dog because he might bite. My husband has always had a job. It wasn't until he was arrested that I had to rely, in part, on welfare. The other issues of family and a job evidently didn't matter to them, nor did the Director even look at the fact that Ethan was now working. He had made assumptions that weren't valid.

I found the Department of Corrections uncaring about the future of one of its parolees. Whether or not his reintegration into society was successful, those bureaucrats couldn't care less. Our legislators had nothing but disdain for the difficulty an ex-offender faces when he is released, and his plight. They did nothing to help.

In the end, I moved to his mother's home town. We have our own house now and we are expecting a baby girl soon. The parole agent assigned to us is supportive and seems to understand the hopelessness most parolees face. We have another three months before Ethan is released from parole. I'm glad it's over, but until then, I sleep light. You never know when they might plant something on us.

*   *   *

COMPASSIONATE RELEASE

AIDS has brought the subject of compassionate release to the forefront. Prisoners afflicted with terminal illnesses in the past have often sought compassionate early release so they could die outside of prison surrounded by their loved ones, but they were few in number.

Now that AIDS is rampant among prisoners, the numbers of such inmates has grown exponentially and their cases have been given more publicity than previously.

Sadly, it's nearly impossible to obtain early release for compassionate reasons. Theoretically, this privilege is available to those serving determinate or indeterminate sentences of life with the possibility of parole, or less, and to parole violators who have been returned to custody (RTC). It is not available to those whose sentences are death or life without the possibility of parole

(LWOP). Those unfortunates are destined to die in prison.

It's easiest for RTC parole violators to get compassionate release because in most cases they can present their request to their parole agent, and do not have to go before a judge. The parole agent has the authority to order their release.

For those serving sentences, it's another story. They have to petition their sentencing judge. Most often the judge denies the request, or says he wants to wait until the person is sicker. This sometimes results in no release at all, or release just a day or two before death occurs.

Frequently this inmate-patient is so sick and weak, he is unable to sip water, let alone hold a cup. Yet they are chained to their hospital beds, administrations's excuse being that they are an "escape risk."

In most cases where families have been successful in obtaining compassionate release at a time when the patient is still capable of benefiting from it, they have done so by being extremely aggressive in their communications with the Department of Corrections, and enlisting the assistance of very assertive organizations and celebrities.

Sadly, families often spend so much time, energy and money fighting for compassionate release that they don't get a chance to deal with their emotional "unfinished business" with the inmate before he dies.

Judy Greenspan, Director of Catholic Charities of the East Bay HIV/AIDS in Prison Project in Oakland, California, has done as much or more than any other individual to obtain the release of terminally ill inmates from California prisons. She works to help all inmates, not just those with HIV/AIDS, and has received kudos from "Dear Abby" for her efforts. At the risk of causing her to be swamped with mail and phone calls, we want Judy to have public recognition for her untiring efforts and perseverance on behalf of the most helpless and powerless members of society.

*   *   *

Parole is supposed to give the ex-inmate a sporting chance at assimilating back into the free world. The problem with parole is that my parole agent demands that I check in with his office between the hours of eight and five during the week. Of course, he's never in during the lunch hour. Most parolees have to check in weekly, then twice a month after that. After a year of parole, I now have to check in once a month. If the parolee has a job, he must take time from that job to check in with his agent. Valuable hours, not to mention pay, is lost and some employers dislike having their employees take so much time off. This doesn't make it easy to keep a job or to stay out of trouble when we lose our jobs because we've had to take too much time off. I feel lucky that my boss is willing to let me take care of business. Not many do.

32-year-old parolee

PART THREE
DEATH PENALTY - WAITING TO DIE
Look in the Tiger's Eye
Death Row Inmate-San Quentin

Once I was asked "What is it like to do time in prison?" After much thought, I tried desperately to explain.

Have you ever been to the Zoo and seen the look in the Tiger's eye, as he looks out at you?

He's just a Tiger, raised by the Laws of the Jungle, but had he broken one? You see the farmer had over sixty sheep, the Tiger had none. Did the Tiger kill from hunger? The farmer claims it was in fun.

Hunted down and sent to a Zoo, pacing endlessly back and forth in his steel cage, hoping to find his way as the watchers walk on by. Some even poke at him with sticks or throw things and run. Why should they care, the judging has already been done.

Months of whips and pain, steel cages and chains, start to erase memories of a Life he once knew. The pacing gets him nowhere now, just a little more lost and confused.

Even his keepers are saying he must be locked-up forever because he's not really a Tiger anymore. He can't even return to the Jungle and live. Hell he doesn't even know now what the sheep was killed for.

And what will become of this Tiger, this once great proud Tiger with eyes filled with Life and Fire? Just look what they've done to you. His soul is slowly dying. Surely yours would die too, if they took everything you ever Loved away from you.

You've asked me what it's like to do prison time? So keeping to the Truth, the next time you're at the zoo, just Look deep into the Tigers eyes, when he's looking out at you.

There is always an easy solution to every human problem: neat, plausible and wrong.
H. L. Mencken

Living on death row is a lot like childhood: the days go too slow and the years go too fast.
Anonymous Death Row Inmate

THOSE WITHOUT THE CAPITAL GET THE PUNISHMENT

Arguments favoring the death penalty are based upon one emotion, revenge: the desire to inflict pain in retaliation for pain. People are afraid of crime, and look to politicians for a solution. Politicians support the death penalty because their "tough on crime" posturing assures them of votes, while it enables them to avoid addressing the real social and economic issues that are the root causes of crime.

There have never been more than 200 executions in the United States in any one year. It's not logical to believe that executing fewer than 200 people who are locked up and out of circulation, whose crimes occurred several years previously, will eliminate crimes that are happening today or prevent those that will happen tomorrow.

Arguments opposing the death penalty are based on fact and logic, not emotion:
* The death penalty is expensive. Contrary to popular belief, it costs less to imprison someone for life than it does to execute him. If life in prison averages 40 years, at the cost of $20,000 a year, the cost of life imprisonment is around $800,000. A New York study revealed it cost $1.8 million to try an indigent defendant in a capital case. Most of that cost is not for the so-

called "endless" appeals. The greatest portion of the cost is at the trial level, spent by the prosecution, not by the defense. Some death cases cost upward of $5 million. A California study showed that taxpayers could save $90 million a year if the death penalty were eliminated there.

* The death penalty is not the only way to deal with the crime of murder. Life in prison without possibility of parole protects the public from the offender. In addition, the murderer can work in prison, pay restitution to his victim's family, pay part of his own living expenses and help support his own family.

* The death penalty is not "fair" (however you define "fair"). "Those who have no capital get the punishment," the saying goes. There is no recorded case of a wealthy person being executed in this country. The death penalty is not reserved for the "most heinous" crimes, but for the unluckiest defendants who have the poorest legal representation and are up against zealous prosecutors who are looking to build their careers on a particular case. Of about 25,000 homicides in the U. S. annually, only about 300 defendants are sentenced to death, and only a few are actually executed. More people have been executed in Texas in 1996 than ever before, but those numbers still hold true in general.

* Innocent people are wrongfully convicted and executed. In this country, in this century, about 400 people are known to have been wrongly convicted for murders they did not commit. Of those, 23 were actually executed, while the rest were exonerated or died in prison.

* The death penalty is racist. Most executions are of blacks who have killed whites. Out of more than 15,000 recorded executions in this country, only 31 have been of whites who killed blacks. Black males represent only 6 percent of the total population but, disproportionately, comprise about 42 percent of the death row population nationally.

* The death penalty does not help victims' families. Prosecutors tell families that the death of the perpetrator will heal their emotional wounds, but this has been proven to be false. Instead,

victims' families who expected to feel a sense of relief or "closure" after witnessing the execution of the person who killed their loved one, tell of feeling empty, disappointed and cheated when the promised healing did not occur. Families of murder victims would be better served if the money spent to execute the perpetrator were instead diverted to provide them with counseling.

* The death penalty has been abolished in virtually all modern industrialized nations. We are in the company of Iraq, Iran, China, Russia, Nigeria, Singapore, Turkey, Saudi Arabia, Japan and Yemen.

* The death penalty has been denounced by most major religious groups. The Roman Catholic Church has revised its official catechism to reflect the position that the death penalty is not acceptable under any circumstances. (Previously the Catholic catechism said it was allowable in certain extreme cases.) Literal interpretation of selected Biblical passages, often quoted out of context by advocates of the death penalty, corrupt the compassionate and redemptive spirit of Christianity.

*   *   *

Mick Mandeville of San Gabriel, California writes in the January/February 1997 issue of *The Pilgrimage*, a publication of the Louisiana Coalition to Abolish the Death Penalty, about the May 3, 1996, execution of his friend Keith "Danny" Williams, at San Quentin:

I am unable to go write off Danny as just another statistic. During the years of our correspondence and when I visited him on the row, I found him to be another human being, one who did indeed commit violence against others, having been convicted of three murders. But he was also a husband, a father and a grandfather. . . as a person [who advocates] the abolition of the death penalty, I pray for the victims of crimes and their families, for those executed and their families, and for those who participate in executions in my name.

*   *   *

> There is no "humane" way to destroy another human. Execution is the most premeditated form of killing and is a necrophilic sado-ritual catering to attitudes of vengeance and retribution, attitudes which are destructive to a just and merciful society.
>
> Jerome D. Gorman, M.D.

Legislators in Arizona and Georgia have introduced bills providing for the harvesting of organs from death row inmates for transplantation. The proposal calls for them to be executed by guillotine before becoming "donors." The Arizona bill was defeated; the Georgia bill remains pending.

*   *   *

Since a man executed by electrocution in Florida was burned alive because of faulty equipment (April, 1997), a bill was introduced in the legislature there to switch to the guillotine. The warden assured spectators that the man, an immigrant from Cuba who protested his innocence until the end, definitely suffered no pain. Even if he did, the governor opined, so what? "We don't want y'all to feel sorry for these killers."

*   *   *

Harvard law professor Alan Dershowitz says "Capital punishment is one of the great scandals [in America]. You are ten times more likely to get the death penalty if you are black and kill a white. Effectively, we have no death penalty for killing a black person. The states are cutting back on defense. Most places give you only $1,000 to defend a death penalty case. Innocent people are being executed." Dershowitz also said in a TV interview that his office "never turn[s] down a death penalty case."

*   *   *

> No laws are binding on the human subject which assault
> the body or violate the conscience.
>   Sir William Blackstone, Commentaries, 1765

"How awful does a lawyer have to be?" asks Bruce Shapiro in an article in *The Nation* (April 7, 1997). Apparently pretty bad, when appellate courts rule that just because a lawyer is drunk, sleeps throughout the trial, presents no defense, or all three, that's no reason to believe his client didn't receive a fair trial.

"The Constitution says that everyone's entitled to an attorney of their choice. But the Constitution does not say that the lawyer has to be awake," said Judge Doug Shaver of the Texas District Court.

The nation's death rows are largely populated with people whose lawyers have never tried a criminal, let alone a death penalty, case; who have legendary drug and alcohol dependencies; and who are utterly unprepared to conduct a defense. Judge Shaver said he thought the lawyer sleeping was "a strategic move on [the lawyer's] part."

         *   *   *

In Kentucky, court appointed lawyers are paid $2,500 for an entire capital trial; in Alabama $1,000; in Mississippi less than $12 an hour.

Fresno County (California) in 1996 instituted a fee cap of $40,000 for a court appointed lawyer in a capital case. The plan has been called by some "HMO law," comparing it to the practice of medicine in health maintenance organizations, where doctors are given bonuses if they don't hospitalize patients. The "HMO" lawyer gets to keep all the money if he doesn't hire an investigator or any expert witnesses: anyone he hires, he pays for out of "his" $40,000.

         *   *   *

A correctional officer who privately deplores the abuse of prisoners told us this story, which typifies the sort of petty meanness prison officials often exhibit towards inmates:

A condemned prisoner was within six hours of execution. He had said good-bye to his family and was sitting, shackled, wringing his hands, in his bare death watch cell. At the very moment the guard was bringing the man his last meal, the phone rang. The guard set the tray down on the desk in front of the cell, in view of the condemned man, and answered the phone. It was the governor's office; the man had been granted a 60 day stay of execution. Without saying anything to the prisoner, the guard proceeded to eat the food, noisily slurping, smacking his lips and commenting on how good it tasted.

"Hey, that's my food, what are you doing?," the prisoner cried out. The guard didn't answer until he had finished eating. "You're not entitled," the guard said, laughing. Only then did he tell the man he had been given a reprieve.

*   *   *

The Catholic Church opposes capital punishment in all cases without exception. Cardinals Pio Laghi and Joseph Ratzinger, high church prefects, announced this change in church policy in May, 1997.

Previously, the Catholic Catechism, containing the official doctrines of the church, said the death penalty was acceptable "in cases of extreme gravity." In a 1995 encyclical "The Gospel of Life" Pope John Paul II wrote that cases in today's world that meet the test of "extreme gravity" are "very rare, if not practically nonexistent."

A new official Latin language Catechism published in the autumn of 1997 dropped the "extreme gravity" clause, and clearly reflects the church's new official position that the death penalty is absolutely and unequivocally unacceptable under any circumstances.

Archbishop Renato R. Martino, the Vatican's delegate to the United Nations, said "In the most serious cases, imprisonment for the duration of one's life protects society, while at the same time it safeguards the community from becoming a vindictive, bloodthirsty murderer itself."

*   *   *

Proponents of the death penalty claim that victims' families receive solace or "closure" when the person who killed their loved one is executed. Some relatives of murder victims say they believed this when it was told to them at the time of the trial by police and prosecutors, but when the execution actually took place, their grief did not magically disappear. Some say they felt "emptiness" or "nothing."

Not all victims' families want the perpetrator executed. Murder Victims' Families for Reconciliation (MVFR) is an organization of those who have chosen to forgive the killer and get on with their lives. They vigorously oppose capital punishment. (See Appendix for more about MVFR).

Comedian Bill Cosby and his wife Camille did not object to the decision of Los Angeles County prosecutors when they announced they would not seek the death penalty against the alleged killer of the Cosbys' son, Ennis.

The unnamed father of a victim of the Oklahoma City bombing said in a TV interview that he felt "compassion" for the father of convicted terrorist Timothy McVeigh. The grieving man said he felt no pity for the younger McVeigh, but that he could see and feel the anguish of the elder McVeigh and felt sorry for him.

*   *   *

When President Clinton signed the so-called anti-terrorism legislation, included was a one year deadline for filing federal appeals of state death sentences. While the Supreme Court is considering the issue, the 9th Circuit Court of Appeals ruled that under certain circumstances the time can be extended.

The intent of the law was to make federal appeals, and thus executions, occur much more speedily than in the past.

*   *   *

The death penalty as currently administered in our country is "marred by unfairness and racial injustice." Robert Gray, a Virginia lawyer, told a meeting of the American Bar Association "it is . . . unacceptable to administer the ultimate punishment in a racially discriminatory way."

*   *   *

According to the Death Penalty Information Center, the number of executions by states since 1976 is:

Texas	119	Nevada	5
Virginia	39	Utah	5
Florida	39	California	4
Missouri	24	Indiana	4
Louisiana	24	Mississippi	4
Georgia	22	Nebraska	2
Alabama	15	Pennsylvania	2
Arkansas	15	Washington	2
South Carolina	11	Oregon	2
Oklahoma	9	Maryland	1
Delaware	8	Montana	1
North Carolina	8	Wyoming	1
Illinois	8	Idaho	1
Arizona	7		

*   *   *

The American Bar Association (ABA) House of Delegates, at a February, 1997 meeting in San Antonio, TX, by a vote of 280 to 119, urged an immediate moratorium on executions until the judicial process meets the Association's standard of fairness. The resolution was approved despite opposition from President Clinton and the Association's own president.

The group did not come out against the death penalty, but only addressed the issue of the unfair administration of it. In a position paper, the ABA reiterated themes familiar to death penalty opponents: discrimination against minorities and a shortage of qualified defense lawyers. The ABA had previously adopted policies that call for competent lawyers for all capital defendants, federal court review of state cases, elimination of racial discrimination in capital cases, and no executions of defendants who are mentally retarded or under age 18.

The ABA urged each jurisdiction that imposes capital punishment not to implement the death penalty unless they ascertain that death penalty cases are administered fairly and impartially in accordance with due process, and that all precautions are taken to minimize the risk of executing an innocent person.

*   *   *

"I am outraged that prison authorities would deny those on death row, soon to be executed, spiritual comfort and forgiveness," wrote Catholic Bishop Walter Sullivan of the Diocese of Richmond to the Director of the Virginia Department of Corrections.

The Bishop had been refused permission in 1996 to administer the Sacrament of the Sick and Dying, also called Last Rites, to three Catholic prisoners who were scheduled to be put to death. Prison authorities gave as a reason that the prison was on a "routine lockdown."

In 1995, Virginia prison authorities pulled a similar stunt when they denied a Baptist minister permission to baptize a prisoner prior to execution. The reason given was that he had already been baptized. Authorities were unmoved by the minister's explanation that those of the Baptist faith often undergo successive baptisms after experiencing religious "rebirths."

California correctional authorities told a condemned prisoner who was scheduled to die in August, 1997 that his spiritual advisor, an ordained minister, could not stay with him during his last hours. The minister had previously been allowed to remain with other condemned inmates until the end. After a law suit, the CDC told the minister she could remain, but could not use the bathroom during the entire evening. After a second law suit, they told her she could use the bathroom, but would be subject to a complete strip search that could take an hour or more each time she used the facility. The necessity for this was not made clear, as she and the inmate would not be in physical contact during the last hours. They would be separated by cell bars in full view of a guard at all times. The issue was rendered moot when the man was given a temporary stay.

*   *   *

The United States has the distinction of being the death penalty capital of the Western World. Texas is the state whose claim to fame is "everything is bigger," and that applies to capital punishment along with everything else. As of June 1997, the

Lone Star State boasts 119 executions since the end of the moratorium in 1976. If it continues at its present pace, it may soon lay claim to more state sanctioned slaughter than all the other states put together.

Executions in Texas have become so boringly routine of late that everyone connected with them, except for the "guest of honor" and his loved ones, is apparently underwhelmed. More than 20 executions have already taken place in the first half of 1997. Media and victims' relatives don't even bother to show up any more. The usual contingents of beer swilling, epithet shouting proponents are noticeable by their absence, as are the hymn singing, candle waving abolitionists. Texas has managed to achieve mass apathy by making executions humdrum non-events.

Instead of killing them just after midnight like all the other states, Texas has moved the witching hour up to 6 P.M. When executions were done in the dark and secrecy of the middle of the night, hundreds often flocked to the killing grounds to enjoy the show. Texas has discovered the secret of making murder by the state go unnoticed: do it at the height of the commuter rush hour and the dinner hour. Nobody cares enough, apparently, to brave the traffic and miss their supper just to watch some guy die. Been there, done that. Ho hum.

At one recent Texas execution, it was reported, an official of the Department of Criminal Justice stood around munching on a pretzel. Then he invited the handful of people who showed up to witness the happening to join him in a betting pool. What time would the executee die? Nobody won that time. One reporter bragged that he had attended 70 or more executions, more than any other person in the country.

The family of the man being executed were kept separate from the other onlookers. The guards who were keeping watch over the man's niece and his 77-year-old mother apparently did not consider the execution a solemn occasion, nor did they seem to respect the grief of the family they were "escorting." They stood about until the end cheerfully chatting about their kids, the Little League team and what they were going to do on their day off.

Harris County (Houston) District Attorney Johnny Holmes boasts he has sent about 30 percent of its 450 inmates to Texas' death row. He brags that he is the "winner" of more death sentences than any other prosecutor in America.

          *   *   *

Columnist Molly Ivins writes:
In my state of Texas, the death penalty is now an assembly-line process: You convict 'em, we fry 'em. We are dead-beddin' folks down here so fast and so often, you can't get people to raise an eyebrow over it, no matter what the specifics of a case are. I remember the first time we executed a man we knew was innocent - you couldn't get anyone excited about that, either.
The common misimpression is that in order to draw the death penalty, you have to be guilty of a truly heinous crime. Wrong. You don't have to be accused of a particularly horrible crime to draw the death penalty; you don't even have to be guilty. Since the Supreme Court reinstated the death penalty in 1976, sixty-three death row inmates have been set free after it was conclusively proved that they were not guilty of the crimes for which they had been sentenced to die. Those guys had some bad lawyers.

          *   *   *

Amnesty International has expressed concern about the situation in Texas. The group said it understood Americans' desire to bring an end to crime and violence, but "the death penalty only foments that violence."

          *   *   *

The United Nations has adopted by a vote of 27-11 a U.N. Human Rights Commission resolution urging nations who have not yet abolished capital punishment to do so. The United States was the only Western nation to vote against the bill. The other 10 "no" votes were cast by Algeria, Bangladesh, Bhutan, China, Egypt, Indonesia, Japan, Malaysia, Pakistan and South Korea.

          *   *   *

A high school student told us:
My teacher assigned us to write an essay on any topic

of our choice. I wrote about why I oppose the death penalty.
The teacher gave me an F. She said the spelling, grammar,
punctuation, and all that were fine, but she gave me an F
because she disagreed with the content. She said I was "stupid"
because "everybody knows those creeps deserve to die."

Other students wrote in favor of such controversial issues
as gay weddings, corporal punishment of children and the
legalization of marijuana, and against abortion, curfews for teens
and school prayer. None of them got an F and none was graded
on the content of their paper.

That F changed my grade for the semester. I petitioned
the principal, and then the school board, and they backed up
the teacher. The principal said I had "no right" to have such
"subversive" ideas. He told me I could re-write the essay with
the opposite viewpoint, but I refused to do it. I kept the F. This
experience has really turned me off about school. The teacher,
principal and school board, all of them are the "thought police."
What gives them the right to tell me what I'm allowed to think?

            *   *   *

"If you knew your brother had committed a serious crime, one
that might possibly get him the death penalty, would you turn him in to
the authorities?" was the question du jour on a radio call-in talk show.

David Kaczynski, brother of accused Unabomber suspect
Theodore "Ted" Kaczynski, had to make that painful decision.
He pleaded that "people see him [Ted] as a human being."

A woman building contractor said "If my brother did what
Ted Kaczynski supposedly did, I'd try to get help for him first. If
I knew the Justice Department was going after the death penalty,
I'd sure think twice about turning him in."

"Two wrongs don't make a right," said Larry, a firefighter.
"The guy sounds to me like he's off balance. Do we want to
execute a guy who's mentally ill?"

A social worker said "The guy needs to be in a locked mental
facility, not in a prison." Another social worker said "He did some
pretty horrible things. I hope he's locked up for the rest of his life."

In a New York Times interview, David Kaczynski said if his
brother is convicted of the bombings, he hopes he will be spared the
death penalty. "If he did attack and kill people, that was wrong. But

it would be equally wrong if he were killed for some notion of justice."

In May, 1997, Attorney General Janet Reno announced the Justice Department would seek the death penalty for Ted Kaczynski.

*   *   *

> He does not sit with silent men
> Who watch him night and day;
> Who watch him when he tries to weep,
> And when he tries to pray;
> Who watch him lest himself should rob
> The scaffold of its prey.
> Oscar Wilde, *Ballad of Reading Gaol*

> Knowingly hanging the wrong man with the blessing of the Supreme
> Court should become the basis for a political and social movement.
> Phil Gaspar, College of Notre Dame

THE SUPREMES SING ABOUT CAPITAL PUNISHMENT

Various past and present members of the Supreme Court have widely divergent opinions on the death penalty in general, and whether or not it's okay to slaughter the innocent with their judicial blessing. Once you've been found guilty, it seems you remain "legally" guilty forever, even though you can show you are "factually" innocent. This legal quirk makes you eligible to be the guest of honor at a lynching. Two who say mere innocence shouldn't disrupt the execution process are:

CHIEF JUSTICE WILLIAM H. REHNQUIST [Herrera v. Collins, 1993] rendered the opinion that some wrongful convictions and even executions of innocent defendants must be tolerated: Because of the very disruptive effect that entertaining claims of actual innocence would have on the need for finality in capital cases, and the enormous burden that having to retry a case based on often stale evidence would place on the State.

JUSTICE ANTONIN SCALIA, concurring [Herrera v. Collins] There is no basis in text, tradition or even in contemporary service for finding in the Constitution a right to demand judicial consideration of newly discovered evidence of innocence brought forward after conviction.

Other Justices express varying degrees of revulsion at the idea of intentionally executing the innocent.

JUSTICE HARRY A. BLACKMUN, dissenting [Herrera v. Collins]
Nothing could be more contrary to contemporary standards of decency, or more shocking to the conscience, than to execute a person who is actually innocent.

JUSTICE BLACKMUN [Herrera v. Collins]
A truly persuasive demonstration of "actual innocence" made after trial would render the execution of a defendant unconstitutional. The question is what a "truly persuasive demonstration" entails.

JUSTICE BLACKMUN, prior to his 1994 retirement
From this day forward I shall no longer tinker with the machinery of death . . . I feel morally and intellectually obligated to concede that the death penalty experiment has failed.

JUSTICE BLACKMUN
The execution of a person who can show that he is innocent comes perilously close to murder.

When declaring capital punishment unconstitutional in 1972 the Supreme Court said it is "arbitrary and capricious" and "harsh and freakish."

JUSTICE LEWIS F. POWELL, 1994
I have come to think that capital punishment should be abolished because it brings discredit to the whole system and it serves no useful purpose.

JUSTICE WILLIAM BRENNAN
It smacks of little more than a lottery system.

JUSTICE THURGOOD MARSHALL
A state has no legitimate interest in killing a man sooner than

later. If there is any chance that a defendant has a valid objection to his conviction or sentence, elementary principles of justice require that his attorneys be afforded a full opportunity to present that claim before the issue is rendered moot by death.

JUSTICE THURGOOD MARSHALL
No matter how careful courts are, the possibility of perjured testimony, mistaken honest testimony and human error remains too real. We have no way of judging how many innocent persons have been executed, but we can be certain that there were some.

JUSTICE WILLIAM O. DOUGLAS, 1972
One searches our chronicles in vain for the execution of any member of the affluent strata of this society.

*   *   *

For each man kills the thing he loves
Yet each man does not die
Oscar Wilde, *Ballad of Reading Gaol*

YOU'RE S.O.L.

The Statute of Limitations, in legal lingo abbreviated S.O.L., refers to the time limit after which an action (law suit) can no longer be brought. The S.O.L. in some civil cases is one year. For some criminal cases, it may be as long as 7 to 10 years. For murder, there is no S.O.L.: you can be arrested and tried whenever they catch you, even if it's 50 years after the crime.

You go to trial, and you are convicted. But you really are innocent. You uncover some exculpatory evidence, proof of your innocence, after you've been in prison for a while. Maybe the real murderer reads about your case in the paper, feels guilty, and confesses to the crime. Or your missing alibi witness suddenly turns up. Your lawyers try to get you a new trial based on this new evidence, which wasn't available at the time of your trial.

Too bad. You're S.O.L., in both meanings of the phrase. The Statute of Limitations says you're S— Outta Luck. This is because the law strictly limits the amount of time during which you can present new evidence. It doesn't matter that the evidence was unavailable previously. That's your problem. Tough luck.

From the day you're convicted, you'll sit in jail until you're sentenced, maybe a month or more. When sentenced, you'll sit in jail until they get around to moving you to a prison, maybe a few weeks more. When you get to prison, they'll hold you in an "Adjustment Center" for a while, maybe from 30 to 60 or even 90 days, so you can "adjust" to your new surroundings. Then they might ship you out to another prison, depending on how you're classified. In this other prison, you may again spend a few days, weeks or months getting "adjusted." You'll be "adjusted" so often, you'll never again need a Chiropractor.

During all the time from when you're convicted until you're fully "adjusted," you will probably have limited or no access to visitors, letter writing materials, phone calls, your lawyer, or the box of legal papers you're going to use to get your appeal started. During this time, your incoming mail will be misdirected, and, if you get it at all, it will take weeks to catch up with you.

Finally, the big day comes. They house you in a permanent cell, and give you back your belongings. You take out your yellow legal pad and the two-inch pencil stub they've generously issued you, and you start to write your motion for a new trial based on the new evidence.

"Don't waste your time," your cellie says, "it's too late. You're S.O.L." He shows you his law book. He ain't jivin'. The time limits on submitting exculpatory evidence are these: in 17 states it has to be filed within 60 days of sentencing, including Virginia, where you're S.O.L. after 21 days and Texas, S.O.L. after 30 days; in 10 states, District of Columbia and Federal - 2 years; in 8 states - between 1 and 3 years; in 6 states - more than 3 years; and in 9 states - there's no time limit.

*   *   *

" . . . we must insist on a change in our own Supreme Court's approach
to new evidence in capital cases. Our Supreme Court has so weakened
the constitutional rights of capital defendants that we have created a
genuine risk that the innocent will be executed. Just as there is no statute
of limitations on murder, there can be no statute of limitations on newly
discovered evidence of innocence, especially in capital cases,"
                Alan Dershowitz says in *The Abuse Excuse*,
                (1994, Little Brown & Company).

        *   *   *

HOW ROGER COLEMAN GOT TO BE S. O. L.

"Virginia law provides no legal remedy for the convicted
if the evidence of their innocence is discovered more than 21
days after trial," the Commonwealth high court ruled in the case
of Roger Coleman. This bizarre miscarriage of justice, which came
to its tragic conclusion with Coleman's 1992 execution for the
murder of his sister-in-law, lives in infamy in the annals of
American jurisprudence. Coleman, who was almost certainly
innocent of the crime, was convicted on circumstantial evidence
manufactured by police and prosecutors, and the testimony of a
jailhouse snitch who swore Roger "confessed" to him. Evidence
pointing to Roger's innocence was concealed by the prosecution
at the time of trial.

When another man confessed to the killing six years after
Coleman's conviction, the Virginia Attorney General's office said
"Even if the alleged confession were true, it would not constitute
grounds for judicial relief because the commonwealth had no
knowledge of any such confession at the time of the trial." No
kidding. Duh. Nobody else did, either, because the man didn't
confess until six years after Coleman's conviction.

Certainly in any other country some court or government
agency would have investigated to see if the confession were
true. Certainly any civilized government would have considered
it more important to save the life of an innocent man than to stick
steadfastly to the letter of the law. In this country, we have no
mechanism by which a person can re-open the issue

of factual innocence once they have been judged guilty. Innocent people are slain in our execution chambers by government officials who shrug and say "Tough luck" rather than concede they convicted the wrong person.

Our "justice" system has no mechanism for the review of a factually innocent person's case, but that well-kept secret is not shared with the general public. The media, TV in particular, gets away with dispensing disinformation that causes the American public to believe the myth that "no innocent person is ever executed in this country."

A case in point is an episode of "The Commish" that aired in 1996. A condemned inmate is shown kneeling in his cell, about to receive Communion and Last Rites from a priest. His wife is in the cell kneeling in prayer beside him. (This would never be permitted in a real prison.) At the very last moment, as the execution is about to take place, the hero of the piece, the police chief, comes running in yelling words to the effect of "Stop the execution. Hold everything. The real killer has confessed." This could not, will not, and has never happened in the real world. Yet the public is deceived once more into reinforcing the erroneous belief that an innocent person can never be executed here.

The commonwealth of Virginia refused to consider the issue of Roger Coleman's innocence, so his lawyers could do nothing but pursue appeals based on judicial error, the unfairness of the original trial. The beginning of the end came when the attorneys inadvertently filed an appeal in state court one day too late. Because of this procedural violation, the court dismissed the appeal without a hearing.

"Tough on crime" advocates often talk about criminals who are released because of a legal "technicality," though this happens rarely, if ever. But what about this innocent man who was executed because of a legal "technicality?" In America, a man is executed because of a technicality, a piece of paper that was filed a day late. A government allowed one of its citizens to die because it had too much pride to say "Oops." Think about that. It could happen to you.

You must love your family as much as you can, and be prepared for it not to be enough.

Wife of death a row inmate

MOTHERS AND OTHER HUMANS

Excerpts from a dialogue with Aba Gayle, mother of a murder victim, death penalty abolitionist and advocate for the humane treatment of prisoners:

My heart breaks for the mothers of the men on death row. They suffer because their sons are going to be killed, too. I'm starting a foundation to teach the healing power of forgiveness and to support a prison ministry that will provide books, educational supplies and spiritual support for men in California prisons and jails.

Proponents of capital punishment always say the death penalty gives closure to the families of victims, "fixes" it for them. The mother of one victim was very disappointed because she felt the man who killed her son didn't suffer at all when he was executed because she didn't feel anything. She felt nothing when he died and this was disappointing to her; she felt something was going to happen, some closure to her anger. She's glad he's gone so he'll never kill again. She said she wanted to sit down and talk with him before he was executed, but the warden wouldn't let her. She did agree that viewing this execution did her no good whatsoever. Isn't that sad? Underneath all this rage she's a nice lady.

Whether you're the mother of a victim or the mother of a condemned inmate, you feel isolated. You can't tell people who you are, you can't share your life experiences with them.

*   *   *

MY SON WAS WRONGLY CONVICTED

Excerpts from a dialogue with Jackie, the mother of a condemned inmate whom she says was railroaded for a murder he didn't commit:

My son was convicted of a murder he didn't commit and he's on death row. The murder was in 1988. He spent two years in jail awaiting trial and he's been on death row six years.

There's no evidence he did it. There was another person involved who obviously did do it. My son had a terrible defense. The Public Defender was a very quiet man. He gave no opening statement and a very short closing argument.

The defense attorney was offered a judgeship and was made a judge right in the middle of the trial, so his heart wasn't in it anymore. He left the trial at the end of the guilt phase and another attorney took over for the penalty phase. I believe he sold my son out for that judgeship. Once they decide they want to get you, the authorities do what they have to do, lie, whatever it takes. The lawyer had tried a capital case before but he never won one. He did very little; he only made a few objections. He was no Perry Mason. If my son had a better quality defense he wouldn't be where he is today.

He always appears to be in a good mood because he doesn't want me to worry about him. One time he was real nervous and he had cuts on his face. I asked if someone hit him, and he said no, he fell over his shoes, but since then he hasn't gone out on the yard; it's been two or three years. He's lost so much weight, probably from stress. When I visit he has an appetite, and I send him a box of food every three months but he's lost over 50 pounds.

At first I almost had a nervous breakdown and had to go on heavy medication and into therapy. I'm still in therapy. I took Prozac for about two years, 60 milligrams a day. I went without any medication for about a year, and now I'm on Zoloft.

The first time I went to visit I was kind of nervous because I'm going to be locked in the room with murderers. I didn't know what to expect. But now it's not like that. I know a lot of the guys. They don't look menacing; they're just like anybody else. If you were to see them walking down the street you'd never know who they were. And the families, they are very ordinary, too.

Therapy has helped. I and some other mothers tried to start a support group, but nobody would participate.

He calls me every Saturday and I see him once a month. For the most part the staff are nice and friendly except for one guard who's not. He glares at you and acts mean. I've never had any trouble with them. I've become very bitter towards the police, lawyers, judges, the whole justice system. I think it's a bunch of bull. When I get summoned to jury duty I go into a rage and write them a nasty letter. I'm having a real hard time with the anger.

I would advise any other mother to be there for her son,

get his friends to visit, encourage him to practice his religion. Try and keep his hopes up by having a good attitude when you visit. Act cheerful and keep praying.

After my son was convicted I was in a state of shock and I just sort of died. When I woke up my daughter said we need to get a lawyer, so my daughter and I shopped around and we found a lawyer in the phone book. The ad said "have you been wrongly convicted," so we called him. He was real anxious to do this case and he wanted $30,000: a $5,000 retainer and $350 a month for 10 years to do this appeal. He said if we got a new trial he'd do the trial for free. About a year after I started paying him, my son was given a lawyer appointed by the state. This one never even filed an opening brief. The state appointed lawyer told me I shouldn't be paying this other guy because he wasn't qualified, but I felt like this man wanted to help my son, so I continued paying him. After three years of paying him, the private lawyer had still done nothing. The appeals attorney from the state finally convinced me I should do something about it. He referred me to another attorney and I called him and he was really nice, the third attorney. He said there was no way anyone could do a death penalty appeal for $30,000 so this man was scamming me. So I took the first lawyer before the bar association and I won partially. They let him keep $10,000 of my money for "comfort and reassurance." He defrauded me. He had contacted the appeals boards and they told him not to take the case because he wasn't qualified to take a death penalty appeal, so he knew that all along, and he took my money and my son's case anyway. He was supposed to pay me back part of the money, so he paid me a few dollars and declared bankruptcy. The other lawyers said that any lawyer knows it would cost from $100,000 to $200,000 for a capital case appeal.

If lawyers know it would cost this much for an appeal, how can the court turn around and give a $30,000 fee cap for a death penalty trial for a court appointed trial lawyer? The prosecution can spend as much as it wants. The defense gets what amounts to a token amount. It's so unrealistic.

My family has stood by me but friends have not. I don't know if it's my depression. I'm not the same person I was eight years ago.

        *   *   *

RAILROADED

Excerpts from a dialogue with Charla:

Four people were killed. The police botched the investigation. The forensic investigator had no experience and didn't know what he was doing. They never even looked for anyone else. More than 75 people walked through and contaminated the crime scene in the first 24 hours. They found one drop of blood on the wall that didn't belong to a victim so, according to the police, it must have been my friend's. All the evidence was tossed in together by the police, so it was contaminated. There was planted evidence, too.

The media was calling my friend a "mad-dog killer." There was so much media hype there was no way he could get a fair trial. The prosecution used up the one drop of blood for testing, so the defense didn't get any blood to test. They used an old form of DNA test that's obsolete. One survivor of the crime said my friend wasn't the killer, that it was three men. But by the time it got to trial, his story changed. He said he saw only a shadow. The witness saw my friend's picture on TV, and said that wasn't him. It's strange how, if a witness identifies the defendant, the D.A. makes a big thing of it. But if the witness says the defendant is not the killer, the D.A. tells the jury to disregard it, this witness doesn't know what he's talking about. There's a double standard depending whose side the witness is on. Prosecution witnesses are supposedly credible; defense witnesses supposedly are not.

There was no motive, no robbery, but a car was taken. Witnesses said they saw three men driving it, but the police didn't even pursue that lead. A pair of bloody pants was found; the sheriff kept them for six months and then destroyed them. My friend was railroaded. There was a lot of hysteria. He has no family here, so I'm his only support system. When I first started visiting him he was so angry. Now he's just numb, but he hasn't given up.

   *   *   *

TIME WILL TELL

Excerpts from a dialogue with Francine (not her real name) who's trying to figure out how to tell time:

I'm involved with a person who's been on death row now

for 14 years. His death sentence was reversed two and one half years ago, but he still had to stay on the row until he got his new trial. We just had the retrial and he was found guilty of second degree murder.

Now we're trying to figure out what his time is, when he is coming home. The judge said he should be eligible for parole right away. It's very frustrating. The sentence on the second degree murder was two consecutive terms of 15 years to life each, which would be the same as 30 years to life. He was sentenced under the old indeterminate sentence law. He was given credit for 21 years. They said he'd be eligible for parole after 20 years, and he's already done 21.

Nobody seems to know how time is computed. If there's a formula or regulation, it's a well-kept secret. His lawyers don't know. Nobody at the Department of Corrections will tell us. They say they have no idea how it's done. Can you believe that? I've talked to various lawyers who said they will look over his papers, but they're not experts. The DOC is very arbitrary. Somebody just tells you what your time is, and nobody checks their math. My friend has been to meetings with people but they don't even introduce themselves, and when he asks their names, they don't tell him. They work for the DOC, though. I was told a counselor would figure his time. This is a person who works at the prison. Nobody can provide me with any documents that show the formula for computing time. I've been to numerous sources. The DOC is so secretive about figuring time, like it's this big military secret or something. What have they got to hide?

Many of us believed he was innocent of the crime. I've only known him for five years, but I worked on his case as his lawyer's assistant for eight years before that. He never even had a parking ticket in his life. The D.A. was up for re-election. His lawyers had never tried a criminal case, let alone a capital case, before.

His family put up over $50,000 to get who they thought was the best lawyer in town. They had never been involved with the law before. When the family ran out of money, the lawyer handed the case over to the next guy down the line, who had never done criminal law in his entire life.

There's so much evidence in this case proving someone else did it: DNA, foot prints, fingerprints. At the second trial, even though there was no evidence he had done the crime, and all this evidence pointing to someone else, the jury believed they shouldn't find him innocent. They thought they should give him second degree, because he had been convicted of the crime before, and somehow that made him guilty in their sight. Some jurors were crying; they weren't comfortable with their decision. I've been in the legal field now for many years as a paralegal and legal assistant, and I know a trial is nothing more than a performance. The defendant isn't even a part of it. It's all orchestrated by the judge, and whoever puts on the best performance wins the trial. It has nothing to do with the crime. By the time it gets to court, nobody cares about innocence or guilt, either, any more. If the prosecutor outshines the defense lawyer, he wins. The prosecution has all the advantages.

*   *   *

HOW MUCH IS YOUR LIFE WORTH?

Excerpts from a dialogue with Fatimah, a paralegal and part time law student:

The prosecution can spend millions on a case. They have all the resources: investigators, crime lab, experts, plenty of support staff, people to do legal research. The public says the system is skewed in favor of the defense, but that's not true. That's political propaganda. The public defender's office doesn't have the same resources available to it. The judge appoints a lawyer for the defense, and gives him a maximum payment, only as little as $1,000 in southern states, $40,000 in Fresno [CA] County.

Psychiatry and psychology experts get $2,000 or $3,000 a day plus expenses. DNA testing costs money. Ballistics. Investigators get as much as $65 an hour. The lawyer has to pay his office rent, secretary, the cost of photocopying documents. So the court gives him a sum of money, and out of it has to come all these expenses. The lawyer gets to keep whatever is left over. If he wants to get paid for his own work, he says don't bother with experts. We don't need DNA, we don't need ballistics, we don't need a psychiatrist, we don't need an investigator. Like a doctor practicing medicine in an HMO: if he doesn't order an x-ray for the patient, he gets to pocket the cost of the x-ray himself. If he does order it, the doctor winds up paying for it out of his own pocket. That's a conflict of interest for a doctor or a lawyer, isn't it?

It's ludicrous to expect anyone to represent a defendant in a capital case under this system. In this country we're supposed to be entitled to fair representation no matter how much money we have. Public defenders are now talking about charging clients. It defeats the purpose. Where will some homeless person get the money?

They certainly shouldn't have a fee cap. They say it's necessary because the system has been abused. That's ridiculous. If a lawyer cheats by overcharging, then penalize that lawyer. Don't penalize all clients and make them pay with their lives for someone else's defrauding the system.

The state doesn't want to pay lawyers what they're worth. They expect them to work for peanuts. Lawyers in private practice make an average of $250 an hour. Court appointed or appellate lawyers make about $65 an hour, and out of that comes all expenses and overhead. Each defendant should be entitled to the same quality defense O.J. Simpson got. That case is the gold standard as defenses go. Sorry, the pun was not intentional. If we did that, prosecutors wouldn't be dragging people into court for absurd three strikes cases, stealing a piece of pizza, things like that.

There should be no fee cap unless you say to the lawyer this money is for your salary, and the state will foot the bill for investigators, experts, and all the rest, and have it accounted for. This fee cap is penny wise, pound foolish. They save a few bucks on defense at the original trial, everybody winds up with a death sentence, and the state goes broke in the end paying for the appeals. Makes no sense. Cases will be railroaded through, executions will happen much sooner, more innocent people will be executed because they didn't get a meaningful trial or appeal. Everybody loses.

Lawyers don't want to take on an appeal for a pittance and have the responsibility for someone's life. There's an ethical issue when it comes to appeals. A lawyer has a responsibility to do what's best for his client. If representing this client means a quicker execution for his client, it's the lawyer's ethical duty not to take on the case. When they don't get paid enough to make a living, lawyers who don't care about the clients will wind up taking the cases, pocketing the money and not working the case. The lawyers who care, the ethical lawyers, won't touch them. They can't afford to work for nothing, and they won't compromise their integrity or their client's lives by taking the case if they don't intend to give it 110 percent. As usual, it's the defendant who loses.

*   *   *

There is no chapel on the day
On which they hang a man;
The chaplain's heart is far too sick
Or his face is far too wan,
Or there is written upon his eyes
Which none should look upon.
Oscar Wilde, *Ballad of Reading Gaol*

Every noise makes you jump
Death row inmate

EXECUTION NIGHT

From a dialogue with the wife of a death row inmate:

There are all kinds of losses people feel, like when someone dies, or when you lose your job, or retire, or have to give up the house you've lived in forever, or go through a divorce or separation, or have a mastectomy. Then there's the loss women feel when their husband, son or brother goes to prison. I say women because most prisoners are men, and most loved ones left behind are women. I know there are women in prison who leave their men folks behind, but I'm just going to say women for now.

Most of these losses are within the realm of human experience, and sooner or later you can cope with them, at least in many cases. They may be sad and tragic, but stuff happens. You know what I mean. But there's a kind of loss that happens to very few of us, and that's when someone you love goes not just to prison, but to death row.

When he gets sentenced, you feel like you're caught in a giant rat trap, and you're the rat, like a huge door has slammed in your face. And you feel like you're a member of this very exclusive club, one that has only about 3,000 members in the whole country, but it's not an exclusive club you want to belong to. Only a very few people understand how you feel, because it's an experience reserved for so few. And if your man is innocent, or you believe he's innocent, I mean really innocent based on the facts, not just some denial fantasy that he's innocent, but honest-to-God innocent, you can't help but feel a good dose of the "poor-me's." And nobody understands because they just haven't been there.

There's another kind of loss that happens to those of us who belong to this "exclusive club." It's when someone on the row is executed. I don't mean my own husband, God forbid, but one of his friends, someone he and I have come to know and care about. You see, when a man goes to the row, and if he's never been in prison before, like my husband, certain men who are predators may try to befriend him, to take advantage of his naivete and abuse him or misuse him for sex or money or drugs or whatever they can think of in their warped minds.

But not all the men on the row are like that. Some are old convicts, which is what they call themselves, men of respect, who may or may not have committed the crime, but underneath, even if they did the crime, they are decent human beings. And they will take a new fish under their wing, show him the ropes, tell him who to watch out for, even protect him in some situations. And if they believe the new fish is really innocent and wrongly convicted, they will take extra care that he's not hurt in the middle of some brawl or when the guards get trigger happy or things like that.

My husband made a friend like that when he first landed on the row. I got to know this man and his family in the visiting room, and sometimes his daughter and his sister and I would go out for coffee after visiting, and we developed a friendship. We are the only ones who can understand what we are going through, you know what I mean?

Anyway, two weeks ago this man, who had become a dear friend for more than nine years, he was executed. My husband and many of the guys on the row, even some of the guards, missed him and grieved for him. He was a good person.

But just when it was happening, that day, my husband told me some of the guys said they hated him and good riddance. Then afterwards, they said they missed him. I think they do that to spare their feelings. If they pretend they hate the man, they think they won't feel any pain when they lose him. After he's gone, it's okay to admit they liked him.

And I miss him and mourn his passing. And so do some of the other women visitors who had gotten friendly with his family. He only had his sister and daughter, because his wife died of cancer about a month after he was sent up, and his son disowned him because he didn't want to be disgraced.

Anyway, the ones who are left behind, once again, are the women, in this case his sister and daughter. Because they not only lost him, but they lost their reason for being allowed into the visiting room, so they have lost their whole support system. They no longer have access to the visiting room, because you have to be on the list to visit a specific prisoner, so now they have lost their contact with all the women friends they made in there, women who could give them support and who could understand their pain. And now they will have to get a life because every weekend was taken up with visiting the prison. Now they'll have to find something else to do to give meaning to their lives or they'll go nuts.

On the night of the execution - they always seem to hold them at midnight - like it's the eerie witching hour or something - several of us women got together with his sister and daughter at a friend's house. They didn't want to go to the media circus in front of the prison. So after the last visit with him, we drove them to this friend's house, and we stayed with them all night.

It was hell. I wouldn't wish it on my worst enemy. We had the radio and TV on, and it showed the hyenas in front of the prison yelling "Fry him." We could see on the TV that some men were up on top of the wall taking pictures. Later we learned they were from the FBI, and they were taking pictures of the abolitionists, and writing down their license numbers, like they were Communists or something. Then the radio said he got a stay, and we all got hysterical. Then a half hour later the TV said the stay was lifted, and they would proceed to kill him, and we all went numb.

The next day, we all went home to our different home towns, and now his daughter and sister don't have us to lean on anymore, just when they need us the most, it seems. So the family of the guy who's executed, they lose both their loved one, and their support network, all at once.

For the rest of us, sitting there trying to comfort them, it was another kind of hell, too. It seemed like a dress rehearsal for the night when, God forbid, our husband or son or brother would be murdered - yes, I said "murdered" - by the state.

Talk about victims! We are victims, too.

Last week I went to visit my husband, it was a week after the execution. It seemed unusually quiet in the visiting room, not as many visitors as usual, not much talking at all, but a lot of loud laughter that sounded faked and too loud, like one of those laugh tracks on TV. It seemed strange not to see this man, our friend, and out of the corner of my eye I kept thinking I saw him. And I missed seeing his sister and daughter, my friends, too. I miss them a lot.

My husband said the scuttlebutt was that the man went crazy

near the end. The talk was that when that stay came down, and then was lifted, he just fell apart and became incoherent, and was crying, but how can we know if this is true or not. There are so many rumors.

Some of the men, a few days or weeks before they are executed, seem go a little crazy, or a little macho, I'm not sure which. They will tell their wife or girl friend "I don't want you to visit any more, I don't love you any more." Most people, even some of the guards, say they do that because they think if you feel angry or hurt then you won't feel any pain when they die, and they think they're doing you a favor to save your feelings. I think that's crazy, but they say desperate people do desperate things. I have heard of people who are dying in the hospital doing something like that. They tell their family not to visit because they don't want you to see them looking awful with all the tubes and such. They don't seem to understand you can't just turn your feelings off and on because they tell you to. Maybe they're not trying to save your feelings - the men on the row, I mean - maybe they're trying to save their own. If they pick a fight then they don't have to suffer through the pain of the last visit and saying good-bye to you. Yes, I do believe that must be why they do that.

*   *   *

As a general rule, a man is undone by waiting for capital punishment well before he dies. Two deaths are inflicted on him, the first being worse than the second, whereas he killed but once ... Such a basic injustice has repercussions, besides, on the relatives of the executed man. The victim has his family, whose sufferings are generally very great and who, most often, want to be avenged. They are, but the relatives of the condemned man then discover an excess of suffering that punishes them beyond all justice. A mother's or a father's long months of waiting, the visiting room, the artificial conversation filling up the brief moments spent with the condemned man, the vision of the execution are all tortures that were not imposed on the relatives of the victim. Whatever may be the feelings of the latter, they cannot want the revenge to extend so far beyond the crime and to torture people who share their own grief.

Albert Camus, *Reflections on the Guillotine*

WHAT TO DO IF YOU HAVE A LOVED ON THE ROW

You will find yourself dealing with paradoxical and contradictory demands, expectations and emotions. You may find yourself needing to:
* be the strong one in the relationship, while allowing him to make whatever decisions are allowable, so that you don't deprive him of his dignity and manhood
* maintain hope while preparing for the eventuality of a possible execution
* accept disappointment whenever an appeal is denied, yet be relieved that the process still has far to go
* hope that the endless waiting will be over while feeling guilty about your desire for the waiting to end.

You might be able to help your loved one by:
* not talking to anyone except the attorney about the case or the appeals, and don't talk to anyone else unless the attorney OK's it
* visiting, writing, accepting his phone calls
* expressing your love and support "no matter what happens"
* not saying things like "Don't worry, it will be OK"
* allowing him to talk about dying if he feels the need

There will be times when you feel as if you're losing your mind. In order to be strong for your loved one and the rest of your family, you have to take care of yourself. You need to preserve your sanity, your physical and mental health. Some things you can do for yourself include:
* join a support group for death row families. If there is no support group in your area, start your own
* get counseling from a professional counselor or clergy
* make friends with others you meet in the visiting room
* accept help from friends and family members who offer it
* avoid people who seem to look down upon you - don't try to win their favor
* take a little time off occasionally to relax, get your hair done, go to the beach, take a trip, get yourself together
* pray.

PART FOUR
RESOURCES

Without help or support from another living, breathing human being, I existed in a void, that place between nothingness and hell.

Mother of daughter in prison

OUTSIDERS LOOKING IN & DEATH PENALTY FOCUS
Group Offers Support To Families Of Prisoners And Death Row Inmates

When someone is accused or convicted of a crime, the invisible and forgotten victims are his or her family, friends and loved ones. Whether the accused is in detention awaiting trial, out on bail, in jail or in prison, the family suffers right along with the families of the other victims.

While the family of the accused have committed no crime themselves, they are often shunned by relatives, ostracized by neighbors, fired from their jobs, even "disfellowshipped" from their churches. Many have nowhere to turn. A few have become suicidal.

FAMILIES OF PRISONERS SUPPORT GROUP provides emotional support. At our meetings, no one is snubbed because of the nature of the crime their loved one stands accused of. Members talk about mutual concerns, ask for and give advice, share information about the criminal justice system, and offer comfort, strength and hope to one another. We do more than talk. Some members provide volunteer help to each other (and occasionally to their attorneys) copying and collating documents, doing research and writing letters to public officials.

Others visit prisons and prisoners, provide transportation to prison for members who don't drive, and attend court sessions. Between meetings, some get together by phone, and two or three meet at each other's homes whenever anyone needs someone to lean on.

Meetings are held monthly at the Center for Nonviolence at 985 N. Van Ness, Fresno, California, 93728.

      *   *   *

CURE
(Citizens United for Rehabilitation of Errants)

Kay Perry asked the warden if there were programs for family participation in her brother's rehabilitation. The warden laughed. Kay became an activist after her brother's incarceration and has served as Vice Chair and Director of Michigan CURE.

A national advocacy organization devoted to reducing crime through prison reform, CURE began in San Antonio Texas in 1972, when citizens went to the legislature in Austin to work against the death penalty. In 1975, CURE formally organized with an annual convention and a constitution.

"It is the responsibility of all citizens to see to it that the corrections system is conscious of the dignity of the human person - victims and perpetrators - and is conducted in a manner consistent with basic democratic principles and constitutional rights."

Contact Charlie or Pauline Sullivan at POB 2310 Washington, DC 20013-2310

*   *   *

FRIENDS OUTSIDE

Friends Outside's basic functions:

1. We assist the families of inmates by: pick up clothing or other items from their loved one in jail and return it to them; act as an intermediary between the family, the accused and the justice system; talk to the families; offer emotional support and discuss the resources available to them and the accused in the community; help identify each family's need and assist them in resolving those issues surrounding the arrest and incarceration.

2. Inmate services: to make sure those who are incarcerated get what they need in prison or jail. Families can contact us if they believe their loved one is being treated unfairly, or if something they've sent to him didn't arrive.

3. We offer the ex-offender: emotional support and information about parole and community referrals. Parolees who are mandated by the courts to perform community service are plugged into Friends Outside. We offer youth and community services like job referrals and counseling, and we set individuals up with training programs.

Our support groups for ex-offenders involve problem solving, breaking the denial of their involvement in criminal activities and helping them accept personal responsibility for their criminal activities. We say to them, "There is always one person there each time you break the law: you." During drug and alcohol counseling, we use confrontive and reality-based therapy to help them learn the difference between making a mistake and intentionally becoming involved in a crime. Some of our clients perceive a "mistake" as "stupidly getting caught." This is wrong.

We help ex-cons resolve their differences with their families through honesty and truth. No more lying and no more bluffing. There are tremendous physical and psychological changes that happen to a person in prison. We try to help the families and the parolee understand how these changes affect his life and the lives of those around him, then we work with them to overcome the problems that result from these changes.

Friends Outside is staffed by volunteers.

SUPPORT GROUPS AND ORGANIZATIONS

ACLU Capital Punishment Project. 122 Maryland Ave NE, Washington, DC. 20002.

ACLU National Prison Project. 1875 Connecticut Ave. NW #410 Washington, DC 20009.

A/G Prison Ministry. 1445 Boonville Springfield, MO 65802.

Aid to Incarcerated Mothers 32 Rutland St., 2nd fl. Boston, MA 02118; or 599 Mitchell St. SW Atlanta, GA 30314.

Aleph Institute. POB 546564 Surfside, FL 33154. Jewish advocacy.

Alston Wilkes Society 2215 Devine St. Columbia, SC 29205. Operates in South Carolina to assist prison inmates and those being released or paroled.

American Friends Service Committee. Contact: Laura Magnani 1611 Telegraph, Suite 1501 Oakland, CA 94612

American Friends Service Committee. 140 Pine St. Florence, MA 01060

Amnesty International USA Program to Abolish the Death Penalty. 322 Eighth Ave. New York, NY 10001.

Amnesty International Western Regional Office. 9000 W. Washington Bl. 2nd fl. Culver City, CA 90232.

Arm The Spirit. POB 6326, Stn.A Toronto, Ontario M5W 1P7 CANADA. www ats@etext.org.

Books Through Bars. 4722 Baltimore Ave. Philadelphia, PA 19143. www taojones@-iww.org. A non-profit agency affiliated with New Society Publishers in Philidelphia.

Books to Prisoners. c/o Left Bank Books. Box A, 92 Pike St. Seattle, WA. 98101. An organization that sends books to prisoners. Needs donations.

Bruderhof Communities. POB 240, Route 40 Farmington, PA 15537. Works to abolish the death penalty. Plough Publications, anti-death penalty books,music

Bureau of Prisons, Central Office. 320 First St. NW Washington DC 20534. 1-800-995-6423. Federal Prison Information.

California Coalition for Alternatives to the Death Penalty. c/o San Jose Peace Center 48 South 7th St. San Jose, CA 95109. www. sjpc@igc.org.

California Coalition for Women Prisoners. 100 McAllister St. San Francisco, CA 94102.

California Department of Corrections Visiting Hotline. 1-800-374-VISIT.

California NORML. contact: Dale Gieringer Berkeley, CA 94704. Works to change laws that criminalize marijuana sales & possession.

California Prison Focus. 2489 Mission Street, #28 San Francisco, CA 94110. Public information and action about conditions in Security Housing Units, especially at Pelican Bay, Corcoran, and Chowchilla.

California Visitor's Corp/CVC. POB 1019 Sacramento, CA 95812-1019.

Capital Punishment Research Project PO Drawer 277, Headland, Al 36345.

CEGA Services, Offender Referrals. POB 81826 Lincoln, NE 68501-1826. Offers pre-release referrals for prisoners for the area they will be released into.

Center for Children of Incarcerated Parents. 65 S. Grand Ave. Pasadena, CA 91105.

Center on Juvenile and Criminal Justice. Contact: Dan Macallair 1622 Folsom Street, 2nd Floor San Francisco, CA 94103.

Centerforce. 64 Main St, POB 336 San Quentin, CA 94964 (415)456-9980 Fax: (415)456-2146. Provides Hospitality Houses at each Calif. Prison for families and their children.

Center of Support Families of Adult Sex Offenders. Lynn Scott POB 460126 San Francisco, CA 94146.

Centurion Ministries.Rev Jim McCloskey. 32 Nassau St, 3rd fl. Princeton, NJ 08542.Advocates for death row inmates who have been wrongly convicted.

Chicago Legal Aid to Incarcerated Mothers. 205 Randolph #830 Chicago, IL 60606.

Children's Center. POB 803 Bedford Hills, NY 10507 Foster Care Handbook for Incarcerated parents $2.00.

Children of Incarcerated Parents. 714 West California Blvd Pasadena, CA 91105.

Citizens United for the Rehabilitation of Errants (CURE). National Office POB 2310 Washington, DC 20013 (202)842-1650 x320.

Claustrophobia ABC. POB 1721 Baltimore, MD 21203. Prisoner's advocacy group

Columbia Human Rights Law Review. 435 West 116th St. Box B-25, New York, NY 10027. Sells the "Jailhouse Lawyer Manual."

Coalition Against Political Imprisonment. POB 56422 Washington, DC 20011.

Commission of Judicial Performance. 101 Howard Street, suite 300. San Francisco, CA. 94105.

Committee to End Marion Lockdown. POB 578172 Chicago, IL 60657-8172. www.nkurshan@aol.com. Individuals interested in prison reform.

Committee for Prisoner Support. POB 12152 Birmingham, AL 35202-2152.

Community Connection. 2144 El Cajon Bl. San Diego, CA. 92103. Reintegrate family unity during/after incarceration.

Concerned Citizens for Prisoners. POB 2331 West Sacramento, CA 95691-2331.

Correctional Service Federation-USA 436 W. Wisconsin Ave., Ste 500 Milwaukee, WI 53203-20009. Voluntary agencies, bureaus, or individuals devoted to the rehabilitation of offenders.

Correctional Association AIDS in Prison Project. 135 E. 15 St. New York, NY 10003. (212)674-0800. Offers resources concerning AIDS in prison.

Criminal Justice Consortium. Naneen Karraker 1515 Webster St. Oakland, CA 94612 (510)548 6364. www. cjc@igc.org. Association of agencies and individuals working for criminal & juvenile justice in California; information and referral.

Criminal Justice Policy Coalition. 99 Chaunch St. Rm 310, Boston, MA 02111. Promote and support progressive justice reform.

Criminal Justice Ministries. Working for Restorative Justice. Jean Basinger 1335 48th St. Des Moines, Iowa 50311-2450.

CURE-ENOUGH. POB 15655 Detroit, MI 48230. Seeks to remove restrictions on ex-felons.

Death Penalty Focus. 74 New Montgomery Street, Suite 250 San Francisco, CA 94105. (415)243-0143 Fax: (415)243-0994 Contact Lance Lindsey. www dpfocus@aol.com Educates the public about the death penalty.

Death Penalty Information Center. 1606 - 20th St. NW 2nd Fl. Washington, DC 20009. (202)347-2531 Fax: (202)332-1915.

Death Row Support Project POB 600 Liberty Mills, IN 46946. A project of the Church of the Brethren that links concerned individuals with prisoners on death row.

Delancey Street Foundation. 600 Embarcadero San Francisco, CA 94107. Residential drug treatment for adults and some juveniles.

Dershowitz, Alan. Attorney At Law, Harvard University Byerly Hall 8 Garden St. Cambridge Mass 02138 Death penalty and appeals.

Disabled Prisoners' Justice Fund. 38 - 13th. St. #1 Richmond, CA 94801.

The Endeavor Project/Endeavor: Live Voices from Death Row Across the USA. POB 23511 Houston, TX 77228-3511.

Equal Justice USA. Quixote Center POB 5206 Hyattsville, MD 20782. www quixote@igc.org.

Equal Justice Initiative of Alabama. 114 N Hull St. Montgomery, Al 36104. Provides legal assistance to indigent defendants and death row prisoners.

Equal Justice USA West/Prison Radio Project. 558 Capp St. San Francisco, CA 94110. www ejuswest@sirius.com

Families Against Mandatory Minimums. 1612 K St, NW #1400 Washington, DC 20006.www.famm@ix.netcom.com.

Families Against Mandatory Minimums. contact: Virginia Resner POB 170375 San Francisco, CA 94117. (415)753-6602. Advocacy to reform federal mandatory minimum sentencing laws.

Family and Corrections Network. Jane Adams Center M/C 309, 1040 W. Harrison St. #4010, Chicago, IL 60607. www.ifs.univie.ac.at.uncjin/mosaic/famcorr/fmcordir.html#california

FamilyNet. 300 Santa Isabel Suite C Costa Mesa, CA 92627. www lwop@ix.netcom.com.

Family Resources Coalition of America. 200 S. Michigan 16th Fl. Chicago, ILL 60604.

Fathers Behind Bars 141 1st St. Coldwater, MI 49036; or POB 86, Niles, MI 49120. Assists fathers in prison reestablish and maintain relationships with children, spouses, family and friends.

Fellowship of Reconcilliation. POB 271 Nyack, NY 10960. Works for peace, justice and freedom through non-violence and conflict resolution.

Fitness For Life 3675 Elder Rd. S. West Bloomfield, MI 48324-2531. To create and develop programs that encourage prison inmates physical and mental fitness.

Fortune Society 39 W. 19th St., 7th fl. New York, NY 10011. Ex-offenders and others interested in penal reform. Addresses needs of ex-offenders and high-risk youth.

Foundation for Inner Peace. POB 598 Mill Valley, CA 94942 Will send inmates a free copy of the spiritual guide "A Course In Miracles."

Freedom Foundation. POB 487 San Quentin, CA 94964. Works only on selected cases concerning those whith claims of being falsely accused or illegal confiscation.

Friends Committee on Legislation. 926 J Street, Rm 707 Sacramento, CA 95814-2707. (916)443-3734. An organization that watches crime bills and conducts workshops

Friends Outside . 3031 Tisch Way, Ste 507 San Jose, CA 95128. (408)985-8807 Fax: (408)985-8839 Assists prison inmates into society, counsels families and has support groups.

Gay and Lesbian Advocates and Defenders. POB 218, Boston, MA 02112.

Gay and Lesbian Prisoner Project. Bromfield St. Educational Foundation 29 Stanhope St. Boston, MA 02116.

Hatcher Center for Human Rights. 120 Amber Road Hamlet, NC 28345.

HIV/AIDS in Prison Project of Catholic Charities/East Bay. contact: Judy Greenspan 433 Jefferson Street Oakland, CA 94607.

HIV Prison Project NYC Commission on Human Rights . 40 Rector St. New York, NY 10006.

Hope Aglow Prison Ministries. POB 3057 Lynchburg, VA 24503.

Housing Discrimination Project. 57 Suffolk St. Holyoke, MA 01040. (413)539-9796. Fair housing for individuals coming out of prison.

Human Rights Watch. 1522 K St., NW Washington, DC 20005 (202)371-6592

Indigenous Women's Network. POB 174, Lake Elmo, MN 55042

Illinois Clemency Project for Battered Women. 4669 North Manor Ave Chicago, Ill 60625. Supports clemency petitions before the Governor for women who have murdered their abuser.

Inside-Out: Citizens United for Prison Reform, Inc. POB 2393 Hartford, CT 06146.

International Indian Treaty Council. 54 Mint St. #400 San Francisco, CA 94103.

International Legal Defense Counsel. Packard Bldg, 24 fl. 111 S. 15th St. Philadelphia, PA 19102. Advocates for prisoners abroad.

International Prison Ministry POB 63 Dallas, TX 75221. Seeks to rehabilitate prisoners through the process of Christian conversion.

Innocence Project. Peter Neufield and Barry Scheck Attorneys. 500 W. 185th St. New York, NY 10033-3299. Cases where DNA is involved.

Iskcon Prison Ministries. 2936 Esplanade Ave. New Orleans, LA 70119. Meditation.

Islamic Prison Foundation. 1212 New York Ave. NW #400 Washington, DC 20005. Works with Muslims in prison.

Islands Support Group 1840 So. Gaffey St. #274 San Pedro, CA 90731.

Jail and Prison Health Committee & American Public Health Association. Corey Weinstein, M.D. 1109 Vicente, #104 San Francisco, CA 94116 Reform in medical services for inmates of CA jails and prisons.

James Markunas Society. 245 Harriet St. San Francisco, CA 94103.Lesbian, Gay, Bisexual prisoners.

Jewish Prisoner Services International. POB 85840, Seattle, WA 98145-1840 www.jewishprisonerservices.org.

John Howard Association. 67 E. Madison, Ste 1416 Chicago, IL 60603. Devoted to prison reform.

Jubilee Plowshares West Support Group c/o Magdalene House. 528 - 25th St. Oakland, CA 94612.

Justice Education and Action Project. 1218 E. 21st St. Oakland, CA 94606. A membership based organization comprised of youth and families impacted by the Juvenile Justice System.

Justice Fellowship POB 17500 Washington, DC 20041-0500. Christians who support prison reform.

Justice Watch. 932 Dayton St. Cincinnati, OH 45214. Works to eliminate classism and racism in prison.

KNOw INjustice Coalition. co/ LSPC, 100 McAllister San Francisco, CA 94102. Prison reform by bringing together every group who works for justice.

League of Lesbian and Gay Prisoners. 1202 E. Pike, #1044 Seattle, WA 98122.

Legal Services for Prisoners with Children contact: Dorsey Nunn 100 McAllister Street San Francisco, CA 94102. Class action litigation, training, and information & referral about prisoners with children.

Leonard Peltier Defense Committee. POB 583 Lawrence, KS 66044.

Lesbian AIDS Project. GMHC 129 W. 20th St. New York, NY 10011.

Liberty Prison Outreach. 701 Thomas Rd. Lynchburg, VA.

Malcolm X Grassroots Movement/New Afrikan Peoples' Organization. POB 2348 Harlem, NY 10027.

Massachussetts Correctional Legal Services. 8 Winter St., 11th fl. Boston, MA 02108.

Middle Ground Prison Reform. 139 E. Encanto Dr. Tempe, AZ 85281

Million Letters for Mumia Campaign FreeMumia Abu-Jamal Coalition. POB 650 New York, NY 10009.

Mothers Against Prison Rape. POB 152 Cary, IL 60013. A support group and organization of mothers who work against the rape of prisoners.

Mothers Opposed to Maltreatment of Service Members. 8285 Black Hawk Court, Federick, MD 21701. Advocates for military prisoners.

Mothers ROC (Reclaiming Our Children) Jeri Silva 4167 S Normandie Ave. Los Angeles, CA 90037 (213)291-1092 http://labridge.com/mroc/.

MOVE / International Concerned Friends and Family of Mumia Abu-Jamal. POB 19709 Philadelphia, PA 19143.

Murder Victims' Families for Reconciliation Pat Bane POB 54 Atlantic, VA 23303-0054 (804)824-0948 Anti-death penalty. Believes in forgiveness.

Murder Victims' Families for Reconciliation. 1555 Fifth Ave, #102 San Francisco, CA 94122. (415)974-4577.

NAACP Legal Defense and Educational Fund, Inc. 99 Hudson St. New York, NY 10013.

National Black on Black Love. 1000 E. 87th St. Chicago, Il 60619. Individuals and businesses united to promote the motto, "Replace Black on Black crime with Black on Black Love."

National Campaign to Stop Control Unit Prisons, West POB 2218 Berkeley, CA 94702.

National Convocation of Jail and Prison Ministry. 1357 East Capitol St. SE, Washington, DC 20003. A national agency for prison chaplains.

National Clearinghouse for the Defense of Battered Women. 125 S. 9th. St. #302 Philadelphia, PA 19107. Provides assistance and information to the defense teams of battered women charged with crimes.

National Coalition to Abolish the Death Penalty 1436 U St. NW, # 104 Washington, DC 2009 (202)387-3890 Fax:(202)387-5590. www.ncadp.org

National Coalition Against Domestic Violence. POB 34103, Washington, DC 20043.

National Council on Crime and Deliquency. 685 Market St. Ste 620, San Francisco, CA. 94104.

National Institute Of Corrections, Information Center. 1860 Industrial Circle, Suite A, Longmont, CA 80501. Directory of programs for families of inmates. 1-800-877-1461.

National Lawyers Guild Prison Law Project 558 Capp St. San Francisco, CA 94110. Jailhouse lawyers.

National Network for Women in Prison. 714 W. California Ave. Pasadena, CA 91105.

National Prison Hospice Association. POB 58 Boulder, CO 80306-0058.

National Prison Project 1875 Connecticut Ave., NW, Ste 410 Washington, DC 20009. Part of the American Civil Liberties Union. Aims to improve prison conditions and develop alternatives to incarceration.

National Women's Law Center Women in Prison Project. 11 Dupont Circle NW, Suite 800 Washington, DC 20036.

Native American Indian Inmate Support Project. 8 Dallas Dr. Grantville, PA 17028.

Native American Prisoners' Rehabilitation Research Project. 2848 Paddock Lane, Villa Hills, KY 41017. Legal and spiritual support.

Native American Rights Fund. 1522 Broadway Boulder, CO 80302-6296. (303)447-8760. Support for jailhouse lawyers.

Navajo Nations Corrections Project. POB Drawer 709 Window Rock, AZ 86515.

New African Women for Self-Determination. POB 2835 Oakland, CA 94609.

Northern California Service League. 28 Boardman Place San Francisco, CA 94103. (415)863-2323 FAX (415)863-1882. Support for San Francisco county jail prisoners and job development for state and county ex-prisoners.

Oberlin Action Against Prisons. POB 285 Oberlin, OH 44074-0285. www sht9195@oberlin.edu.

On the Outside: Prison Activist Radio. Free Radio Berkeley (Oakland, CA) 104.1 FM:Every other Mon 9-10 p.m., Radio Libre San Francisco Mission Dist. 103.3 F.M. Every other Tuesday 9-10 p.m.

Osborne Association 135 E. 15th St. New York, NY 10003. Implements programs to decrease population in prisons and jails.

Out of Time c/o Out of Control Lesbian Committee. 3543 18th St. San Francisco, CA 94110. Free Newspaper for women in prison.

Packages From Home. POB 905 Forestville, CA 95436. Sells mail-order food packages for prisoners for about $20.00.

Parent Resource Association. 213 Fernbrook Ave. Wyncote, PA 19095. Offers information and referrals to incarcerated parents.

The Peace Museum. 314 W. Institute Place Chicago, IL 60610 (312)440-1860

PEN, Writing Program for Prisoners. 568 Broadway, NY 10012. Offers resource books for prisoners who write.

Penal Law Project. California State University, Chico. Chico, CA 95929. Provides legal information to prisoners at Susanville Correctional Institution.

Pleasanton AIDS Counseling and Education St. Augustine's Catholic Church - AIDS Ministry. 3999 Bernard Avenue Pleasanton, CA 94566.

Police Harrassment, Amherst. Jean Sherlock, 103 Meadow St. Amherst, MA 01002.

Pro Family Advocates. contact: Vivian Hagan POB 341247 Los Angeles, CA 90034-9247. Network of families of prisoners; advocates on issues such as family visitation.

Prison Activist Resource Center (PARC). contact: Eli Rosenblatt POB 3201 Berkeley, CA 94703 (510)845-8813   FAX   (510)845-8816 www. parcer@igc.org. Information and referral about prisons and prisoners across the U.S. and Canada.

Prison AIDS Project, Gay Community News. 62 Berkeley St. Boston, MA 02116.

Prison AIDS Resource Center. POB 2155 Vacaville, CA 95696-2155

Prison-Ashram Project Rte 1, Box 201-N Durham, NC 27705. Provides advice to prisoners and other shut-ins who want to expand their spiritual training.

Prison Book Program. 92 Green St. Jamaica Plain, MA 02130.

Prison Connections, Western Mass. Prison Issues Group. POB 9606 N. Amherst, MA 01059-9606 www.wmpig@persphone.hampshire.edu

Prison Family Foundation. POB 1150 Auburn, AL 36831. Supports family education in prison.

Prison Fellowship International POB 17434 Washington, DC 20041. Organizes Christian ministry in prisons.

Prison Fellowship Ministries. POB 17500 Washington, DC 20041. Encourages Christians to work in prisons.

Prison Law Office, Davis. UC Davis POB 4745 Davis, CA 95616. (916)752-6943 Fax: (916)752-0822. Provides legal assistance to prisoners at Folsom and Vacaville State Prisons in Calif.

Prison Law Office. General Delivery San Quentin, CA 94964. (415)457-9144 Fax: (415)457-9151. Undertakes class action litigation related to conditions in California State prisons.

Prison MATCH. 595 Kenilworth San Leandro, CA 94577. An advocacy group for children of prisoners, serves as a national clearing house on maternal incarceration.

Prison Ministry of Yokefellows International POB 482 Rising Sun, MD 21911. Helps serve religious needs of those in prisons. Tries to bridge the gap between the outside and the inside by promoting employment, halfway houses and counseling.

Prison Project. SYDA Foundation, 371 Brickman Rd. Hurleyville, NY 12747-5313. Correspondence course in meditation.

Prisoners Justice Day Committee of Toronto. #237 - 517 College St. Toronto, Ontario M6G 4A2 www.sage!zoltan@noc.tor.hookup.net

Prisoners Rights Union. 2308 J Street P.O.B 1019 Sacramento, CA 95812-1019. (916)441-4214. Advocacy and information about prisoner rights in California. Produces Resource Guide and The California State Prisoners' Handbook.

Prisoners with AIDS. Rights Advocacy Group POB 2161 Jonesboro, GA 30237.

Prisoner Visitation and Support. 1501 Cherry St. Philadelphia, PA 19102. Provides institutional visits in military and federal prisons.

P.R.O.O.F. (Project Reaching Out to Overcome Failure). POB 2265 Minden, NV 89423.

Project for Older Prisoners (POPS) National Law Center. 2000 H St. NW, Washington, DC 20052.

Rehabilitation Research Foundation Box 1425 Columbia, MO 65205-1425. Plans funds and evaluates programs of prison reform, offender re-socialization and mental health.

Rosenberg Fund For Children. 1145 Main St. Springfield, MA 01103. Supports prison rights activists and provides for the emotional needs of children whose parents have been harrassed by the system. www.rfc.org.grants.htm

Sacramento Area Coalition Against the Death Penalty. GJRC 2110 Broadway Sacramento,CA 95818.

Safer Society Programs and Press POB 340 Brandon, VT 05733-0340. Provides referrals for specialized assessment and treatment of youthful and adult sexual victims and offenders. Is a national project of the New York State Council of Churches.

San Jose Peace Center. 11154 La Paloma Drive, Cupertino, CA 95014. (408)257-1360.

The Sentencing Project 918 F. St., NW, Ste 501 Washington, DC 20004. (202)628-0871 Fax: (202)628-1091. Provides public defenders and other public officials with information in establishing alternative sentencing programs.

Set Free Prison Ministries. POB 5440 Riverside, CA.92517-9961.

Silent Warriors. Andover Newton Theological School 210 Herrick Rd. Newton Centre, MA 02159. (617)524-4266. For mothers with sons or daughters behind bars.

Southern Poverty Law Center. POB 548 Montgomery, AL 36195. (205)264-0286.

Southern Prison Ministry. 910 Ponce de Leon Ave. NE, Atlanta, GA 30306.

Stop Prisoner Rape, Inc. 333 North Ave 61 #4 Los Angeles, CA 90042 spr@ix.netcom.com, web page: www.igc.apc.org.spr.

The Poetry Wall. Cathedral of St. John. 1047 Amsterdam Ave. New York, NY 10025. Displays poetry written by prisoners.

Transfiguration Prison Ministry c/o Convent of the Transfiguration. 495 Albion Ave., Glendale Cincinnati, OH 45246. The spiritual welfare of prison inmates.

Turning Point of Central California. contact: Jeff Fly, Executive Director 119 South Locust Visalia, CA 93291. Operates several residential programs for state prisoners.

Vera Institute of Justice 377 Broadway 11th fl. New York, NY 10013. Helps people who are considered unemployable move into the regular work force.

Volunteers of America. 7677 Oakport St., 3 fl. Oakland, CA 94621. (510)568-9214 Operates several residential programs for state prisoners.

Washington Coalition to Abolish the Death Penalty. 705 Second Ave, #300 Seattle, WA 98104.

We Care. Rte 2, Box 33M Atmore, AL 36502. Helps deter juveniles from a life of crime.

Western Massachusetts Prison Issues Group WMPIG. POB 9606 North Amherst, MA 01059-9606. Prison Connection Newsletter with issues for prisoners and families.

William James Association. 303 Potrero St. #12-B Santa Cruz, CA 95060-2756. Runs the art programs in the state prisons.

Women Hurt in Systems of Prostitution WHISPER. 1135 Raymond Ave. St. Paul, MN 55108-1922.

Women's Prison Association 110 2nd Ave New York, NY 10003 Aids women who have been in conflict with the law. Promotes alternatives to incarceration.

Women Prisoners Convicted by Drugging. Bamberg B1146-L, Frontera, CA 91720.

Women's Advocacy Project. POB 833 Austin TX 78767.

Women's Prison Book Project. Arise Bookstore 2441 Lyndale Ave South, Minneapolis, MN 55405. Free books.

WORLD Women Organized to Respond to Life-Threatening Diseases. POB 11535 Oakland, CA 94611. (510)658-6930 Fax (510)601-9746. Works for compassionate release of women inmates who are dying of HIV/AIDS.

Youth Law Center. 114 Sansome St. Suite 950 San Francisco, CA 94104. (415)543-3379 FAX (415)956-9022. Class action litigation on behalf of youth in the juvenile justice system nationwide.

INTERNET RESOURCES & WEB PAGES

Activists Resources. www.ocms.ox.ac.uk 'comfort/ACTIVIST_BOOKMARKS_2.html sexuality

Black Peoples' Prison Survival Guide. www.cs. oberlin.edu/students/pjaques/etext/prison-guide.html

California Correctional Peace officers Association. (CCPOA) www.cj.nmu.edu.cj.ccpoa/rs.html. E-mail addresses of correctional officers

Criminal Justice Links. www.fsu.edu/'crimdo/cj.html. Home page with links to other important resources.

Criminal Justice Reform in California. www.sonnet.com/Criminal Justice Reform.

Families of Adult Prisoners. www.ifs.univie. at.uncjin/mosiac/famcorr/fmcorrpt.html

Find Law. Internet legal Resources www.findlaw.com

How to Break the Law. Arrest etiquette. www.unicorn.com//lib/law.html

Inmate Classified. www. inmate.com/inmates.html. Inmates who have access to the internet. Can communicate with them.

Know Your Rights. www.execpc.com/'wrfincke/RIGHTS.html

Justice Net. www.igc.apc.org/prisons Extensive information about prisons and prison issues.

LAO Analysis of 97-98 Budget Bill Judiciary & Criminal Issues Part 1. www.ca.gov/crim-justice-depts.1a.anal97.html.#_1_2.

Legal Resources on the Internet. www.usc.edu/dept/ law-lib/legal/topiclst.html#Prevent. Access legal resources from the law library.

Nolo Press. www.nolo.com On line legal book store that has dozens of easy to read pamplets you can download for legal information.

Prison Issues. www.sonic.net/'doretk/archive/ ARCHIVE/prison/prissues.html. Homepage with dozens of links to other prison resources.

Prison Law Page. www.www.wco.com/'aerick/ prison.html. Written by attorney Arnold Erickson, a staff attorney for the Prison Law Office, this excellent homepage has links to other prison related topics, plus links to magazines and articles written by prisoners.

Webactive Directory, Civil Rights. www.webactive.com/webactive/cgi-bin/ wniadirsearch? Civil Rights.

INTERNATIONAL

Howard League for Penal Reform 708 Holloway Rd. London N19 3NL, England. Aims to educate the public about issues related to criminal justice Believes that "prison is the severest penalty on the statute book, and to use it more than can be shown to be the minimum necessary to protect the public is wrong in principle, besides being ineffective and costly." (See John Howard Assoc.)

International Prisoners Aid Association University of Louisville Department of Sociology Louisville, KY 40292. Agencies and individuals in 45 countries concerned with aid programs for prisoners.

International Probation Organization 813 Burden St. Federiction, NB, Canada E3B 4C5. Fosters the use of probation as an alternative to prison.

RECOMMENDED READING

Abbott, Jack Henry. In the Belly of the Beast. Vintage Books (1981)

Abramson, Leslie. The Defense Is Ready. Simon & Shuster (1997)

Aman, Reinhold. Hilary Clinton's Pen Pal. Maledicta Press (1996)

Andrews, Lori. Black Power, White Blood: The Life and Times of Johnny Spain. Pantheon Books (1996)

Aptheker, Bettina and Angela Davis, eds. If They Come in the Morning. Signet (1971)

Arguelles, Marilla, ed. Extracts from Pelican Bay. Pantograph Press (1995)

Bertsch, Steve. Crisis in Our Courts. Gollehon Books (1993)

Blake, Stephen. Arrested! Now What? A Self-Help Guide to the Crimial Justice System.

Brenzel, Barbara. Daughters of the State. MIT Press (1983)

Brown, Joyce Ann. Justice Denied.

Browne, Angela. When Battered Women Kill. The Free Press (1987)

Bruchas, Joseph. Light From Another Country. Greenfield Review Press (1984)

Bull, Steven. Trial by Jury. American Lawyer Books (1989)

Burkhart, Kathryn Watterson. Women in Prison. Doubleday (1973)

Camhi, Morrie. The Prison Experience. Charles Tuttle Co. (1989)

Camus, Albert. Reflections on the Guillotine

Casper, Jonathan. American Criminal Justice: The Defendant's Perspective. Prentice-Hall (1972)

Chesney-Lind, Meda. The Female Offender: Girls, Women and Crime. Sage Publications (1997)

Chinosole, ed. Schooling the Generations in the Politics of Prison. New Earth Publications. (1995)

Cooper, Cynthia L. & Sheppard, Sam Reese. Mockery Of Justice: The True Story of the Sheppard Murder Case. Onyx Book (1997)

Aronoff, B.R., Dead Man Walking: A Matter Of Time. Eagle Publishing, (1991). This book can be ordered from OLINC Publishing, P.O. Box 6012, Fresno, CA 93703-6012

Christenson, Jean Marie. Keepers and the Caged. Kendall Hunt Publications (1996)

Churchill, Ward & J. J. Vander Wall, eds. Cages of Steel. Maisonneuve Press (1992)

Cromwell, Paul, ed. Jails and Justice. 1975

Cummins, Eric. Rise and Fall of California's Radical Prison Movement. The Stanford University Press (1994)

Currie, Elliott. Confronting Crime. Pantheon Books (1985)

Datesman, Susan K. and Frank Scarpitti. Women, Crime, & Justice. Oxford University Press (1980)

Davies, Joan. Writers in Prison. Basil Blackwell, Inc. (1990)

Davis, Angela Y. Women, Race, & Class. Vintage (1981)

Davis, Kevin. The Wrong Man. Avon Books (1996)

Denfeld, Rene. Kill The Body The Head Will Fall: A Closer Look at Women, Violence and Aggression. Warner Books. (1996)

Dershowitz, Alan. Reasonable Doubts: The Criminal Justice System and the O.J. Simpson Case. A Touchstone Book (1997)

Di Iulio, John J., Jr. No Escape: The Future of American Corrections. Basic Books(1991)

Donaldson, Stephen. Manual Overview of the Prisoner Rape Education Project. Brandon, VT: Safer Society Press. (1993)

Donziger, Stephen. The Real War on Crime. (1996).

Duffy, Clinton. San Quentin Story. Doubleday (1950)

Earley, Pete. Circumstantial Evidence. Bantam Books (1995)

Earley, Pete The Hot House: Life Inside Leavenworth Prison. Bantam Books (1992)

Editorial El Coqui. Can't Jail the Spirit. (1992)

Edna McConnell Foundation. Seeking Justice. (Free Book) Office of Communications, Edna McConnell Foundation. 250 Park Ave. New York, NY 10177.

Fallis, Greg and Greenberg, Ruth. How to be Your Own Detective. (1989)

Faith, Karlene. Unruly Women: The Politics of Confinement & Resistence. Press Gang Publishers (1993)

Foucault, Michel. Discipline and Punishment: The Birth of the Prison. Vintage Books (1977)

Franklin, H. Bruce. Prison Literature in America: The Victim as Criminal and Artist. Oxford University Press (1989)

Freedman, Estelle. Maternal Justice: Miriam Van Waters and the Female Reform Tradition. University of Chicago Press (1996)

Friedman, Lawrence M. Crime and Punishment in American History. Basic Books (1993)

Gillespie, Cynthia K. Justifiable Homicide: Battered Women, Self-Defense and the Law. Ohio State University Press (1989)

Goldman, Emma. Living My Life, Vol. 1 and Vol. 2. Dover Publications Inc. (1970)

Gramsci, Antonio. Selections from the Prison Notebooks. International Publishers (1971)

Griffith, Lee. The Fall of the Prison: Biblical Perspectives on Prison Abolition. Erdmans (1993)

Hagen, Margaret. Whores Of the Court. (About expert witnesses who can be bought.)

Hall, Douglas Kent. In Prison. Henry Holt & Co. (1988)

Hickey, Eric. Serial Killers and Their Victims. (1996)

Hogshire, Jim. You Are Going To Prison. Loomponics Unlimited (1994)

Human Rights Watch. Prison Conditions in the United States: A Human Rights Watch Report. Human Rights Watch (1991)

Institute for the Study of Labor and Economic Crisis. Iron Fist and the Velvet Glove. The Crime and Social Justice Associates (1992)

Irwin, John et al. It's About Time: America's Imprisonment Binge. Wadsworth Publishing Company (1994)

Jackson, George. Soledad Brother: Prison Letters of George Jackson. Bantam Books (1970)

Jackson, George L. Blood in my Eye. Black Classic Press (1990)

Jacobs, Nancy, Seigal, Mark, Quiram, Jacqueline, eds. Prisons and Jails: A Deterrant to Crime?

Jones, Ann. Women Who Kill. Ballantine Books. (1981)

Johnson, Robert. Hard Time: Understanding and Reforming the Prison. (1987)

Kaminer, Wendy. It's all The Rage. Addison Wesley (1996)

Kappeler, Victor et al. Mythology of Crime and Criminal Justice. The Waveland (1993)

Knight, Barbara, Early, Stephen Jr. Prisoner's Rights In America. Nelson-Hall (1986)

Kubler-Ross, Elizabeth. On Death and Dying.

Laws, Lewis. (Warden at Sing Sing). 20,000 Years at Sing Sing.

Leech, Mark. Prisoner's Handbook. Pluto Press (1995- 1997)

Lesce, Tony. The Big House: How American Prisons Work. Loomponics Unlimited. (1991)

Leve, Paul. Prison Life and Human Worth. (1974)

Loftus, Elizabeth. Witness for the Defense. St. Martins Press (1991)

Long, Harold S. Surviving in Prison. Loompanics Unlimited (1990)

Lyon, David. Electronic Eye. The University of Minnesota Press (1994)

Magnani, Laura. America's First Penitentiary: A 200 Year Old Failure. American Friends Service Committee 2160 Lake St. San Francisco, CA 94121 (415)752-7766

Martin, Danny & Peter Y. Sussman. Committing Journalism: The Prison Writings of Red Hog. W. W. Norton and Company (1993)

Menninger, Karl, M.D. The Crime of Punishment. The Viking Press (1968)

Messerschmidt, James. Capitalism, Patriarchy, and Crime: Toward a Socialist Feminist Criminology. Rowman & Littlefield (1986)

Mitford, Jessica. Kind and Usual Punishment. Knopf (1973)

Mones, Paul. When a Child Kills. Star Books, (1991)

Morris, Ruth. Penal Abolition. Canadian Scholars Press (1995)

Morgan, Seth. Homeboy. Vintage Books (1990)

Morris, Mark, ed. Instead of Prisons. Prison Research Education Action Project (1976)

Morris, Norval and Rothman, David, eds. Oxford History of Prisons. Oxford University Press (1995)

Newton, Huey P. To Die For the People. Writers and Readers Publishing Inc. (1995)

O'Donnell, H. I Cried, You Didn't Listen. Feral House Press (1991)

Ortega, Nancy E., J.D. & Joel R. Wells, J.D. Prisoners' Legal Manual for Selected Problems. Southern Poverty Law Center (1993)

Orwell, George. 1984 . New American Library (1961)

Parmelee, Allan. How to Win Prison Disciplinary Hearings. 2802 E. Madison, Suite 168 Seattle, WA 98112 (1995)

Perske, Robert. Unequal Justice? Abingdon Press (1991)

Platt, Tony & Paul Takagi. Punishment and Penal Discipline: Essays on the Prison and the Prisoner's Movement. Crime and Social Justice Associates (1980)

Rafter, Nicole Hahn. Partial Justice: Women, Prisons, and Social Control. Transaction Publishers (1990)

Ray, Don. A Public Records Primer & Investigators Handbook. (1992)

Reed, Little Rock, ed. The American Indian in the White Man's Prisons: A Story of Genocide. UnCompromising Books (1993)

Reiman, Jeffrey. The Rich Get Richer and the Poor Get Prison: Economic Bias in American Criminal Justice. Allyn & Bacon (1996)

Richie, Beth E. Compelled to Crime: The Gender Entrapment of Battered Black Women. Routledge Press (1996)

Rideau, Wilbert & Ron Wikberg. Life Sentences: Rage and Survival Behind Bars. Times Books (1992)

Rierden, Andi. The Farm: Life Inside a Women's Prison. University of Massachusetts Press (1997)

Rudovsky, David, Alvin J. Bronstein, Edward I. Koren, Julia Cade. Rights of Prisoners, The: A Comprehensive Guide to the Legal Rights of Prisoners Under Current Law; fourth edition Southern Illinois University Press (1988)

Rosenblatt, Eli, ed. "With the Power of Justice in Our Eyes": A Handbook for Educators and Activists on the Crisis in Prisons." Western Institute for Social Research (1993)

Serna, Idella. Locked Down: A Woman's Life in Prison. New Victoria (1997)

Shakur, Assata Autiobiography of Assata Shakur (born Joanne Chesimard). Assata Zed Books (1987)

Sherman, Allen. Rape of the A.P.E. (American Puritan Ethic) Playboy Press (1973)

Simon, Rita James. Women and Crime . D.C. Heath and Company (1975)

Snedecker, Michael. Down in the Valley. Clear Glass Publications (1992)

Smart, Carol. Women, Crime and Criminology: A Feminist Critique. Routledge & Kegan Paul (1976)

Storr, Anthony. Solitude: A Return to the Self. The Free Press (1988)

Sullivan, Larry. The Prison Reform Movement. (1990)

Thurston, Linda M. Call to Action. A Third World Press (1993)

Wachtler, Saul. After the Madness. (1997)

Walker, Lenore E. Terrifying Love: Why Battered Women Kill and How Society Responds. Harper Perennial (1989)

Wooden, Kenneth. Weeping in the Playtime of Others. McGraw-Hill (1976)

Wooden, Wayne S. and Jay Parker. Men Behind Bars: Sexual Exploitation in Prison. Da Capo Press (1982)

Wright, Eric Olin. The Politics of Punishment. Harper & Row (1973)

DEATH PENALTY

Ainsworth, Steven King Writings from Death Row. Sacramento Area Coalition Against the Death Penalty (1994)

Bailey, Lloyd. Capital Punishment: What the Bible Says. Abingdon Press (1987)

Bedeau, Hugo The Death Penalty In America. Oxford Press (1982)

Brown, Edmund. Public Justice, Private Mercy. Weidenfeld & Nicolson (1989)

Cabana, Donald, A. Death at Midnight: The Confession of an Executioner. Northeastern University Press, Boston (1996)

Capote, Truman. In Cold Blood. (1970)

Dicks, Shirley. Congregation of the Condemned. Prometheus Books (1991)

Drimmer, Frederick. Until You Are Dead: The Book Of Executions in America. Pinnacle Books (1990)

Gilmore, Mikal. Shot in the Heart. Doubleday (1994)

Gray, Ian & Stanley, Moira. A Punishment in Search of a Crime. Avon books (1989)

Gunterman, Joe & Thomas, Trevor. This Life We Take: A Case Against the Death Penalty. (1987) This book can be ordered for $1.00 from Friends Committee on Legislation of California 926 J St. Sacramento, CA 95814 (916) 443-3734.

Johnson, Robert. Death Work. Wadsworth, Publishing Co. (1990)

Lesser, Wendy. Pictures at an Execution. Harvard University Press (1993)

Mailer, Norman. The Executioner's Song.

Marquart, James W. & Sheldon Ekland-Olson, Jonathan R. Sorensen. The Rope, the Chair, and the Needle, Capital Punishment in Texas 1923-1990. University of Texas Austin Press (1994)

Miller, Kent S. & Betty Davis Miller. To Kill and Be Killed: Case Studies from Florida's Death Row. Hope Publishing House (1989)

Perske, Robert Deadly Innocence? Abingdon Press (1995)

Prejean, Helen, C.S.J. Dead Man Walking. Random House (1993)

Radelet, Michael L., Hugo Adam Bedau, Constance E. Putnam. In Spite of Innocence: Erroneous Convictions in Capital Cases. Northeastern University Press (1992)

Radelet, Michael. Executing The Mentally Ill: The Criminal Justice System and the Case of Alvin Ford. Sage Publications (1992)

Radelet, Michael. Facing the Death Penalty. Temple University Press (1989)

Trombley, Stephen. The Execution Protocol: Inside America's Capital Punishment Industry. Anchor Books (1992)

Von Drehle, David. Amongst The Lowest of the Dead. Random House (1995)

Weinglass, Leonard. Race for Justice: Mumia Abu-Jamal's Fight Against the Death Penalty. Common Courage Press (1995)

Zehr, Howard. Death as a Penalty. Mennonite Central Committee, U.S. Office of Criminal Justice.

BOOKS, ARTICLES FROM ORGANIZATIONS

Amnesty International. The Machinery of Death. 322 8th Ave. New York, NY 10001.

Amnesty International. When the State Kills. 322 8th Ave. New York, NY 10001.

Bedeau, Hugo. The Case Against The Death Penalty . ACLU Capital Punishment Project. 122 Maryland Ave NE. Washington, DC 20002.

National Coalition to Abolish the Death Penalty. The Death Penalty: The Religious Community Calls for Abolition. 1436 U St. NW #104 Washington, DC 20009.

Human Rights Watch. All too Familiar: Sexual Abuse of Women in US State Prisons. Human Rights Watch, 485 fifth Ave. New York, NY 10017-6104

National Institute of Justice. Issues and Practices. (1988) Office of Justice Programs Washington, DC 20531

National Institute of Justice. Work in American Prisons: The Private Sector gets Involved. (1988) Office of Justice Programs Washington, DC 20531

Worth, Robert. A Model Prison. Atlantic Monthly. Nov 95.

NEWS PUBLICATIONS, WEB PAGES, INTERNET CONNECTIONS

Angolite Magazine. Wilbert Rideau, Editor. Louisiana State Prison Angola, Louisiana 70712. Award-winning inmate publication. $20 per year for six issues

Bay View. Willie and Mary Ratcliff, 4401 3rd St. San Francisco, CA 94124. African-American newspaper, deals with African-American prisoners.

Behind the Walls. 5 Star Press POB 4167 Halfmoon, NY 12065.

Black Fist. 15110 Bellaire Box 317 Houston, TX 77083. Phone: 713-845-7730 Fax: 713-686-9526 Email: BlackFist3@aol.com.

Black Scholar. POB 2859 Oakland, CA 94609.

The Blast! POB 7075 Minneapolis, MN 55407. Email: hein0134@maroon.tc.umn.edu.

Human Rights Held Hostage: A Prisoners' Newsletter Committee for Freedom Publications. POB 14075 Chicago, IL 60614.

Journal of Prisoners on Prisons. POB 54 University Centre, University of Manitoba Winnipeg R3T 2N2 CANADA.

New Jersey Crime Line. NJ Speakout Publication. POB 1214 Belle Mead, NJ 08502. Email nj-speakout@igc.apc.org.

Out of Control: Lesbian Committee to Support Women Political Prisoners and POWs. Out of Time Newsletter 3543 - 18th. St. #30 San Francisco, CA 94110.

Prison Connection. POB 9606 North Amherst. MA 01059-9606. A newsletter

Prison Dharma-Network. POB 912 Astor Station Boston, MA 02123-0912. Buddhist meditation material.

Prison Legal News. 2400 NW 80th St. #148 Seattle, WA 98117. An excellent newspaper describing legal issues prisoners face.

Prison Life Magazine. 1436 W. Gray, # 531, Houston TX 77019 Under new management. Sometimes late. $28 for 1 year for 6 issues.

Prison News Service / PSC Publishers. POB 5052, Stn. A Toronto, ONTARIO M5W IW4. Email: pns@pathcom.com.

PWA Coalition Newsletter. 31 West 26th. St. New York, NY 10011.

Raze the Walls: Prisoner Resource Guide. POB 22774 Seattle, WA 98122-0774. Phone: 206-328-8571. e-mail waji@waji.seanet.com

Rites of Passage Legal Journal. 558 Capp Street San Francisco, CA 94110.

Rocky Mountain Peace and Justice Center/ Prisoner's Rights Project/Shut Them Down Newsletter. POB 1156 Boulder, CO 80306-1156. Phone: 303-444-6981 Fax: 303-444-6523

Shut Them Down Newsletter Social Justice: A Journal of Crime, Conflict and World Order. POB 40601 San Francisco, CA 94140.

South End Press. 116 St. Botolph St. Boston, MA 02115. Phone: 617-266-0629 Fax: 617-266-1595

Straight Low: Louisiana Prison News Magazine Dixon Correctional Insitute. POB 788 Jackson, LA 70748.

SMALL BOOKS & PAMPLETS

Austin, James, Ph.D. America's Growing Correctional-Industrial Complex. The National Council on Crime and Delinquency (1990)

Baun, N. and Brooke, B. Trading Books for Bars. Center on Juvenile and Criminal Justice (1994)

Bloom, Barbara, Meda Chesney Lind, and Barbara Owen. Women in California Prisons: Hidden Victims of the War on Drugs. Center on Juvenile and Criminal Justice (1994)

Browne, Julie. The Labor of Doing Time: Convict Labor Exploitation in the Development and Practice of Imprisonment in the United States. (1995)

Buck, M. , Evans, L . Rosenberg, S. , and Whitehorn, L. Conspiracy of Voices Emergency Committee to Defend the Human and Legal Rights of Political Prisoners. (1990)

Chevigny, P. Police Brutality in the United States Human Rights Watch. (1991)

Cochran, Johnnie L. and Bernstein, David L. Free - Waiting for History - The Case of Geronimo Pratt. (1996)

Concrete and Crowds: 100,000 Prisoners of the State. The Center on Juvenile and Criminal Justice (1991)

Dowker, Fay and Good, Glenn. From Alcatraz to Marion to Florence: Control Unit Prisons in the United States.

Ervin, Lorenzo Komboa. Draft Proposal for an Anarchist Black Cross Network, An Anarchist Black Cross Network Handbook.

Excerpts From International Human Rights Treaties That Need To Be Ratified by the United States. Meiklejohn Civil Liberties Institute.

Falcon, Luis Nieves, Coordinator. Special International Tribunal on the Violation of Human Rights of Political Prisoners and Prisoners of War in United States Prisons and Jails Special International Tribunal. (1990)

Fighting Back! Attica Memorial to the People. Attica Now (1974)

Foote, Caleb. The Prison Population Explosion: California's Rogue Elephant. Center on Juvenile and Criminal Justice (1993)

Fried, Jonathan. Operation Blockade: A City Divided. American Friends Service Committee (1994)

Gardner, J.L. California Prison Visitors' Handbook. Gardners Press (1994)

Godfrey, Michael J and Schiraldi, Vincent. How Have Homicide Rates been Affected by California's Death Penalty? Center on Juvenile and Criminal Justice (April 1995)

Greenfeld, Lawrence A. & Stephanie Minor-Harper. Women in Prison. U.S. Department of Justice (1991)

International Symposium on Human Rights Violations of Political Prisoners and Prisoners of War in the U.S. International Tribunal on Political/POW Prisoners in the U.S. (1990)

Jurgens, Ralf. HIV/AIDS in Prisons: A Discussion Paper. Canadian AIDS Society and Canadian HIV/AIDS legal network (1995)

Koetting, Mark & Vincent Shiraldi. Singapore West: The Incarceration of 200,000 Californians. Center on Juvenile and Criminal Justice (1994)

Kojimoto, Carrie. AIDS Information for Prisoners Legal Services for Prisoners with Children. (1992)

Kondo, Sharon. Be Good To Yourself: A Self-Care Manual for Inmates Living with HIV. AIDS Project of Los Angeles (1993)

Lee, Michael. Alternatives: An Anarchist View of Prisons, Crime and Violence. Raze the Walls (1994)

Lee, Michael. Raze the Walls! Prisoner Resource Guide. Raze the Walls.

Lichtenstein, A.C and Kroll, M.A. (Ed. Kamel, R) The Fortress Economy. American Friends Service Committee (1990)

Mauer, Marc. Americans Behind Bars: The International Use of Incarceration, 1992-93. The Sentencing Project. (1994)

Mauer, Marc et al. Young Black Americans and the Criminal Justice System: Five Years Later. The Sentencing Project (1995)

McIntyre, Jennifer and Alissa Riker From Beyond Shelter to Behind Bars Center on Juvenile & Criminal Justice. (1993)

Meierhoefer, Barbara S. General Effect of Mandatory Minimum Prison Terms, The Federal Judicial Center. (1992)

Political Women Prisoners in the U.S. Revolting Lesbians (1987)

Prete, A (ed.) The Lessons of Marion. American Friends Service Committee (1993)

Prison Discipline Study : Shattering the Myth of Humane Imprisonment in the United States. Prison Discipline Study, Sacramento (1990-91)

Rosenblatt, Eli, ed. The Labor of Doing Time..." in Criminal Injustice: Confronting the Prison Crisis. South End Press (1996)

Singer, Mark I., Ph.D. Women Serving Time. Center for Practice Innovations, Mandel School of Applied Social Sciences, Case Western Reserve U. (1993)

The Criminal Justice Process / Over-Reliance on Prisons / Alternatives to Incarceration. Criminal Justice Consortium, Oakland, CA (1996)

Vincent, Barbara S. and Paul J. Hofer. The Consequences of Mandatory Minimum Prison Terms: A Summary of Recent Findings. Federal Judicial Center (1994)

Voices from Inside: Prisoners Respond to the AIDS Crisis. ACT/UP San Francisco (1993)

25 Years on the Move. MOVE Organization (1991)

Frady, Marshall. Death in Arkansas. The New Yorker. Feb. 22, 1993

HOW TO OBTAIN CONGRESSIONAL DOCUMENTS

Congressional bills, reports and public laws are available free. However, the number of copies that may be obtained at one time is limited. Information on the status and availability of Senate legislative documents. Call (202) 224-7860 Only one request per day will be filled. For single copies write

Senate Document Room
B-04 Hart Bldg.
Washington, DC 20510

For House documents,

House Document Room B-18,
House Annex No 2.
Washington, DC 20515
Phone (202) 225-3456.

Six items may be requested in person, 12 by mail and 6 by phone

Order extra copies of
Outsiders Looking In

We verified each of the addresses in this section immediately prior to publication. Most of the groups and organizations subsist on contributions, memberships and donations. Some have newsletters or books they sell to help raise money, others conduct conventions or workshops. Almost all are in dire need of funds to keep their organizations from disappearing. Most are located in member's homes or they share office space with other like-minded organizations. Therefore, they are always on the move in search of cheaper digs. If the group you are searching for isn't here or has moved, write to another group in the same area. They may be able to help you locate your party.

Family or friends need this valuable information? Don't let them go without it!

Additional copies can be ordered.

Please send $21.95 ($19.95 + $2.00 S.& H., California residents add sales tax) to:

OLINC Publishing
P.O. Box 6012
Fresno CA, 93703-6012

About The Authors

Toni D. Weymouth, Ed. D. is a sexologist and educator. She has worked for the California Youth Authority and an inpatient mental health hospital, and is a community organizer. She lives in California with her husband and a special friend she rescued from doggie death row. She has a son, a daughter, and a brand new granddaughter.

Maria Telesco, R.N., B.A. has had multiple careers as a journalist, registered nurse, teacher, investigator, columnist, and free lance writer. She is now retired and working harder than when she was employed. Maria has one daughter, five grandchildren and one great grandaughter.